PART ONE: SENTENCE ELEMENTS & THEIR RELATIONSHIPS

PART TWO: THE ALPHABETIZED HANDBOOK-GLOSSARY (pp. 381-417)

For quick reference on many questions of grammar and usage as well as for explanation of the special errors listed in the **CORRECTION KEY** (see page 380 and the inside back cover).

A COLLEGE RHETORIC

A COLLEGE
RHETORIC

by Jim W. Corder and Lyle H. Kendall, Jr.

TEXAS CHRISTIAN UNIVERSITY

RANDOM HOUSE
NEW YORK

We wish to thank these publishers for permission to use material from the books cited:

Alfred A. Knopf: H. L. Mencken, *The Bathtub Hoax,* copyright 1958 by Alfred A. Knopf, Inc.; William Alexander Percy, *Lanterns on the Levee,* copyright 1941 by Alfred A. Knopf, Inc.; Farrar, Straus, & Cudahy, Inc.: Robert Graves, *The White Goddess,* copyright 1948 by Robert Graves; The Macmillan Company: Horace Kephart, *Camping,* copyright 1919 by The Macmillan Company; James Winny, ed., *The Frame of Order,* copyright 1957 by The Macmillan Company; E. P. Dutton & Company, Inc.: Anthony Standen, *Science Is a Sacred Cow* (Dutton Paperback Series), copyright 1950 by E. P. Dutton & Co., Inc.; Time, Inc.: "Rape in Kivu," copyright 1961 by *Time* Magazine; Harcourt, Brace, and World, Inc.: George Orwell, *Shooting an Elephant and Other Essays,* copyright, 1945, 1946, 1949, 1950, by Sonia Brownell Orwell; Charles Scribner's Sons: Thomas Wolfe, from "Circus At Dawn" (copyright 1934, 1935 Modern Monthly, Inc.) from *From Death to Morning;* Thomas Wolfe, *Look Homeward, Angel,* copyright 1929 Charles Scribner's Sons, renewal copyright © 1957 Edward C. Aswell, as Administrator, C.T.A. of the Estate of Thomas Wolfe, and/or Fred W. Wolfe; Random House: William Faulkner, *Absalom, Absalom!,* copyright 1936 by Random House; Harper and Brothers: Mark Twain, *The Autobiography of Mark Twain,* copyright 1924 by Harper and Brothers.

PREFACE

This book exists because of our conviction that the freshman course in composition as it is generally conducted, and as we ourselves taught it until a few years ago, often wastes more time than it properly uses by not returning at once to the first principles of writing but instead by attempting to review and summarize grammar, punctuation, spelling, all of which the college instructor has a right to assume have been mastered in secondary school.

The book exists also because of our further conviction that there is a rather specific body of subject matter and techniques which it is the purpose of the first-year course on composition to explore fully and consider carefully. This body of knowledge, moreover, is continuous, each part fundamental to and indicative of the next part. It is a body of knowledge of such coherence that the individual instructor may find detailed and systematic methods for making everything he does in the classroom—discussion of word, sentence, paragraph, essay, examination of text readings, study of current printed matter—a vital part of a unified whole.

Our materials have been developed laboriously and tested at length in the classroom. Wherever possible, therefore, the outlines, paragraphs, and essays used for illustrative purposes have been written by our own students. We have edited these materials in a few cases, but only to emphasize a point at issue.

We are indebted to a host of students and friends, whose

unstinting assistance has been both willing and gracious.
Several student writers provided illustrative material for use
here; we wish especially to thank Tad Cecil, Philip Welsh,
Carl Lane, as well as others who shall remain anonymous.
To Miss Martha Whitaker, Miss Ann Allen, Miss Jacqueline
Gregory for their typing, and to Miss Frances Aman, who
typed all but a chapter or so of the final draft, we are ever-
lastingly grateful. We owe a special debt to Mr. John Graves,
who very kindly provided for us an exercise on sentence
style.

Last (and first, as husbands of good wives all know) we
would acknowledge if we could what we owe to our wives.
Their particular contributions we may cite: To Aubyn Kendall
our gratitude for some bibliographical research and for mow-
ing the lawn; to Patsy Corder our gratitude for providing the
children who appear in many illustrations in this book. Their
real contributions are incalculable, as our enduring gratitude
is inexpressible.

                                                          J.W.C.
                                                          L.H.K.

CONTENTS

A COLLEGE RHETORIC

Chapter One

❋ INTRODUCTION

The Province of This Book

Whatever else we may decide about him, whatever else may be decided for him, we are probably agreed that man has an inquiring and a communing spirit, and that he has a voice and a language to express both the inquiry and the communion. The purpose of this as of any textbook in composition is to aid that expression. Specifically, its purpose is to help the student become articulate, and further to help him to *know* that he is, so that at his choice he may with deliberation articulate his feelings and his ideas and those of his race. The province of this book is, therefore, writing and the attendant problems of effective style.

There must be many college freshmen who spend an academic year with an English instructor or two and ever afterwards are unable to decide whether the overdose was grammar, poetry, or philosophy. All of these are legitimate disciplines whose right to a place in the English curriculum is traditional and unchallenged. But they are certainly separate disciplines, and to attempt to deal with them coherently

3

in one college course is to invite confusion and to obscure an even more basic consideration.

We assume decent writing—not high school grammar, not *belles lettres*, not the history of ideas—to be the sole concern of a freshman course in English. Decent writing, if the writer has something to say worth saying, presupposes a careful choice of words and idioms and a close attention to the principles of organization and style. These are rhetorical principles. They make this a conservative, a rather systematic book: principles of any sort are largely unaffected by the passage of time. So that it may properly develop these principles, *A College Rhetoric* touches on fundamentals obliquely. Such matters as the working stock of grammatical terms, a knowledge of mechanics and elementary diagraming, and avoidance of the traditionally egregious error are discussed only as they affect style, with commentary in the Handbook-Glossary and suggested readings at the end of pertinent chapters to aid the student whose background is less solid than he would like it to be.

The concentration on the principles of rhetoric that this permits involves a clear gain (not to be spent in excessive contemplation of essay subject matter) for the instructor as well as the student, and a consequent freedom to read, write, and analyze essay materials in the classroom.

Because of a fairly common tendency among both instructors and students to dwell on grammar, form, or subject matter of assigned essays, a course in freshman English sometimes lacks unity and coherence. The student may find himself submerged in the intricacies of the nominative absolute and the dangling modifier for six weeks, struggling to the surface only to discuss at length the mores of dating or the sociological implications of the two-income family, succumbing at last when he is plunged back into the sink of sentence style. Assuming that coherence and unity are possible in the freshman English course, *A College Rhetoric* has, as far as possible, a progressively logical organization, beginning with a study of effective diction and an exploration of sentence and paragraph style. Succeeding chapters cover preparation for the full-length essay and practice in the various types of prose composition: exposition, argumentation, description, and narration. Last are a chapter on the research paper, with sample typescripts, and a handbook with glossary of usage.

This plan, by which the student may begin with the language itself and thereafter accumulate some information and understanding regarding successively larger units of composition until he is prepared for the composition of full-length essays, is, we feel, a workable plan that helps to guarantee some continuity for the course, provided that assigned readings are always subordinate to the principles they are meant to illustrate. It need not, however, be the *only* workable plan. Instructors who, for example, prefer to have their students begin writing full-length essays immediately and then pick up the details of style could well begin with Chapters Five and Six on organization and exposition, then go back to the beginning and proceed with the study of the other chapters in their present order.

As a possible guide for the use of *A College Rhetoric*, the appendix contains some suggested syllabi for a course in freshman composition. Four possible plans are suggested: the first is for a full-year composition course following the order of the chapters in the text; the second is for a full-year composition course following a different order of study; the third and fourth are for one-semester composition courses, one using the present order of chapters, the other a variant.

Aside from the body of the text and the suggested syllabi, there are additional features that, we feel, considerably enhance the value of *A College Rhetoric*. The book has at the end of each chapter suggested exercises in which we have tried to avoid the customary bunching of sentences with words to be underlined, in favor of assignments that require both reading and considerable writing—writing of a sort calculated to be of immediate benefit to the achievement of a good prose style. And, although it is designed to accompany a volume of essays, where pertinent each chapter recommends supple-

mentary readings—usually from the classics of our language—
to explain and illustrate stylistic problems as they arise. An
incidental benefit deriving from these listings is the possible
encouragement to library prowling.

One special concern of this book we assume to be both
dear to the hearts of English instructors and central to the
educational process itself. Freshman composition courses are
in many universities followed by a year or more of advanced
study of literature, usually surveys of English or American or
world literature, or courses introducing the student to different
kinds of literature. In many universities the freshman course
itself includes an introduction to literature. For these reasons,
considerable attention is devoted in this book to the composition of the literary essay: a section of Chapter Five discusses
the organization of the literary essay; a part of Chapter Six
discusses and illustrates several kinds of literary essay; and
Chapter Ten uses the literary research paper as a means of
discussing research writing in general. The book thus is suitable for use in connection with or in preparation for the study
of literature.

Preliminary Suggestions about Writing

An educated man should be able to write a literate essay.
Conversely, the student who is unable during or at the end
of his university career to write a literate essay cannot in all
likelihood satisfy either traditional or recent standards of
educational accomplishment.

To help the student acquire the ability to compose a literate
essay is one of the goals of this book, which is accordingly
arranged so that the student may gradually accumulate the
skill and the understanding of style that he will need. In many
cases, however, the student is required to write full-length
essays from the beginning of his first semester of study, even
while he is acquiring the necessities of a good style. Some
English instructors prefer to have their students start writing
essays immediately, and instructors in other disciplines have

their own writing assignments that the student must follow. Hence the student may find it useful to consider briefly at the beginning some of the requirements of a good essay.

The preliminary principle that the beginning writer must master is not a principle of grammar or of mechanics. To be sure, the writer must control both grammar and mechanics, but he can easily learn to do so through practice and with the help of glossaries and guides to usage, like the Handbook-Glossary included in this book. The central problem of the beginning writer as of all writers is the eternal difficulty of communication: how to make the writer's expression coincide with his intention so as to arouse the desired reaction in the reader. If the writer has something to say worth saying, his problem, in other words, is to say it precisely and economically so that his reader will understand and share the thing that was worth saying.

While he must soon gather to himself other elements of style, in order completely to fulfill this obligation, the writer may from the first rely on this preliminary principle: a good essay must have a beginning, a middle, and an end.

The Beginning of the Essay.   The writer must have a subject about which he has some information, some ideas, some feelings, or some convictions. Often in the freshman English course the instructor will provide a specific subject, a list of specific subjects, or general subjects from which the student is to evolve his own specific subject. If the student has a specific topic, he is ready to proceed with his essay once he has provided the brief orientation suggested below. If he begins with a general topic of his own or of the instructor's choosing, he then must limit his subject in such a way that it is suitable for development in an essay, and he must begin his commentary on this subject at an *understandable* place, furnishing at the beginning sufficient information regarding necessary antecedents for his reader to appreciate his concern for the subject and the significance that the subject has for him.

The Middle of the Essay.   Once he has announced a specific, limited subject and has provided whatever information is necessary to inform his reader of the pertinence and background of the subject, the writer then is obliged to explore this subject in the middle of his essay. A beginning, which comes from conviction, thought, or feeling, necessarily has consequences; such things are never static. Hence the writer who knows his subject may be led to examine what exactly is involved in this subject, to examine, for example, the minor problems that constitute the major problem that is his subject, or to examine his subject as it may be seen in its different aspects. Whatever direction this section of the essay may take, the writer must at all times keep his subject before him so that everything he says has direct bearing on the matter he is developing.

The End of the Essay.   Having started his prey and having pursued it with wounding gunfire, the hunter, sportsmen tell us, is honorably bound to kill. Literate men know that once a writer has begun his discourse and followed it with telling points, he too is honorably bound to end what he has begun. The writer cannot simply *stop* his work; he must conclude it, investigating his subject and its possible consequences so well that the reader is left with no unfulfilled expectations.

The Beginning, the Middle, and the End Illustrated.   The three parts of the essay we have been discussing may be illustrated in this way:

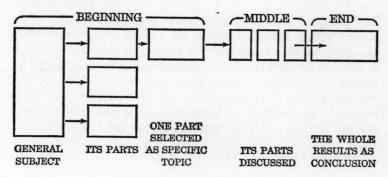

Beginning with a general subject, the writer resolves it into parts, *one* of which becomes the specific subject of his essay, thus providing a *beginning*. This specific segment of a general subject in turn then may be resolved into its parts, discussion of which constitutes the middle of the essay. These smaller segments are then presented, each of them sufficiently well to represent the whole again.

Consider, as a further example, an actual writing assignment. The student, let us say, has been asked to write an essay of 500 words on a topic of current interest. Because of his recent reading in newspapers and magazines and because of his little brother's experiences during the past summer, the student-author happens to hit upon current discussions of Little League baseball. He has, at this point, a general subject. He should see then that many things—how many depends on the extent of his interest in and knowledge of the subject— are involved in Little League baseball. Interest in this subject could lead a student to write, for example, about the organization of the leagues, their equipment and rules, their usefulness as physical training or as social training, about the merits or the demerits of Little League baseball. Let us suppose further that the student has recently read a number of adverse criticisms of the Little Leagues, that he has watched many games, that he has at times acted as umpire, and that his little brother habitually became sick immediately after each game. This combination of circumstances might lead the writer to settle upon one aspect of his general subject, the demerits of Little League baseball. When he announces this special interest and shows the circumstances mentioned above that aroused his interest in this special subject, he has a *beginning* for his essay.

A moment's thought is likely to reveal here that in order to follow this beginning and to expose the weaknesses of Little League competition, he will once again have to consider several aspects of what is now his specific problem. His observation of the games, his participation as umpire, his reading, and his closeness to the sickened brother might suggest to him for example that three specific features of the competition have created conditions unsuitable for boys—excessive organization, excessive stress on winning performance, and excessive parental zeal. When he has fully explored each of these individual weaknesses, keeping always before him the central topic and never allowing irrelevant matter to intrude, he has a *middle* for his essay.

Now he is ready to return to his central position, that Little League competition is marred by serious flaws. If he can state this with a reasonable degree of assurance, reasonably well convinced that he has left no questions unanswered, no alleys unexplored, he has an *ending* for his essay. He has, moreover, an essay that will probably adhere to most of the principles it is the purpose of this book to discuss in detail.

The importance of such a progression in writing may be illustrated by an essay that does not observe strictly this preliminary necessity of establishing a beginning, a middle, and an end:

IS MONEY THE TRUE BASIS FOR HAPPINESS?

(1) The definition of money as found in the dictionary is "metal, as gold, silver, or copper, coined or stamped, and issued as a medium of exchange; any form or value of coin or currency lawfully used as money." (2) A more common definition is that money is something which if you have enough of, nothing will be too far out of reach.

(3) Money has a special meaning to everyone. (4) For the majority of people, money is a lease on life which can be bought through the investment plan. (5) But through this investment plan we lose something. (6) It might be love or our self-respect which we lose, but usually it is our happiness.

(7) How many people do you know that have at least twenty credit cards? (8) These are the people who have beautiful homes, servants, two or three cars in the garage, and nothing in the bank. (9) They get very little compensation from what they do have. (10) I doubt very much whether they know what true happiness is. (11) Today most people feel that if they don't have money there is nothing in life for them. (12) This was true of Jean A., who said "If I didn't have money, I think

I would go off and die." (13) Of course this is rather far-fetched thinking on her part, but this is what she honestly believed. (14) And she never said she was happy.

(15) Happiness is something you can have whether you have money or not. (16) Some of the happiest people are the ones who have little money in the bank. (17) Take for instance a dirt farmer. (18) He will probably never have anything, but he is contented with what he does have. (19) Happiness is a thing of the mind which is always needed but not always found.

(20) Sometimes when you have money you will feel superior to those who have not as much as you do. (21) But you will find that you are really inferior to them. (22) They have something that you as an individual will never have—self-respect.

(23) When you have money, everyone is your friend. (24) When you have none, only a few will be your friends. (25) As in the poem "Solitude" the author says, "Laugh and the world laughs with you; Weep and you weep alone." (26) This is the effect money has on many people. (27) When you have risen to the top, you find yourself very lonely.

(28) The lonely people are the ones who have great wealth. (29) Go to your library and read the life stories of many of the great philanthropists and I think you will see what I mean.

(30) I will agree that money is needed. (31) But I don't think that money is something that you couldn't live without. (32) Money will always be around, but we shouldn't let it have a hold on us.

Important, but not to the purpose at the moment, are numerous weaknesses in form and usage throughout the essay—contractions, shifted constructions, faulty sentence structure, colloquialisms, and other stylistic problems. Such problems would prevent even a good, well-organized essay from being acceptable, but they may be corrected with relative ease. More difficult to cope with is the larger problem of direction and sense that is illustrated in this work.

This essay has no beginning, middle, and end; rather it is a kind of maze.

Consider the title and the first paragraph of the essay. The title itself indicates probable weakness in the essay to follow, a question of so little force being insufficient to indicate the approach the writer is following to the subject. The first paragraph begins well enough, albeit with a commonplace definition of what is to be one of the key terms in the discussion. The last sentence in the paragraph might have been effective, but in an effort to bring the subject close to home, the author has used incorrectly what must have been intended to be a colloquial expression. Neither the title nor the first paragraph indicates precisely what the subject of the essay is: we do not know whether the author feels money is or is not the basis for happiness; we learn nothing in fact save a common definition of one of the terms. Nor do we learn any reason why the author is talking about money—he has not communicated the subject, the purpose, or the background of his essay. The essay thus has no beginning.

Neither does it have a middle if by that term we mean the section which extends fully from the beginning to the end, for the bulk of the essay moves in totally unrelated directions. Having been informed in the second paragraph of the "special meaning," "the lease on life" that money represents, we are then told that we lose something in the quest for money. What we lose may be love or self-respect, but usually, the author tells us, it is happiness. He does not, however, explain his justification for separating love, self-respect, and happiness into distinct categories. The fifth sentence is also a *non sequitur*, the loss of something not necessarily following from the quest for money.

Having announced that we lose something in the search for money, the author goes on, in the paragraph beginning with the seventh sentence, presumably to illustrate how this loss occurs. But we are told in sentence eight that the people he is discussing, while they have other things, have no money in the bank. The author has, unknowingly it appears, shifted his subject. In the preceding paragraph he has spoken of how people who get money lose something, but in the present paragraph he is actually talking about people who do not have money. At this point it is quite clear that the author has not sufficiently decided on his direction. But his shifting is not yet done. Sentences seven through ten speak of people who have "nothing in the bank," but sentences eleven through fourteen speak of people who do have money. Since neither those at the first without money nor those at the last of the paragraph with money are happy, we can only conclude at this stage of the essay that there seems to be no basis for happiness, for there is no happiness.

We turn then, in the fourth paragraph, to those who are happy without money. Hoping to convince his audience that happiness does not depend upon money, the author cites the dirt farmer, who is "contented with what he does have" although he "probably will never have anything." The author here asserts that the farmer who *never has anything* is content with *what he has*—which is both an impossibility and a *non sequitur*.

Paragraph Five speaks of superiority and inferiority—neither necessarily related to what the author has been discussing—and speaks of the loss of self-respect, a characteristic presumably dismissed in sentence six.

Paragraph Six, beginning with the twenty-third sentence, tells us first that everyone is the friend of the man with money, then announces last that those at the top (presumably with money) are alone. In between he speaks of weeping and laughing, their connection with money and happiness not being made explicit.

Paragraph Seven reasserts the loneliness of those who have money, although sentence twenty-three earlier told us that they have many friends, and asks the reader to provide a point which the author fails to make clear.

The middle section of the essay follows thus a sequence such as this:

1. men lose something in the search for money
2. what they lose is happiness
3. people who have no money in the bank are not happy
4. people who do have money are not happy
5. some people are happy without money

6. some people feel superior when they have money, but they are really inferior
7. men with money have many friends
8. men with money are alone

Items 1 and 2 are negated by item 3, which is in turn negated by item 4. Item 5 stands alone, with no appreciable connection to other points, and item 6 is self-canceling. Item 7 is contradicted by items 8 and 9. In other words, the middle section of this essay disappears, one part negating the other. The essay has no middle.

It does have an end, the assertion that while money is necessary, it should not be dominant in our lives. But an end that follows no beginning and no middle is hardly an end. In a sense, the writer of this essay has only arrived at a beginning when he stops.

To avoid such confusion in thinking, feeling, and writing, the student-author is urged to remember at all times the preliminary necessities discussed earlier. And he is specifically urged to read with some care the book which follows.

Assignments

Examine the following essays for sensible and continuous development. Note especially whether each essay begins clearly, proceeds fully, and ends conclusively.

IS FOOTBALL A DANGEROUS SPORT?

Football is becoming a more dangerous sport every day. There were tentative plans last year to ban high school and college football because of the many injuries encountered. The game is an extremely rough one.

I have had my share of football injuries. In the 1959 season I encountered three serious injuries involving trips to the hospital. One of my injuries has damaged me permanently.

The game is a very good one. It is the injuries that are giving football a bad name.

In the United States last year there were six players to die from injuries received from this game. This game has proved to be a very damaging one.

The equipment available today is not sufficient. If football is going to stay in the sports world, someone is needed to devise better and safer equipment.

It seems to me that the schools in the United States are more interested in making a profit from the game. They are not too interested in their football players' safety.

I believe football is going to end in the very near future.

A WOMAN'S PLACE IS IN THE HOME

Success in home management means far more than having an attractive, comfortable home, and a well-fed family. It creates a social, spiritual, and physical environment in which each member can grow in ability, understanding, and ideals. It calls for the cooperation of all members of the family, although the mother, as homemaker, is the natural leader.

Being the leader of the home is a full time job and carries with it much responsibility. The training of the children is one of the most important of these responsibilities, and only the true mother of the children can lead her young in the direction in which she wants them to go. If a mother works and is forced to leave her children with strangers, she can never be sure of what they are being taught while she is working. During the young and tender years it is most important for a mother to be with her children, for during these years the ideas of right and wrong are formulated. Later in life, if her child has become a law breaker, she may find that all the money she has made in previous years will not redeem him now.

Also, the emotional stability of the child is endangered if the mother works. Being kept by first one stranger and then another, the child will never know just exactly whom he can turn to for love and comfort. This may result in a complex which will stay with him the rest of his life. If a mother will not or cannot stay with her children while they are young, she should never have them.

Aside from being a good mother, the leader of the home should also be a good wife. If she is working she cannot have a hot meal ready when her husband arrives home, nor will she feel like turning a sympathetic ear to his problems. In the Bible it says that the wife's palace is her home. If this is true, she should stay there where she will be of more benefit to the whole family.

The Bible also states that woman was made as a helpmate for man, and that she is to be in subjection to him. However, if she is working and making as much money as he, it will be hard for her to be in subjection because she will feel she is equal to him. If she stays at home with the children, she will be a helpmate by bearing and caring for his children, but she will also be in subjection to him.

I believe that marriage and children are the most important thing in a woman's life. All the money in the world cannot buy a husband and wife a child of their own, nor will it buy a woman a good husband, or a man a good wife. The material things of life are not really important at all in comparison to the happiness of a family. Therefore, I think that marriage and home life are the full time responsibility of the woman; and if she works, it will be detrimental to the happiness of her family.

Readings

David Hume, "Of Simplicity and Refinement in Writing," *Essays and Treatises on Several Subjects* (London, 1870).

W. Somerset Maugham, "Lucidity, Simplicity, and Euphony," *The Summing Up* (New York, 1938).

Jacques Barzun, "How to Write and Be Read," *Teacher in America* (Boston, 1945).

Ernest Hemingway, *Green Hills of Africa* (New York, 1935).

Max Beerbohm, "Habit," *A Selection from "Around Theatres"* (New York, 1930).

"Corruption of Our English Tongue," *The Tatler*, no. 124 (London and New York, 1953).

E. B. White, Introduction to William Strunk, Jr., and E. B. White, *The Elements of Style* (New York, 1959).

Granville Hicks, "Clarity, Clarity, Clarity," *Saturday Review*, Aug. 1, 1959 (on *The Elements of Style*).

F. L. Lucas, "What Is Style?" *Holiday*, Mar., 1960.

Mario Pei, "English in 2061," *Saturday Review*, Jan. 14, 1961.

Bonamy Dobrée, "The New Way of Writing," *Modern Prose Style* (Oxford, 1934).

H. L. Mencken, "A Short View of Gamalielese," *The Nation*, Apr. 27, 1921.

Margaret Nicholson, "What Is Good English?" *Atlantic*, May, 1957.

Arthur Quiller-Couch, *On the Art of Writing* (New York, 1916).

Chapter Two

❀ EFFECTIVE DICTION

The student of writing, if he is serious, must learn first that no good writer ever uses a word, a phrase, or a punctuation mark accidentally. Every symbol put on paper by the good writer is a deliberate choice, calculated to fulfill some desired function. In the creative process that culminates in a written work, the writer may deliberate a long while on what he wishes to say and on the order in which he wishes to say it; but when he comes at last to express his ideas on paper, his first care must be the words that will best give life to those ideas. And if the words are to serve their purpose, they must be proper and precise. They must suit the author, his audience, and his intention; and they must be the exact expression of his ideas.

The Proper Word

LEVELS OF USAGE

Although we customarily announce that we speak or read or write the English language, we must recognize from the beginning that we have several languages, all in one way or another native to us. We speak one language in the dormitory, but we write quite another in a letter home to mother, and still another in a semester research paper. Hence a living language changes, and its standards change. Yet there is always available to the student a tradition of conventional and appropriate standards for acceptable English. Experimentation with language is an admirable thing. Through experimentation writers have sometimes achieved great results including both fanciful poetry and profound fiction. But experimentation is usually not suitable for oral communication and is never proper for a first-year student of rhetoric, whose first obligation is to catch up with his race by learning what his race has learned, by achieving himself what the human race has already achieved. A body of consistently useful and appropriate standards for communication is one of those achievements.

Among these standards is what might be called a principle of moderation. The student of writing will ordinarily want to avoid the opposite extremes of unnecessary formality and unforgivable illiteracy. These two extremes and the middle ground between them coincide with the usual classification of the many varieties of English into three principal categories—formal English, informal English, and vulgate.

Most often used in written discourse, *formal English* is used in oral discourse among formal groups in formal situations. Stylistically, this variety of English is characterized by a somewhat broader vocabulary than is used in everyday discourse, by longer and more complex sentences than appear in popular magazines or in ordinary conversation, and by a somewhat more conservative practice in style, grammar, and mechanics than one finds elsewhere. Formal usage is most often seen in scientific and technical journals, academic papers, and in essays and articles written for professional and learned journals.

The language of those who are largely uninfluenced by the factors that determine educated usage is called *vulgate English*. Standard English is the product of much more than school instruction, being formed in part by newspapers, motion pictures, magazines, advertising, radio and television, ordinary conversation, and other agencies. The kind of language that follows its own unique and local standards, without regard to prevalent standards announced by schools and other informing institutions, is inappropriate to student writing. This kind of language, vulgate English, is found in regional dialects, in vocabularies peculiar to special crafts and occupations, and in slang.

The common language of educated people, the third principal variety of English, is called *informal English*. A language refined of crudities, of slang, and of any uninformed usage, it differs from formal English in several respects. The written vocabulary of informal English is closer than that of formal English to the spoken vocabulary. Short, simple sentences and compound sentences predominate, and the practice in grammar and mechanics is usually more liberal. This is the language of the classroom, of domestic conversation and familiar letters, and of much popular and literary writing. It is with this level of usage that this book is primarily concerned, though in some sections, such as that on research writing, the emphasis will be on more formal usage.

VARIATIONS IN USAGE WITHIN LEVELS

Our language is constantly changing, and even within these general levels of usage there are further variations. Time and place, for example, have their effect on one's language. Words once in common use have disappeared, and new words constantly confront us. Words that once were current but are no longer in use are called *obsolete*. *Archaic* terms are those words, such as *beau* and *kine*, which are disappearing from common use but which are still used occasionally in special contexts. The disappearance of *beau*, incidentally, leaves us without a single good term to be used in naming a male lover. *New* words, of course, are constantly being added to our current vocabulary. Developments in technology in the twentieth century, for example, have added many words such as *kodak* and *television* to our common usage.

Some variations in usage arise from locale and from habit. *Provincialisms* or *localisms* peculiar to one region or another sometimes creep into written usage, particularly in idiomatic constructions. In Fort Worth, Texas, for example, one usually says "out at Lubbock," "over in Dallas," "down in New Orleans," and "up in Oklahoma City." In Lubbock, Dallas, New Orleans, and Oklahoma City, one would undoubtedly use different constructions. Informed usage prohibits such local terminology in written discourse, as it does the use of those expressions called colloquialisms, which are common in speech, but not proper to written forms. Such expressions as "I haven't got any" and "I'll be right over" are common enough in our speech, but their acceptance there does not qualify them for written use, except in dialogue.

SOME STANDARDS OF PROPRIETY

Since there are so many varieties of usage, the beginning writer is often faced with the problem of determining what usage is appropriate to his speaking and to his writing. Although there are some absolute standards of usage, the writer has to be careful nonetheless, for the same style will not work in different situations. The physicist who serves on weekends as a lieutenant in the reserves would hardly use the same style of speech in his military capacity that he would in addressing a formal gathering of his academic colleagues, but he needn't say "They was here" in either situation.

The writer should first take care to use a natural diction, one that suits him, his background, and his expectations. The beginning writer who uses *expectoration* instead of *spit*, *domicile* instead of *home*, or *inebriated* instead of *drunk*, is laboring under some kind of misapprehension. Neither one's teachers nor one's audience expects polysyllabic words when short words will do. Students sometimes seem to feel that writing in college must be formal—they usually call it "flowery." Such is not the case. Writing which is unnatural is bad writing; the student therefore should avoid excessive formality, particularly an exaggeratedly complex vocabulary. The use of a word like *progenitor* for *father* can only be attributed to a misguided attempt to be funny or to an equally misguided attempt to affect a pretentious style. Both are inappropriate.

The writer, then, should use a vocabulary that is natural to him. This is not to suggest that he remain content with a static vocabulary. Any student who would be educated understands that a vocabulary must grow in order for its user to express his enlarged consciousness. To insert strange words in one's essays in an unnatural manner, however, may not be the best way to learn them.

The writer should also take care to use a vocabulary that is proper to his audience and to his purpose. Affecting an exalted style is dishonest, and writing down to one's audience is insulting. Usually the writer's natural mode of expressing himself will also be proper for his audience, though some audiences, both for the written and the spoken word, require a more formal usage. The purpose a writer has in his work may also determine the diction he uses. A research paper, for instance, demands formal usage, but a speech on the social significance of comic strips requires a more informal style and may, for the sake of illustration, demand even the vulgate.

Through various departures from acceptable usage, the language of the following excerpts from student essays reveals some common mistakes and misunderstandings:

1. *Getting in shape* for a track meet can logically be compared to studying for an examination. A sincere track competitor realizes that he must begin early to develop his body to *top condition* in order to compete well.

Here the italicized phrases, common to speech, are inappropriate to the tone of the passage, which is generally formal.

2. The character in *Psycho* who is trying to *make himself out* as a very unadventurous person is actually schizophrenic.

In this sentence the colloquial usage, "make himself out," is ineffective, particularly from a student who can use the term *schizophrenic*.

3. My first urge to become independent provoked a profound conflict between my parents and me. Perhaps this urge arose in me earlier than in the average person for I first experienced the blessings of independence at the young age of thirteen. Having been blessed with a gift of musical talent, I had developed this gift to an appreciable degree so that *it afforded me an opportunity to become self-supporting* at an early age for it became the *motivating factor in stimulating my interest* in individualism. Individualism breeds the desire to be independent and independence, unfortunately, breeds conflict. The conflict, in this particular case, arose between my narrow-minded parents, *who refused to take cognizance of my desires* to become an individual, and myself.

In the first two passages inappropriate mixtures of different levels of usage mar the author's efforts. The third passage illustrates a different, and more difficult, problem. The diction and tone here are uniform; there is no mingling of different usage levels. Here the usage is inappropriate to the situation. The author is describing a highly personal episode in his life. Although we can appreciate his effort to be objective, his use of an elevated style compounded of long sentences, long words, and long thoughts almost transforms this serious episode into a comic one. The italicized passages, for example, indicate a pomposity that tends to make the author ridiculous rather than justify him.

The Precise Word

The writer's choice of the precise word to express his meaning is, unfortunately, not always an easy task. Indeed, good writing is not easy. But however uncomfortable it may make us, we cannot argue that "it's not important how I say it, just as long as I get it said." No matter how clear an idea may be in one's mind, it will never be so clear in his reader's mind unless it is couched in words that precisely express the writer's intention. In some ways the principal problem in writing is that of bridging the distance between the writer and the reader. To bridge this distance, the writer must express himself with minute attention to the details of vocabulary, to the literal, implied, and associative values of the words he may use. Failure to do so results in the common complaints of beginning writers, "I know what I meant, but I just couldn't seem to say it," or "What I meant to say was . . . ," or "You know what I mean."

Weaknesses in diction often take two common forms. The student who is not sure of his language or the student who is not careful with his language will frequently either totter around his point but never make it or obscure his point through the inadequacy or inaccuracy of his vocabulary. The following excerpts from student essays indicate these failures.

1. The rough and unpredictable aspects of football were shown in the Baylor vs. Texas Christian University game on Saturday. *The rough part was expressed by the many injuries* to both teams throughout the game.

The italicized passage shows that the author is not in control of his work. The word *part,* for example, indicates that there is a specific segment of football which is rough. The author unquestionably wanted to show that roughness was a constituent element in the game, not a separable segment. Further, injuries do not *express* roughness, though they may *illustrate* or *reveal* roughness. The author has not made his desired point.

2. Each year many students who are not properly prepared for the demands of a college enroll. Many students are helpless when they are given original works to read that have not been abridged, outlined, or condensed. *This helplessness may apply to the students' former education.*

This student is on his way to making a point, but if it is clear in his mind, it has not yet begun to emerge clearly in his writing. A present helplessness can hardly *apply to* a past study; such helplessness may, however, *result from* past study.

  3. The world today is in a state of unrest and fear. Two world powers poise, ready to strike and annihilate an enemy's industrial wealth. Once an attack has begun, it cannot be stopped. *Destruction is the final result of a difference of two countries.*

The difference *between* two countries may be almost anything, but not necessarily destruction. The only necessary result of a difference between two countries is that there will be two countries. Again, the author has not gotten to his point, which presumably would have involved political differences.

In the passages above, each of the authors failed to get at his point because of inadequate control over diction. In the passages below difficulty arises from inaccurate or confused use of words.

  1. If the faith is strong, there is no *extent* to the love.

The author here probably meant to suggest that if faith is strong, love is limitless. His use of the word *extent* with the negative, however, gives precisely the opposite meaning. His sentence literally says that if faith is strong, there is no love— a quality having no extent presumably not existing.

  2. The realists, on the one hand, often become neurotic, but the romantics, *equananimously,* often go insane. The choice presents itself, then. Shall I choose *neurosy* or insanity?

The author here has tried to use a vocabulary that was not natural to him, with rather foolish results.

  3. "All men are created equal." So say the supporters of *segregation* in the United States. This *question* has been with us since the War Between the States, yet there is still no satisfactory answer to it.

Misuse of *segregation* makes this passage illogical and contradictory. Use of the word *question* is also misleading, no questions having been brought up.

The student writer who is concerned to use the proper word should make the dictionary his constant companion. Any of the recent standard college dictionaries such as those listed below is satisfactory.

The American College Dictionary, Random House, New York.
Webster's New Collegiate Dictionary, G. & C. Merriam Co., Springfield, Mass.
Webster's New World Dictionary, The World Publishing Company, Cleveland.

The student should also become acquainted soon with any special dictionaries that might be helpful to him. And finally, the student should immediately learn to use the standard unabridged dictionaries listed below.

A *Dictionary of American English*, 4 vols., University of Chicago Press, Chicago.
New Standard Dictionary of the English Language, Funk and Wagnalls, New York.
The New English Dictionary, 10 vols. and Supplement, Clarendon Press, Oxford.
Webster's New International Dictionary of the English Language, Second Edition, G. & C. Merriam Co., Springfield, Mass.

THE USE OF THE DICTIONARY

If the writer recognizes his obligation to be precise, he should also soon recognize that the dictionary is an indispensable companion. It is not indispensable, however, simply for its list of words and definitions. The dictionary is much more than this: it is a complete guide to the language, and it is a remarkably accurate index to our culture. A good dictionary is useful in the ordinary business of reading and writing; it may be useful also as a tool for advanced research. The standard desk dictionaries listed above provide information of linguistic, geographical, biographical, and historical nature sufficient to the needs of most classroom requirements.

For further study or for advanced study at any time, *The New English Dictionary,* listed above, is in itself a library of information. It provides not only the standard information available in all other dictionaries, but also gives a complete history of each of the words included, giving sources and uses, with copious examples in context, and noting how these uses have changed through the years. Knowledge of the historical changes in word uses, made possible through these accounts, is invaluable to the understanding of the problems of precision in word usage and of cultural, political, and social changes reflected in changed word meanings.

But the standard desk dictionaries furnish all the information necessary for most collegiate uses, more, indeed, than most of us are ever aware of. The prefatory materials in most good dictionaries, too often unused, are effective essays on language and usage. In The *American College Dictionary,* for example, one can find introductory discussions of the selection of entries and definitions, pronunciation, the treatment of etymologies, synonyms and antonyms, usage levels and dialect distribution, and British and American usage. Also provided is a table of common English spellings and an explanatory note describing the kind of information presented in the body of the dictionary and the order in which it is presented.

Within the body of the dictionary, given with each entry, are the proper spelling and division of the word; a key to pronunciation; grammatical information, the part of speech being indicated; inflected forms of the word; usage labels, where pertinent, to indicate restrictions when the word is limited in usage to one level, region, subject, or time; definitions, with grammatical context ordinarily provided; variant spellings; etymologies; and synonyms and antonyms. All of this information is customarily given, along with special information wherever necessary, as the sample pages on pages 28–29 illustrate.

In addition to the standard desk and unabridged dictionaries, there are, as indicated earlier, numerous special dic-

Running Head	**beauty**
Vocabulary Entry	**beau·ty** (bū′tĭ), *n., pl.* **-ties. 1.** that quality of any object of sense or thought whereby it excites an admiring pleasure; qualification of a high order for delighting the eye or the aesthetic, intellectual, or moral sense. **2.** something beautiful, esp. a woman. **3.** a grace, charm, or pleasing excellence. [ME *beute*, t. OF: m. *beaute*, der. *beau.* See BEAU] **—Syn. 1.** loveliness, pulchritude.
Idiomatic Phrases	**beck**[1] (bĕk), *n.* **1.** a beckoning gesture. **2.** *Scot.* a bow or curtsy of greeting. **3. at one's beck and call,** ready to obey one immediately; subject to one's slightest wish.
Syllabication Dots	**—***v.t.. v.i.* **4.** to beckon. [short for BECKON]
Pronunciation	**be·di·zen** (bǐ dī′zən, -dĭz′ən), *v.t.* to dress or adorn gaudily. [t. BE- + DIZEN] **—be·di′zen·ment.** *n.*
Example Contexts	**be·fore** (bǐ fōr′), *adv.* **1.** in front; ahead. **2.** in time preceding; previously. **3.** earlier or sooner: *begin at noon, not before.* **—***prep.* **4.** in front of; ahead of; in advance of: *before the house.* **5.** previously to; earlier than: *before the war.* **6.** ahead of; in the future of; awaiting: *the golden age is before us.* **7.** in preference to; rather than: *they would die before yielding.* **8.** in precedence of, as in order or rank: *we put freedom before fame.* **9.** in the presence or sight of: *before an audience.* **10.** under the jurisdiction or consideration of: *before a magistrate.* **—***conj.* **11.** previously to the time when: *before we go.* **12.** sooner than; rather than: *I will die before I submit.* [ME *before(n)*, OE *beforan*, i. *be* by + *foran* before]
Antonyms	**—Ant. 1.** behind. **2.** afterward. **3.** later.
Part of Speech and Inflected Forms	**be·gin** (bǐ gǐn′), *v.,* **began, begun, beginning. —***v.i.* **1.** to enter upon an action; take the first step; commence; start. **2.** to come into existence; arise; originate. **—***v.t.* **3.** to take the first step in; set about; start; commence. **4.** to originate; be the originator of. [ME *beginne(n)*, OE *beginnan*] **—be·gin′ner,** *n.*
Synonym Study	**—Syn. 3.** BEGIN, COMMENCE, INITIATE, START (when followed by noun or gerund) refer to setting into motion or progress something which continues for some time. BEGIN is the common term: *to begin knitting a sweater.* COMMENCE is a more formal word, often suggesting a more prolonged or elaborate beginning: *to commence proceedings in court.* INITIATE implies an active and often ingenious first act in a new field: *to initiate a new procedure.* START means to make a first move or to set out on a course of action: *to start paving a street.* **4.** institute, inaugurate, initiate. **—Ant. 1.** end.
Variant Principal Parts	**be·jew·el** (bǐ jōō′əl), *v.t.,* **-eled, -eling** or *(esp. Brit.)* **-elled, -elling.** to adorn with or as with jewels.
Variant Spelling	**be·la·bor** (bǐ lā′bər), *v.t.* **1.** to beat vigorously; ply with heavy blows. **2.** to assail persistently, as with ridicule. **3.** *Obs.* to labor at. [Also, *Brit.*, be·la′bour.]
Hyphenated Entry	**belles-let·tres** (bĕl lĕt′r), *n.pl.* the finer or higher forms of literature; literature regarded as a fine art. [F] **—bel·let·rist** (bĕl lĕt′rĭst), *n.* **—bel·le·tris·tic** (bĕl′lĕ trĭs′tĭk), *adj.* **—Syn.** See literature.
Word Element	**bene-,** a word element meaning "well", as in *benediction.* [t. L, comb. form of *bene, adv.*]
Consecutive Definition Numbers	**be·neath** (bǐ nēth′, -nĕth′), *adv.* ① below; in a lower place, position, state, etc. ② underneath: *the heaven above and the earth beneath.* **—***prep.* ③ below; under; *beneath the same roof.* ④ further down than; underneath; lower in place than. ⑤ lower down on a slope than: *beneath the crest of a hill.* ⑥ inferior in position, power, etc., to: *a captain is beneath a major.* ⑦ unworthy of; below the level or dignity of: *beneath contempt.* [ME *beneth(e)*, OE *beneothan*, i. *be* by + *neothan* below] **—Syn.**
Etymology	**3.** See below. **—Ant. 1.** above.
Usage Note	**bent**[1] (bĕnt), *adj.* **1.** curved; crooked: *a bent stick, bow, etc.* **2.** determined; set; resolved (fol. by *on*). **—***n.* **3.** bent state or form. **4.** direction taken (usually figurative); inclination; leaning; bias: *a bent for painting.* **5.** capacity of endurance. **6.** *Civ. Eng.* a transverse frame of a bridge or a building, designed to support either vertical or horizontal loads. [pp. of BEND[1]]
Synonym List	**—Syn. 4.** tendency, propensity, proclivity, predilection.
	bent[2] (bĕnt), *n.* **1.** bent grass. **2.** a stalk of such grass. **3.** (formerly) any stiff grass or sedge. **4.** *Scot. and N. Eng.* a grassy tract, a moor, or a hillside. [ME; OE *beonet*, c. G *binse* rush]
Short Pronunciation Key	ăct, āble, dâre, ärt; ĕbb, ēqual; ĭf, īce; hŏt, ōver, ôrder, ch, chief; g, give; ng, ring; sh, shoe; th, thin; ṯh.
	b., blend of, blended; c., cognate with; d., dialect, dialectal; m., modification of; r., replacing; s., stem of; t., taken

brunch

bi-, a prefix meaning: **1.** twice, doubly, two, as in *bilateral, binocular, biweekly.* **2.** (in science) denoting (in general) two, as in *bicarbonate.* Also, **bin-.** [t. L, comb. form of *bis* twice, doubly, der. L *duo* two] — **Prefix**

Bi, *Chem.* bismuth.

B.I., British India. — **Abbreviation**

bi·son (bī′sən, -zən), *n., pl.* **-son.** *Zool.* a large North American bovine ruminant, *Bison bison* (**American bison,** or **buffalo**), with high, well-haired shoulders. [t. L. t. Gmc.; cf. G *wisent*] — **Illustration**

American bison. *Bison bison* (10 to 12 ft. long, ab. 6 ft. high at the shoulder) — **Caption**

blood·mo·bile (blŭd′mə bēl′), *n.* a small truck with medical equipment for receiving blood donations. — **Geographical Entry**

Bos·ton (bôs′tən, bŏs′tən), *n.* **1.** the capital of Massachusetts, in the E part: the largest city and seaport in New England. 801,444; with suburbs, 2,354,507 (1950). **2.** (*l.c.*) a game of cards, played by four persons with two packs of cards. **3.** (*l.c.*) a social dance, a modification of the waltz. —**Bos·to·ni·an** (bôs tō′nī ən, bôs tō′-), *adj., n.* — **Run-on Entry**

bot·tle¹ (bŏt′əl), *n., v.,* **-tled, -tling.** —*n.* **1.** a portable vessel with a neck or mouth, now commonly made of glass, used for holding liquids. **2.** the contents of a bottle; as much as a bottle contains: *a bottle of wine.* **3. the bottle,** intoxicating liquor. **4.** bottled milk for babies: *raised on the bottle.* —*v.t.* **5.** to put into or seal in a bottle; esp. in England, to can or put up fruit or vegetables. **6. bottle up,** to shut in or restrain closely: *to bottle up one's feelings.* [ME *botel,* t. OF: m. *botele,* g. LL *butticula,* dim. of *buttis* BUTT⁴] —**bot′tle·like′,** *adj.* —**bot′tler,** *n.* — **Homograph Numbers**

bot·tle² (bŏt′əl), *n. Brit. Dial.* a bundle, esp. of hay. [ME *botel,* t. OF, dim. of *botte* bundle]

bou·fant (boo fän′), *adj.* French. puffed out; full, as sleeves or draperies. —**bou·fante** (boo fänt′), *adj. fem.* — **Foreign Word Label**, **Two Word Entry**

brain washing, systematic indoctrination that changes or undermines one's political convictions. —**brain-wash,** *v.*

brain wave, 1. (*pl.*) *Med.* electroencephalogram. **2.** *Colloq.* a sudden idea or inspiration.

brass (brăs, bräs), *n.* **1.** a durable, malleable, and ductile yellow alloy, consisting essentially of copper and zinc. **2.** a utensil, ornament, or other article made of brass. **3.** *Mach.* a bearing, bush, or the like. **4.** Music. **a.** a musical instrument of the trumpet or horn families. **b.** such instruments collectively in a band or orchestra. **5.** Brit. a memorial tablet incised with an effigy, coat of arms or the like. **6.** metallic yellow; lemon, amber, or reddish yellow. **7.** *U.S. Slang.* **a.** high-ranking military officers. **b.** any important officials. **8.** Colloq. excessive assurance; impudence; effrontery. **9.** *Brit. Slang.* money. —*adj.* **10.** of brass. **11.** using musical instruments made of brass. [ME *bras,* OE *bræs*] —**brass′·like′,** *adj.* — **Subject Label**, **Geographic Label**, **Usage Label**

brig·and·age (brĭg′ən dĭj), *n.* the practice of brigands; plundering. Also, **brig′and·ism.** — **Variant Form**

Bron·të (brŏn′tĭ), *n.* **1.** Anne, (*Acton Bell*) 1820–49, British novelist. **2.** her sister, Charlotte, (*Currer Bell*) 1816–55, British novelist. **3.** her sister, Emily Jane, (*Ellis Bell*) 1818–48, British novelist. — **Biographical Entry**

brown·ie (brou′nĭ), *n.* **1.** (in folklore) a little brown goblin, esp. one who helps secretly in household work. **2.** *U.S.* a small, highly shortened chocolate cake, often containing nuts. **3.** (*cap.*) a trademark for a type of inexpensive camera. **4.** any inexpensive camera. **5.** (*cap.*) a member of the junior division (ages 8–11) of the Girl Scouts or (*Brit.*) the Girl Guides. —**Syn. 1.** See fairy. — **Capitalization**, **Cross Reference**

Brum·mell (brŭm′əl), *n.* See Beau Brummell.

brunch (brŭnch), *n.* a mid-morning meal that serves both as breakfast and lunch. [b. BREAKFAST and LUNCH]

oil, bŏŏk, ōōze, out; ŭp, ūse, ûrge; ə = a in alone; that; zh, vision. See the full key on inside cover.

der., derived from; f., formed from; g., going back to; from; ?, perhaps. See the full key on inside cover. — **Short Etymology Key** tionaries. These include dictionaries of slang, underworld terminology, synonyms and antonyms, dictionaries for special professions, and many other special-purpose dictionaries.

EXERCISE:

Compile a list of at least ten special dictionaries, indicating the subject matter and the specific purpose of each.

The dictionary cannot be one's only guide, however, for words change in their meanings and sometimes accumulate associations that a dictionary cannot record. In the history of the English language words have often changed. Some of the changes seem almost whimsical, but others follow fairly definite patterns. Some words, for example, have become generalized, losing their original specific meaning. *Quarantine,* for instance, once meant the forty days' isolation period for ships suspected of carrying disease, but now is used to indicate any kind of isolation for any duration. Other words have lost original general meanings and become more specific. *Meat* once referred to food in general, but now of course refers to flesh used as food. Other words have experienced a pejoration, their meaning changing from an original reference to something good to the present unpleasant implication. *Lust,* now used exclusively in immoral associations, once meant simply *pleasure,* and *hussy* originally meant *housewife.* Still other words have undergone an amelioration. For example, our word *steward* earlier meant *sty guardian.* A curious example of both amelioration and pejoration, the word *queen,* once simply designating a woman, has been used to refer to both the women of the streets, and *the* woman of the realm.

Countless other kinds of changes have occurred, and are still occurring. It is because words do change and because they continually take on new associations that the student must be so careful in his choice of them. The dictionary is his surest guide. It is a record of usage, not a law of usage as so many think, but it does provide the standard definitions of words, showing how they are customarily used in educated society. Dictionary definition is not always enough for the student, it must be remembered. In order to choose the *precise* word, he must be aware not only of the literal meaning of a word, but also of its implied or suggested meanings. He can choose the precise word only if he knows it to be exact in denotation or in connotation.

EXACTNESS IN DENOTATION

A word comes to have a literal or denotative value when the people who use the word agree completely on what the word signifies. The person or place or thing or idea that a word stands for is called the word's *referent*. When a student uses the word *desk*, then the thing that holds his books, upon which he writes, and in front of which he sits, is the referent of that word. When we all use a word and agree upon its referent, we may say the word has a central, specific meaning, a denotation. We all agree, for example, that the word *mother* signifies a female parent. The word may mean more than this for us—we know that sometimes mothers are nags and hags and pals and sweethearts and saints, but we agree on that one central meaning.

The writer, unless he is deliberately trying for suggestive appeal in his writing, must be careful, then, to use words that denote the exact referents he has in mind. This is one of the most crucial tasks of the writer. It is his way of showing precisely what he means. Suppose, for example, the writer wishes to describe a person moving from one end of a room to another. The tendency in most beginning writers would be to say simply, "He walked from one end of the room to another." But consider how much more specific, effective, interesting, and descriptive the account would be if the writer could find the word whose meaning exactly defines the movement. A person may stagger, reel, stroll, amble, wander, limp, waddle, roll, wiggle, saunter, mosey, weave, stumble, or almost anything else to the end of the room. The more accurate a writer is in choosing the word that precisely identifies the movement, the more apt he is to communicate precisely what he wishes to his audience.

The writer will be most successful in doing this who makes greatest use of specific, or *concrete* words. The most specific words in our language are concrete nouns, which name one specific person, place, or thing. Next to these are those words usually labeled *concrete words*. These are words whose referents are clear and undisputed. Less specific than these are *relative words* such as *warm, cool, poor,* whose meanings depend on their contexts. Words having no specific meanings at all, no commonly agreed on referents, are called *abstract* words. Such words as *honor, glory,* and *beauty* have no meanings at all other than those conferred upon them by their contexts. The free and easy way to sure communication is clearly through the use of concrete words.

1. George Orwell, in his essay "Politics and the English Language," discusses the common failure of modern writing to be detailed and precise:

> . . . I am going to translate a passage of good English into modern English of the worst sort. Here is a well-known verse from *Ecclesiastes*:
>
>> I returned, and saw under the sun, that the race is not to the swift, nor the battle to the strong, neither yet bread to the wise, nor yet riches to men of understanding, nor yet favor to men of skill; but time and chance happeneth to them all.
>
> Here it is in modern English:
>
>> Objective consideration of contemporary phenomena compels the conclusion that success or failure in competitive activities exhibits no tendency to be commensurate with innate capacity, but that a considerable element of the unpredictable must invariably be taken into account.
>
> This is a parody, but not a very gross one. . . . It will be seen that I have not made a full translation. The beginning and

ending of the sentence follow the original meaning fairly closely, but in the middle the concrete illustrations—race, battle, bread—dissolve into the vague phrase "success or failure in competitive activities."

—George Orwell, *Shooting an Elephant and Other Essays* (New York: Harcourt, Brace and Company, 1946).

2. Study the following paragraph:

Tolerance is a quality which most every person hopes to acquire during his life time. Following closely along the pattern that most worth-while things in life are not passed out on a *golden platter*, tolerance is certainly not an easily obtained characteristic. However, it is a quality which is essential as well as most useful in various vocations. For example, *teachers* must always have an abundance of toleration in order to maintain self-control in their *classrooms*. Many unnecessary questions are always being asked by *students*. On these instances as well as many others, tolerance is the answer needed to solve the problem. The acquisition of toleration toward others is an attribute of which any man may be most proud.

This student paragraph illustrates the weakness of writing that depends too much on relative and abstract words. Words of this sort can only have meaning from their context, but in this case the context itself is so generally vague that no meaning is achieved. The four italicized terms are more specific than the rest, but of the four, one is a cliché and the other three denote classes of things rather than single objects or persons.

Another way the writer has of achieving preciseness in denotation is through his use of synonyms. The English language is particularly blessed with synonyms, but they are sometimes misleading. Even though words may have the same general referent, their specific meanings may vary slightly. For this reason, the writer has to be very cautious in choosing his words. The casual writer, for example, may see no major difference between the words *crowd, mob, throng,* and *multitude;* but the careful writer will see a difference. The words do agree up to a point in that they each refer to a group of people, but beyond that point their meanings vary. The words do not, for instance, denote groups of the same size. Most of us would agree that a multitude is bigger than a throng, and we all know that a crowd is the smallest of the four (it only takes three to make one). We also would probably agree that *mob* differs from the other three, suggesting as it does something about the nature of the group.

Distinctions that must be made among synonyms can be seen in the following:

1. We may *build* a barn, but we probably would not say we were *constructing* or *erecting* one.
2. We may call ourselves *average*, but we will fight at being called *mediocre*.
3. If we visit the rooms of a favorite professor and find that he does not attend to his housekeeping duties, we might say his place was *cluttered*, but out of deference to him we probably would not say it was *squalid* or *messy*.
4. When I see injustice, I may be *indignant;* you will belittle me if you say I am simply *angry*.

The writer who would speak of the whole range of human affairs is inevitably faced with a different kind of precision. His first obligation is to be exact in the literal meanings of the words he chooses. But beyond that the writer is confronted with the moral, ethical, and social values that have accumulated around some words, and he is confronted with the expression of qualities and ideas that cannot easily be communicated with simple literal words. Just as in our lives, at moments, experience crowds in upon us, filling a second with meaning, so experience crowds in upon language, packing some words with suggested and implied values. The writer's second obligation, in other words, is to be precise in the use of words with a high degree of connotative value.

EXACTNESS IN CONNOTATION

Meanings other than the literal denotations have become associated with many words. The writer must be aware constantly of the possible implications, or connotations, of the words he uses. The writer who ignores the suggestive power that words have dooms himself to failure. The imaginative appeal of all our literature depends in good part on just this quality in words, and the effectiveness of student writing depends on the alertness with which the student recognizes and uses the packed meanings that words can have.

These packed meanings occur in several ways. The way a word is customarily used may sometimes alter its denotative value. The word *proletariat*, for example, denotes the unpropertied class of workers, but because of its common use to label the revolutionary class in Russia, we cannot safely use it to denote unpropertied American workers. Customarily we *give* a panhandler a nickel for a cup of coffee, but, because of common usage in more dignified settings, we say we *donate* to charity. The writer can make or break his work, depending on what use he makes of the connotative values that words have. The actual meaning that a composition has is determined to a great extent by the writer's manipulation of these accumulated meanings. Consider the vast difference between the two passages below, each of which describes the same thing but does so with words of varied connotative value.

His home? Why it's what you'd expect of an intellectual, I guess. The minute you walk in the door you can tell he and his family have decided that appearance doesn't count much. It's a warm place—there are stacks of books on the arms of all the chairs and on the mantel and on the floor. Some of them are stacked open as if he had just left them. Some original oils were leaning against one wall. They were striking impressionistic pieces. When I came in, there was in the air still the sweet-strong bite of good tobacco. The huge black polished pipe he usually smokes lay in an ashtray filled with other pipes and ashes and matches and dottle. He was at the typewriter, pausing from his work with a cup of coffee.

His house? Why it's just exactly what you might expect of an egghead, I guess. The minute you walk in the door you can tell he and his family have rationalized that appearance doesn't count much. It's a cluttered, messy place—there are piles of books littering the chairs, the mantel, and the floor. Some of them were carelessly left open. Some pictures were collecting dust on the floor against one wall. The painter couldn't draw very well. When I came in, the air was still heavy with the acrid odor of poorly-mixed tobacco. The unwieldy dark pipe he usually smokes lay in an ashtray filthy with pipes and ashes and dottle. He was at the typewriter, dawdling over a cup of coffee.

Words may also come to have connotative value through their context. Everyone has heard new parents trying to settle on a name for their child. What often happens is that when one parent suggests a name, the other rejects it because he has known some unpleasant person with the same name. The name, in other words, has previously been used in an unpleasant context. The effect of context on the meaning of a word can be seen in the following passage in a famous western novel by Owen Wister, *The Virginian*. The hero is in a conversation with an old friend, during the course of which the following exchange takes place:

> "Take a man that won't scare. Bet yu' drinks yu' can't have the American's."
> "Go yu'," said the Virginian. "I'll have his bet without any fuss. Drinks for the crowd."
> "I suppose you have me beat," said Steve, grinning at him affectionately. "You're such a son-of-a —— when you get down to work. Well, so-long! I got to fix my horse's hoofs."
> I had expected that the man would be struck down. He had used to the Virginian a term of heaviest insult, I thought. I had marvelled to hear it come so unheralded from Steve's friendly lips. And now I marvelled still more. Evidently he had meant no harm by it, and evidently no offence had been taken.

A short while later, in a card game with a group of men, the Virginian is addressed in the same way by a man who is not his friend:

> "*And* twenty," said the next player, easily.
> The next threw his cards down.
> It was now the Virginian's turn to bet, or leave the game, and he did not speak at once.

Therefore Trampas spoke. "Your bet, you son-of-a ———."
The Virginian's pistol came out, and his hand lay on the table,
holding it unaimed. And with a voice as gentle as ever, the
voice that sounded almost like a caress, but drawling a very
little more than usual, so that there was almost a space between
each word, he issued his orders to the man Trampas:—
"When you call me that, *smile!*" And he looked at Trampas
across the table.
Yes, the voice was gentle. But in my ears it seemed as if
somewhere the bell of death was ringing; and silence, like a
stroke, fell on the large room.

Much of the appeal of good writing comes from the writer's deliberate use of words with packed meaning. We recognize that life is not simple; we know that the smallest stone
can cause many ripples in the water. It is only proper that our
language should be involved in this way, single words sometimes being filled with a world of meaning.
Early in William Faulkner's *Absalom, Absalom!* the following passage appears:

Then hearing would reconcile and he would seem to listen
to two separate Quentins now—the Quentin Compson preparing
for Harvard in the South, the deep South dead since 1865 and
peopled with garrulous outraged baffled ghosts, listening, having
to listen to one of the ghosts which had refused to lie still even
longer than most had, telling him about old ghost-times; and
the Quentin Compson who was still too young to deserve yet
to be a ghost, but nevertheless having to be one for all that,
since he was born and bred in the deep South. . . .
                    —William Faulkner, from *Absalom, Absalom!*
                    (New York: Random House, 1936), p. 9.

In these lines the sad sense of life incomprehensibly pouring
in upon the boy emerges clearly, largely because of the highly
suggestive diction. Divested of the colorful diction, the passage is bare and inadequate:

Then hearing would reconcile and he would seem to listen to
two separate Quentins now—the Quentin Compson preparing
for Harvard in the South, the deep South lifeless since 1865
and filled with strange, vital memories, calling back in particular

one of the memories which seemed more persistent than others, reminding him of old times; and the Quentin Compson who was still too young to be memory-filled, but was even so, being born and bred in the deep South. . . .

Words also accumulate additional meanings when they are used figuratively. One of the most common mistakes made by beginning writers is their assumption that figurative language is merely ornamental, something added to writing to make it seem handsome. Figurative language, properly used, is a kind of shorthand by which writers can say more in few words than they could if they used literal terms. Figurative language, in other words, is functional; it is a way of compressing meaning into brief space and arousing the emotions of the reader. The most common figurative usages are listed below.

1. **Simile**—This is a figure of speech based on some unique resemblance between two things otherwise unlike, the comparison between them usually specifically stated with *like* or *as*. Using some resemblance as a beginning, the writer can transfer from one of the things to the other the qualities he wishes to show in his subject. When Shakespeare has a character say

> As flies to wanton boys are we to the gods,
> They kill us for their sport,

he transfers the insignificant quality of flies to mankind and the cruel nature of the wanton boys to the gods. In this way he makes tangible the abstract qualities of insignificance and cruelty.

2. **Metaphor**—Similarly based on resemblance, the metaphor assumes a comparison but does not state it. Metaphor informs our daily conversation and all of our writing, from the best to the worst. It is one of the methods writers and speakers have customarily used to grasp difficult or abstract matters and to explain them in manageable forms. The Psalmist, when he says "The Lord is my Shepherd," establishes at once the

serenity and security of the religious mood, not by trying to describe the abstraction, but by picturing it in human terms.

3. **Analogy**—Another figure based on resemblances, analogy is usually a more detailed comparison of subjects having some similarity, the purpose ordinarily being to explain the more difficult term by showing its similarity to the more familiar term. The fairly commonplace explanation of the human nervous system, which we cannot see, by comparison with the telephone exchange system, which we can see, is an example.

4. **Synecdoche**—This figure is based on the association in our minds of some important part with a whole it represents. When a writer says "The mill hired forty hands today," he is associating hands with what they represent, the means of working. It is a shorthand way of calling attention to the thing that, in this context, is important about the forty men.

5. **Metonymy**—Also based on association, this is a figurative usage that substitutes for the subject a thing which represents it, thus again calling our attention to a special quality or feature. The word *guts* is often used to signify courage or bravery, perhaps because originally the word would have called to our minds the whole complex of glandular and adrenal activity, toughness of stomach, strength, and flexibility which partly constitute bravery.

6. **Hyperbole**—Deliberate exaggeration, used to startle, strike the fancy, and attract attention, is hyperbole. The two raftsmen in *Huckleberry Finn* who in long passages brag of their fierceness, saying "Contemplate me through leather; don't use the naked eye," are exaggerating in hope of calling attention to themselves and possibly scaring off their opponents.

7. **Litotes**—This is deliberate understatement, calculated to call attention to a subject by appearing to avoid it. After the

fight between Grendel and the hero in *Beowulf*, a fight in which Heorot, the great hall, is almost destroyed, the poet says "That was a bitter spilling of beer," directing our attention to the devastation through modesty and through the implication that the vigor was so great as to affect even the most insignificant of things in the hall.

Some Precautions Regarding Diction

For various reasons several kinds of particularly weak usage have become popular with us. These weaknesses usually result from careless or uninformed efforts to be polite, impressive, or flowery. All must be avoided.

Wordiness. We often take the longest way around to get home. Unnecessary words are often used because of the writer's need to achieve a required length, because of some notion that the more words he uses the more effective he is, or because of simple carelessness. Examples can be seen in the following sentences:

1. When winter comes, all of the missing winds suddenly find a way to get into my dormitory, and *due to the fact that* most of the windows are broken, my room becomes very cold.

Aside from other mistakes appearing in this sentence, the five words italicized could be replaced by one word, *since,* without altering the meaning.

2. The Beast is pictured as a very ugly and evil-appearing creature.

The word *very* here—and nearly everywhere else—is unnecessary. We can accept *ugly* by itself without the qualifying word. *Appearing* is also unnecessary.

3. Time, like space, is so vast *or large in scope* that we should not think in hundreds but in thousands of years.

The italicized words are unnecessary, their meaning having already been established by *vast*.

4. My opinion of dormitory is that it is hell on earth.

This sentence would be much more direct, vivid, and effective if it simply said, "My dormitory is hell on earth." We can assume that this is an opinion.

Euphemisms. In unnecessary and unfortunate efforts to elevate status, to soften hardships, or to blunt reality, many writers habitually use what they deem "polite" words. The straightforward, plain word is always preferable.

1. Notice, for example, that we can easily buy *reconditioned* cars or furniture, but we can hardly find *second-hand* goods.

2. Consider how often *-rama* is added to plain words in some kind of effort to make them sound up-to-date, technical, and stylish. We have *sellaramas,* instead of sales, *smellaramas,* instead of perfume exhibitions, *vistaramas,* instead of home demonstrations, and the list goes on and on.

3. There is an almost endless list of euphemistic expressions used in place of *die* and *death*: pass on, pass away, cross the great Divide, check out, check in, cash in one's chips, meet one's Maker, expire, go to Heaven, and so on. Death is a natural event, which we need not try to disguise.

Redundancy. Many of us are guilty of repeating, within the same sentence, things that we have already said. This usually results from carelessness, from unsure thinking, or from the necessity of padding out the length of the paper.

1. Today, since science is highly thought of *as being of great importance,* it is usually never questioned.

The italicized passage here repeats what is already suggested in *highly thought of.*

2. They cannot be an asset *of value* without some form of modesty.

The italicized words here are repetitive, *asset* suggesting value.

Clichés. Our language is filled with *clichés*—phrases and terms that are habitually used in certain situations. All movies are colossal, and the eyes of all pretty girls are like deep velvet pools. These worn-out expressions, usually figures of speech, have been used so often that what little value they originally had is lost. They should be avoided always. If you have seen a figure of speech in print, it is generally wise not to use it again.

1. Every shot I hit was flying *as straight and true as an arrow*.

This was old the day after arrows were invented.

2. It clings to the sharp cry of a new-born baby and the *inner glow* which pours from his mother's eyes.

This might have meant something once; now it is only a poor substitute for specific meaning.

3. The worst feeling man can experience is being alone and helpless in a *cold, cruel world*.

Please!

Jargon. One of the worst abuses in writing is the twisted misuse of formal English called *jargon*. It is common among advertising men, public relations men, and the men who write government documents. One form it often takes is the use of circumlocutory expressions in informal writing, as in the following example:

Having been blessed with a gift of musical talent, I had developed this gift to an appreciable degree so that it offered me an opportunity to become self-supporting at an early age as it became the motivating factor in stimulating my interest in individualism.

Madisonese. This is a relatively new misuse of our language—the increasingly popular phrasing that seems to have come from advertising and public relations. The most flagrant abuse is the addition of *-wise* to the most unlikely words.

Assignments

1. From an essay assigned by your instructor list all the words of whose meaning you are not completely sure. Then consult a standard desk dictionary to determine (a) the pronunciation, (b) its first meaning, (c) its source, and (d) the level of usage each word represents. This activity should become habitual with the reading of any assigned work.

2. Consult a reference dictionary such as the *New English Dictionary* to determine the history of each of a similar group of words.

3. Using a similar list of words, show whether each word is being used essentially for its denotative or for its connotative value. If for its connotative value, explain what associations the author evokes through the use of the word.

Readings

Reference

Albert Baugh, *History of the English Language* (New York, 1935).
H. L. Mencken, "The American Language," *Yale Review*, XXV (March, 1936), 538–552.

Illustrations

George Orwell, "Politics and the English Language," *Shooting an Elephant and Other Essays* (New York, 1946).
Mark Twain, "Fenimore Cooper's Literary Offenses," *The Portable Mark Twain* (New York, 1946).
Arthur Quiller-Couch, "On Jargon," *On the Art of Writing* (New York, 1916).
Frank Sullivan, "The Busy Cliché Expert," *A Pearl in Every Oyster* (Boston, 1938).

Bergen Evans, "Fell Swoop on a Fine Cliché Kettle," *New York Times Magazine,* July 27, 1958.

Joseph Wood Krutch, "Great Cliché Debate (Cont.)," *New York Times Magazine,* Aug. 31, 1958.

Noel Perrin, "Don't Give Me One Dozen Roses, Give Me a Nosegay," *New Yorker,* Apr. 4, 1959.

Roger Angell, "Department of Amplification," *New Yorker,* Apr. 25, 1959.

Chapter Three

❋ SENTENCE STYLE

A writer's words determine the tone of his work and help to determine its effectiveness, but the basic structural unit in composition is the sentence. A sentence is in many ways a miniature composition, having many of the characteristics of the full-length work. It must be clear, coherent, and unified; it must be concise and interesting. The old definition of a sentence as the expression of one complete thought is especially meaningful. A sentence is an expression of thought, but, to be effective and significant, it must express not unformed but coherent thought. The record of one's private reveries, half-formed, is sometimes important in imaginative literature, but it can never be of any value in expository or argumentative writing, or in most description and narration. The writing one is most often concerned with involves explaining something, convincing someone of the truth of some position, describing something, or relating some sequence of events. To do any of these things properly requires conspicuous care in the construction of every sentence. No sentence should ever be the accidental expression of the writer's ideas; all sentences must be the result of deliberation. The

writer will consciously debate not just the grammatical construction of his sentence, but also its sound, its appearance, the
location of its parts for emphasis, and the arrangement of its
parts for interest.

For this reason the writer must not concern himself only
with the syntax of the sentence. It is one of the convictions
on which this book is based that an understanding of grammar
does not necessarily produce capability in writing. Grammar
must be the servant of other considerations in writing the sentence. The good writer should of course be able to analyze
his sentences grammatically, but one may be able to spot the
antecedent of a pronoun at ten paces and still not be able to
write an effective sentence. Writing effective sentences requires, in addition to grammatical sense, a sound understanding of style. Grammar is, for our consideration, important only
as a tool for rhetoric; it is not important in itself. The efficacy
of a sentence usually depends not on grammatical units, but
on units of sound and sense, their location and arrangement.

The subject of this chapter, then, is the rhetorical nature of
good sentences, not their grammatical nature. To understand
this distinction clearly, consider the following sentence:

> The student may find himself submerged in the intricacies of the
> nominative absolute and the dangling modifier for six weeks,
> struggling to the surface only to discuss at length the mores of
> dating or the sociological implications of the two-income family,
> succumbing at last when he is plunged back into the sink of
> sentence style.

Grammatical analysis of this sentence would indicate that it
is a simple sentence with a singular subject and verb and a
direct object followed by three lengthy participial phrases.
This, however, while it reveals an *accurate* sentence, does
nothing to indicate whether or not this is a *good* sentence.
The effect of the sentence—and, considering its origin, perhaps we may be pardoned a moment's reflection on its merit
—depends not on the grammatical nature of the sentence, but
on its stylistic and rhetorical features. What effectiveness the

sentence demonstrates depends first on the pertinence and force of the sustained metaphor, the implied comparison of the freshman English student with the floundering swimmer who struggles, escapes temporarily, then falls back again. The effect of the metaphor, in turn, depends in part upon the sequence of the actions, failure—momentary success—failure, to which attention is directed by another stylistic technique, alliteration, which appears in the key words *submerged, struggling,* and *succumbing,* as well as elsewhere. The author has used sound to good effect here, too. The hushed, conspiratorial tone created by some fourteen sibilants is appropriate to what may at first appear to be the sinister and brooding nature of a freshman English course.

Consider a sentence which is rhetorically ineffective:

> Everyone had praised this short story so he thought this might be his talent.

Here is a compound sentence with an independent clause at the beginning followed by a second independent clause. Knowing this, however, does not help us to explain its weakness and lack of color. It is never going to be a particularly striking sentence, but we can see a way to help it along. The independent clause at the beginning of the sentence states a cause; the second independent clause states an effect. We can probably assume that the effect in this sentence should get more attention, should, in fact, be the dominant part of the sentence. In its present form the sentence emphasizes the cause by putting it in the first major element and thereby diminishes the effect. We can correct by revising the sentence to read

> Since everyone had praised this short story, he thought that writing fiction might be his talent.

Now what is probably the main idea has been put into the main part of the sentence, where it should be.

The effectiveness of a sentence depends upon its style. Effective style in sentences demands *clarity, conciseness,* and *interest.*

The Clear Sentence

Perfect clarity in a sentence requires that it be free of any ambiguity, that its parts be logically related, and that its important elements be adequately emphasized so that the reader cannot miss them. There are several basic techniques for guaranteeing clarity.

CLARITY THROUGH GRAMMATICAL ACCURACY

While this book avoids any detailed discussion of grammar, it must not be taken for granted that grammar is unimportant to the sentence. The student, it is assumed, will have, from his previous schooling, adequate grasp of the fundamentals of grammar. An ungrammatical sentence is no true sentence at all, but an unformed thought. Grammar is a system of relationships that enables the writer to rid his work of ambiguity and to assert the logical relationship of the parts of his sentence. The grammatical problems that most often create confusion in the sentence are the following:

> fragmentary sentences
> shifted constructions
> dangling modifiers
> split constructions
> improper case
> subject-verb agreement
> pronoun-antecedent agreement
> pronoun reference

For discussion and illustration of these problems, see the Handbook-Glossary.

CLARITY THROUGH ADEQUATE PUNCTUATION

The rules of punctuation, which are restated in somewhat different form in the Handbook-Glossary, are included in this chapter because the style, or rhetorical pattern, of a sentence usually determines its punctuation. Hence punctuation is an aspect of rhetoric.

Punctuation also serves to satisfy certain conventions and to clarify difficult passages.

A. Punctuation Reflecting Sentence Structure

RULE 1. Depending upon the nature of its content, a sentence ends with a period, a question mark, or an exclamation mark (see Handbook-Glossary on exclamations).

RULE 2. A comma follows (a) an introductory adverbial clause, of whatever length, or (b) a long introductory phrase.

(a) *As Claude Rhomboid ran across the street to greet Henrietta Mood,* his shoes filled with water.

(b) *Dodging puddles and rivulets and islands of mud,* Henrietta tiptoed toward Claude.

RULE 3. (the rule of *and, or, but, nor*) Regardless of clause length, if the two independent clauses of a compound sentence are separated by one of the conjunctions *and, or, but, nor,* the conjunction is preceded by a comma. In the absence of one of these conjunctions a semicolon replaces the comma. (See *for* in the Handbook-Glossary.)

Comma

(a) Henrietta screamed joyfully, *and* Claude gathered her somewhat impatiently into his arms.

(b) "I will perish by my own hand, *or* you must have pity on me," Henrietta murmured.

(c) Claude—and never more than now—had always yearned for the life of a pirate, *but* for reasons of respectability he was committed to a clergyman's existence.

(d) Henrietta never loved Claude as he deserved, *nor* was she likely to let any man sweep her off her feet.

Semicolon

(a) She screamed joyfully; he gathered her somewhat impatiently into his arms.

(b) I will perish by my own hand; perhaps I will change my mind if you show some pity.

(c) He had always yearned for the life of a pirate; nevertheless he settled regretfully for a parson's pittance.

(d) Henrietta never loved him as he deserved; however, she was not likely to love any man more determinedly.

RULE 4. Nonrestrictive or parenthetical sentence elements are set off by commas. (See *restrictive* in the Handbook-Glossary.)

Words

(a) Nonrestrictive: Claude's youngest brother, *Jim,* died yesterday after revealing his love for Cecily Mood.

(b) Restrictive: Claude's brother *Jim* died yesterday after revealing his love for Cecily Mood.

Phrases

(a) Nonrestrictive: There were three words, *I love you,* tattooed among the roses on Jim's forearm.

(b) Restrictive: The words *I love you* were also tattooed across the small of Claude's back.

Clauses (adverbial)

(a) Nonrestrictive: Henrietta regards Claude Rhomboid with distaste, *although she is secretly attracted to him,* because he has conceived a passion for her only sister.

(b) Restrictive: Henrietta regards Claude Rhomboid with distaste *because he has conceived a passion for her only sister.*

Clauses (adjectival)

(a) Nonrestrictive: Claude Rhomboid, *whom Henrietta is just now regarding with extreme distaste,* has fastened his vulture-like attentions upon her only sister.

(b) Restrictive: The only man in this room *whom Henrietta regards with distaste* is Claude Rhomboid.

RULE 5. Sentence elements in a series are set off by commas beginning with the second item of the series. The final item is not followed by a comma.

Words

Claude screamed, ranted, harangued, shouted, and blustered without making the slightest impression on Henrietta.

Phrases

In the town, in the country, on the high seas, even in his beloved suburbia Claude Rhomboid thinks of nothing but Henrietta's only sister.

Clauses

Whenever I go, wherever I see, howsomever I touch, however I kiss Henrietta, her only sister, Cecily, is still uppermost in my mind.

RULE 6. Depending upon the violence of the interruption, sentence interrupters are set off by dashes or parentheses. (But see the Handbook-Glossary on both devices.)

(a) Claude began (and Henrietta began to ape him behind his back) to applaud the virtues of Cecily Mood.

(b) Cecily Mood, whatever her faults—can she actually have any—is an ideal mate for Claude Rhomboid.

B. Punctuation According to Certain Conventions

See QUOTATIONS in Handbook-Glossary.

RULE 7. The second and all subsequent items in dates and addresses are set off by commas.

Claude and the radiant Cecily were eventually married at six P.M., Friday, June 1, 1962, at her ancestral home, 6, The Cloisters, Puckering Valley, Dorset, England, whence they departed for an out-of-the-way hotel in Wales.

RULE 8. Formal introductions, which are complete statements, are followed by colons. Informal introductions are usually followed by commas, but if what is introduced is the object or complement of a verb, no punctuation is needed.

Formal

> During their first night at the hotel Claude and Cecily unpacked these wedding presents: a hot water bottle, an electric toaster, a jar of watercress marmalade, a Norfolk jacket, and a set of tea napkins.

Informal

> During their first night at the hotel Claude and Cecily telephoned to say that they required some hot water, three English muffins, a patent opener, and some note paper.

RULE 9. Degrees and titles following names are set off by commas.

> May I introduce our rector, Claude Rhomboid, D.D., Henrietta's brother-in-law, you know.

C. Punctuation Needed to Clarify Certain Passages

RULE 10. If punctuation is required only for the purpose of clarification, rewrite the sentence or passage so that its meaning is clear and specific.

CLARITY THROUGH SUBORDINATION

The surest indication of a student's mastery of the problems of writing is his ability to subordinate. If a sentence is the expression of a complete thought, surely the best sentence shows that its author has weighed that thought, determined what about it is most important, and constructed his sentence to emphasize whatever he found to be most important. Effective subordination may be the single most important feature of a good style, for it is through subordination that the writer points to his reader what he wishes that reader to remember. Simple sentences, the expression of one complete thought, and compound sentences, the expression of two or more complete thoughts, are important to a writer's style, but the basis of his style must be the complex sentence, the expression of a major thought and a minor thought. In some ways the complex sentence is the clue to education, for it is an act of judgment. By writing a complex sentence, the writer testifies to his judgment, showing that he can determine what is important and what is relatively unimportant.

Subordination is thus the key to forming thoughts into sentences. The writer's exercise of judgment upon unformed experience and unformed thought can best be handled through subordination in the complex sentence. Such an exercise of judgment makes the sentence a miniature composition, with minor segments unified around a central idea.

Failure to exercise this judgment occurs in several ways. Probably the most frequent are failure to subordinate at all (the fault of excessive coordination) and failure to subordinate logically (the fault of illogical or upside-down subordination).

Sentences that pile ideas together indiscriminately in coordinate elements are invariably failures. If we can assume that there is order somewhere in this world—as we usually do—then we must believe that ideas have relative value and cannot, therefore, be treated as if they all were the same. Even if there is no order in this world, it is the writer's privilege and obligation to impose order. One way he has of doing so is to distinguish between ideas. Consider the following sentences.

> Football is a remarkable sport in that *it instills in every player the will to give the very best he has to offer,* no matter what the price may be, and *it brings out some of those qualities which help to make a gentleman* and *one of these more important qualities is sportsmanship.*

The three elements italicized, linked as they are by the coordinate conjunction *and,* are apparently meant to be equal in importance. A gifted reader, seeing them so connected, will assume that this is what the author meant. The three elements, however, are obviously not equal in importance, the first two being reasons for the remarkability of football and the third being only further clarification of the second. The first two elements, then, may be equal in importance, but the third is logically *a part of* the second.

> Some people do not believe that there is a God. *These people are called atheists.* Others do not deny God, but say that it is impossible for man to know whether there is a God. *These people are called agnostics.*

Here we have a slightly different problem in which several ideas are not coordinated in one sentence but are instead placed in separate sentences. But since sentences are units of thought, a careful reader has to assume, unless he is shown otherwise, that they are equal to each other. The two simple sentences italicized in the passage above illustrate the need for subordination, since it is illogical to separate meanings in this way. The first sentence identifies a class of people, but the term for that class is in another sentence. The same pattern is repeated in the third and fourth sentences. The same meanings could be expressed more concisely and logically (with the term and the identification in the same sentence) in several ways:

> Those who are called atheists do not believe in God.

or

> Atheists do not believe in God.

> Very few limitations are put on boys at most schools about their dress, but there are a few schools that require the men to wear coats and ties to class.

This sentence illustrates one of the most common failures in subordination. Two independent elements are joined here by the coordinate conjunction *but,* which signifies that they are equal in importance. There is some logic in this connection— this may be, in fact, an acceptable sentence. But it is not as effective as it could be if the author would plainly indicate the statement and contradiction to us by subordinating one of the statements. Which he subordinated would depend on what he wanted to emphasize.

> Although very few limitations are put on boys at most schools about their dress, there are a few schools that require the men to wear coats and ties to class.

Subordinated in this way, the revised sentence places the emphasis on the exceptional schools.

> Although there are a few schools that require the men to wear coats and ties to class, very few limitations are put on boys at most schools about their dress.

Handled in this way, the sentence emphasizes the general rule. Incidentally, the sentence needs revision in other ways. Here is the original sentence again:

> Very few limitations are put on boys at most schools about their dress, but *there are* a few schools *that* require the men to wear coats and ties to class.

At most schools intrudes between the more important ideas of limitation, boys, and dress. The italicized words in the latter part of the sentence are unnecessary. Revised (before subordination), the sentence looks like this:

> At most schools very few limitations are put on boys about their dress, but a few schools require the men to wear coats and ties to class.

To summarize, then: we have looked at three common problems of inadequate subordination (or excessive coordination). First, the writer must avoid lumping ideas together haphazardly, making no distinctions between them. Second, the writer must where possible avoid putting into separate sentences ideas that logically belong together in one. Third, the writer must remember his reader and make the relationship between ideas as clear as possible by subordination. Subordination, it must be remembered, is a way of making yourself clear to your reader by showing him how you distinguish between ideas, by letting him know what you consider to be of major importance and what of minor importance.

Even when elements have been subordinated, however, the meaning of a sentence may remain confused unless that subordination is logical. The second most frequent failure in subordination is illogical subordination. This usually occurs when the writer, through carelessness or ignorance, puts the principal idea of the sentence into the dependent element and the minor idea into the independent element. A careful reader (there he is again—you will have to watch out for him) will assume that you are a sufficiently responsible writer to get your most important idea into the most important part of the sentence. If you don't, he may still assume you are responsible, but he will worry about your mentality. In the following sentences, the writers have mistakenly put major ideas into minor sentence elements:

> I have found others who believe as I do, so I know that what I believe has some reasoning behind it.

Two things are wrong here. First, there is a cause and effect relationship that the author has not clearly stated. Second, he has minimized what would obviously be most important to him, his conviction that there is some logic in his position. The revised version corrects both these errors:

> Since I have found others who believe as I do, I know that what I believe has some reasoning behind it.

In this version, the major idea has been put into the independent element of the sentence.

> A good friend of mine had bought a new car and thought that it ran pretty well, so one night he decided to go out and drag it.

One only has to read this sentence to discover that dragging is apparently going to be the important idea in the discussion that follows. But the decision to "go out and drag it" is here relegated to a dependent element. Meaning could be given to this idea by careful subordination:

> Convinced that the car he had bought ran pretty well, a friend of mine decided to go out and drag it.

For clarity in sentences, a writer must distinguish the relative importance of ideas, and he must make that distinction logically so as to put major ideas into major sentence elements, thereby emphasizing their importance to the reader.

Subordination is a major stylistic device as well. Through careful manipulation of a complex sentence, the writer can get the effect of certain stylistic patterns. He can, for example, make his sentence build to an effective climax, or he can begin with the striking idea and then furnish support, or he can in innumerable ways vary the rhythm, movement, and emphasis of the sentence.

Look at the following sentence and then consider the suggested revisions that follow, each of which shows a different way in which the sentence can be handled to get different effects. The sentence was taken from a student essay titled "The Scientific Sell," the main purpose of which was to discuss ways that scientific images have been used in advertising.

> It is logically impossible for every product to be better than every other of its kind, but this is what one must believe if the advertising used is true.

In its original form above this is a compound-complex sentence which by its structure indicates that the two independent elements are equal in importance. The sentence can stand as it is, although there is some question whether we should coordinate (signify as equal) a logical impossibility and the necessity for belief. The writer can make this sentence clearer and more effective by rearranging the elements to emphasize one or the other or to show which of the elements is going to be more important in the rest of the discussion.

> Although it is logically impossible for every product to be better than every other of its kind, this is what one must believe if the advertising used is true.

This version subordinates the first clause and calls attention to the second, thereby emphasizing the foolishness of what we are asked to believe. The writer can call still more attention to this foolish belief if he puts it at the very end of his sentence:

> Although it is logically impossible for every product to be better than every other of its kind, if the advertising used is true, this is what one must believe.

This puts the startling demand advertising makes on us—that we must believe falsehood—at the end, usually the most important part of the sentence. Assuming that one wants to emphasize the necessity of this belief, it is important to show the reader its significance by subordinating all other elements. It would be particularly effective to place the idea at the end of the sentence if the sentence were the last in an essay or the last in a paragraph. As the last sentence in an essay, the final version above would be an effective movement toward a climax, ending as it does with the major idea. As the last sentence in a paragraph, this version would be an effective transition, reminding the reader of the key idea before he moves on to the next unit of the essay.

The writer can change the whole emphasis and effect of his sentence by subordinating other elements:

> It is logically impossible for every product to be better than every other of its kind although this is what one must believe if the advertising used is true.

Arranged in this way, the sentence emphasizes the logical impossibility by placing it in the independent element and subordinating the other elements. This idea can be further emphasized by rearranging the sentence again:

Although this is what one must believe if the advertising used is true, it is logically impossible for every product to be better than every other of its kind.

or

Although this is what one must believe if the advertising used is true, for every product to be better than every other of its kind is logically impossible.

Subordination such as is illustrated above is also a useful technique in maintaining the unity of a paragraph or of an essay. By subordinating carefully, the writer can keep constantly before his reader the central idea of his essay. If he minimizes corollary or secondary ideas in the sentence by subordinating them, the writer clearly shows in the remaining independent element what is most important to the essay. The last two versions of the sentence above, for example, would be appropriate to an essay developing a thesis about the logical impossibility of advertising. The first versions, however, would not, because they subordinate the idea of logical impossibility.

Subordination is an act of judgment by which a writer commits himself to the belief that this is more important than that. As such, it is a service to readers, informing them of the relative significance of ideas grouped together in sentences. *With careful subordination the writer can make his sentences clear by minimizing secondary ideas and emphasizing primary ideas. With careful subordination the writer can make his sentences more interesting by varying their order and by altering the points of emphasis. He can, moreover, help to maintain unity in all of his writing by keeping secondary ideas in subordinate elements.*

CLARITY THROUGH COORDINATION

Proper coordination, a further service to the reader, also requires careful exercise of the writer's judgment. Coordination of sentence elements, whether clauses, phrases, or words, signifies that those elements are equal in importance. It is therefore useful only when the content of the elements can logically be construed as equally significant. That careful reader who has appeared before intrudes again here. He is conscious of what the writer is doing. When he reads, he sees. Beginning writers in particular are sometimes reluctant to admit that syntactical structure is either important to their meaning or noticeable to their readers. But it is both important and noticeable, and the writer who ignores this is invariably going to fail as a writer. To succeed, the writer must remain consistently aware of what he is doing, leaving no pen mark to chance.

Writers who fail to coordinate sentence elements deliberately most often err in two ways. The first of these, excessive coordination, is the piling up of several coordinate elements without attempting to distinguish their relative value or significance. This flaw has already been reviewed above in the discussion of subordination. Be reminded here only that words or phrases or clauses cannot be indiscriminately treated as if they were equal to each other time after time. Indiscriminate coordination is like piling forty people and three cats in a room and pronouncing them all alike.

Many times the writer will need to use coordinate elements either for stylistic or for logical purposes. In this case, he must be careful of the second common error in coordination—putting together two or more elements that because of some incongruity do not belong together. This error occurs in the following sentence, taken from an otherwise imaginative description of a campus student center as it might appear to a nineteenth-century student:

> Not only is there a feeling of magic in the very air, but the people eat such odd foods.

This sentence could be made more effective in several ways. Subordination of the second clause would be one method of eliminating the strange mixture of ideas found here. The two ideas as they are expressed above simply do not go together— one refers to a quality, the other to a thing; one invites, rather tritely, a sense of mystery and strangeness, the other forces us back to earth with talk of food. Most important, the first clause tells us of a quality of which the second is only a condition. The odd foods in the second clause are presumably only one of the reasons for the feeling of magic expressed in the first clause. Subordination of the second clause would be an effective way of improving this sentence. If the writer wants to retain the coordinate structure for stylistic reasons, he is obliged to find a way to coordinate elements that actually belong together, as in the following revision:

> There is a feeling of magic in the very air—the people eat odd foods, they wear unholy clothes, they listen to ungodly music, they talk of unlikely things, and they do it all at an unseemly time.

This is somewhat better, stating in coordinate form the factors contributing to the sense of magic in the first clause. One still worries about that "feeling of magic in the very air," however. It is a trying piece of triteness.

A similar mistake appears in the following sentence from an essay trying to describe the same scene (a student center) from the point of view of a Congolese student seeing it for the first time:

> Everybody was white and seemed to be pointing his finger at him and making weird noises.

Here not clauses but verbs and modifiers are coordinated. The hinted fear could be made more noticeable, and the whole sentence could be made more striking, by a greater emphasis on the coordination:

> They were all white, and they were all pointing at him.

The two coordinate clauses are simpler here, making the starkness of their meaning more apparent. They are, moreover, logically coordinated, the whiteness and the pointing being in this case equally troublesome things.

Coordination, then, helps to insure clarity by showing readers which ideas are equal in value to each other; it is in this sense both logically and stylistically useful. In closely-related situations coordinated elements are useful in showing similarity or contrast between two or more ideas. The balanced sentence is particularly advantageous. Here the coordinate parts are structurally identical to each other.

> I share your disgust for dishonesty among students, and I admire your campaign for honor on the campus.

The structure of the two clauses is identical, both having in the same order a subject, verb, modifier, direct object, and two prepositional phrases. Although it is a bit stilted, the sentence clearly shows the similarity of the two ideas by putting them in equal constructions. Contrast can be shown even more effectively: while the similarity of the constructions leads a reader to expect similarity of ideas, he will be more forcibly struck if the content of the second construction is opposite to that of the first, as below:

> I deplore your lack of ambition, but I appreciate your frankness of manner.

Careful coordination gives an advantage to the writer and performs a service for the reader. It is another technique the writer has for making himself clear and for making his sentences interesting. By careful coordination, he can establish which ideas in his work have the same value, showing at the same time how they differ from or resemble each other.

CLARITY THROUGH PARALLELISM

Parallelism is a specialized technique of coordination that enables a writer to express effectively a series of related or identical ideas. It gives the added attraction of a decided rhythmic appeal in the sentence. The sentence below is a classic example of the telling use of parallelism:

> The notice which you have been pleased to take of my labors, had it been early, had been kind; but it has been delayed till I am indifferent and cannot enjoy it; till I am solitary and cannot impart it; till I am known and do not want it.

This is from the famous letter of Samuel Johnson to Lord Chesterfield on the subject of patronage. Beginning with "till I am indifferent" Johnson writes three equally devastating renunciations of Chesterfield's patronage; by putting all three in exactly identical form, he creates the effect of a rhythmic flail, cutting down relentlessly on its target. The similarity in the structure of the three statements can be seen more clearly in this arrangement:

> The notice which you have been pleased to take of my labors, had it been early, had been kind; but it has been delayed
>
> > till I am indifferent and cannot enjoy it;
> > till I am solitary and cannot impart it;
> > till I am known and do not want it.

Like other forms of coordination, parallelism is a technique for showing the equality of separate elements. For this reason it is useful in clarifying the meaning of a sentence by showing immediately which elements are correspondent. The common error beginning writers make in this regard is to fail to make parallel the form of ideas whose contents are equally significant, as in the following sentence taken from a student essay on the advantages of fraternities:

> One will *make everlasting friendships, learn to be a gentleman, to practice manners,* and *many other beneficial things.*

The four elements italicized are pretty obviously meant to have equal significance, each of them listing presumably major advantages of the fraternity. But the spirit of that careful reader grows restive here, for the writer has not demon-

strated this equal significance, as is obvious in this rendering
of the sentence:

One will

1. make everlasting friendships, (verb, modifier, object)
2. learn to be a gentleman, (verb, infinitive phrase)
3. to practice manners, and (infinitive phrase)
4. many other beneficial things (modifiers, object)

If this writer wants to treat his fraternity decently, he will
have to revise this sentence in any one of several ways, of
which the following is an example:

One will make everlasting friendships, learn gentlemanly discipline and manners, and do many other beneficial things.

In addition to its function as a means of clarifying meaning,
parallelism is also a valuable stylistic device. Effectively used,
it gives the reader through its rhythm a sense of the inevita-
bility of the correspondence of its parts. The following sentence errs by confusing the necessities it speaks of:

What has been pounded into their heads for two decades must
now be removed, and they must learn tolerance, understand,
and respect the faiths of other people.

The sentence can be made both clearer and more interesting
through parallelism:

What has been pounded into their heads for two decades must
now be removed, and they must learn to tolerate, to understand, and to respect the faiths of other people.

The following sentence is inadequate for lack of parallelism,
the writer failing to make the form of his sentence show the
equal importance of three occasions when red cells are needed:

These cells are needed when there has been severe loss of blood,
when major operations are to be performed, and to combat
anemia occurring in convalescence.

Revision can make the three occasions more evident:

> These cells are needed to check severe loss of blood, to prepare for major operations, and to combat anemia occurring in convalescence.

or

> These cells are needed when there has been severe loss of blood, when major operations are to be performed, and when convalescent anemia must be checked.

Careful parallel construction serves both reader and writer. It is a method for showing the equality of a series of ideas and for arousing interest in those ideas through rhythmical expression.

OTHER METHODS FOR ACHIEVING CLARITY

Although subordination, coordination, and parallelism are probably the first techniques the skilled writer must master, there are others he must not forget.

The simple sentence, for example, may be a noble instrument of rhetoric if properly used. No better method exists for calling attention to and emphasizing a single idea. Often relatively short and usually straightforward, the simple sentence by its very form attracts the reader's eye and in so doing calls attention to the meaning it expresses. Over-used, as in the passage that follows, the simple sentence may well be an abomination, betraying the writer's unwillingness to commit himself to active judgment:

> His name was John. He was having trouble making decisions for himself. He went to a psychiatrist for help.

Properly used, however, the simple sentence is effective as a sign pointing to the writer's major point. In the following paragraph a simple sentence is used as a climax, expressing the author's principal point:

Much too frequently freshman composition classes are little more than grammar reviews. Often the freshman composition course is not a freshman composition course at all, but a class in sociology, philosophy, current events, or what have you, as teachers devote excessive time to study of the content of text readings. Even now the recent and continuing tiff over structural linguistics as opposed to conventional grammar in the freshman class is working against our proper interests. Neither of these fine disciplines is the proper subject matter of first-year composition courses. The proper subject matter is rhetoric.

The periodic sentence, already discussed indirectly in the section on subordination, is another tactic for guaranteeing clarity. By definition a structure withholding major sentence elements until the last of the sentence, the periodic sentence emphasizes these major elements by putting them in the most noticeable part of the sentence, its conclusion. Consider the following example, this time from a different form of composition:

> Dim as the borrow'd beams of moon and stars
> To lonely, weary, wand'ring travelers
> Is Reason to the soul. . . .

Had he been a different writer, John Dryden might have written the sentence in this way:

> Reason is as dim to the soul as the borrow'd beams of moon and stars to lonely, weary, wand'ring travelers.

But he chose not to, for the periodic construction of his version of the statement gives him several advantages. First, by putting *Reason* near the end of the construction, he calls attention to it as his subject. Furthermore, by separating that subject from its modifier *dim*, which also gets some emphasis by being at the beginning of the statement, he makes the form of his sentence suggest the obscurity he is talking about. Periodic construction could help the following student sentence, which appeared near the beginning of an essay attempting to evoke the visual impressions aroused by a dormitory and its environs:

> Right in front of me was Milton Daniel Hall, which was constantly noisy from the yelling and shouting from all the fraternity sections.

Since the student who wrote this wanted to stress in the rest of his essay the appearance of this hall and its surroundings, he would have done well to stress his introduction of the hall in a periodic sentence such as this:

> Right in front of me, constantly noisy from the yelling and shouting from all of the fraternity sections, was Milton Daniel Hall.

The last special technique for maintaining clear sentences that is to be discussed here is the responsible use of connecting words. Coordinate conjunctions, subordinate conjunctions, and conjunctive adverbs are nice, neat grammatical facts, but much more significantly they are also stylistic strategies. Connectives such as these serve as directions to readers, letting them know in which direction the writer is taking them next. The word *but*, for example, when it connects two independent clauses, suggests that a contrast exists between them. A dependent clause beginning with *although* is quite clearly some kind of concession the author has made in order to stress some other point; *since* introducing a dependent clause just as obviously sets up a cause and effect relationship between the dependent clause and the element that follows it. In the same manner *moreover* indicates a continuation of the same line of thinking; *however* reveals that a line of thinking is being broken for an alternative. Connectives should no more be used whimsically than any other words or groups of words. As transitional devices, they assume a greater importance than their function in the single sentence gives them. For this reason, their use is discussed more fully in the section on transition in Chapter Five.

The Concise Sentence

Although separated here for ease in discussion, the ideals
of clarity and conciseness in the sentence are inseparable,
each being a function of the other. The clear sentence is by
definition concise; the concise sentence is inevitably clear if
by conciseness we understand not mere brevity, but the economic usage that employs only *necessary* words to convey
meaning. Even though good writing must be straightforward
and concise, we cannot assume that it is therefore simple.
Obviously, complex ideas require complex expression; the
problem is to form that expression out of necessary words
only. The most involved kind of figurative writing, as in
Donne's Meditation XVII for example, remains concise, the
figurative expression being a necessity for articulation of the
idea.

Economic usage, then, is another device of sentence style.
Economy is crucial to sentence style because it contributes
to sentence clarity by freeing the reader from the chore of
weeding out waste before he gets to the meaning. The writer
is obligated himself to throw out this waste. His obligation,
moreover, does not end here for when he has removed unnecessary items, he must in what is left direct his reader precisely
to his meaning. Conciseness, in other words, is a twofold
problem: the sentence must be free of non-essential elements;
and the elements that remain must be the *exact* expression of
the writer's meaning.

For this reason, the study of sentence economy or conciseness is also inseparable from the study of diction. The discussion in Chapter Two of exactness in denotation, exactness in
connotation, and of some common weaknesses in diction is
consequently pertinent here. The writer must diligently pursue
the first two and avoid the last if he is to write effective, clear,
and concise sentences. In doing so, he faces several specific
problems, which once again reflect the twofold difficulty of
economy. He must discover the exact word through his understanding of the denotative and connotative qualities of lan-

guage, and he must rid his language of everything that does not contribute to this exactness.

It is in this second area that the most obvious failures in economy occur. Because of misunderstanding or misinformation, beginning writers often feel that the most heavily-syllabled and profusely-worded writing is the best writing. Feeling so, they too frequently become pretentious, employing inappropriate formalities, euphemisms, and multisyllabic jargon. Or, at the other extreme, beginning writers ignore the discipline that is necessary for effectiveness. Their writing almost invariably is vague, filled with unnecessary words, repetitions, clichés, and other weaknesses.

The following student essay reveals many of the common problems of sentence economy; unfortunately, its inexactness is further burdened with countless non-essential elements.

COLLEGE FRESHMEN

(1) Each year many students who are not properly prepared for the demands of a college or university enroll. (2) Many such seekers of knowledge are helpless as babies when they are given original works to read that haven't been abridged, outlined, or condensed. (3) This helplessness may apply to the student's former education.

(4) Throughout high school subjects are presented in such a way that there is actually no need for a student to cultivate the habit of studying or thinking for himself. (5) Secondary materials are always available. (6) Teachers, tending to forget that a part of learning is thinking for oneself, give their students subject matter that can be absorbed with little effort. (7) The memorizing of facts is the ultimate goal of high school study. (8) In colleges or universities, the theories and opinions upon which these facts are based become prevalent.

(9) High school teachers give many subjects a once-over-lightly, but never give their students a microscopic view of them. (10) Many times teaching aids are beneficial, but these aids should be presented along with the original material. (11) In this way all phases are visible. (12) Many times the teachers

do not have the time in which to present the subjects as thoroughly as this.

(13) I agree with Alexander Pope: "A little learning is a dangerous thing." (14) Many high school students feel they have much of the vital preparation necessary for college when, in reality, they have only begun their preparation for life. (15) Trying to give a broad education rather than a concentrated one is the common feeling of most high school educators. (16) This plan should be true in the first two years of high school, but the final two years should begin to prepare students for the intensified demands of a higher education.

(17) It might be well if educators would remember that in this modern world of today, high school should be more of a preparatory school rather than an education in itself.

There are a number of inadequacies in this essay that it is not to the purpose to examine at this time. Consider now the writer's failure to achieve conciseness. A number of mistakes are obvious and can be dismissed briefly. The title, of course, is inadequate, failing as it does to signify the precise subject of the paper. In sentence two "seekers after knowledge" is pretentious; *students* is sufficient. In the same sentence *abridged* and *condensed* mean the same thing, one of them therefore being sufficient. In sentence nine the cliché "once-over-lightly" is ineffective. An example of redundancy appears in sentence fourteen: if a preparation is *vital*, we can assume it is *necessary*. A similar redundancy occurs in sentence seventeen, where "modern world of today" says the same thing twice.

Other mistakes in this essay are more troublesome because they reveal a more deep-seated weakness in handling the language. The author has two particular faults that relate to the present topic of economic usage. He is often quite vague, and he frequently fails to use words in quite the right sense. The third sentence, for example, makes little or no sense, the inaccuracy of the wording seeming to reveal the author's incomplete grasp of his material. Most of us would agree, probably, that the sentence should read, "This helplessness may *result from* the student's former education." The eighth sentence reveals a similar lack of control over the material. Contrary to the suggestion there, it seems unlikely that *facts* are based on *theories* and *opinions*. The word *microscopic* in the ninth sentence probably betrays the author. In the context, it is evident he wants to say that students do not get detailed views of their subjects. If we accept the word *microscopic* in its literal implications, however, it will probably signify a *close-up view* of *part* of a subject. The term *teaching aids* in sentence ten is somewhat ambiguous; specific illustrations would be useful here. The matter of the teaching aids is further complicated by the *secondary materials* of the fifth sentence. The reader is at a loss as to whether there is a distinction between these two objects. The eleventh sentence, "In this way all phases are visible," is meaningless. A reader cannot know here which phases of what thing are visible to whom. Finally, the fifteenth sentence uses a number of words that are both inaccurate and unnecessary. The sentence could be revised as follows: "A broad education rather than a concentrated one is the goal of most high school educators."

To follow the image of economy in language, one might say that this essay, whatever its other virtues or flaws, reveals an embarrassment of riches that are conspicuously and recklessly thrown about. Unnecessary and inexact words, phrases, and sentences mar the whole work.

The exact and necessary word in the exact and necessary place—this is the goal for the writer who would achieve the clear and concise sentence.

Interesting Sentences

If a sentence is clear and concise, it is likely to be an interesting sentence. However, a responsible writer cannot depend on this alone, for a new problem appears when the writer begins putting his sentences together. Ten clear and concise sentences fashioned into a paragraph may construct a delightful passage; they may just as easily become a monstrosity.

Even if each of these sentences is perfectly exact and clear, all of them together may be grotesque unless the writer takes care to maintain a sufficiently interesting pattern of sentence constructions. Ten good sentences that are all the same length, or ten good sentences that begin the same way, or ten good sentences that have the same kind of construction—these are no longer good sentences, for the reader is apt to bog down in their midst from simple boredom. The efficacy of the individual sentence is lost in the morass of uniformity, as in the following passage from a student essay describing the ideal teacher:

> The portrait of an ideal teacher represents many things and qualities to me. The most important quality represented is a genuine love for children and young people. A teacher without this is hopelessly striving to do a job for which he is not suited. Neither he nor his students will benefit if the teacher is not wholly dedicated to his work.
>
> A second required trait is a desire to teach and thus to help others. Young children have a great desire for learning which may either be stimulated or discouraged by teachers. Constantly a teacher must challenge students with new ideas in order to develop this desire more fully.
>
> Another important quality which a teacher must possess is originality in his teaching methods. He should make even the dullest course interesting by various methods of teaching which he has devised.

Taken individually, the sentences in this passage are generally acceptable (except for the first one). They are correct, clear, and typically concise. Taken as a whole, however, the passage is dull and ineffective. There are many reasons for this, but one of the most important is that the author took no care at all to keep the sentence structures interesting and varied. The sentences, for example, are all about the same length, the shortest being twelve words long, the longest only sixteen. Although there is nothing wrong with short sentences, so many of them in a row begin to sound like a list instead of a composed essay. These sentences also begin in about the

same way, either with the subject, or with the subject near
the beginning and preceded only by a connective or modifier.

A writer has many techniques he can bring to bear on the
problem of interest. For example, careful subordination, coordination, or parallelism could eliminate the monotony of the
passage—and at the same time eliminate some of the repetition
—as follows:

> The most important qualities of an ideal teacher are a genuine
> love for young people, without which he is hopelessly striving to
> do a job for which he is not suited; a desire to teach, without
> which he is unable to stimulate students who must be challenged;
> and originality, without which he is unable to interest students
> who are in his class.

Emphatic breaks following long sentences such as this,
breaks that can be accomplished with a good crisp simple
sentence, furnish another method for creating interest (see
paragraphs on pages 66, 100).

In addition to the standard methods of achieving clarity
and interest (subordination, coordination, parallelism, use of
the simple sentence, and other methods described above),
there are some special methods for helping to maintain interest
in sentences grouped into paragraphs or essays. Simple *variation in sentence length* is sometimes helpful. No one (except
that careful reader who broods over these pages) is going to
count words in your writing, but the length of sentences is a
thing that impresses itself on a reader, consciously or otherwise. Neither will anyone suggest that you count as you write.
It is only necessary to be aware of what you are doing. No
mark should be put on paper without deliberation. Look at the
first paragraph of the paper on page 72, revised so as to alter
sentence lengths:

> The portrait of an ideal teacher represents many things to me.
> The most important quality represented is a genuine love for
> young people, without which the teacher is hopelessly striving to
> do a job for which he is not suited. Unless the teacher is dedi-
> cated, no one benefits.

Here the effect of the paragraph is somewhat improved by moving from a short to a longer to a still shorter sentence. The effect is considerably heightened by the appearance of the shortest sentence in the climactic position. The revision also illustrates another method for creating interest. In the original version every sentence was constructed loosely, the major elements coming early in each sentence. The short periodic sentence at the end of the revised version is a sample of *variation of loose and periodic sentence structure*. Finally, the revised version illustrates still another technique for creating interest. In the original version, all of the sentences began in about the same way. The final sentence in the revised form destroys that uniformity by putting a long modifier at the first, illustrating the *variation in sentence beginnings* that often helps to avoid monotony.

Not illustrated in this passage is a fourth method for creating interest: *variation in sentence types*. Too many sentences of the same grammatical type in a row will inevitably create a deadly rhythm, which will so lull the reader that he may not awaken.

The writer, then, has certain fairly reliable methods for creating and maintaining interest in his sentences. *He has the standard methods discussed in the sections on clarity and conciseness. He has, in addition, four special methods: variation in sentence length, variation in loose and periodic structure, variation in sentence beginnings, and variation in sentence types.*

❀ *Deliberate Sentences*

One of the greatest problems for the young or inexperienced writer is the deliberation that is necessary in order to write well. No word, sentence, or paragraph can be written by chance; no part of the meaning can be left for the generosity or wit of the reader to divine. The special form this problem takes is the necessity for the writer to remain conscious at every moment of what he is doing and why he is doing it. As a means of helping to enforce this consciousness, at least in the first six or eight essays, we suggest the use of one or the other or both of the following schemes. Both require the writer to look at what he is doing.

The first scheme is a chart that can be constructed at the end of the essay, with the following headings:

Sentence Number	Sentence Length	Sentence Type	Sentence Beginning
1	18	Simple	Subject
2	21	Complex	Prep. phrase
3	25	Complex	Dep. clause
4	9	Simple	Subject

From the samples given in each column, it is fairly obvious what the purpose of this chart is. A glance at the last three columns will tell the writer whether he is writing too many sentences of the same kind, the same length, and with the same kind of beginning. The chart, of course, should be only a guide to the writer, but it may help him to remain alert to what he is doing.

The second scheme is a key to be used in the margin by each sentence.

s	simple sentence
c	compound sentence
cc	compound-complex sentence
A-1	complex sentence, beginning with an adverbial clause
A-2	complex sentence, ending with an adverbial clause
A-3	complex sentence, with an adverbial clause elsewhere
N-1	complex sentence, beginning with a noun clause
N-2	complex sentence, with a noun clause elsewhere
ADJ	complex sentence, with one adjectival clause
xx	complex sentence, with two dependent clauses
xxx	complex sentence, with more than two dependent clauses

Careful use of this key in the early essays of the writer's career may also help him to deliberate as he composes.

Assignments

Effective Sentences and Subordination

1. Each numbered paragraph below is a group of related ideas. Take each group and combine its ideas into single sentences in *four different ways*, according to the manner in which their emphases would probably fall in each of the following compositions:

> (a) a discussion of range conditions in West Texas
> (b) an essay on the pioneers of this part of the country
> (c) an article about Graham, Texas
> (d) an argument in favor of more dams on the Brazos River

Each sentence you write should be clear, consistent, and concise, and *above all* should use well the principle of subordination. Each must have only one main clause and one or two dependent clauses, the least important ideas being expressed in phrases and words. While you may occasionally omit one or more of the ideas in one of your individual sentences, your papers will be graded partly on the basis of your success in working them all in.

1. Buffalo grass holds rainwater and prevents floods. It is also highly nutritious. It grows in Young County, Texas. Graham is the county seat. The Indians who used to live there were savage. They ate buffalo and antelope. So did the first white men. Buffalo and antelope ate buffalo grass. Cattle eat it now. Drought and overgrazing have left much bare ground. The water that runs off this bare ground into the Brazos River causes floods. Graham is a prosperous cattle town.

2. Sometimes you find log cabins near Graham. You find oil wells too. They represent the pioneer past and the industrial present. In between these periods came a ranching era. Ranching still goes on. Lack of a dependable water supply limits industrial progress.

3. Early settlers knew nothing about scientific farming and ranching. They plowed up the prairies and the rain washed away the topsoil. They put too many cattle in their pastures. This makes the land poorer now than it was then. With better land Graham would be richer. Also, lakes would bring fishermen and hunters and prosperity into Graham.

4. Bill Hynes is a rancher. His grandfather built up a ranch near Graham in Indian times. Graham has a Chamber of Commerce. Bill is its president. The Brazos runs beside his ranch. Sometimes it goes on a rampage and drowns cows. He likes his ranch. It has fed three generations of his family.

5. Possum Kingdom Dam makes a lake close below Graham, Texas, on the Brazos. There are no dams above Graham. Higher up, in West Texas, the Brazos runs through many kinds of country. There are plains and prairies and some stretches which are almost desert. In dry years sometimes it does not flow and these parts of the country are nearly waterless. Lakes would help this condition. When the pioneers came, it was the same.

2. Summarize in one sentence each paragraph of an essay assigned by your instructor. Make each summary sentence a complex sentence, with the topic of the paragraph in the independent clause,

all other elements being subordinated in dependent clauses, phrases, and words. If your sentence follows the organization of the paragraph closely, this should give you widely varying kinds of sentences. If, for example, the paragraph builds toward establishment of the topic at the climax, then your sentence should build toward the independent clause at the end. If, on the other hand, the paragraph starts with a statement of the main idea, then your summary sentence should reflect this structure. Because of its possible value in demonstrating the endlessly varying effects one can achieve with sentence structure, this should become a regular exercise, performed on each essay read. With a little practice, incidentally, this may become a remarkably efficient method for taking notes.

3. Rewrite the sentences in a passage from an essay assigned by your instructor, excepting simple sentences. Invert complex sentences so that the clause which in the original was independent now becomes dependent, dependent constructions appearing now in the independent clause. Subordinate one or more parts of compound sentences to make them complex. Invert compound-complex sentences in much the same way suggested for handling complex sentences. When you have done this, explain why the author chose to handle the sentence as he did.

Readings

Johnson, Letter to Lord Chesterfield, *Selected Letters* (Oxford, 1951).

Donne, selected Meditations, *Complete Poetry and Selected Prose* (Modern Library).

Lincoln, selected Letters and Speeches, *Life and Writings of Abraham Lincoln* (Modern Library).

Churchill, *Blood, Sweat, and Tears* (New York, 1941).

Faulkner, Nobel Prize Speech, *Faulkner Reader* (New York, 1946).

Chapter Four

❀ PARAGRAPH STYLE

No conclusion, no idea, no notion comes to us all in one piece. If, having arrived at some conclusion or having formulated some idea, we should look back on the antecedent musing, meandering, and malingering out of which that conclusion or idea emerged, we would discover that we have put together into one form what had earlier been unrelated ideas. These unrelated ideas, when they suddenly cohere, give us a new formulation, a new idea (new at least to us), a new perspective. This fusion of ideas represents approximately the function of paragraphs. They are the little pieces of truth that we must find a way of putting together in order to articulate a bigger truth.

No one, therefore, can dogmatically pronounce exactly what the form of the ideal paragraph is. Its length, its form will depend on the idea it develops and on how that idea fits into a larger scheme developing a more important idea. In near and in far antiquity, when few people read and when communication was primarily oral, the paragraph was of little concern. The tone, mood, and gesture of the reader or speaker served adequately to inform audiences of the introduction and management of new material, as did obvious transitional devices. Today, writers serve notice by blank space and indentation that they are introducing new topics that, accumulated, will establish a major topic.

This is what paragraphs are for. They are the author's device for determining minor points necessary for the statement of a major point. They are a device that allows the author to take his reader with him through the various steps in his thinking so as to arrive at the conclusion of that thinking. Obviously the length of paragraphs depends on what kind of minor points or steps in thought must be established. Paragraphs may run anywhere from fifty to five hundred words. More important than the number of words is the necessary sense of completeness in each paragraph. An essay cannot be a coherent whole unless its parts are coherent wholes as well.

A paragraph is subject to the same restrictions as the sentence is subject to: it must be clear, concise, and interesting. Like the sentence, the paragraph can be manipulated so as to achieve these goals. But the paragraph creates new problems, too; because it is a collection of sentences, it is more immediately concerned than the sentence need be with movement from idea to idea and with the coherence of ideas. The standards for good paragraphs and the manipulation necessary to achieve and maintain those standards are the subject of this chapter.

Characteristics of a Good Paragraph

The good paragraph has two specific functions: it must develop its own topic, that minor contributing idea, and it must show how that idea merges into a larger composition, helping to develop a more important idea. To perform these functions well, the paragraph, like the sentence, must be clear, concise, and interesting; it must also be unified and coherent.

THE SENTENCE IN THE PARAGRAPH

Quite clearly there is no hope for the paragraph unless the sentences which make up the paragraph are themselves effective. The following paragraph illustrates the failure of a paragraph composed of ineffective sentences:

(1) Everyone has seen what is commonly referred to as niggertown. (2) All towns have them and the reason for this situation is plain. (3) The colored town is the slum area. (4) The houses are dirty and run-down, and an atmosphere of poverty surrounds them. (5) If the average Negro gets enough to eat and a place to sleep, that is all he wants. (6) As long as these conditions are prominent, the white man will never accept the Negro as being on the same level with him; the Negro seems to be in no hurry to change.

Inexactness and fuzzy thinking and writing make this a hopeless paragraph. In the first sentence, for example, the phrase "what is commonly referred to" seems apologetic. One wishes the writer had either avoided the term or used it without embarrassment. The second sentence combines two independent clauses, the first of which makes a statement and the second of which points vaguely to some kind of reason for some kind of situation. The third sentence is a remarkable example of circular reasoning: the colored town is the slum area is the colored town is the slum area. Nothing striking is wrong with the fourth sentence, except that there is no reason for two independent clauses. Beginning with the fifth sentence, the writer changes his subject altogether. In the first part of the paragraph he is talking about slum areas; in the second he has turned and is discussing what he imagines to be the character of the Negro. The fifth sentence itself is a foolish and hasty generalization. The long sixth sentence is troubled too: the word *prominent* is misused, and the writer seems otherwise oblivious to current events. The paragraph, in other words, is no paragraph at all, but a wobbly attempt to put together *two* poorly conceived ideas, an attempt which, far from making any point, simply reveals the author's failure. To avoid such a failure, a writer must begin with disciplined sentences that are clear, concise, and interesting, and with them he must construct an equally clear, concise, and interesting paragraph.

CLARITY, CONCISENESS, AND INTEREST
IN THE PARAGRAPH

We may use these same terms again briefly to discuss some features of paragraph style. A little later we will also see that clarity, conciseness, and interest are the goals of some specific techniques in paragraph design.

An author's work is presumably clear to the reader when that reader can understand (1) the author's ideas, and (2) the relationships between those ideas. A writer can help to make these things clear by manipulating his paragraphs in much the same way he does his sentences. Consider the following paragraph:

> Rhetoric is the neglected art. In the wilderness of papers to be graded, we have been as prophets, crying, "Our students cannot write, they cannot write." Indeed, many of our freshman students cannot write—and the responsibility is at least partially ours: we have not taught them to write. We have studied grammar, we have studied the contents of nice essays, we have written sweet autobiographical themes, but we have not studied rhetoric. We have given our students no models, we have given them no techniques. All too often we have given them no understanding at all of the strategies and techniques that create effective style.

The paragraph is clear enough. The author has called attention to his main point by expressing it in the first sentence of the paragraph. He could call attention to it in another way. In the discussions of subordination and of the periodic sentence in Chapter Three, it was suggested that the end of a unit is usually the most important section of the unit. The author, then, could call attention to his point in the same way he would in a periodic sentence, by putting it at the end of the unit:

> In the wilderness of papers to be graded, we have been as prophets, crying, "Our students cannot write, they cannot write." Indeed, many of our freshman students cannot write—and the responsibility is at least partially ours: we have not taught them to write. We have studied grammar, we have studied the contents of nice essays, we have written sweet autobiographical themes, but we have not studied rhetoric. We have given our students no models, we have given them no techniques. All too often we have given them no understanding at all of the strategies and techniques that create effective style. Rhetoric is the neglected art.

Again, the paragraph is clear enough, perhaps a little clearer than in the original version because the author has taken us through his subordinate points to a climax in the brief simple sentence. He can, moreover, find still other ways of emphasizing this same point:

> Rhetoric is the neglected art. In the wilderness of papers to be graded, we have been as prophets, crying, "Our students cannot write, they cannot write." Indeed, many of our freshman students cannot write—and the responsibility is at least partially ours: we have not taught them to write. We have studied grammar, we have studied the contents of nice essays, we have written sweet autobiographical themes, but we have not studied rhetoric. We have given our students no models, we have given them no techniques. All too often we have given them no understanding at all of the strategies and techniques that create effective style. Rhetoric is forgotten.

Here the author has both begun and ended with his main point, repeating it in the two most important parts of the paragraph in order to keep it before us.

For the sake of clarity in the paragraph the author can, in other words, use many of the same techniques he would use to achieve clarity in the sentence. He can emphasize his

MAJOR POINTS *by getting them into independent elements at strategic places in the paragraph, using subordination, coordination, parallelism, simple sentences, periodic constructions, and other techniques for clarification discussed in Chapter Three.*

Conciseness in the paragraph, while it is as we shall see associated with problems peculiar to the paragraph, is also dependent on the conciseness of the sentences. That is, the principles that make sentences concise likewise help to make paragraphs concise. Like the sentence, the paragraph should consist of exact and necessary elements. It should, therefore, be free of pretentious diction, redundancy, clichés, deadwood, and all the other unnecessary elements discussed in the section on conciseness in Chapter Three.

The suggestions regarding interesting sentences in Chapter Three are also pertinent here. Nothing makes for an interesting paragraph as well as having a good subject well organized, clearly realized, and concisely executed. The writer may, however, also contribute to the interest of his paragraph through use of some of the methods mentioned in Chapter Three. Special efforts should always be made to get a pleasing variety within the paragraph by varying sentence length, sentence types, and sentence beginnings. The chart and key given at the end of Chapter Three are particularly useful in helping writers to stay conscious of these problems as they write.

A CORRELATION OF SOME TERMS

Throughout Chapter Three and to this point in Chapter Four, the terms *clarity, conciseness,* and *interest* have been used as standards for an effective style. At this point it becomes necessary to see how these three terms relate to two special terms that are used in analysis of paragraphs and essays, *unity* and *coherence. Unity* is a term used to denote the singleness of effect that occurs in a paragraph when all the constituent parts harmoniously contribute to that effect. This special problem, the elevation of a single major effect through the contributions of subordinated ideas, obviously is both a part of the general problem of *clarity* and one of the methods of achieving *conciseness*. *Coherence* is a term used to denote the continuity that is necessary to gain a unified effect. It is therefore likewise a method for obtaining *clarity* and *conciseness*. Both *unity* and *coherence* help to maintain *interest*, since a single effect smoothly rendered inevitably creates a certain appeal.

UNITY IN PARAGRAPHS

A paragraph is unified when every element in the paragraph contributes directly to the establishment of a single effect. Writing is perhaps more than anything else an act of faith, by which the author assumes that some kind of order can be imposed upon experience. The establishment of order, the discovery of insight or perspective—in one way or another these are the common goals of most writing. Meaning in this world must be discovered; it must be worked out through the discipline of the mind and of the heart. The lowly paragraph is one means to such discovery. It is the author's assertion that *this* and *this* and *this*, accumulated and arranged in a design, point to *that*. One of the two most common mistakes in the construction of paragraphs is the failure to direct all sentences in the paragraph toward one end, the failure, in other words, to establish meaning through a unified effect. Consider the following paragraph, concluding a student essay entitled "The Invention of the H-Bomb Was a Boon to Mankind."

1 The world today is in a state of unrest and fear. Two world
2 powers poise, ready to strike and annihilate an enemy's indus-
3 trial wealth. Once an attack has begun, it cannot be stopped.
4 Destruction may be the final result of continued differences be-
5 tween these two countries. Will the people of tomorrow live in
6 peace, knowing the wealth and convenience of atomic power;
7 or will there be but a few witnesses to the bomb's fury, a civili-
8 zation reduced to cooking over wood fires and living in make-
9 shift houses surrounded by rubble? Atomic power is wonderful.
10 It has given to mankind a cheap and compact fuel, but will it

11 also be the destruction that denies man the enjoyment of its
12 power? Atomic power is a boon to mankind, but it is up to the
13 heads of the governments to settle the differences without war,
14 so that everyone may know the pleasure of an easier way of life.

One might spend an hour or two on incidental errors in diction and on ineffective sentence structure and other mistakes in this passage. Note, for example, the questionable logic of the title itself, which argues that a bomb, a weapon for killing masses, is beneficial. Despite the plenitude of weaknesses, the most obvious fault in the passage is its failure as a paragraph. The failure is primarily the result of a split in emphasis that destroys the possibility of unity. The title, remember, states the beneficent qualities of the H-Bomb. Yet in this the last (and therefore most important) paragraph, five of the eight sentences lament the devastation and destruction that threaten us, while only one sentence speaks vaguely of the beneficial features. The two remaining sentences speak of possibilities for both evil and good. The paragraph starts off pretty well, dealing consistently with the same general idea, although it is not the idea announced in the title. Then, in the middle of line 9, the author reins up short and shifts horses and directions between sentences, introducing us in the next breath to the wonders of atomic power—which also has nothing directly to do with the H-Bomb, by the way. From the middle of line 9 to the latter part of line 10 the author continues in his new direction, only to shift again, this time in the middle of a sentence, back to the expected grief. He pursues this course again until early in line 12, at which point we leap again to the meditation upon the benefits of atomic power, which the author stays with, somewhat restively, until the end. At this point one is reminded of *Tristram Shandy*. Let us chart the course of this paragraph:

5 sentences take us this way

————————————————————————→

                               1½ sentences take us
                               back this way

←————————————————————

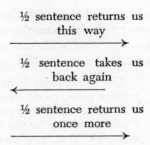

½ sentence returns us
this way

→

½ sentence takes us
back again

←

½ sentence returns us
once more

→

If we were to lose our heads completely and add and subtract, we would discover what we knew all along, that this paragraph doesn't proceed very far from its beginning—and, remembering the title, we would see that the direction it moves longest in is the wrong direction.

The paragraph, to be brief at last, has no unity; it creates no single major effect. Reading it, we do not know what the author's point is. To avoid this kind of failure, the author may resort to a number of strategies that help to create unity.

One of these methods is simply close scrutiny of the subject matter of the paragraph. Even a casual examination of the first draft of most paragraphs is enough to tell an alert writer whether or not everything he says in the paragraph belongs together. The writer of our bomb paragraph neglected this step. If we revise this paragraph, leaving out everything that doesn't help to establish the benefits of the H-Bomb, we of course don't have much left, but what we do have is more nearly unified:

> Because of the wonders of atomic power, the most spectacular form of which is the H-Bomb, people of tomorrow may live in peace, knowing the wealth and convenience that come with this new power. Because it has given mankind a cheap and compact fuel, everyone may soon know the pleasure of an easier way of life.

This is somewhat better, all references to the destructive power of atomic energy having been eliminated.

Another technique the writer may use to achieve unity is to

take special care with the order of his sentences. In the bomb paragraph, for example, we can keep all of the sentences, even those dealing with destruction, and by rearrangement build toward a more unified paragraph:

> The world today is in a state of unrest and fear. Two world powers poise, ready to strike and annihilate an enemy's industrial wealth. Once an attack has begun, it cannot be stopped. Destruction may be the final result of a difference between two countries. Tomorrow there may be but a few witnesses to the bomb's fury, a civilization reduced to cooking over wood fires and living in makeshift houses surrounded by rubble; or, if heads of government can settle these differences, the people of tomorrow may live in peace, knowing the wealth and convenience of atomic power. It has given to mankind both a terrible threat and a potential boon in the form of a cheap and compact fuel. With it, everyone may know the pleasure of an easier way of life.

This is still not the best paragraph in the world, but some improvement is certainly noticeable. All but one of the references to possible destruction have been put in the first half of the paragraph, with the benefits withheld for the last half. There is some justification for handling the material in this way, as if the author were conceding at first the potential disaster but asserting anyhow the possible blessing at the end. A third method, involving several different techniques, is more useful for creating and maintaining unity. The author may retain all of his original statements and by careful subordination, coordination, parallelism, by effective use of periodic and simple sentences, minimize some elements in his paragraph and emphasize those that lead toward the main point. Painstaking subordination, for example, can make the bomb paragraph almost decent:

> Although the world today is in a state of unrest and fear with two world powers poised, ready to strike and annihilate an enemy's industrial wealth with atomic attacks that once started cannot be stopped, people of tomorrow may live in peace, knowing the wealth and convenience of atomic power. While de-

struction may be the final result of continued differences, with only a few witnesses to the bomb's fury remaining and civilization reduced to cooking over wood fires and living in makeshift houses surrounded by rubble, the wonders of atomic power may prove a boon to mankind. It has given mankind a cheap and compact fuel; consequently, if the heads of government can settle our differences, everyone may know the pleasure of an easier way of life.

In this version of the paragraph every reference to the destructive power of atomic energy has been subordinated. With these elements diminished, we can see more clearly the points the writer makes about the potential good of atomic power. The effect here is to call our attention only to those points that help to establish the blessings of atomic power.

The writer thus has several techniques for unifying his paragraphs. Careful study of his subject matter may help him to eliminate all non-essential or incongruous items. Rearrangement of his sentence order may help him to emphasize what is most important. Subordination and other tactics of sentence style may help him to minimize unimportant elements and attract attention to the points that contribute to the single effect he wants. The most useful method, which we have not discussed yet, is the development of a paragraph from a topic sentence.

The Topic Sentence. Either by choice or by chance most paragraphs contain a single sentence that expresses the central idea of that paragraph. This is the topic sentence. It may appear anywhere in the paragraph. The author may choose to begin with the statement of his central idea and then develop the contributing points. He may choose to begin with the contributing points and build toward statement of his central idea at the end of the paragraph. He may just as well choose to put the topic sentence somewhere in the middle of his paragraph; he might, for example, prefer to take a moment to set his scene, then state his central idea, and afterwards develop the necessary minor points. Some paragraphs, however, may not have *one* sentence which states the key idea. Some paragraphs develop a central idea by accumulation rather than by statement and development. But always, whether it is stated or implied, the paragraph has as its focus one central idea. The topic sentence is the articulation of purpose in the paragraph. Every paragraph must have such a ruling purpose; the topic sentence is simply its formal statement.

As such, it is an efficient tool for guaranteeing unity in the paragraph. If the writer commits himself to a definite statement of the purpose or central idea of his paragraph, he has a standard by which he can measure the rest of the paragraph. If the central idea of the paragraph is actually stated, the writer can by constant reference to it insure the close relationship of the other sentences in the paragraph.

(1) To achieve the results we want—acceptable, intelligent writing—through the study of rhetoric, we must first of all assume some knowledge on the part of the students. (2) We must assume a basic knowledge of grammar, syntax, and punctuation. (3) Even if these were proper materials for a university composition course, there would simply not be enough time adequately to consider these things as well as the more important matter of rhetoric. (4) Accordingly, we must conduct our classes as if everyone there had proper preparation for college work, devoting class energies to writing, re-writing, and analysis of writing. (5) We must be obstinate in the cause of the university. (6) A semester or even a year is all too little time for the proper study of writing, and we can ill afford to waste any of that time on elementary study.

In this paragraph the first sentence is the topic sentence. Note the close relationship between it and the succeeding sentences. The topic sentence announces the central idea, that some knowledge on the part of the student must be assumed. Sentence 2 then states what kind of knowledge must be assumed, and sentence 3 explains why this knowledge must be assumed. Sentence 4 indicates briefly one effect this assumption would have on classroom activities. Sentences 5 and 6 show further why this knowledge must be assumed, reiterating for effect the reason advanced in sentence 3. Using the topic sentence as a point of reference, the author here established a logical relationship between each sentence and the central idea of the paragraph.

Unity in the paragraph, by whatever means it is achieved, is a feature of writing that (1) *fixes the reader's attention on a dominant idea and thus helps to insure the* CLARITY *of the paragraph;* (2) *minimizes or eliminates non-essential material and thus helps to insure the* CONCISENESS *of the paragraph; and* (3) *enables the reader to see the writer's ideas developing more clearly and thus helps to insure the* INTEREST *of the paragraph.*

COHERENCE IN PARAGRAPHS

At the beginning of the discussion of paragraph unity it was pointed out that one of the two most common problems in paragraph construction is the failure to direct all the sentences in the paragraph toward one end. Even when this problem is solved, however, the writer cannot rest on his laurels, for the second of these common problems then occurs. Unity among the sentences of a paragraph is not enough—indeed unity is not fully achieved—unless there is a clear, continuous movement from the first to the last of the paragraph. This is the problem denoted by the term *coherence*. Earlier defined as the continuity necessary to achieve a unified effect in the paragraph, coherence is that quality which gets the reader through a paragraph smoothly, enabling him to follow the development of the author's ideas without any break in his own line of thinking as he follows the author. Here is a paragraph illustrating what happens when that quality is missing (taken from an essay arguing against integration):

(1) "All men are created equal." (2) So say the supporters of segregation in the United States. (3) This question has been with us since the War Between the States, yet there is still no satisfactory answer to it. (4) The people of the South have been

taught and they are teaching their children to look down on the colored people. (5) They were suddenly ordered by the highest court in the land to do just almost the opposite. (6) It is against human nature to suddenly change what has been accepted as right for years. (7) Any man with a reasonable amount of intelligence knows that integration will never be practical, especially in the South.

Once again let us, in a gesture of sweet charity, do our best to overlook errors that are not immediately pertinent to our discussion. The major problem facing us in this paragraph is incoherence: for obvious reasons we cannot follow the author's thinking with any assurance. For example, his misuse of the word *segregation* in sentence 2 destroys any possible connection this sentence might have had with the first sentence, which quotes a passage presumably dear to *integrationists*. In sentence 3 the author goes on to say, "This question has been with us. . . ." In doing so, he once again blocks the reader in his effort to follow the pattern of reasoning, for no question has been introduced. We can see that there is some connection between sentences 3 and 4, but it is tenuous; we are forced to jump from a question that has no answer to consideration of the training of Southern children. The introduction of the court order in sentence 5 is clear enough in itself, but cannot stand in clear relationship to the preceding sentence unless some indication of time is given. From sentence 5 to sentence 6 we move readily, the order to "do just almost the opposite" preparing us well enough for the resistance of human nature. We probably will assume that a cause and effect relationship exists between sentence 6 and sentence 7, the perversity of human nature being the cause for the impracticality of integration. But the author has not *shown* us that cause and effect relationship. He merely makes two statements, offering no connection between them.

Coherence in a paragraph is a convenience for the reader, a necessity for the writer. The writer, whoever he is, must have some purpose in writing, and that purpose cannot be fully realized unless the reader stays with the writer throughout his work. The writer cannot succeed unless he accomplishes one fundamental task: conveying the reader by means of coherence easily from first to last. Several useful methods for doing so are available. The most obvious of these is using familiar material for the paragraph. If the writer uses familiar material about which he has a complex of ideas, it is likely that the thought development of the paragraph will be continuous, with no major breaks to sidetrack or lose the reader.

But the writer cannot depend on this alone, for sometimes ideas and their relationships, however commonplace or familiar to the author, will seem quite alien to the reader. Hence the writer is obligated to direct his reader in the way he wishes him to go. The direction may be accomplished by judicious pronoun reference, literally demonstrating a connection with an antecedent that might otherwise be overlooked. He may on rare occasions want to effect this direction by repetition of key words in key places, or by near-repetition in a theme-and-variations sequence. Or he may be able to establish coherence by the thoughtful use of *transitional expressions,* whose sole purpose is to connect sentence and paragraph elements (see Chapter Five, pp. 134–137).

"All men are created equal," the supporters of *integration* in the United States *constantly say.* The problem this dogma raises has been with us since the War Between the States; yet there is still no satisfactory *solution to the* problem, for while supporters of integration say this, the people of the South have been taught and they are teaching their children to look down on the colored people. *But suddenly in 1954* they were ordered by the highest court in the land to do almost the opposite. *Feeling that it is against human nature* to change suddenly what has been accepted as right for years, *Southerners think* that any man with a reasonable amount of intelligence knows that integration will never be practical, especially in the South.

As the italics (indicating a pattern of organization) help to show, the segregation paragraph has been revised to give the appearance of rationality, even though its content is still deplorably irrational.

The following paragraph further illustrates the methods of achieving coherence:

(1) In the study of rhetoric we have found outside reading requirements to be very helpful. (2) Since students can usually do at least twice what we ask them to, this energy can well be used in study of essays and selections by the great stylists—authors inexplicably neglected in most anthologies of readings for freshmen. (3) The standards we usually have in mind for writing are the standards that have been attained by the great writers we ourselves have studied and cherished; yet we seldom make them available to writing students.

A sense of continuity can be discovered in several features of this paragraph. "Outside reading requirements" in the first sentence is echoed by "study of essays and selections by the great stylists" in the second. The introduction of the dependent clause in sentence 2, *since*, sets up a cause and effect relationship between the dependent clause and the independent clause that follows. Repeated use of almost synonymous terms such as *great stylists, authors,* and *great writers* helps to keep the goal of good reading before the reader. *Yet,* in the next to last line, establishes a contrast to which the author calls attention.

This kind of direction is a service the writer is obliged to perform, and he must direct the reader's attention not only from sentence to sentence within the paragraph, but also from one paragraph to another. This special problem of transition is discussed in Chapter Five.

The achievement of coherence in a paragraph is a way of pointing out precisely the line of development the paragraph follows and thus insuring its *clarity*. It is a way of directing the reader to the crucial steps, and only the crucial steps, in the development and thus guaranteeing *conciseness* of effect. It is a way of effecting continuity and movement in the paragraph and thus attracting *interest*.

The Development of Ideas in the Paragraph

Great writers, ordinary writers, and hacks have over the centuries discovered functional techniques for writing, methods that have proved reliable in almost all situations where written communication is called for. Among these are techniques for the development of ideas in paragraphs, techniques that have long since become standard and traditional approaches to the construction of good paragraphs. These methods are not good because they are traditional; they are traditional because they are good. They have proved effective and satisfying, in good part at least, because they reflect customary ways of thinking.

Some methods for the development of ideas in a paragraph suggest themselves immediately because they follow some kind of inevitable order. Suppose you live next door to the Boliver P. Taliaferros, man and wife, and suppose you discover when you come home from work one day that they are in the midst of a blind, falling-down sort of family argument. Entranced, you watch the unfolding of this domestic tragicomedy and then rush to the back fence to tell Mrs. Simon Cadwallader the news. Almost invariably your account will follow one of four courses: (1) you will begin with something like, "Well, as I got home and was getting out of the car, I saw . . . ," and go on to relate the events of the bout in about the order they occurred; (2) you will begin with something like this, "Well! I could hardly believe it when I saw them standing there on the front porch . . . ," and then go on to describe the action, from porch to living room to kitchen (the latter views of course through a window); (3) you will rush pell-mell up to Mrs. Cadwallader and blurt out, "That man hit Mrs. Taliaferro across the face with a book and she has a black eye and he said awful things and I wouldn't blame her if she left him for good," going on then to relate the events that led up to this calamitous culmination; or (4) you will, if you savor a story with a good punch line, mosey up to Mrs. Cadwallader and say, "Well, you'll never guess what I saw today," and then, tantalizing her, build your story out of bits and pieces up to its black-eyed crescendo.

These four gossip techniques correspond exactly to four simple plans for developing ideas in paragraphs: chronological order, spatial order, support order, and climactic order. These and other methods may be expanded for use in developing full-length essays, which may also be developed with combinations of these techniques.

1. CHRONOLOGICAL ORDER

Paragraph topics that involve an event or a sequence of events in passing time sometimes naturally demand a chronological development. Paragraphs, for example, in biographical or autobiographical essays or in narratives of special days or special events can usually be worked out pleasingly with simple chronological order. Two special precautions are worth noticing in developing material in this way:

a. The chronological order where possible should be unobtrusive. Handle time references ordinarily in subordinate elements since time is a medium in which things of importance are happening and is not the thing of importance itself.

Not this:

It was nine o'clock when I first saw Winona Walrus, and it was ten o'clock when I saw her again. As I saw her for the third time, when I knew for sure I loved her, the big clock above us was chiming eleven.

This:

I had already seen her twice that morning, once as I hurried into my nine o'clock class and again when I left it. When I saw her the third time, I knew I loved Winona Walrus, for my heart began to pound, racing ahead of the chimes vibrating eleven in the tower high above us.

The most frequent mishandling of time occurs when students fall into a toy-clock rhythm, saying "First I . . . . Then I . . . . Next I . . . ."

b. In chronological development the writer shouldn't treat all time alike. We don't often live high. Unfortunately, we don't even live importantly very often. In a paragraph developed chronologically the writer needn't feel bound by the clock. He must give that important two minutes most of his attention, even if it means slighting the other fifty-eight. The paragraph should be paced so that the most space is given to the most important moments, regardless of their duration, while ordinary moments are passed over quickly. In the following paragraph notice the quick dismissal of time and the pacing that gets us quickly to the point. The author does not dwell on hour and minute, but uses a brief sequence to set a scene. Then he passes quickly over the minutes he must have spent in looking at the painting by saying simply "I came finally . . . ," *finally* here foreshortening the time by calling our attention to the end of a period only so that the author can get quickly to the crucial problem:

> That afternoon I arrived early at the museum and went past the receptionist, past the man who had his gear set up before the Eakins painting and was copying it, and past a couple, one of each type, in black pants and some kind of sweater. I went into the inner exhibition room to the painting they had told me about and stationed myself before it. I tried diligently to explore all the nuances of color, the conformation of the abstract design, the play of shape against shape and color into color. I knew that the artist was internationally recognized, and I knew that his work had been praised in journals and books. Still, standing there, trying as hard as I could to bring to the picture some valid kind of aesthetic judgment, I felt somehow inadequate as I looked past the horned triangle to the mauve parallelogram. I came finally to one succinct conclusion. Somebody was addled.

2. SPATIAL ORDER

An equally natural plan for the development of ideas in a paragraph is some kind of arrangement in space. Topics that deal with objects or places or scenes or with the things that go on in or around these things can easily be handled with a spatial plan. The problem here is to adopt some kind of perspective, to make some kind of order in space. You will often be asked to write descriptive paragraphs or paragraphs explaining a concrete object. Two suggestions may be useful in this event:

a. The simplest way to organize such paragraphs is to begin at some point in space and move systematically to its opposite extreme.

b. The point from which the writer begins and the direction in which he goes from there will depend on what his subject is and what kind of emphasis he wants to give to which parts of it. There are several plans for this kind of development:

Movement from: large to small
small to large
right to left
left to right
inside to outside
outside to inside
far to near
near to far
dominant to subdued
subdued to dominant

In the passage that follows (a classic piece of description, incidentally), the narrator moves from the far distance to things closer at hand, minimizing those things which do not help to evoke the impression of the scene:

The first thing to see, looking away over the water, was a kind of dull line—that was the woods on t'other side; you couldn't make nothing else out; then a pale place in the sky; then more paleness spreading around; then the river softened up away off, and warn't black any more, but gray; you could see little dark spots drifting along ever so far away—trading-scows, and such things; and long black streaks—rafts; sometimes you could hear a sweep screaking; or jumbled-up voices, it was so still, and sounds come so far; and by and by you could see a streak on the water which you know by the look of the streak that there's a snag there in a swift current which breaks on it and makes that streak look that way; and you see the mist curl up off of the water, and the east reddens up, and the river, and you make out a log cabin in the edge of the woods, away on the bank on t'other side of the river, being a wood-yard, likely, and piled by them cheats so you can throw a dog through it any-wheres; then the nice breeze springs up, and comes fanning you from over there, so cool and fresh and sweet to smell on account of the woods and the flowers; but sometimes not that way, be-cause they've left dead fish laying around, gars and such, and they do get pretty rank; and next you've got the full day, and everything smiling in the sun, and the song-birds just going it!

—Mark Twain, *Adventures
of Huckleberry Finn*

The two methods of development we have looked at so far are partly determined by factors outside our control. Time and space, we like to assume, are there; what we must do is find a way of looking at them. These are methods resulting from the exercise of our little judgment upon materials already largely shaped for us. The two plans that follow, however, are determined entirely by the exercise of our judgment. They de-pend completely upon what the writer decides to do with his experience.

3. SUPPORT ORDER

This is a term used to denote that method of paragraph development in which the writer starts with a statement of his central idea, developing subordinate ideas thereafter. This plan has some decided advantages, the most important of which is that by beginning with the dominant idea the writer has a good chance of getting and keeping his reader's interest. In the paragraph that follows the author begins with his topic sentence, the statement of the central idea of the paragraph. The rest of the paragraph is devoted to elaboration of that point and its possible consequences:

Complete concentration on rhetoric in the freshman composi-tion class would inevitably mean increased mortality rates among

first-year students, at least at first. Grading would be stricter as
teachers tended to become less and less tolerant of below-stand-
ard English, ultimately perhaps even refusing to accept papers
not written in correct English. But even if the loss of students is
great, it would be, though deplorable, only a temporary loss. If
we should establish and maintain high standards for writing,
demanding some prior intimacy with the English language, very
little time would pass before students would begin arriving on
campus better prepared for the business of a university course
in composition.

4. CLIMACTIC ORDER

This mode of development has the same advantages as the
periodic sentence; it withholds the dominant idea until the
very last. Carefully handled, this method can hold the reader's
attention well by accumulating subordinate ideas like a crescendo and building toward the major point at the end of the
paragraph. The paragraph that follows uses this technique
beautifully. Relating in the early sentence the incidents of
actual horror, the paragraph culminates in a final sentence
that, because of the suggestion of even greater *possible* horror,
has the impact of a blow.

> After the brutalities had gone on for weeks, U. N. Malayan
> troops finally got moving. They shepherded 35 missionaries into
> a hotel in the town of Kindu, got 20 out to Leopoldville. No one
> died, though a nun whose breasts were badly burned with
> lighted cigarettes wakes up at night screaming at the memory.
> The U. S. last week protested the "outrages" and demanded that
> the culprits be brought to justice. But 250 missionaries were still
> trapped in Kivu.
>
> —"Rape in Kivu," *Time,* LXXVII
> (March 24, 1961), 25

A Parenthetical Note. These four methods have many uses.
Not the least, for the student writer, is their possible use in
handling essay examinations. Although each of these methods
is simple, each is also reliable and effective. Any one of them

could be appropriately used in planning the answer to an essay question. In most essay examinations professorial exasperation results not so much from inadequacy of students' knowledge as from students' unwillingness or inability to shape the knowledge they do have into some coherent and unified form. It is, after all, permissible to organize one's answers to essay questions.

Some Special Plans for Paragraph Development

Also traditionally reliable and effective are some rather more specialized methods of developing ideas in paragraphs. Because they correspond to our typical modes of reasoning and analysis, these remain satisfactory techniques for analyzing or explaining whatever subject the writer must deal with. The writer can, for example, explain his subject by pointing to an illustration; he may help to explain the subject by showing how it came into being, that is, by process analysis; or he can help to explain his subject by defining it. He may also contribute to the explanation of his subject by describing it, by comparing it with something his reader knows better, by classifying it, or by studying either the causes of its existence or its possible consequences.

Each of these methods may be elaborated into schemes as complex as would ever be needed for the examination of the most involved subject, or each may remain a simple procedure for the development of ideas. Whether simple or complex, these methods are the results of reasoning processes that men have found successful for centuries. Because of the complexity of this reasoning, because of the occasional complexity of the methods, and because of the importance of the methods, men have spent volumes in the discussion of these techniques. Although we recognize the dangers of oversimplification, we feel that the writer's first goal in this connection should be to become acquainted with some relatively simple suggestions and precautions regarding each of the methods. In this way he will have available some standard and reliable procedures to be used in almost any situation where writing is required. The sincere and alert student, if he possesses this fundamental information, may easily discover from his own reading increasingly sophisticated usages of each method.

1. ILLUSTRATION

The first and simplest—and possibly most important—of these techniques, illustration actually frees the writer from the responsibility of developing an idea or explaining a subject. He simply *shows* it to his reader. The reader thus does part of the work, inferring from the example given whatever piece of truth the writer wanted to express about his subject.

a. Use either one extended illustration or several brief illustrations. Ordinarily, the more complex the topic of the paragraph becomes, the better it is to use one extended example in order to have ample space, time, and opportunity to develop it fully. As a subject becomes more complex, it becomes more difficult to point to an illustration, the complex subject having so many different aspects that it requires a fully realized illustration to exemplify them all.

b. If the illustration is to have any real significance, it must be specific. The writer must evoke an actual thing or place or person or idea for the reader to look at.

c. To make the illustration specific, present it realistically so that the reader can see that it clearly is a piece of experience. The fault most commonly found in the use of illustrations is the failure to use *specific* examples, vividly realized, as in the following paragraph:

> A sandpile, while it provides exciting entertainment for the children, may break a father's back and a mother's heart. When they can get outside the children can have lots of fun playing and digging in a good sandpile. Sometimes digging and preparing one is hard on the father, of course. Mothers sometimes get very upset if the children bring a lot of sand into the house on the clothes and feet and hands.

The weakness of this paragraph can be corrected with more concrete language and with more specific examples clearly related to the topic of the paragraph:

A sandpile, while it provides exciting entertainment for the children, may break a father's back and a mother's heart. On the afternoon when I finished our sandpile, I called the children out, and they came in eight and five and two-year-old fury to the urgent matter of excavation. Listening and watching from the kitchen window, we did not hear the usual rages and roars, only the business-like exchange of instructions for this hole, that road, and yonder cave. Watching their squatted concentration we knew again how large and free is the child's world, and I could see my wife's eyes grow misty seeing their straight backs, arms hooked over bent knees. She very nearly cried, but remembered that I was supposed to empty the trash. I tried to get up, discovered that at least three of my vertebrae had gotten fastened together a new way from the digging and found that though I was not in a chair, I was still in the posture. And so I very nearly cried. A balding goblin, I started out the door, only to meet face to face—I was broken, please remember—with the unholy three who sought a spoon, a big spoon, and a drink, and brought on seat and knee and face and hand the entire top surface of the sandpile in a massive transfer of topsoil from outside to in. And so my wife very nearly cried again.

Topic sentence states 3 consequences

Digging and concentration illustrate their pleasure

Mother's reaction illustrates emotional effect

Father's reaction illustrates physical effect

Mother's second reaction illustrates further emotional effect

2. PROCESS ANALYSIS

Often a topic can be explained by showing its origins, its functions, and its purpose. To reveal each of these things would require a process analysis to indicate the sequence of events, either movement from beginnings to the present state, operation within the present state, or movement from present to ultimate state.

a. Since process analysis ordinarily requires chronological arrangement, refer to the discussion of development by chronological order earlier in the chapter.

b. In developing a chronological process, keep the sequence of events straight, pacing the discussion so as to give proper emphasis to the more important steps.

c. In developing a mental process, preserve the chronological sequence if it is possible and proper and indicate the principles or associations by which the steps in the process occur.

d. In developing a material process, preserve the chronological sequence and indicate the principle by which the process occurs.

Getting a sandpile built can sometimes be exacting business. In order to get ours ready this summer, my wife and children started last September, all four of them knowing by now that I am hesitant to undertake physical labor of even the tenderest sort. So they mentioned it along ever so often, during Christmas holidays got me to inquire about the price of sand, mentioned it some more, at Easter encouraged me to find some boards for siding, and early in June hinted that the summer might be over with no sandpile for all they could tell. Circumstances and conscience permitting no further delay, I bor-

Process announced

Early steps mentioned in right order but dismissed quickly

rowed a shovel the first week in June,   *Intermediate steps*
a wheelbarrow the second week,   *mentioned and dismissed*
bought a small pick the third week,
and in the fourth week got under way
when my oldest daughter asked if she
could go visit a friend across town
who *had* a sandpile. Not liking this
kind of thing very much, I firmly
resolved to do the whole affair in one   *Ultimate steps presented*
day to have it done. We had agreed   *in detail*
to dig about twelve inches down in
the arranged plot, board the sides,
and then pile in the dirt. I started
digging at eight in the morning. At
nine I thought perhaps a little water
might soften the soil for digging, and
having wet it down, thought I had
better wait a little while until it dried
to just the right consistency. After I
had gotten the children out of the
mud and helped clean them up—after
all, the mud *was* my doing—I started
to dig again.

3. DEFINITION

One of the most useful of the methods of paragraph development, definition depends upon logical distinctions that show how the topic differs from all other members of its class.

a. To define your topic, first put it into its proper class. Since almost any term can be put into any number of classes, determine the appropriate class by its usefulness in developing the topic and by its familiarity to your readers. The term *Petrarchan sonnet* could be put into any of these classes: sonnet, poem, or lyric. The first, while it is logical, is not helpful to the development of the idea because it uses part of the same term. The last, while it also is logical, is not useful because it might not be familiar to your reader. The second is the proper class.

b. Having put your topic into a class, show then how it differs from all other members of that class. To do so, use language that is concrete.

c. Avoid words that are more complex than the term you are defining.

d. Avoid using in your definition any form of the term being defined.

e. Where necessary and useful, use examples in conjunction with definition.

f. Avoid hasty or dogmatic definitions. Because of shifting connotative values a word or a term may not have the same meaning in different contexts.

A sandpile is a bunch of dirt. But all in one place and circumscribed by board, cement, or other restraining materials, it is the setting for children's cavorting, the occasion for dad's dexterity in arranging it, and otherwise the source of parental pouting. Composed of sifted sand, forty-seven toy soldiers, eight trucks, one tractor, one road-grader, three spoons, one shovel, and innumerable incidental children, both indigenous and immigrant, a sandpile, unlike other bunches of dirt, is informed by the vision of children.

Term to be defined, sandpile, *placed in a class,* bunch of dirt

Term differentiated from other members of the class

4. COMPARISON OR CONTRAST

One of the most widely used methods of explanation and development is to compare or contrast the topic with one that is better known to the reader.

a. In comparison, show how the topic *resembles* the thing it is being compared to.

b. In contrast, show how the topic *differs from* the thing it is being contrasted with.

c. Develop comparisons or contrasts of simple terms by presenting the characteristics of the more familiar first and then relating the characteristics of the less familiar to these points.

d. Develop comparisons or contrasts of complex terms by alternating characteristics of the more familiar and the less familiar. The reader has more to keep up with here; serve him by establishing similarity or difference immediately.

e. Develop figurative comparisons or contrasts just as you would literal comparisons or contrasts. Refer to the definition of *analogy* given in Chapter Two.

The careless observer may conclude that a sandpile is like any other pile of sand, such as, for example, the truck-dumped pile awaiting the concrete mixer alongside the membraned structure that will be a new dormitory.	*Two terms for comparison established in first sentence*
He will see that the sandpile, like the sand for cement mixing, is usually sifted and free of any more than dime-sized pebbles. He will see that	*First point of similarity*
the sandpile, like the other sand, is limited and solitary, set off from other areas of the same material. He will	*Second point of similarity*
see that they share the same colors and the same texture. And he will see	*Third point of similarity*
that like most things here on earth, they both are perpetually shifting.	*Fourth point of similarity*
But if he sees only this, he does not understand sandpiles, for a sandpile is a cultural fact of sedimentary significance quite unlike the builder's	*Contrast implied*
pile of sand. The builder's pile is after all only a means to an end, a partial constituent of other means to other ends. A sandpile is a thing in itself, an	*First point of difference*
end, sand made entire in castle, road, cave, and fort. Watchers of sandpiles know that while other sand may find use in the exercise of one man's vision articulated in another man's blueprint,	*Second point of difference*

and find form in the construction of a
third, a sandpile is vision whole and
unimpeded, world on top of world,
world beneath world, the formed
fancy of that great philosopher, the
child.

5. CLASSIFICATION

Comparison, definition, and classification are closely related
techniques, moving in different directions to arrive at the same
goal. Comparison requires the writer to show the similarity of
his subject to some other member of the same general class.
Definition requires the writer to show how his subject differs
from other members of the same general class. Classification
requires the author to show what his subject has in common
with other members of the same general class. It is equivalent
to the first step in a definition.

a. Classify the topic appropriately. Find a class that will
help to develop the topic in the way you want it to go. Eutha-
nasia can logically be classified as either killing or kindness.
The way a writer chooses to classify it depends on what
effect he wants to create.

b. Classify the topic by showing what characteristics it
shares with all other members of an appropriate class.

Watchers of sandpiles know that
not all sandpiles are alike. They know
that there are sandpiles in public
playgrounds, they know that the
beach is a haven of other public sandpiles, and they know that at last
there are SANDPILES, though pro-
ficiency in sandpile-watching may
demonstrate the existence of other
classes. The expert knows that the
sandpile in the public playground has
the same composition as any in
private yards, save for the greater

Sandpiles classified
1. public sandpiles
2. beach sandpiles
3. private sandpiles

Distinctions among the
classes of sandpiles

incidence of rocks, toy soldiers,
spoons, and shovels, but he also
knows that it doesn't permit that
sovereign sense the child has in his
own domain. The expert also understands that the beach sandpile,
composed much like that in the public
playground but for a new ingredient,
shells, and a new sense, the sound of
ocean which makes forts all the more
desirable in sand, likewise forbids the
exercise of monarchy except temporarily. But he who *knows* sandpiles,
knows that the private sandpile in the
backyard is an empire untroubled
except by brothers and sisters and
occasional friends, and they can be
managed when the vision is strong.

6. CAUSAL ANALYSIS

One of the most intellectually satisfying methods of explanation and development is that by which a writer seeks out the
logical antecedents or the possible consequences of a given
topic.

a. In causal analysis, distinguish between immediate and
original causes, original causes pursued too diligently presumably leading all analysis to Adam.

b. Distinguish between conditions and causes. Causes do
not occur in a vacuum; many circumstances may be associated
with a cause; some circumstances may even contribute to the
creation of the effect. Do not, nevertheless, confuse these circumstances with the causes you seek.

c. Be hesitant about pinpointing one cause for a given effect.

d. Where possible, examine more than one case where the
cause or effect you are interested in occurred. Characteristics
shared by more than one case are good guides to the logical
discovery of cause or effect.

Because my wife had a sandpile
and enjoyed it and because I didn't
have a sandpile and missed it, we
agreed that the children should have
a sandpile. Perhaps, in a maze of
fancy I could even say that long ago
in the West Texas of the thirties, I
found a need for sandpiles, in the
midst of the long copper-black dust-
storms envisioning restrained and
controlled sand. And perhaps long ago
in her West Texas of the thirties she
knew a freedom in her sandpile, a
freedom transferable even to city and
cement in its sandy form. Perhaps.
But wife shakes her head. She knows
that sandpiles have their own myriad
pasts fitting each child's conceit, and
she knows that I could not be stirred
to shovel and haul by even such
whimsy as this, and she knows that I
built a sandpile because the oldest
asked for one and the middle asked
for one and the youngest had a
falling-down fit when she could not
break through the rocky soil of our yard.

*The effect: construction
of a sandpile*

Original causes

Immediate causes

7. DESCRIPTION

Paragraphs dealing with persons, places, or things may often
be developed by description. This can be the most vivid of all
the methods, for the writer is obligated not to tell about his
subject, but to show it to his reader and to give his reader the
same impression of it that he has. For this reason it is effective;
the writer shares his experience with the reader, thereby making the reader's understanding of the topic more immediate.

a. Refer to Chapter Eight, "Description."

b. In description, adopt a consistent point of view. Either
look at your topic the same way at all times or inform your
reader when your view shifts.

c. Unify your paragraph around one dominant impression. Find the most striking feature of your subject and subordinate all other features to it.

d. Observe accurately and report concretely. The most common failing in descriptive paragraphs is lack of concreteness. Your reader must see the subject as you do; he cannot do this unless you present vividly the sensory impressions which the subject creates.

> Our sandpile is about three feet wide and nine feet long. We built it against the curb of the driveway, which serves as one side. Wide boards bound it on the other three sides. It is in the shade falling from the big tree in our neighbor's yard. The pile is very light brown and smooth.

The weakness of this paragraph can be corrected by more accurate reporting, by closer observation, and by more concrete diction.

> Our sandpile is one child wide and three children long. It is built against the curb of the driveway outside the kitchen window, and the curb serves as one side. Around the other three sides are old wide boards I found greying behind the garage. Sand spills over the curb onto the driveway all the time, and over the wide board in the back which isn't after all quite wide enough to stand high enough. The shade falling from the big tree in our neighbor's yard cools the sandpile almost all day. Here and there sunlight twisting through the leaves touches the sand and glints of gold and red and white in grain and pebble mottle the sand piled and tracked and fingered in microcosmic landscape.

Assignments

---

1. Read assigned essays in your reading text and be prepared to demonstrate (a) the author's methods of unifying his paragraphs, (b) his methods for maintaining continuity within and between paragraphs.
2. Write paragraphs utilizing each of the methods discussed in this chapter.

3. Write several two-paragraph essays combining two methods of paragraph development to make one controlling method. For example, write a two-paragraph essay developed by cause and effect in which the first paragraph establishes cause by some means of development such as illustration and in which the second paragraph establishes effect by another method, such as definition.

Readings

Reference

Aristotle, *Rhetoric and Poetics* (Modern Library).
Herbert Read, *English Prose Style* (New York, 1928).
James Sutherland, *On English Prose* (Toronto, 1957).

Illustrations

Hazlitt, *Selected Essays* (New York, 1944).
Thoreau, selections from *Walden and Other Writings* (Modern Library).
Milton, "Of Education," *Complete Poetry and Selected Prose* (Modern Library).
Bacon, *The Essays of Francis Bacon* (New York, 1936).

(Illustration) Bertrand Russell, "The Functions of a Teacher," *Unpopular Essays* (New York, 1950).
(Process analysis) Anthony Standen, "They Say It's Wonderful," *Science Is a Sacred Cow* (New York, 1950).
(Definition) Russell Lynes, "The Part-Time Lady," *A Surfeit of Honey* (New York, 1957).
(Comparison or contrast) Edmund Wilson, "War," *A Piece of My Mind* (New York, 1956).
(Classification) Francis Bacon, "Of Simulation and Dissimulation," *Essays of Francis Bacon* (New York, 1936).
(Causal analysis) Rachel Carson, "The Global Thermostat," *The Sea Around Us*, rev. ed. (New York, 1961).
(Description) William Laurence, "The Atom Bomb," *Dawn Over Zero* (New York, 1946).

Chapter Five

✻ ORGANIZATION OF THE ESSAY AS A WHOLE

Once the writer has acquired a reasonable mastery of sentence and paragraph style, he will begin to project technique into the essay as a whole. To do so successfully requires careful and methodical preparation, failing which the essay will fall short of the mark whatever its merits of content and style. Such preparation normally involves five closely related operations: (1) *selecting the subject,* (2) *choosing an approach to the subject,* (3) *forming the thesis,* (4) *breaking down or analyzing the thesis,* and (5) *developing the outline.* It is the purpose of this chapter to pursue these steps, to demonstrate several useful patterns of formal and informal organization, and to convince the writer of the absolute necessity for adherence to the written outline during the stages of actual composition.

I. Selecting the Subject

A. *For the documented paper.* A research paper is nothing more nor less than an expository or argumentative essay with footnotes and possibly a bibliography. Chapter Ten develops the particular problems in subject area for the research paper.

B. *For the undocumented paper.* A *College Rhetoric* is designed for use with a book of expository and argumentative essays. (For an explanation of the nature of argumentation and exposition, see Chapter Six, pp. 141–142.) Guided closely by his instructor, the student will choose subjects for his own essays that are closely related to, in most cases dependent upon, the readings assigned by the instructor, who may himself assign essay subjects arbitrarily. His assignment will usually be a list of topics from which the student may freely choose. These considerations should influence his choice:

1. The extent of his disagreement with the author of an assigned essay. If the disagreement is substantial, concrete, and specific, the student may decide to write an argumentative essay.

2. The possibility of pursuing the author's discourse in a new direction, perhaps by expanding an idea introduced but not elaborated by the author. (Exposition)

3. The need for redefining the author's terms to agree with recent experience—historical, social, political, economic. (Exposition)

4. The desirability of examining the author's unstated assumptions. (Exposition)

5. If the author makes recommendations, the possibility of predicting the consequences, granting the adoption of the recommendations. (Argumentation or Exposition)

6. The likelihood that the author has not dealt with some vital aspect of the essay problem. (Argumentation or Exposition)

II. Choosing the Approach to the Subject

A. The subject should be chosen with an eye to avoiding the trite, the hackneyed, the obvious. Hence any writing problem involves a certain amount of original thinking on the student's part. Thought is a painful process, an impossible one if the student is unwilling to concede that he owns a set of long-cherished prejudices or hitherto unchallenged preconceptions. Fortunately, to write well he need not rid himself of prejudice, but he does need to understand what he already "knows," so that he can decide whether his approach to a subject will be admittedly subjective, giving perhaps full play to the dogmatic, or whether it will be objective—lofty, disinterested, impartial. Both approaches have their uses and limitations, the subjective being mostly preferable for private problems, the objective for public problems. Once the point of view has been decided upon, however, it must be scrupulously maintained; the pronoun *I* throughout an essay will sufficiently indicate a subjective point of view.

Examples of subject areas which tend to dictate point of view:

Subjective	Objective
Personal experience	Education
Religion	Science
Choice of husband	Philosophy
Politics	Government
Cooking	Taxation
Vacations	Law
Books	History
Morals	Health
Art	Culture

B. Most college freshman essays are restricted in length, the average falling somewhere between 400 and 800 words. The scope of the essay must therefore be severely restricted, preferably to one or two specific aspects of the subject under consideration, if the essay is to be expository or argumentative. If it is to be narrative or descriptive, the actual time covered by the narrative should be perhaps only a few minutes; the space covered by description no more than one or two walls of a room, the central figure of a painting or a person's shoes.

Examples of essay titles indicating more or less restricted subject area:

Personal experience
1. Two Minutes to Go
2. Nose Dive
3. Learning a New Dance Step

Religion
1. Missing Sunday School
2. Two Churches Next Door to Each Other
3. Ecclesiastical Clothes for Summer Days

Morals
1. No More Cheating for Me
2. White Lies
3. Fixing Tickets

Education
1. Arithmetic and Algebra
2. Listen and Learn
3. Mental Block

Health
1. Walking to Work
2. The Great Pill Conspiracy
3. Acids and Alkalis

Taxation
1. Free Air
2. Take-Home Pay
3. Private Highways for Trucks

III. *Developing the Thesis*

A satisfactorily restricted subject, conveniently phrased in a tentative title, is the basis for the thesis or *statement of the essential content of the essay in one sentence.* The useful thesis sentence has these properties:

1. It is a complex sentence whose main or independent clause states the central idea of the essay. It is not necessary that the thesis sentence actually appear in the essay, but it may do so.

2. This central idea is clear and specific.

3. The sequence of clauses or phrases reflects the planned organization of the essay.

4. Illustrative material is excluded from the thesis. (It is always understood, however, that illustrations or examples are the ultimate measure of success with the essay.)

Examples of thesis sentences developed from several of the foregoing essay titles (main clause italicized; each example is followed by a suggestion as to a suitable form of discourse):

1. Learning a New Dance Step—Although my sister is an excellent dancer, *she can't teach me to rumba* because she is too bossy. (Narration)

2. Ecclesiastical Clothes for Summer Days—Although there is something to be said for being able to identify a minister by the clothes he wears, *he has the right of every human being to wear a suit that is in season.* (Exposition or Argumentation)

3. Fixing Tickets—Although there may often be good reasons why a mayor or judge or county clerk grants favors to influential persons, *such actions destroy the faith of the voter in government,* for the standards of public morality are absolute. (Exposition or Argumentation)

4. Mental Block—When a pupil develops a psychological resistance to learning in a particular area, *probably his total education, in regard to increasing the power to think, has ended.* (Argumentation or Exposition)

5. Free Air—As civilization becomes increasingly complex, *the tax burden becomes ever heavier,* although the tentacles of the tax collector do not extend infinitely. (Exposition)

6. The Great Pill Conspiracy—The testimony of radio and television advertisements to the contrary, *pills cause more ills than they cure.* (Argumentation)

IV. Breaking Down or Analyzing the Thesis

It is absolutely essential that the main clause of the thesis sentence have a single idea. Contributing ideas are in dependent clauses or phrases; any ideas that do not contribute must be edited out of the sentence. The central idea and those supporting it, then, are closely related, and it is largely the nature of the contributing ideas that determines the patterns of idea development in the essay. An examination of the foregoing six thesis sentences should help to show how these patterns emerge.

1. This sentence has two dependent clauses, both describing the writer's sister. Hence at least a three-paragraph essay is suggested. The material of the first clause can be developed in several ways—cause and effect, description, illustration, even process analysis. The second dependent clause again permits process analysis, description, contrast (with the brother's character), cause and effect, possibly description. As already indicated, narration by means of a series of illustrations or one illustration carefully worked out will serve for the main clause.

2. Here there are three dependent clauses, but the first (enclosing another, "he wears") contributes most heavily to the main line of thought. Two or three paragraphs of argumentation, using contrasting illustrations, are a possibility. Definition is one good way to proceed with the main clause.

3. The rhetorical pattern of this sentence is not greatly different from that of the first sentence. In the first dependent clause "favor" and "influential persons" may need defining, and "good reasons" can be contrasted with "real reasons" by definition and—especially—illustration. In regard to the final clause description and definition may be applied to "standards of public morality." Cause and effect (or its first cousin, process analysis), with an illustration or two, is fairly obvious for the independent clause.

4. Cause and effect or process analysis seems suitable for this sentence over-all. The words of the main clause point up the need for defining a term.

5. Process analysis will serve better than cause and effect. The last clause calls for an illustrative contrast.

6. Description is the best way to reveal the nature of advertisements. Illustrations may also be used to develop the opening phrase. The main clause has several possibilities: contrast, narration, cause and effect, process analysis, illustration. Probably two or more of these should be used in two or three closely related and well-considered paragraphs.

SAMPLE STUDENT-PRODUCED THESIS SENTENCES
FOR FURTHER ANALYSIS AND CRITICISM

1. We are very independent in the United States, which has always enjoyed independence.

2. No one is so completely independent that he does not need someone; therefore I am no exception.

3. Wealth today is the abundance of riches, property, material objects, and personal wealth that directly contributes to making a person industrially efficient.

4. Even though we are all supposedly endowed with certain inalienable rights, the restraints with which one pursues his rights determine the extent of his independence.

5. Politics have greatly affected the class system in my home town ever since revolutionary times, and they still affect social classes today.

6. Although I am able to provide a living for myself now, time and education will bolster my ability and ego.

7. The people in my home town try to avoid being classed so that they may serve others and help themselves.

8. Since there are a number of specialized fields of study which attract people of widely varying interests and great diversity in the social and economic means of these students, on our campus, as at any large university, definite linguistic communities are evident.

9. Too much liberty turning into license is shown by many countries falling into a state of license because they were not taught the way of liberty.

10. I know that our faith is not in vain because faith and desirable goals give our lives meaning and purpose.

11. The physically handicapped worker has proved himself to be a great asset to many people, and live the same life as the physically capable.

12. The person with the higher education has a better chance in life to really make something of his career.

13. There is no such thing as a non-essential item.

14. Being handicapped strengthens a person and makes him better than he was before he was limited physically.

15. Because of the existence of social classes in American high

schools, our young people are being prepared for a life in which one's social position will be more important than any other single factor.

16. My home town possesses a patronage and an appreciation of the arts which cannot be excelled by any city of comparative size in the United States.

17. The qualities exemplified by a gentleman are most often instilled at an early age and remain distinguishable throughout his entire life.

18. Many great achievements have been made by scientists since advertising men were helping.

19. Because of the growing need of business firms to sell their products, a verbal magic came into advertisements, in which certain devices are used to make the advertisement attractive and appealing to the public.

20. Although one must diligently apply himself if he wishes to learn another language, he is soon rewarded for his efforts when his philosophy of life takes on a cosmopolitan aspect rather than a provincial one.

21. Americans often tend to neglect, even omit, cultural arts and sciences from their education, homes, social enjoyment, and lives.

22. When we compare farms of the past and farms of the present, we are able to realize the decline of rural characteristics in farm culture.

23. As modern stoves and heaters replaced the old wood stoves, American culture lost not only its most durable and practical method of heating but also the last vestige of genuine family fellowship.

24. Although the pioneers of our country made the best use of their tools, their homes were at best crude and inefficient and their work slow and difficult, thus bringing the results that the frontiersman invented the new and better methods of accomplishing his work so that he could devote more time to study.

25. When the West was in the process of being settled, six-shooters were carried as a means of protection but are almost never used now because of the changing culture of man.

It is presumed that by this stage of preparation the writer will be making notes on specific material, especially illustrations, suited to the pattern of the paragraph and of the essay as a whole. This is a process that continues until he is ready to produce the final draft.

V. Developing the Outline (and Staying With It)

The outline is an organized analysis, or breakdown, of the thesis sentence. The parts of the outline may be words, phrases, clauses, or sentences, depending upon the complexity of the ideas, but in any case they (the parts of the outline) must be parallel in grammatical structure, or as nearly so as it is possible to make them.

The most useful types of outline are the noun phrase—or topic—outline and the sentence outline. The following outlines demonstrate the form of organization, which must be scrupulously observed.

NOTE: Five classes of essay division deserve special headings, (1) Introduction, (2) Transition, (3) Summary, (4) Conclusion, (5) Thesis. As he studies the essay, the student should number its paragraphs consecutively. In the outlines below, the numbers of the paragraphs concerned follow the topic or sentence. (The essays for which these outlines have been done are listed in "Readings" at the end of this chapter.)

A. **The partial topic outline** (or skeleton outline), particularly useful with the brief essay, or the essay which follows a relatively uncomplicated line of development.

Partial Topic Outline of Aldous Huxley, "Comfort"

Thesis: There is no point in material progress except insofar as it subserves thought. (13)

Introduction: (1)

I. The voluntary nature of discomfort in the past (2–11)
   A. Sub-thesis (2–3)
   B. Comfort and spiritual life (4–5)
   C. Central heating (6)

    D. Baths and morals (7–9)

    E. Clothing (10–11)

  II. Comfort as an end in itself (12)

Thesis: (13)

B. The complete topic outline (transition devices italicized).

Topic Outline of T. H. Huxley, "The Method of Scientific Investigation"

Thesis: Although there is a common notion that hypotheses are largely untrustworthy, they are nevertheless at the foundation of human progress and are scientifically valuable in direct proportion to the care and completeness with which their bases have been tested and verified. (14)

Introduction: The human mind as *necessarily* employing theories, hypotheses, deduction, and induction (1–2)

    A. The scientific method as the expression of the *necessary* mode of working of the human mind (1)

    B. *This mode's* employment of theories, hypotheses, deduction, and induction (2)

I. The establishment of law by the layman or scientist resulting from the use of the *principles* of deduction and induction (3–6)

    A. The basing of man's actions on the *principles* of deductive and inductive philosophy (3)

    B. *These principles* demonstrated by the "hard green apples" illustration (4–5)

        1. The conclusion that a third *hard green apple* will be sour if the first two tasted are sour (4)

        2. The rejection of the *third apple* as the formulation of a law based on a syllogism (5)

    C. Although more precise and delicate, and aimed at the verification of universal experience, the similar reasoning and experimentation of the scientist (6)

Transition: In view of *this* universal way of establishing laws, a look at the universal way of dealing with causation (7)

II. The stolen-teapot-and-spoons hypothesis as a demonstration of the *similar* trains of reasoning about cause on the part of scientists and laymen alike (8–13)

A. The way in which the conclusion that the silver was stolen can be experimentally verified (8–12)

    1. The "stolen" *hypothesis* as over against other theories accounting for the absence of the silver (8–11)

        a. The relative strength of the *hypothesis* (8–9)

            (1) The *hypothesis* as based on a long train of inductive and deductive reasoning (8)

            (2) In the absence of absolute proof, the relative strength of the *hypothesis* (9)

        b. The possibility of advancing *other,* if less probable, hypotheses (10–11)

            (1) The hypothesis that the spoons were taken by a monkey (10)

            (2) The *even less* probable hypothesis that the deductions and inductions were baseless because of the suspension of the laws of nature during the night (11)

    2. The verification of the *original* hypothesis by the apprehension of the burglar (12)

B. The use by the scientist, even when examining the most occult phenomena, of the *same* train of reasoning as that leading to the silver thief (13)

Thesis: (14) [Since the thesis is found at the beginning of the outline and since the whole thesis is in paragraph 14, it need not be repeated here.]

C. The complete sentence outline.

Sentence Outline of T. H. Huxley, "The Method of Scientific Investigation"

Thesis: [as above] (14)

Introduction: The method of scientific investigation reflects the *necessary* mode of working of the human mind, which in all its thinking uses theories, hypotheses, deduction, and induction. (1–2)

A. Since the only difference between the activities of the man of science and the ordinary man involves the use of precision instruments, the method of scientific investigation is nothing but the expression of the *necessary* mode of working of the human mind. (1)

B. Everyone employs theories, hypotheses, deduction, and induction in his thinking. (2)

I. The establishment of law, whether by the scientist or the layman, results from the use of the *principles* of deduction and induction. (3–6)

A. During all their lives people act on the *principles* of deductive and inductive philosophy. (3)

B. An examination of the processes involved in tasting sour apples will demonstrate how people act in *this way*. (4–5)

1. If you find that two hard green apples tasted in a shop are *sour,* you will conclude that a third hard green apple is sour. (4)

2. In rejecting the third hard green apple you formulate a law which may be tested by further experimental verification, performing the operation of induction, and found a deduction by constructing a syllogism. (5)

C. Although in a *more* precise and delicate manner, the scientist *also* establishes the existence of a law and exposes it to every possible kind of verification, his final objective being the verification of universal experience on the part of mankind. (6)

Transition: Having seen that all men establish laws in the same way, let us *now* look at the method by which we regard certain phenomena as standing in a causal relation to other phenomena. (7)

II. A *hypothesis,* whether it has to do with concluding that a thief has stolen some missing silver or with experimenting to discover the origin and laws of the most occult phenomena, results from exactly the same train of reasoning. (8–13)

A. The *hypothetical* conclusion that a thief has stolen some missing silver can be experimentally verified. (8–12)

1. *This* conclusion, although based on a long train of inductive and deductive reasoning, is not the only conclusion that can be based upon all this reasoning. (8–11)

a. *It* has relative strength in the absence of absolute proof. (8–9)

(1) If you were to discover that a teapot and some spoons were missing from your parlor, your conclusion that they were stolen would be a *hypothesis* founded on a long train of inductions and deductions. (8)

(2) Since you furnish no absolute proof for your "stolen" *hypothesis*, it is rendered only highly probable by your train of reasoning. (9)

b. If *less* probable, other hypotheses may be advanced by helpful friends. (10–11)

(1) Before you go for the police, a friend might come in with the *less* probable hypothesis that the silver was taken by a monkey. (10)

(2) *Another* friend might advance the even *less* probable hypothesis that your deductions and inductions may be baseless because the laws of nature may have been suspended during the night. (11)

2. *But* if you go to the police and the police apprehend a person with your property in his pockets, the jury will agree with you that your hypothesis has been experimentally verified. (12)

B. *And* scientists, conducting experiments to discover the origin and laws of the most occult phenomena, even when using infinitely greater "scientific" care to avoid flaws or fallacies in their hypotheses, use the same train of reasoning which led to your "stolen" hypothesis. (13)

Thesis: [as above] (14)

This is a detailed outline, *accounting for every paragraph with an individual topic for that paragraph,* of an essay which is easily 5,000 words in length. But the principle of at least one topic for each paragraph holds true no matter how long the essay is. And so a good student essay of no more than three or four paragraphs will reflect careful organization. In regard to short essays probably the most useful kind of outline is a one-level sentence outline, as in the following examples from uncorrected student papers, which should be examined critically as to how well they follow the principles thus far developed.

FRATERNITIES

Thesis: Are our fraternal programs aiding or hurting our students of today?

I. Fraternities teach their members to be friendly, gentlemen, and to practice manners always.

II. Fraternities are helpful in campus life.

III. A fraternity is a free man's home.

IV. A fraternity does more good than harm.

STATEHOOD AND ITS SOCIALLY SIGNIFICANT CONNOTATIONS TO ALASKANS

Thesis: Many Alaskans felt that statehood would effect a more benevolent union between Alaska and the United States while the contrasting view held that Alaska's economic progress would be endangered by such a union.

I. Alaska, from its early pioneer days, has been a province owned by the United States but governed economically as well as politically by the will of rugged individualists who have continuously prospered in a capitalistic atmosphere.

II. The contemplation of statehood brought two schools of thought into existence, those who felt that political representation in Congress would increase Alaska's economic development and those who maintained that statehood would hinder Alaska's economic progress while bolstering the economy of the United States.

III. Having been a state a little over a year now, one can vaguely perceive statehood's effects by realizing that Alaska's natural resources are being utilized more today than ever before although the question of who is reaping the rewards of these natural resources is omnipresent.

LIBERTY AND LICENSE

Thesis: Although all men have liberty in many things, they are also restricted by certain ideas or rules.

I. Because liberty means complete freedom, restrictions, license, must be made of the best practice for the people.

II. Liberty means complete freedom and independence, but license means restrictions and regulations.

III. Because human nature is as it is, people use freedoms for purposes other than good.

IV. Since our forefathers worked for our freedoms, we must work to deserve these privileges.

HOW INDEPENDENT AM I?

Thesis: A person is not ever completely independent of responsibilities since to live and be a wholesome person requires men to hold responsibility.

I. The United States was founded on the principles of freedom, liberty, and independence, although today's citizens are restricted by laws which have been passed by both legislature and society.

II. Throughout a person's life he is constantly dependent upon someone or something, whether he admits this fact or not, as long as he has responsibilities or duties to fulfill.

III. Total independence is not possible to a man since it would make him a helpless human being.

IV. College does not offer unlimited freedom, either.

POLITICS—THAT DIRTY WORD

Thesis: If all the men who run our local, state, and national governments were honest, trustworthy, and loyal, *politics* would not be a dirty word.

I. Most American parents would be disappointed if their child chose politics as a career.

II. Most of our politicians are lawyers or businessmen who have sacrificed their careers to labor in governmental work.

III. Until 100 years ago American politicians were not even paid a salary for what they did.

IV. If we hope to improve the quality of our politicians, we must attempt to make politics a rewarding profession, socially and financially.

SOCIAL SITUATION AS REVEALED BY LANGUAGE HABITS

Thesis: Language habits reveal noticeable traits that distinguish a person's social situation so that his background and culture are very obvious.

I. Although language has served to classify and separate people for many centuries, it now serves an additional purpose in that it reveals the social situation of a person.

II. A person's language habits readily reveal the social class that he is in.

III. Whether a person is accepted or rejected by a social class depends upon his language habits.

IV. The language habits which a person employs illustrate his background and culture.

Each of these five student outlines follows an informal pattern of organization. It is suggested in passing that the first two lend themselves to development by means of argumentation; the others are expository. How effectively they can be developed depends first upon the position of the thesis in the completed essay. There are four useful positions: (1) at the beginning, (2) following the introduction, (3) preceding the conclusion, (4) *at the end.*

Unquestionably the best position for a thesis paragraph is at the end (as in the outlines of the Huxley essays above), if the pattern of organization for the essay is not to be determined completely by the clause structure of the thesis sentence. There are several excellent reasons for waiting until the end, or almost the end, to present the thesis:

1. Not the least of these, especially from the standpoint of the reader, is the suspense or concealment or climax or even surprise inherent in such a plan (see Chapter Three, p. 66).

2. The writer will find it easier, as a rule, to develop material and to demonstrate the consequences rather than to state a thesis and be burdened with proving it from then on. There is little freedom left for the writer he has stated his thesis.

3. If the final paragraph deals with the thesis, there is no need for a conclusion, which is always a difficult writing problem. (Conversely, beginning with a thesis does away with the need for an introduction.)

4. In argumentation it is a relatively easy matter to deal with the opposition if the thesis is, in effect, concealed.

The foregoing discussion implies the necessity for brevity of introductory or transitional material. Seldom is it necessary, in the short essay, to begin with an introductory paragraph—a sentence or two will suffice. Similarly, the most effective transition device is the word or phrase.

The *conclusion,* however, poses a quite different problem. An awkward or useless introduction may be redeemed by what follows it, but there is nothing to follow a conclusion. Hence the conclusion must not merely bid farewell to the reader but must *say* something about as important as anything said before the conclusion. There are at least three ways to write a successful conclusion:

1. Return to and expand upon a so far undeveloped idea in the essay.
2. Examine the implications of the thesis.
3. Make a prediction.

To an appreciable extent all three of these approaches to a conclusion may be seen in the final paragraph of Thomas Henry Huxley's "On the Advisableness of Improving Natural Knowledge," which has forty-two paragraphs:

> If these ideas be destined, as I believe they are, to be more and more firmly established as the world grows older; if that spirit be fated, as I believe it is, to extend itself into all departments of human thought, and to become co-extensive with the range of knowledge; if, as our race approaches its maturity, it discovers, as I believe it will, that there is but one kind of knowledge and but one method of acquiring it; then we, who are still children, may justly feel it our highest duty to recognize the advisableness of improving natural knowledge, and so to aid ourselves and our successors in our course towards the noble goal which lies before mankind.

The balanced structure of this sentence, incidentally, is worthy of careful study in the light of Chapter Three, pp. 62–65, "Clarity through Parallelism."

The following paragraphs, produced by students as conclusions, are furnished for analysis and discussion.

1. Thesis: Since the daydream can help make or destroy a person, it must be used like medicine—a little doesn't hurt but helps while a lot destroys.

Concluding paragraph: Where does a person draw the line between a little and too much daydreaming? Everyone should daydream a little to keep the world from being a place of near desolation. People who let their daydreams rule their bodies and souls won't ever reach their little worlds of contentment. One thing will always be in their way, the world around them. Meanwhile people who only daydream a little understand the world around them. When something the daydreamer doesn't like confronts him, he simply withdraws to his island of serenity. On the other hand the non-daydreamer will take his pleasure in stride. He may not like it but will accept it. Where does a person draw the line on daydreaming? I say when he withdraws from the world every time something doesn't please him. However, it is a good idea to daydream some on plans for your future, for they will help you in every way to achieve your world of serenity.

2. Thesis: Although I misunderstood my parents' actions, I now admit that my education has become more meaningful and more valuable.

Concluding paragraph: Well, so what? So my views are changed. So now I feel that I have a real goal, a real reason for being in college. It is no party. Surely, you can make it one, but that comes after work. My goal happens to be a career. Teaching school shall be my role. But should I marry, I can either continue as I hope to do or quit and fall back on the profession in case I need to. I plan to aid my family and my country. I believe that all parents should instill this sense of education's necessity in life and make it valuable to their children. As a result, I'm working my way through, paying all my expenses except that I receive a small, a very small allowance. This paying yourself makes you want and cherish education.

3 Thesis: The arrival of spring has caused me to lose interest in the deep, dry study of life's philosophy and long for the opportunity to live it.

Concluding paragraph: However, all this daydreaming is getting me absolutely nowhere. You see, I have a theme due in thirty minutes. What an ugly word is *theme*. It sounds rather like a clod of cement falling from a truck. Yet, though I dread writing a theme today, I can recall a time not so long ago when my mind craved knowledge and work just as my body desires food. What sort of dilemma has gone over me? Why do I suddenly loathe and despise everything but soporific skies and warm, gentle breezes?

4. Thesis: Although psychiatrists have dealt with timidity for decades, it still remains a major problem for many people who are trying to find confidence in a world which is obsessed with conflict and selfishness.

Concluding paragraph: Timidity is one of the worst enemies of the human race. It is caused by a lack of confidence or by a frightening childhood experience. The result is that many people will bear the burden of timidity all through their lives. Unless they seek professional guidance from a psychiatrist, their timidity will cause them to miss a great deal in life. Indeed, some people cannot handle the ordinary problems of life because they are timid. These people will not be able to experience the joy in rearing a family or pursuing a career. They will never know what it is to accomplish a goal or to set up high ideals for themselves. These people will be burdened with the everyday drag of life.

5. Thesis: That advertisements are sometimes misleading because of the use or misuse of words by an advertiser is primarily the fault of the public.

Concluding paragraph: Although some advertisements are straightforward and upright, the majority are schemes which are meant to sway the thinking and get the money of the American public. This propaganda, even though it is misleading, is not altogether misrepresentation. It is primarily successful because of the gullibility of the public and the failure of the public to check, before buying, to determine the quality of the intended purchase. If a person keeps an open-minded view of products and their advertisements, he can eventually put the advertisements to work for him.

Formal Patterns of Organization

The kinds of outlines thus far analyzed partake of varying degrees of formality. All of them are in a sense formal because they are written and because they commit the writer to a predetermined plan that he should not willingly depart from. (The completely informal outline, then, has some kind of fragile and dangerous existence in the writer's mind.) As a written plan, the partial topic (or skeleton) outline has the least formality and is therefore useful as the organization for an impromptu essay or for an essay type of examination. It serves well, too, as a preliminary outline while the writer is deciding upon his materials. But once the materials are settled upon, the outline should immediately assume a formal character owing to its completeness, as in the topic and sentence outlines of "The Method of Scientific Investigation." Each element of the sentence outline is, in effect, a miniature thesis.

THE PLAN OF THE CLASSICAL ORATION

Sufficient for the task, in the short essay of four or five paragraphs, is the outline that is an analysis or breakdown of the thesis sentence. Most college courses, however, demand one or more research or term papers of some length. Although length in itself does not imply increased complexity, the long paper may very well require an organization which the structure of the thesis sentence will not adequately reflect. A convenient and reasonably flexible plan for the long paper (and often, as will be seen, for the short paper as well) is fortunately available in the form of the *classical oration,* a literary type of great antiquity that nevertheless continues in use among scientists—the laboratory report is a good example—professional speech writers, and essayists today. *As employed in argumentation* the classical oration has eight parts:

1. *Exordium* or *Proem.* The beginning or introduction.

2. *Narratio.* The general statement of content or the summary of the background to the matter under consideration.

3. *Propositio.* The statement of what the writer intends to demonstrate or to prove. Usually the thesis in the classical oration.

4. *Partitio.* Analysis of the proposition or thesis. Announcement of the way in which the subject is to be divided.

5. *Confirmatio.* The body of the discussion. The material supporting the proposition or thesis. Logically the most fully developed part of the oration.

6. *Reprehensio.* Refutation of the opposition, which may already exist or be anticipated. (The basic difference between argumentation and exposition resides in the presence or absence of *reprehensio.*)

7. *Digressio.* Subsidiary or nonessential remarks. Designed to reduce tension or to illustrate ideas not strictly applicable to the proposition. (A measure of the flexibility inherent in the classical oration is that the digression may come—and more than once—anywhere after the *exordium* and before the *peroratio.*)

8. *Peroratio.* General conclusion. (As indicated above in the remarks on the conclusion, this is the place for a prediction.)

As employed in exposition the classical oration has seven parts, following the plan for argumentation except for the omission of *reprehensio.*

The serious student of writing will profit from a study of organization in several famous essays that are, in effect, classical orations: (1) Sir Philip Sidney, "An Apologie for Poetrie"; (2) John Milton, "Areopagitica"; (3) John Dryden, "An Essay of Dramatick Poesy"; (4) Jonathan Swift, "On Abolishing Christianity"; (5) Thomas Henry Huxley, "On the Advisableness of Improving Natural Knowledge," the final paragraph of which is quoted earlier in this chapter. Huxley's essay, to cite one example, has this pattern:

Proem	(paragraphs 1–6)
Narratio	(paragraphs 7–22)
Propositio	(paragraphs 23–26)
Confirmatio	(paragraphs 27–28)
Partitio	(paragraphs 29–37)
Reprehensio	(paragraphs 38–41)
Peroratio	(paragraphs 42–43)

Huxley's essay is argumentative, for one of its parts is *reprehensio*, the refutation of the opposition. It should be noted, further, that he has organized one part (*partitio*, the division, or analysis of the *propositio*) within the framework of the *confirmatio*. And, in the interests of greater cohesion of content, he has omitted *digressio*.

The so-called "short form" pattern for the classical oration, equally ancient and respectable as the "long form," permits further streamlining:

Argumentative	Expository
Exordium or *Proem*	*Exordium* or *Proem*
Narratio	*Narratio*
Confirmatio	*Confirmatio*
Reprehensio	*Digressio*
Digressio	*Peroratio*
Peroratio	

Even further tightening of form is possible, again, through the omission of *digressio*, which may, as circumstances dictate, occur anywhere after the opening remarks and before the closing remarks. A final variation, in argumentation, is possible by beginning with *reprehensio*—always a strong opening.

The Transition Device

The transition device, which looks backward and forward at once like the double-faced Roman god Janus, is an important means of strengthening the internal organization of the essay. But it must never be used as a substitute for organization; an excellent essay can be written without resorting to the transition device. To put it another way, the best kind of transition device goes unnoticed, for it involves either a contrast or the repetition of ideas in somewhat different terms.

A good writer, however, can scarcely do without a substantial stock of what may be called *bare transition devices,* words or phrases which have specific (often severely limited) denotative meaning and serve therefore as directions to the reader. The student is invited to expand the following list, which is by no means exhaustive.

THE DEVICE	ITS FUNCTION OR MEANING
1. *"Pure" or coordinate conjunctions (only four of these)*	
and	links parallel or equivalent constructions or ideas
or	regards what it connects as alternatives
but	suggests a contrast between what it connects
nor	excludes what it connects as alternatives (opposite of *or*)
2. *Subordinate Conjunctions*	
although (though)	makes a concession
because	shows a causal relationship
for	means *because*
if (often used with *then*)	predicts a causal relationship
since	indicates a cause-and-effect relationship
unless	qualifies a prediction
when	shows a close temporal relationship
whether	precedes alternatives
while	shows that two happenings take place at the same time (not to be used meaning *although*)

THE DEVICE	ITS FUNCTION OR MEANING
3. *Conjunctive adverbs*	
also	approximates *and* (to use with *and* involves redundancy)
hence	precedes an effect
however	reveals that a line of thinking is being broken for an alternative
moreover	continues the same line of thinking
nevertheless	shows that opposites must be equally considered
so	connects causally related elements
then	shows a close temporal or causal relationship
therefore	(see *so*)
whereas	points out a contrast
yet	(see *nevertheless*)

An additional list of words and phrases commonly used as transition devices:

accordingly

another (often used with *one* in the preceding construction)

as a result

at the same time

at times

both . . . and

by contrast

certainly

consequently

conversely

different

especially

even

finally

first (probably followed by *second,* etc.)

for another

for example

for instance	on the other hand
for one thing	on the whole
frequently	other
granted (that)	similar
here	similarly
in addition	some . . . other
indeed	sometimes
in general	specially
in other words	specifically
in short	still (more, other)
just as	that
largely	there
less	these (those)
more	thus
much	to be sure
no doubt	to conclude
not only (. . . but also)	too
often	to sum up
once	usually
on the contrary	

Personal pronouns are also useful as transition devices provided the reference is incapable of ambiguity.

CAUTION: The pronouns *this* or *it* should be used sparingly, if at all, as transition devices beginning a sentence. Strictly speaking, *this* or *it* must refer to a noun or noun clause.

❀ The Organization of the Literary Essay

The kind of material with which an essay deals *never* dictates organization. An essay is either expository or argumentative, whether its concern is with biology, sociology, education, theology, philosophy, literature, or whatever, although certain disciplines like law or mathematics may resort to a symbolic language, or jargon, and a unique way of presenting their ideas, as in a formula or legal brief. Except for a few special cases, then, either the structure of the thesis sentence or the plan of the classical oration is the foundation of organization. Certainly in all cases, even legal and mathematical, the essay worth writing presents original ideas, where possible supported by evidence—illustrations, statistics, various factual material.

The literary essay is something of a special case. Its "evidence" is literary art, or would-be art: poetry and prose. There are three distinct types of literary essays whose province is artistic poetry and prose, (1) *Appreciation*, (2) *History*, (3) *Criticism-Interpretation*. The student's first problem in organizing the literary essay is deciding which of these is best suited to his assignment. Appreciation has almost wholly to do with demonstrating excellence. Hence a thesis sentence devoted in large part to the shortcomings of a story or poem or novel is not appropriate to appreciation. Similarly, a thesis sentence for an essay in literary history aims at showing how a piece of imaginative literature came to be what it is, because of sources, analogues, and other influences upon its creation. For the critical-interpretative essay, finally, the focus of the thesis may be one of several aspects of the work under consideration: meaning, significance, value, relationship with similar works, technique, the establishment of a reliable text.

The second problem involves presenting new material, or at least a new look at old material. The principles involved in gathering evidence will be taken up in Chapter Ten: "The Research Paper." But the rules governing its use, since they have to do with planning the paper, are stated here in the hope of solving the third problem.

1. Start with twice as much evidence as you plan to use. Short quotations are more vivid, more direct, more pertinent than long quotations.

2. Severely restrict the scope of your subject.

3. Unless absolutely necessary in a historical essay, stay away from recounting an author's life or any part of it.

4. Synopses or summaries are appropriate only in an appreciation or "book report." (A book review, since its subject is a recent publication, may summarize content, however.)

5. Assume that you are writing your paper for a person who is as familiar with what you are writing about as you are.

6. Whenever possible, use chronological, spatial, support, or climactic order as the basis of your plan (see Chapter Four, pp. 96–101).

7. If comparing or contrasting two or more works, deal with the same aspects of these works side by side, so to speak; *do not* discuss the works separately and then summarize your findings.

8. Keep your introduction short. Get to the heart of the matter.

9. Dispense with minor considerations first. Work toward your thesis.

10. Save a good idea to present in your final paragraph.

Assignments

1. A study of the organization of several essays in the reading text.
2. The formulation of partial and complete outlines of these essays.
3. The writing of thesis sentences (ideas developed from studying essays in the reading text) and the formulation of outlines breaking down or analyzing these thesis sentences.
4. A study of one or more of the readings listed below in regard to how well they follow the pattern of the classical oration.
5. A search for additional essays which follow this pattern.
6. The construction of an original outline, with a thesis sentence, using the plan of the classical oration.
7. A detailed study of transition devices in essays assigned from the reading text.

Readings

John Dryden, "An Essay of Dramatick Poesie," *Selected Works of John Dryden* (New York, 1953).

Aldous Huxley, "Comfort," *Proper Studies* (London, 1927).

Thomas Henry Huxley, "The Advisableness of Improving Natural Knowledge," *Method and Results* (New York, 1895).

————, "The Method of Scientific Investigation," *Readings from Huxley* (New York, 1920).

John Milton, "Areopagitica," *Complete Poetry and Selected Prose* (Modern Library).

Sir Philip Sidney, *An Apologie for Poetrie* (London, 1928).

Jonathan Swift, "The Abolishing of Christianity," *Gulliver's Travels and Other Writings* (Modern Library).

Chapter Six

❊ EXPOSITION

Thus far the student has had considerable, but more or less isolated, practice in several related techniques: (a) *choosing the proper word* (Chapter Two), (b) *consciously varying sentence structure patterns* (Chapter Three), (c) *developing an idea within a coherent and forceful paragraph according to what the idea seems to require* (Chapter Four), and (d) *organizing a group of ideas on the same subject from a predetermined plan* (Chapter Five). Every sentence he has written, and every paragraph, has been governed by a specific intention to illustrate, define, classify, contrast, compare, analyze cause or process. The essay as a whole is similarly governed. That is to say, the thesis sentence, by its very nature, makes a strong suggestion about how it should be demonstrated. Definition, for example, may be the whole purpose of an expository essay of some length, but if for nothing more than the sake of variety, as many other methods of idea development as possible should be used in conjunction with—subordinate to—definition.

141

Exposition, which may be called the art of written enlighten-ment, unifies these techniques, separately or in combination with description, narration, argumentation, within the frame-work of organization made explicit by the thesis sentence and the outline. Most of what the college student has been reading or writing (except for fiction and poetry), and most of the writing he deals with in college courses, is expository. (*Argu-mentation—the art of written disagreement*—does not differ from exposition in regard to how it uses these techniques; other special aspects of argumentation are discussed at length in Chapter Seven. As a matter of convenience *description* and *narration* are also considered in later chapters.) This enlight-enment for the most part involves telling the reader something he does not know or explaining to him something he fails to understand. It can also be concerned with clarification of what he *thinks* he knows or understands, and with re-analysis of what may already have been analyzed, elsewhere, a number of times. Hence the province of exposition extends from auto-biographical explanation of self to objective views of the uni-verse, from exploration of personal and immediate experience to rationalizations of world history. So distant are its bound-aries, embracing man's daydreams, ideas, and activities, that it is rather an empire than a province. A certain amount of classification—consistent with *selecting the subject* and *choos-ing the approach to the subject* (see the beginning of Chapter Five)—in regard to the basic kinds of exposition is therefore desirable: (1) *exposition of persons,* (2) *exposition of things,* (3) *exposition of sequences,* (4) *exposition of ideas.*

NOTE: There can be no substitute—no instructions, no lists of admonitions—for close and continued study and imitation of how the masters of English prose develop their ideas. Hence it is assumed that whatever value this chapter has depends almost completely upon sentence-by-sentence and paragraph-by-paragraph analysis and emulation, in the classroom as well as in the study, of essays assigned by the instructor.

Exposition of Persons

SELF-ANALYSIS

Essays of an autobiographical character and explorations of personal experience drop easily into the first of the above classifications, just as objective views of the universe belong to the last. By far the simplest kind of exposition problem to handle, of course, is the personal essay, because of the copious "information" readily available, if only subconsciously. A man knows himself pretty well; consequently, his first full-length expository writing assignment ought to involve self-analysis of some sort. The opportunities for such analysis are virtually unlimited, and so a conscious effort must be made to limit its scope. These titles, taken from student themes, are offered for class discussion in regard to whether their scope seems satisfactorily limited.

1. Conclusions from a Week in the Wilderness
2. I'm a Fool
3. Hypocrisy Goeth before a Fall
4. What Went Wrong in High School
5. Two Minutes to Disaster
6. My Prejudices
7. My Sister and I
8. Why I Am in College
9. Sources of Personal Satisfaction
10. Inferiority Complex
11. How Football Changed My Life
12. Final Exam
13. Never Again
14. A Corner of My Mind
15. Broken Dates
16. Am I a Coward?
17. Changing Churches
18. White Liar
19. Mental Cripple
20. Unsophisticated—That's Me

21. Studying Life's Philosophy or Living It?
22. Daydreamer
23. Egotistical or Introverted?

Commentary: Evidently each of these subjects invites narration, which can under certain circumstances be the backbone of an expository essay. But if the essay consists completely, or almost so, of narration, then the purpose of exposition has not been met satisfactorily; probably the reader has not been sufficiently enlightened. Here the enlightenment must consist of character revelation. This revelation must be stated specifically in the independent clause of the thesis sentence, the organization of which (unless the form of the classical oration is employed) determines the progression of ideas in the essay.

EXERCISES:

1. The formulation of appropriate thesis sentences for ten of the titles listed above. At least five of these sentences should be broken down into sentence outlines.

2. The composition of ten theme titles indicating possibilities for development by means of self-analysis.

3. The formulation of five thesis sentences, and accompanying sentence outlines, using the titles from Exercise 2.

4. The composition of a theme based upon one or more of these outlines.

Consider the following student-composed essay, a maiden effort in exposition. The assignment was to write a four-paragraph paper, with a different method of idea development in each paragraph but with a central method pervading the whole essay. The writer chose *cause and effect* as his central method, and decided to *illustrate, compare, show process,* and *define* in the four succeeding paragraphs.

HOW I ACQUIRED EMOTIONAL DEPTH

(1) As well as I can remember them, I believe my years in Crestwood Elementary School were the best of my short life. I had many friends who were with me constantly every day

of the year. At school I was a patrol boy, an honored position. My "girl friend" was the best looking girl in the class. I led my life with an ease and confidence I have never since known. But after my family moved me during my sixth grade year, my confidence was rocked. I didn't seem to be able to break into the group at Alice Carlson Elementary or McLean Junior High. I knew no boys who liked to play baseball or football in someone's front yard. Everyone except me was on the school team; I knew no girls and lacked the confidence to start an acquaintance. My new life left me alone for the first time.

(2) This aloneness resulted in the greatest change of my life. I never went out with other boys, and never took a girl out. Our untimely move had occurred at just the age when young students take dancing lessons, and I had missed out. Dances horrified me, and I never lost my fear of them until Senior High School. I started throwing a paper route, which left me to my own thoughts every afternoon. I began to prefer being alone and pursuing my own personal philosophies.

(3) My solitude became a pleasure and my philosophizing a fascination. I plunged into an ocean of new thought and reality. I philosophized on life and its meaning. Finally I reached the decision that life must be lived to the fullest. But how? I began to plan the kind of life which would be the fullest for me. Somehow I would acquire wealth and travel extensively. I would like to be a writer and bring new reality to people through my own experiences. I would like to be a playboy type living a life of ease and fun. But to achieve any of this I must forsake my seclusion and experience much of life. This led to my decision to go out into the social world around me, and eventually to discontinue my philosophizing, which had been the answer to my problem.

(4) This period of change left me with my "emotional depth." I keep the highest ambitions and reach the lowest levels of disappointment when it seems to me that I am making no progress toward them. Changes of mood dominate me always. I have an eternal hope of success, and an extreme sadness over any failure.

Commentary: This is not a successful essay, but it does not miss success by very much. Its author obviously has thought deeply and long—he is making a real attempt to understand himself. He uses transition devices well and is beginning to grasp the importance of a *noun and verb vocabulary*, although his diction is sorely damaged by the most banal sort of teenage jargon. A look at his outline, submitted with some reluctance, shows how narration, or preoccupation with narration, has tended to obscure self-analysis:

1. Cause—Comparison—got along easily in elementary—didn't get along too well in Jr. High & with difficulty
2. Illustration—of narrowing and inward life—paper route—much spare time—not able to dance
3. Process—spare time—thinking, philosophizing some, worrying —planning (writer, traveler, wealth, girls, etc.)—disappointment
4. Definition—high ambitions and disappointment over my slow expansion and aloneness. Eternal hope of success & extreme sadness over my failure

This is not, strictly speaking, an outline at all, but merely notes on material, notes that have at any rate guided composition. These notes do suggest, however, a possibility of unifying the material: the recurring word *disappointment*, suggesting that a thesis sentence could be written embodying the mixed optimism and sadness, owing to disappointment, so characteristic of youth. The fourth paragraph, then, is properly the focus of the essay, containing as it does three sentences charged with honest self-appraisal. But this paragraph seems almost an afterthought, following three paragraphs of narration. As for the methods of idea development, *cause and effect* as advertised takes charge in the first paragraph (cause: moving; effect: loneliness), which also uses *illustration. Comparison* is supposed to be the method of paragraph two; perhaps there is an implied comparison between the life before the move and afterwards. Also there is satisfactory *process analysis* in paragraph three, but paragraph four fails to *define* anything. Indeed, there is no need to define. To sum up, the essay has three basic faults: haphazard organization, failure to emphasize the central idea (which the writer himself may not have grasped), and failure to follow the announced plan of idea development.

EXERCISE:

A study of the variety of sentence structure and sentence length in the foregoing essay, according to the schemes proposed at the end of Chapter Three (pp. 75–76). It is understood that in regard to the essays written by the student himself this is a standing assignment unless the instructor specifies otherwise.

ANALYSIS OF OTHERS

In writing an essay analyzing a person or persons other than himself, the writer is forced to change his approach. His knowledge of others is seriously limited; often suspicion takes the place of knowledge, and there are secrets that men carry with them to the grave. This is one major difficulty in regard to the essay of self-analysis, which may be a confused effort at self-concealment. The writer analyzing others labors under no such difficulty. He can appraise his friends and enemies with dispassion—that is to say by putting aside his prejudices—if he applies the following indices to character, *to what a person is.* They are listed in probable order of importance:

1. his actions
2. the reactions of others to him
3. what others say about him
4. his words

No matter what he says, there is no way of knowing what he thinks. If he does nothing, he may *be* nothing. Hence actions and reactions form the basis of an expository essay developing the character of another person. These subjects are offered for class discussion as to their suitability in regard to such an essay, or one of character contrast or comparison.

1. Golfers I Have Known
2. My Brothers (or Sisters; or Brothers and Sisters)
3. Scoutmaster

4. The Most Unforgettable Person I Have Ever Met
5. Conclusions from a Week in the Wilderness
6. Hypocrisy Goeth before a Fall
7. Superiority Complex
8. Two Ball Players
9. Final Examination
10. Salesmen
11. Broken Dates
12. Egotistical or Introverted?
13. What Is a Professor?
14. Actions Speak Louder than Words
15. Town Bum
16. Closets
17. Chatterbox
18. Blowing off Steam
19. People Who Make Me Nervous
20. Coward or Hero?
21. Why People Leave My Home Town

That several of these titles are taken from the first list in this chapter indicates, it is hoped, that practically any title can inspire a good essay on practically any subject.

EXERCISES:

1. The formulation of a thesis sentence for each of these subjects. The development of at least five sentence outlines from these thesis sentences.

2. The composition of one or more essays using these outlines. It is not a bad idea for students to trade outlines, *in the classroom,* and accordingly to write essays from outlines that they have not seen before.

The following student-composed essay, written on the first of the titles listed above, is offered for analysis and criticism.

GOLFERS I HAVE KNOWN

Thesis: Though character reveals itself in existence alone, the very nature of the frustrations, anxieties, and competitiveness in a sport such as golf enables us to perceive a genuine revelation of self that rarely occurs in portraying the existence of a mere being.

Outline

I. One readily discerns from observation and cartoons of golfers that golf produces an idealistic situation for the revelation of character.

II. Although golfers are vastly similar in their emotions, they become unique in their attitudes and quest for perfection.

III. The perfectionist is the most dedicated golfer so that there is little doubt concerning the outcome of his career.

IV. The nonchalant golfer possesses the natural ability and the attitude which enables him to succeed.

V. The golfer who possesses neither of the specific abilities that I have mentioned is doomed never to rise to stardom in golf.

GOLFERS I HAVE KNOWN

(1) Upon observing two typical golfers, a person would have to acknowledge that it is perhaps the most frustrating sport that was ever conceived by man. Not only is the frustration revealed in score but in every aspect of the golfer's personality. More than frequently it is said that a person has a completely different personality when he plays golf. It is little wonder that you often see the little reminder in the golf shop that says, "Golf is a revealer of character. Make it pleasant for those about you as well as yourself." Nevertheless golf continues to produce a variety of emotions which are expressed in numerous ways. Largely though, the golfer gives vent to these emotions in one of two ways, club throwing or cursing. One is reminded of the cartoon expression of the golfer who throws his club in anger only to have it clobber his playing partner. Although this mode of expression is dangerous, it is probably not quite so offensive as profane language. Language on the golf course is characterized by the minister who said that he would have to give up golf or preaching because he didn't have the vocabulary for both. (Illustration)

(2) Such are the characteristics of the typical golfer. It might lead one to think that golfers are a group of stereotyped personalities. Nothing could be further from the truth. Virtually

every type of personality enjoys golf. However there is a most interesting contrast that occurs between the perfectionist and the nonchalant golfer. Here I am assuming that both are good golfers and differ greatly in their approach to the game. You might consider that they differ in ability as well as intelligence. Both are successful, and for different reasons. The mediocre golfer is not a member of the two previously mentioned categories. I will attempt to explain the nature of his failure later in my essay. (Contrast)

(3) First let us consider the perfectionist or the intelligent person. They are a very unique type of golfer in their attitudes, ambitions, and willingness to work. Although one might wonder why intelligence and perfection are related, it will become evident as we analyze the two unique types of golfers. For the perfectionist there are not enough hours in the day to play golf. The perfectionist attitude is best expressed by Ben Hogan's saying that he spent all of his waking hours and a great deal of his sleeping hours in quest of perfection. Every thought is dedicated to one ultimate goal: finding a secret or superior way of striking the ball. Every minute aspect of the swing is considered. Concentration is their most precious possession on the course. The perfectionist approach to the game might be analyzed from several different viewpoints. It is perhaps the most rewarding with regard to hitting the ball. However there is an apparent lack of confidence which is perceivable from this attitude. Unless everything is precisely figured, their entire swing might collapse. This type of golfer is not what might be termed a "natural," but it would be equally ridiculous for one to assume that he is not fairly coordinated. His success rests upon his intelligence to analyze his swing and convey this thinking to his muscles till it becomes committed to muscle memory. (Process Analysis)

(4) By contrast there is the casual type of player. He is best described as the fellow who is exceedingly gifted in muscular coordination, and is not intelligent enough to realize the many aspects of golf that could go wrong. He is not nearly so negative in his attitude as the perfectionist. He hits the ball without giving much thought to how he did it. He is not afraid his game will collapse because he is not willing to consider all the possibilities of what might go wrong. The very nature of his being is not golf, and once he is through with his round he is

off to enjoy something else. He is the person who might be termed the natural athlete. If he starts playing badly, he has to rely on his natural ability to snap him out of his slump. His only thought is for the club to hit the ball. He does not need to consider every aspect of the swing because they are engrained in his natural ability. (Contrast)

(5) Specifically I have analyzed the good golfer who falls into two categories. Each is unique in what enables him to succeed in golf. As I have already mentioned, the mediocre golfer is the guy who does not possess one of these unique traits but displays a rather weak sample of a combination of both of these traits. He is not a natural athlete, thus rendering him incapable of accidentally becoming a good golfer, nor is he intelligent enough to analyze his swing and concentrate on making the necessary adjustments. Thus it can be observed that good golfers are a select group which are determined at birth and virtually nothing can be done to change the aspect of endowed human ability. (Definition)

Commentary: Getting at the virtues and faults of this essay will be facilitated by finding answers to the following questions, which can be posed of any expository or argumentative paper.

1. *The title*

    a. Is it short?

    b. Is it interesting?

    c. Is it closely connected with the content of the essay?

2. *The thesis sentence*

    a. Is the central idea of the thesis sentence in its main clause?

    b. Are the title and thesis sentence consistent with each other?

    c. Does the thesis sentence indicate the line of development the writer *ought to* follow? (The author of this essay is obligated, according to the principles of exposition proposed thus far, to write about how golf reveals character—presumably character in general as revealed by its manifestations in specific illustrations.)

3. *The outline*

a. Is the outline a breakdown or analysis of the thesis?

b. Does the outline follow the organization of the thesis or of the classical oration?

c. Is there anything in the outline that does not contribute to the thesis?

4. *The essay*

a. *Sentence structure.* Are the sentences correctly written?

b. *Sentence style.* Are the sentences *clear, concise, interesting?* Is the diction appropriate to the subject and consistent in level of usage?

c. *Transition.* Are there any breaks in continuity *within* the paragraphs?

d. *Paragraph style*

(1) Does each paragraph reflect its content as advertised in the outline?

(2) Is there a method of idea development central—and suitable—to each paragraph? Is this method actually what the author says it is? Is there enough variety of idea development from paragraph to paragraph?

(3) Is each paragraph *clear, concise, interesting?*

(4) Are the paragraphs closely related by transition devices?

e. *The essay as a whole*

(1) Is there a method of idea development central—and suitable—to the essay as a whole?

(2) Does the essay accomplish what it sets out to do?

(3) Is it expository or argumentative?

(4) Is there sufficient concrete illustrative material?

(5) Is it a success or a failure? Is what it says worth saying? If it fails, does it have redeeming characteristics? By now it should be abundantly clear that "Golfers I Have Known" fails (although it does not handle contrast and comparison badly) in its fundamental approach to the writing problem: it is about *golf* rather than *golfers.*

1. A revision of "Golfers I Have Known," taking into account all of its shortcomings as revealed in answering the questions.

2. A similarly inspired revision of the exposition-of-persons essays thus far written.

Exposition of Things

The questions posed in connection with "Golfers I Have Known" can be invoked in analysis of any essay. That is to say, whatever the subject of a discourse may be, the rhetorical or stylistic principles and patterns making the discourse a success or failure are much the same. What people talk about may change in appearance and even substance from time to time, but the way they talk about it—*or ought to in a good essay*—does not change. Hence the ambitious student will find himself referring again and again to these questions. They constitute his rhetorical frame of reference.

And so when he proceeds to write about *things* instead of *persons,* the writer has a familiar system to rely on. It is a system conditioned by his own prejudices, of course, for he will have a desire—deep-lined in his subconscious being—to express himself on certain matters of universal interest. He has an equally stubborn wish to avoid thinking or talking or writing about other matters. This sensitive emotional and mental constitution of his is not altogether unfortunate. It proceeds from good impulses as well as intellectual laziness and cowardice: man, it is clear, does not wish to be unhappy, nor does he care to see his neighbor suffer. Consequently he applies taboos to what reminds him of his own infinite capacity for unhappiness, of his neighbor's infatuation with misery. And he shuts out the unhappiness and the misery in a passionate devotion to a philosophy of *things.* Analysis of things therefore will indicate something of man's nature (an underlying purpose of exposition), just as analysis of persons will.

For well-directed analysis things can be classified, according to their nature, from various points of view.

Private Things	*Public Things*
food	roads
clothes	meeting places
shelter	stores
cleaning tools and solvents	jails
cooking tools	buses
eating tools	restaurants
things to store things in	schools
bicycles	factories
substitutes for bicycles	trucks
books	motion pictures

Necessities	*Luxuries*
food	champagne
clothing	mink coats
shelter	fall-out shelters
diversion	night clubs

New Things	*Old Things*
television sets	radio receivers
space suits	cowboy clothes
electric typewriters	fountain pens
transistorized wristwatches	pocket watches
comic books	novels
filter cigarettes	snuff
frozen foods	chicken and dumplings
outboard motors	oars
air conditioners	Franklin stoves
electric razors	shaving mugs
aluminum siding	paint
dishwashers	scrub boards
fluorescent lamps	light globes
SLR cameras	box cameras
elevators	stairways
penicillin	aspirin
power steering	stick shifts
refrigerators	ice boxes
tape recorders	phonograph records
instant coffee	tea leaves
hydrogen bombs	hand grenades

Angular Things	*Circular Things*
boxes	balls
television sets	phonograph records
filing cabinets	wheels
fences	hoops
windows	portholes

This is no more than a beginning. As always, the student is invited to compile his own lists. What is hinted here is that the very act of classification, involving a choice of alternatives, will provide subjects for exposition. It is immediately apparent, for example, that angular things often have a negative connotation and that circular things tend to suggest recreation. Further contemplation of lists and classes of things reveals man's infinite inventive capacity, if it is to be measured in terms of recent productive performance (a very good expository essay subject, by the way, for it allows the writer to make a prediction—ever a sound procedure in bringing the essay to a close). Even further probing and thinking might force the writer to come up with more than one fairly significant thesis for expository purposes. Consider the following examples, *student-composed in class* (with some help from the instructor) during compilation of a list of old and new things.

1. People would rather spend money than save it.

2. That we do not pay cash for most of what we purchase indicates a universal tendency to think in terms of getting something for nothing.

3. Although people form lodges and luncheon clubs and organizations of all kinds at an apparently increasing rate, the things they set most store by indicate that they are really antisocial at heart.

4. Man expects most of his possessions to be worn out by the time they are paid for.

5. Man is inventive because he is lazy—physically, not mentally.

6. That man is a natural specialist has caused the tremendous growth of urban populations.

7. Although people, especially young ones, eat almost con-

tinuously, they care little about either taste or nutritional quality in their food.

8. Although inventive and antisocial man specializes in his activities, the things he surrounds himself with demonstrate his eagerness to conform.

9. A glittering surface is more important to man than a solid interior.

10. In his spare time, inventive and antisocial and conforming man wishes to be diverted, not aroused.

The following student essay, based on the third of these thesis sentences and written as a final draft during the class meeting following that in which the list of old and new things was compiled, is offered for analysis.

BOXES

Thesis: Although people form lodges and luncheon clubs and organizations of all kinds at an apparently increasing rate, the things they set most store by indicate that they are really antisocial at heart. (Process analysis chosen as the pervading method of idea development)

Outline

I. There is apparently a club for everyone—indicating a universal tendency to "join." (Illustration)

II. But joining is done in pretense, on orders "from above," so that the joiner can have security and buy the things he wants. (Process analysis)

III. What the joiner buys and the way he lives show that he is antisocial at heart. (Cause and effect)

BOXES

(1) They pervade man's existence. He is born in a box-shaped room, with little holes cut in it for spying on the occupants, and imprisoned in a cradle, shaped like a box with the lid off. When released he crawls about a box-shaped building, from room to room—that is, from box to box. Later on, when he has

been civilized and can sit up to eat, he makes a mess at a table shaped like a box lid, with food that comes out of boxes, preserved in a box called a refrigerator. As soon as his mother can get rid of him, she packs him off to a box called a school, where, during recess, he plays in an area shaped like a box lid. After he has been schooled in a series of boxes, the main object of the process being to accustom him to life in boxes, he goes to work (in a conveyance shaped more like a box than anything else) in a tall, more or less windowless box, surrounded by a jungle of tall boxes. And when he has been exhausted by boxes, a procession of boxes on wheels escorts him to where, as a last irony, he is imprisoned permanently in a box hidden underground. What does he do to escape, while he still has the energy to resist? He lunches with his fellow prisoners, who romantically call themselves Rotarians or Lions or Kiwanians, in a large box which reverberates unpleasantly to the noise of chatter and group singing because it is not constructed so that it will absorb rather than reflect noise. On week nights he joins the other romanticists, who now refer to themselves as Elks or Masons or Shriners, and it is ten to one he is happy after the ritual and more chatter and group singing to return to his private box, a low composite of rectangular shapes jammed up against others just like it. (Illustration)

(2) Nevertheless he loves his private box; he pretends to accept the public boxes of Rotarianism at noon and Masonry at night only because he sells insurance or stationery or real estate—or boxes. To sell boxes he needs a circle of acquaintances; so he sits in the box he calls his office just long enough to communicate with other boxes by telephone. An appointment made, he drinks coffee in a box called a restaurant with pretended friends who try to sell boxes to each other. At lunch he joins hands with his fellow box salesmen, and they agree to sell each other boxes later in the day. All this, all this pretense and self-abasement, enables him to live in his private box at some distance from the box jungle. He is, of course, not likely to be independent as a box salesman, for he has a supervisor, a super-box-salesman, who controls his existence away from the private box and who demands that he join with other joiners in something called a country club, where all the box salesmen walk about together, selling each other boxes but

ostensibly preoccupied with knocking—at last!—a small white *sphere* into a *cylindrical* depression. (Process analysis)

(3) Curiously enough, all this joining does not cause the box salesman to change his basically antisocial nature, for he is not a box salesman by choice. He is a human being, and he does not care greatly for the society of other hypocrites. His private box in its every aspect is designed to insulate him from box salesmen. Its lawn is quite small, so that when he tends it he will not have to spend much time where they can see him. Its garage is attached to the house, so that he can enter his private box unseen, from the moving private box which brings him there. It is air-conditioned, so that he cannot easily communicate with his neighbors, nor they with him. The windows, because of air-conditioning, are tiny and set so high in the walls that further privacy is assured. And he spends the remainder of his waking hours, eating from a box labeled "TV Dinner," in a boxlike cell decorated only by a balefully glowing box which enables him—so he imagines—to watch the world without its watching him. (Cause and effect)

Commentary: Once again, the questions proposed in connection with "Golfers I Have Known" should be applied to "Boxes," but some preliminary remarks may be useful.

"Boxes" will bear considerable revision. It does not always follow the outline, it fails to illustrate sufficiently, its diction is on at least two usage levels, and it is guilty of lapses in taste and point of view. "Boxes," however, succeeds far more than it fails. Especially to its credit is that "Boxes" is expository throughout: it never deviates from the initially announced purpose, to show how boxes pervade man's existence. Also, its point of view, though not maintained rigorously, is well adapted to the subject. Finally, it projects an idea well worth developing, in forceful and spirited terms; there is a unifying scheme of idea development (process analysis) and a sufficient variety of method in the paragraphs.

Perhaps comparison with another student essay, written under the same conditions, will show how successful "Boxes" turns out to be.

THE HOME

Thesis: If one considers the various aspects that influence a person and society, he would undoubtedly have to say that the home itself is the biggest single influence in the life of any person. (Over-all method of development: cause and effect)

Outline

I. The attitudes which are propagated by students are the direct influence of the home. (Contrast)

II. The feelings which the home provides are essential for a coherent personality. (Description)

III. Although the home is forgotten at times, the importance of it when it is needed cannot be underestimated. (Process analysis)

THE HOME

(1) The influence of the home reveals itself in every aspect of a person's life. The home will produce attitudes, feelings, and memories that will last a lifetime. One rarely realizes that every culture in the world has a home whether it be a tent or a mansion. The only inference then is that the home is basic to human nature and that man is going against the grain of his nature when he does not have a roof over his head. It is not hard to predict what type of home various people have come from. The studious type of person comes from a home which believes in hard work and using time conservatively. It probably does not have a television, and a great deal of time is spent reading various materials. The son or daughter is not permitted to listen to the radio all day long. Hard work and achievement are fostered by the atmosphere of the home. Quite to the contrary is the home where time is nothing but leisure. All the gadgets in the home give but little meaning to existence. This attitude propagated by the home will be one of artificial complacency regardless of existing conditions. (Contrast)

(2) However, regardless of the attitude fostered at home, a person's feelings toward his home will be favorable. It will pro-

vide him with a feeling of acceptance when life throws problems at him that are hard to cope with at first. American culture is unique in that it provides a moratorium before students become adults. More than any other culture the home plays a bigger part in the development and adjustment of a student. When the student goes away to school and is in unfamiliar surroundings, he knows that home will be waiting for him at vacation time. In his old room he can recount past experiences and remember how he solved his problems so that those facing him now and in the future seem to appear in their proper perspective. The home may be compared to the parents in many aspects in that the student has to rely on familiar surroundings for a long time before he is able to make the transition to adulthood. (Description)

(3) However, the mores of the culture are such now that many students refuse to acknowledge the love of their home for fear of being ostracized. Generally speaking, this is only a phase of growing up. There is rather a stable syndrome that each student seems to follow. Until he reaches the fourth grade in school, he is still captivated by the television and his parents. From the fourth till the seventh he is finding new companions and is mingling with them at times. By the time he is thirteen and up until he is fifteen, he will rebel somewhat so that he goes out at night frequently. And when the student reaches high school, he will enjoy being away from home as much as he can. Thus the progress of the mores of the culture has prepared the student for going away to college. But there is one thing the parent can be sure of. Son or daughter will appreciate the home more than ever before when they return from college. (Process analysis)

Exercises:

1. Using the questions appended to "Golfers I Have Known," a point by point comparison of "Boxes" and "The Home."

2. Revisions of both essays.

3. As assigned by the instructor, practice in writing essays expository of things.

4. As assigned by the instructor, précis of essays in the reading text, with outlines of the essays.

Exposition of Sequences

The student papers which have been presented thus far in this chapter demonstrate a continuing difficulty in exposition: the writer's understanding what his writing assignment consists of and visualizing it in the proper terms. The authors of "How I Acquired Emotional Depth" and "Boxes" have surmounted this difficulty; "Golfers I Have Known" and "The Home," both ending in a confusion of platitudes, show that their authors have not. The third kind of expository essay, *exposition of sequences,* presents a new problem: dealing with a succession of events and seeing what they mean when viewed as a totality.

At first glance, exposition of sequences may, because of its typical chronological arrangement, seem inseparable from narrative writing (see Chapter Nine). Certain similarities do of course obtain, but there is one major difference between the two forms. Exposition of sequence is meant to explain to an audience a process the outcome of which it already knows, the emphasis being upon *how* that outcome occurred. Narrative writing, as we shall see, relates sequences the outcome of which is not known to the audience at the beginning of the essay, or which is deliberately withheld from the audience.

The writer of expository sequence deals with things or ideas which already exist, which already are public knowledge, his burden being then the explanation of why they came to exist. Many subjects students are familiar with patently call for this kind of exposition:

> How I Became a Man
> How Little Rock Became Notorious
> Dallas and Desegregation
> The Home Run Becomes Common
> Bribery Enters Basketball
> How I Got Lost
> The Last Minutes Before Disaster
> Things Went Wrong in High School

How to Break a Date
I Change Churches
Preparing for Final Exams
I Gave Up Daydreams
How I Blow Off Steam
My Town Buys a Museum
A Small Town Disappears

The list could go on. Every student writer remembers, sometimes with anguish, sometimes with pleasure, sequences of
events in his own life or in the life of his society past or present
that, viewed as a whole, have meaning.

Such sequences can be handled best by extended process
analysis (see "Process Analysis," Chapter Four). Since he is
dealing with a sequence of events, the writer is obligated from
the first to keep things straight, to keep events in their proper
chronological perspective. This is not to suggest that every
exposition of a sequence must be straightforwardly chronological. The writer may wish, for example, to speak first of the
total meaning of his sequence and then back up to get at the
events comprising the sequence. More often, it may become
necessary for the writer to keep more than one sequence of
events going at the same time, in which case he may treat them
as parallel, presenting the first sequence, then the second, both
of which contribute to a larger sequence. The last item in the
list of subjects above, for example, might require first, explanation of a sequence of climactic misfortunes and crop failures;
second, an explanation of a sequence of wartime urgency and
urban promises in order to explain the total sequence and its
total meaning, to explain how a small town disappeared.

With these qualifications, chronology nevertheless remains
the ruling pattern of organization since the writer is explaining
significant things that happen in a sequence. In addition to the
necessity then of keeping things straight, the writer will also
find it necessary to pace his explanation of the sequence properly, spending his time on events of importance, minimizing
events which are in the sequence but which haven't major
importance for the whole subject. In the sequence discussed

above, for example, should there be a gap of some few years between the crop failures and the promise of urban prosperity, the writer, while noting the gap, could minimize it in order to deal with the two minor sequences of events that together form the subject sequence.

One last admonition: life is chancy, but order is nevertheless discernible in most of our doings. In his explanation of a sequence of events, the writer ordinarily will want to make clear the principle or the association by which sequences occur. In the account of the disappearing small town, for instance, the basic principle of self-preservation informs both minor sequences, crop failure creating the need for removal, the promise of urban prosperity providing the opportunity.

HOW I GOT LOST

Things have always bothered me. Once upon a time somebody called me "excitable Eddie," and I suppose he was right, for I perpetually have the tremors. And it has been like this since the beginning, particularly when I was faced with any manner of authority. I was scared when I went to school. Always a paragon of deportment, I lived nonetheless in dreadful fear of the principal. Homework I always did promptly because I assumed that something sinister would happen if I didn't. A little later when I began to read and study about science, that baffled me too. I knew all those men must be right about gravity and vectors and things even though in my most isolated and private moments I somehow suspected that the world was operated by gremlins, elves, and fairies, and that things happened because other things were either ugly or nice. Later still, when I got old enough to move around town or even have dates I often missed buses because, not having anything but perhaps a five-dollar bill, I would be alarmed at facing the bus-driver and asking him to change it. Then when I went into the army I stayed bothered for two years, knowing perfectly that everyone in all the ranks above me was watching and that the sanitary condition of my weapon was a matter of immediate concern to all sergeants and lieutenants. And I have been bothered ever since, first by clerks and people like that, then by many other things such as how in a corporation the size of a desk has mystic affinity with the degree of authority possessed by the man who sits at it, more recently by my own children who are watching everyday to see whether I make out as a parent.

That is how I happened to be lost. Even apparent authority always sets me off, and the surest sign that one is confronting authority, as everyone knows, is that he has to fill out forms. It all started when I had to fill out some kind of form in high school, one section of which asked for place of birth. Now I was born in a farmhouse several miles outside Jayton, Texas, but I didn't think I had room to put all that down and it didn't seem like they would want all of that anyway, so I put down Jayton as the place of birth. I waited for some weeks expecting charges of some kind of fraud, but nothing happened and everything seemed to be all right. Then, some while later, I was drafted, and there was another form. But this time it was the army I was dealing with and I felt that Jayton would never do since I was face to face with the awesome agent of a still more awesome agent, the United States government, at least one official of which, I felt sure, would know, what with statistics and all. Jayton is in one county, and the farmhouse where I was born is in a neighboring county. I couldn't put down either Jayton or the town in the other county because of course you can't mess around with the United States Army. I finally just put down Stonewall County. Even that bothered me a little. It was presumptuous. Well, nothing happened, and I was safe for awhile, but the sorry business doesn't end there. Shortly after I got out of the army I got married. A thing that has the sanction of church, state, and my wife is really something to be careful with, and there was another form to fill out before we could get the marriage license. I knew that I had been flirting with criminal charges with my variant answers. This time I placed all my faith in authority and announced that the place of my birth was Aspermont, Texas. I have never been in Aspermont more than three minutes, but since that is the county seat of the county in which the little farmhouse was located, I somehow felt that I must be recorded there. The rest is brief to tell. In due course, we had a son who in due course was given a birth certificate. And there was another form to fill out. This time, in sheer and desperate bravado because I had escaped all these years, and in my pride at being a father, I threw caution to the winds and wrote down that the place of my birth was Spur, Texas, which was the nearest town that anyone in the outside world might ever have heard of. It seemed unfitting that my son should go through life saddled with a father who might have been born in a relatively-unknown town or a relatively-unknown county. I therefore chose the status symbol and cited Spur.

And that is how it all came about. That is how I got lost. As far as I know no one on earth knows for sure where I was born. My parents could say, but I believe even they are a little confused. Perhaps if I overcome some of the tremors and become famous or something I can someday say I was born in a little weatherbeaten but rugged farmhouse. But for now, no one knows. Sometimes I am not too sure myself.

Two processes have been presented here parallel, the two together constituting the major sequence of events it is the apparent purpose of the paper to explain. In the first paragraph the author shows how his own diffidence and timidity made him increasingly less able to cope with the world. In the second, he explains another process, this time reversing himself to show that as his own weaknesses piled up in the first paragraph, so the world at the same time continually confronted him with obstacles to his sense of well-being. The combined processes, accumulating weaknesses and accumulating obstacles, form the major process, which explains how the author got lost. This combination of processes serves most clearly to distinguish exposition of sequences from process analysis, which it otherwise closely resembles. Though process analysis is typically a single direct development, the writer of expository sequence may often combine several processes, as this author has done, or he may, as this writer also has done, use paragraphs developed by process in order to establish a larger method of development. Here, for example, while each *para-*

graph is developed by process analysis, the *essay* is controlled
by cause and effect organization, the first process being the
cause of the second, which in turn creates the final effect, the
loss.

EXERCISES:

1. Compare "How I Got Lost" and "Boxes," showing especially
how the organization of "How I Got Lost" differs from that of
the earlier essay.

2. As assigned by the instructor, practice in writing essays
expository of sequences.

Exposition of Ideas

A long time ago Matthew Arnold, noted for his pessimism,
wrote: "The mass of mankind will never have any ardent zeal
for seeing things as they are; very inadequate ideas will always
satisfy them." Nevertheless, Arnold devoted his life to the
cause of mass education, of putting useful ideas into everyone's
head. This book is similarly devoted to a hard principle: a
college student with normal intelligence and a willingness to
learn and work can become a competent writer.

When a student arrives on the college campus, his ideas on
most subjects are admittedly inadequate; likely he feels the
inadequacy deeply—however he may continue to resist efforts
to make him read and think. But his possibly meager stock of
ideas, his ability and willingness to comprehend, and his accumulated experience must serve at the start as the fodder
for his compositions. The purpose of the volume of essays accompanying this book is to expand the student's intellectual
experience and to furnish him with some sort of mental spark
plug, a kind of impetus to writing. In this regard the considerations influencing the choice of essay subject outlined in Chapter Five (pp. 113–114) are pertinent and should be referred
to frequently. It is also advisable for the student to cultivate
at least one metropolitan daily newspaper, for its often slanted
columns and editorials—sound as they generally are—will fur-

nish him with a marvelous panorama of inadequate ideas. (To deal with these ideas properly he will need to have occasional recourse to the section in Chapter Seven, "Support through Reasoning.")

In studying the column or editorial he must habitually determine first of all whether the material is intended to be expository or argumentative, and whether it holds true to the intention. If this practice is sufficiently habit-forming, the student will have profited greatly in his own writing, for one of the stumbling blocks to satisfactory organization and content is the writer's inability to realize that he is arguing rather than enlightening. Consider the following example, part of an essay on the United Nations, which, by the way, is probably a thing as well as an idea:

> The League of Nations perished because its humanitarian dreams were hazy and at best premature. What economic and cultural relations existing in the nineteen-twenties among nations—great and small, east and west, Fascist and Democratic—were not enough to produce a lasting instrument for peace. But as a civilized beginning for the expression of international opinion the League of Nations remains as a monument to the human search for reasonable solutions to the interminable bickerings which so often lead to war.
>
> Born like the League of Nations out of war's agony, the United Nations at times like its predecessor seems idealistic and premature. There is cause for hope, however. If the Marshall Plan, the North Atlantic Alliance, the Common Market, and even the long discussed political union with Canada and perhaps England bear fruit, it is not too much to envision a further extension of these areas of political and economic cooperation, and the acceptance of Western democratic ideas on a worldwide basis.

This material is clearly expository. It may—probably will, because of man's contentious nature—*lead* to argument, but as it stands there is no attempt to deal with opposition or to anticipate opposition.

Consider another example:

Why I cannot sleep at night:

The Communist-inspired efforts of the United Nations, abetted by socialists and leftwingers in the United States, to take away our independence under the proposed "one-world" government.

Efforts by misguided administrators, who want the President to have lawmaking powers, to change the structure of our government.

In the face of its own pleas for disarmament, the Executive department's submission to Congress of a demand for nearly five billions of taxpayer money for foreign aid and defense.

The undetermined source of this fantastic sum—certainly not my own empty pocketbook.

The departure of our highest court from its proper judicial function, in favor of misguided and probably vicious attempts to influence the course of legislation.

Communist-inspired laborite radio broadcasts by alleged "Newscasters" who are out to assassinate the characters of decent conservative Congressmen and patriotic organizations like the American Legion.

"We must all sacrifice," coming from the President at a time when there isn't anything left to sacrifice, not even the Constitution.

Public apathy to the warnings of the few patriots who will speak their minds.

Spreading atheism.

This is not, properly speaking, an essay at all. There is no paragraph development, no attempt at organization, no beginning or end, but the writer knows what he wants to say. He takes a positive stand on *issues;* hence his work is argumentative.

Consider one more example:

(1) Why does the administration continue to waste enormous sums annually?

(2) Billions of dollars go annually to foreign countries. This "foreign aid" scheme, in effect since the Roosevelt era, is the

most ridiculous program we have ever given our reluctant consent to.

(3) The humanitarian principles behind foreign aid may be sound, but principles must be sacrificed if foreign aid ruins the economy of the benefactor country. Aid must anyhow be curtailed. For thirty years the tax dollar has gone abroad to create jobs and build industry, whose products then invade the United States to be bought by those responsible for their existence. This game of financial pat-a-cake has got to stop, especially because foreign products are cheaper than United States products, whatever their quality. This business is surely foreign aid, but it cnly increases our unemployment.

(4) Doubtless many countries need our aid to keep their people from freezing and starving. It seems better therefore to send them surplus food and clothing, both of which are excessively stockpiled. Let us send these things, not the tax dollar.

(5) The tax dollar will buy only enemies; money never makes friends.

At first glance this appears to be a successful short essay on foreign aid. It is forcefully written, and its author is in no doubt about his position in regard to the issue at stake. But a closer examination of this essay reveals a confusion of expository and argumentative material. The opening rhetorical question (a weak device stylistically) seems to promise an expository explanation of government waste. The following paragraph involves a shift in both technique and content: now the writer is arguing against the foreign aid program. The first sentence of the third paragraph appears to return to exposition for a moment (to explain the basic principle of foreign aid), but the writer again shifts in mid-sentence to argue, rather effectively, against the program. Paragraph 4 shifts technique once again to exposition, coming fairly close to defining foreign aid as charity—not necessarily what the writer advocates at the beginning of paragraph 3. The final paragraph is again expository, as far as it goes, but it involves still another shift in material, being in disagreement with the beginning of paragraph 3 and all of paragraph 4. It is a *non sequitur*.

A second stumbling block in exposition of ideas involves the inability to distinguish between *ideas* and *things*. Here is an example of this kind of confusion:

(1) We ought to pause once a day to ask ourselves what made America strong and rich. Are our great natural resources responsible? No—there are more than a few undeveloped countries rich in resources. Is our ingenuity responsible? Again no. Every country has had its great inventor. Is ours a superior race? Once again no. America is a mixing bowl of races. Is our freedom responsible? Well, the American Indian was free.

(2) America no doubt was destined to become the leader of all countries because of principles, those written down in the Declaration of Independence and the Constitution of the United States. *These documents respected the laws of God and recognized the wants and liberties of our own people and all of humanity, and promised to uphold and protect them.*

(3) There is but one excuse for government: to protect *man's natural rights found in the Declaration of Independence and Constitution.* The Creator endowed man with natural rights and freedoms, and this means that man has the duty to join with other men in forming a government to protect his rights. *While the Declaration of Independence and the Constitution exist,* they will be protected.

This is a broken-backed essay because the connection between paragraphs 2 and 3 is not established. But, as indicated by the italics, its central weakness from the standpoint of exposition is failure to distinguish between a document and what the document represents.

Perhaps the problem remaining unsolved in these paragraphs can be demonstrated by still another list, which can be expanded almost infinitely.

Persons	Things	Ideas
a man	the world	philosophy
a taxpayer	a tax	taxation
a postman	the Civil Service	government
a congressman	Congress	law
a clergyman	a seminary	religion
a professor	a university	education
a soldier	an army	war

Persons	Things	Ideas
Christ	the Cross	Christianity
a salesman	an insurance policy	insurance
a prisoner	a prison	imprisonment
an executive	a corporation	corporation finance
a writer	a book	criticism
an artist	a painting	art
a housewife	a pancake	cuisine
a forester	a tree	conservation
a doctor	an operation	surgery
a criminal	stolen money	crime
a politician	an election	politics

The third stumbling block in exposition of ideas has application as well to the other kinds of exposition and to argumentation: *the failure to set limits to a discourse.* Chapter One has shown that any essay must have a beginning, a middle, and an end. This precept is clear enough. The difficulty in obeying it arises from the "open end" nature of the world process, and of the infinity of processes into which the world process can be analyzed. Young as he is, man cannot conceive in rational terms of the beginning. Nor is he old enough—it is hoped—to foresee the end. His limitations in this regard do not, however, prevent him from thinking and talking about the beginning and the end. In short, he sets artificial limits to his world vision, just as the writer of an essay dealing with the least complex of ideas must set limits to his discourse. He cannot possibly examine all aspects of any problem, however simple, and he cannot pretend to have the last word on any subject. Consider the following student essay in regard to whether it knows *where to begin, how to apologize for its limitations,* and *where to stop.*

FREEDOM

Thesis: There is no ideal that equals freedom so that man is in constant search for it whether it be freedom from tyranny or freedom of self. (Over-all method of development: cause and effect)

Outline

I. The cycle of life before one reaches maturity provides startling insight into the nature of freedom. (Process analysis)

II. When one observes the rebellion of a person who is denied freedom, the only inference that can be made is that bondage is alien to human nature. (Description)

III. Dictatorship and Democracy provide insights by which the merits of freedom may be judged. (Illustration)

FREEDOM

(1) From the moment a baby is born there is a process that is ushered in which in a vague connotation may be labeled freedom. The infant is destined to mature into a unique being unless something blocks this maturation process. For the first six months attention is the essence of his being. He relies upon his parents alone for food, clothing, satisfaction, and love. Gradually the infant becomes aware of distracting objects in the world about him. That his attention has become diverted from his parents and focused elsewhere so that pleasure and satisfaction come from alien sources reveals minute growth in progress. There are many such processes resembling the one which I have just cited, some more important than others and much more obvious, so that it would indeed be foolish to consider the many aspects of personality in chronological order. However it is important that one realizes the nature of these events. The infant will grow toward maturity. The search for independence reveals itself in many complex ways so that one may wonder at times whether it is the child or the parent who has a problem. Nevertheless there is one thing that we can be sure of. The infant will gradually become a unique being who can feed, clothe, and provide satisfaction for himself. No longer is he just loved but he too loves. (Process analysis)

(2) However in order to gain a more complete analysis of the necessity of freedom, one has to observe the reaction of a person who has been denied freedom. There are endless illustrations which are but manifestations of the denial of freedom. Perhaps the most classic one is the child who is told not to do

something and it becomes the first thing that he wants to do. You can be sure that if you demand that your child not do a certain thing it will become a compulsion for him to do it just to defy parental authority. However a distinction must be made between defiance and seeking to gain a concept of self. The above illustration might be termed defiance and seeking to gain a concept of self in a very elementary sense. Where freedom and denial become more involved is vocation. Many a counselor can cite numerous examples of parents wanting their child to become something that he himself did not want to be. If the eccentric parent triumphs in his quest of absolute authority, he will have a very dependent, somewhat neurotic, and very miserable offspring. (Description)

(3) On the other hand the merits of freedom and manifestation of bondage are readily observable if we consider history and the aspects of many cultures. The Greeks, who have affected every culture, were great believers in individual responsibility. The Christian faith embraces the same belief as the Greeks and has lasted longer than any religion. Democracy has always triumphed where there were courageous persons to support it. Quite to the contrary are the gloomy aspects of bondage. Hitler and Mussolini rose to power but failed because they tried to rule the human mind. Communism tries to do the same thing today. Hitler and Mussolini fell because their ideal did so much evil. You can do so much evil and then a vomiting process occurs. Communism may continue to flourish even though it produces evil. Bondage may be compared to the child who tries to rebel but fails. He can never be free now because he craves being dependent. So may it be with the Communists. For only if you change the nature of man can you change his ideals. (Illustration)

Commentary: Evidently the author of "Freedom" has been exposed to a course in psychology, whose jargon has left scar tissue on an otherwise fairly adequate and unpretentious vocabulary. Further, this is another broken-backed essay, its spine having been broken not once but twice (in effect a new discourse is begun in each paragraph), despite the effort to patch it at the end by referring to the child of the first paragraph.

The cause of fragmented organization is not far to seek: limits have not been set to the discourse. As an idea liberty is extraordinarily vast in scope; "Freedom" might have achieved some modest success had it been content only to contemplate a child's freedom, continuing to explore the ideas in paragraph one.

EXERCISES:

1. An analysis of "Freedom" in regard to whether the advertised methods of idea development, for the whole essay and for each paragraph, have been observed.

2. A thoroughgoing revision of "Freedom," based upon the questions appended to "Golfers I Have Known."

3. An expansion of the list of persons, things, and ideas.

4. The composition of at least ten thesis sentences on *ideas* in the list.

5. The formulation of at least five sentence outlines from these thesis sentences.

6. At the instructor's discretion, the writing of one or more exposition-of-ideas essays from these outlines.

A Final Word on Exposition

Despite its length the following chapter on argumentation discusses a single technique, the art of disagreement. And so the serious writer has thus far come nearly all the way in acquainting himself with the various aspects of rhetoric. He understands that his mind and tongue have begun to comprehend a decent vocabulary, that he has a grasp of the nuances of sentence and paragraph style, that he can write a coherent and cohesive expository essay. His further progress depends upon a comprehensive, concentrated reading program and frequent practice in writing, self-imposed if necessary, emphasizing (a) careful organization, (b) a method of idea development basic to each paper, (c) illustration, illustration, illustration.

Assignments

1. The compilation of a substantial list of titles dealing with contemporary problems, suitable for essays developed by the four methods of exposition.
2. The writing of several full-length (500–750 words) expository essays. At least one of them should be an attempt at combining two or more of the four methods of exposition.
3. As assigned by the instructor, extended analysis of expository essays in the reading text.
4. As assigned by the instructor, a detailed written analysis of at least two of the essays in the list of illustrative readings, which the instructor may well wish to expand. The list of readings at the end of this chapter emphasizes recent essays in American periodicals noted for their attention to quality in content and style.

Readings

I. *Exposition of Persons*

Charles Lamb, "The Two Races of Men," *Complete Works and Letters* (Modern Library).

Thomas Whiteside, "The Time Is Twenty-one After," *New Yorker,* Sept. 5, 1959 (on Dave Garroway).

Mollie Painter-Downes, "Kingsman," *New Yorker,* Sept. 19, 1959 (on E. M. Forster).

Norman Cousins, "Talk with the PM," *Saturday Review,* May 27, 1961 (on Nehru).

Joseph Lash, "The Man on the 38th Floor," *Harper's,* Oct., 1959 (on Dag Hammarskjold).

Leo Rosten, "The Lunar World of Groucho Marx," *Harper's,* June, 1958.

Catherine Drinker Bowen, "Bernard De Voto: Historian, Critic, and Fighter," *Atlantic,* Dec., 1960.

Clifton Fadiman, "A Traveler in Reality," *Party of One* (Cleveland, 1955) (on E. B. White).

James Thurber, "E. B. W.," *Saturday Review of Literature*, Oct. 15, 1938.

II. *Exposition of Things*

E. B. White, "Letter from the East," *New Yorker*, Feb. 20, 1960 (on Maine railroads).

Berton Roueché, "Alcohol," *New Yorker*, Jan. 9, 16, 23, 1960.

Bruce Bliven, "San Francisco: New Serpents in Eden," *Harper's*, Jan., 1958.

David Boroff, "Imperial Harvard," *Harper's*, Oct., 1958.

E. B. White, "Here Is New York," *Holiday*, April, 1949.

Ralph McGill, "Boss Crump's Town," *Atlantic*, Jan., 1960.

E. B. White, "Walden," *One Man's Meat* (New York, 1944).

Elizabeth Hardwick, "Boston: The Lost Ideal," *Harper's*, Dec., 1959.

III. *Exposition of Sequences*

Emmanuel Anati, "Prehistoric Art in the Alps," *Scientific American*, Jan., 1960.

Oliver La Farge, "The Enduring Indian," *Scientific American*, Feb., 1960.

Stringfellow Barr, "Enter the Machine," *The Pilgrimage of Western Man* (New York, 1949).

Douglas Schwartz, "Prehistoric Man in Mammoth Cave," *Scientific American*, July, 1960.

Bernard De Voto, "The Third Floor," *The Easy Chair* (Boston, 1955).

————, "Sacred Cows and Public Lands," *The Easy Chair* (Boston, 1955).

Richard Rovere, "The Invasion of Privacy: Technology and the Claims of Community," *American Scholar*, Autumn, 1958.

Robert Graves, "Homer's Winks and Nods," *Atlantic*, Nov., 1959.

Thomas Davis, "Man Alive in Outer Space," *Atlantic*, Mar., 1960.

Erroll Whittall, "To Fight or to Go: The Dilemma of White Africans," *Atlantic*, Sept., 1960.

IV. *Exposition of Ideas*

Russell Lynes, "Time on Our Hands," *Harper's*, July, 1958.

William Hastings, "Strait Is the Gate," *American Scholar*, Winter, 1957–58.

Arthur Schlesinger, "Our Ten Contributions to Civilization," *Atlantic,* Mar., 1959.

George Kennan, "Foreign Policy and Christian Conscience," *Atlantic,* May, 1959.

Howard Jones, "The American Concept of Academic Freedom," *American Scholar,* Winter, 1959–60.

Roy Lewis and Angus Maude, "The Middle Classes," *The English Middle Classes* (New York, 1950).

Julian Huxley, "Life Can Be Worth Living," *Man Stands Alone* (New York, 1939).

T. V. Smith, "The Double Discipline of Democracy," *Virginia Quarterly Review,* Winter, 1937.

❀ The Précis and the Paraphrase

Unwilling to rely on a notoriously untrustworthy memory, a professor of political science at Princeton University has since his high school days observed a virtually inflexible daily custom: he reads a book and transfers more or less extensive notes on its contents to cards which are carefully filed for quick reference. His professional competence, according to the professor, owes much to this system, to his knack for extracting essentials and recording them briefly, coherently.

The college student, who is in a sense beginning his own professional or occupational life—however occasional and haphazard his devotion to purely intellectual concerns—from sheer necessity works out a similar system; when at last he turns to serious study, few are the hours not devoted somehow to outlining, summarizing, or restating the matter of articles, books, and lectures. The horizons of knowledge in all disciplines are expanding at such a rate that (especially for examination purposes) it is not possible for him to look back. Like the professor he depends, in short, on his "notes."

Much of his note taking is likely to be informal in character, to possess no more organization than, say, a lecture by a professor who tends to let his mind wander in the classroom. But there is no doubt that the better organized a set of notes is, the easier it will be to study and remember. There are two traditional methods of organizing, condensing, and restating: the *précis* and the *paraphrase*.

A. The *précis* may be defined as *a summary of the essential content of an original*. These are its characteristics:

1. *Suitable length*. This may vary anywhere from less than five to as much as twenty or thirty per cent of the original because of the relative density and complexity of the ideas, or, to put it another way, because of the incidence of statistics, examples, or illustrations, which are usually excluded from the précis. (The samples that follow are partly an effort to demonstrate problems of density and complexity.)

2. *Retention of the original arrangement of ideas*. It may be possible to improve upon this arrangement, but it is not the business of the précis to do so.

3. *Exclusion of illustrative material*, unless it contains, by implication, essential ideas not developed elsewhere in the original.

4. *Maintenance of point of view*. If the author of the original writes from the standpoint "I," the précis will preserve the first person approach. It will not resort to such phraseology as "the author says," "in the article it says," "Mumford maintains," and the like. The précis writer, then, assumes the identity of the author, as if he were producing a short version of his own work. Similarly, if the approach of the original is from the second-person "you" or third-person (objective) point of view, the précis maintains it scrupulously.

5. *Stress on transition devices* (see the list of devices in Chapter Five). Where possible, the précis should retain the transition devices of the original. But since nonessentials are edited out of the précis, the use of additional "stitching" words and phrases becomes an important consideration.

6. *Retention of the language of the original*. This is to be encouraged so long as it serves the purposes of the précis writer. The précis makes no pretension of originality. (CAUTION: The student is earnestly exhorted not to dabble, when

reading for profit or pleasure, in book or magazine digests. Many of these are mediums of popular entertainment whose vocabulary is deliberately simplified and whose content may well mirror an editorial compromise involving the sacrifice of essentials owing to commercial or even more obscure motives. The perceptive and honest reader suffers under what amounts to a moral obligation to get his information first hand.)

Samples of précis writing, transition devices italicized:

ROBERT LOUIS STEVENSON, "Pulvis et Umbra" (*Across the Plains,* New York, 1892)

Though in this world on every hand we seem to see wrong and meaninglessness triumphant, faith can nevertheless read a bracing gospel in the harsh face of life. It is, *of course,* true that in the appalling and unsubstantial Kosmos defined by science, matter rots uncleanly into something repulsive we call life. It is *also* true that, being *alive,* we know something about how miraculous and terrible and loathsome an experience *life* is, and know *too* how the *Kosmos* moves on indifferent to it.

But despite his weaknesses and *repulsiveness,* man is astonishingly capable of conceiving and sacrificing himself to a principle called duty—to an ideal. Men and women everywhere, enduring adverse and degrading circumstances, obscurely fight the lost fight of virtue and cling to an idea of honor. *Furthermore,* observation of nature shows us that through all living things a *similar* marvelous devotion to the *ideal* exists. Let men, *then,* take consolation and not complain.

BERTRAND RUSSELL, "The Functions of a Teacher" (*Unpopular Essays,* New York, 1950)

Although throughout history teachers have been subjected to varying controls and restrictions, first-rate men have usually managed to function. In modern times, *however,* state education, by helping to produce bigoted nationalism in the young, has contributed to the decline of our common international culture. *This* new phenomenon is seen most clearly in education in the totalitarian countries. *But* since the First World War the decay of *cultural internationalism* has proceeded everywhere at a continually increasing pace.

What services should teachers perform? *For one thing,* in a democratic society, they should be the main safeguard against dangerous dogmatisms, standing outside of party strife and training the young in impartial inquiry. *For another,* more positive, they should know what civilization is and should want to civilize their pupils. Their *knowledge* should include an intellectual awareness of the universal framework of things, and an emotional awareness of mankind's great achievements. *Furthermore,* unlike propagandists, who thwart and twist their pupils' minds and produce cruelty in them, good teachers should reduce the quantity of repressive and persecuting passion present in the world by showing their pupils the way to wise happiness. *These* are the functions of teachers.

Their fulfillment of *these functions, however,* is obstructed in various ways under state education. Because authorities do not understand the expense of spirit involved in education, teachers are overworked and unable to do their jobs right. *Worse still,* they are expected to subordinate their own opinions to what are regarded as "correct" opinions and to teach morally indefensible "edifying" lies, to the consequent confusion of the young. Their most important *function* of discouraging collective hysteria by instilling tolerance is, like their *other functions,* made difficult or impossible by the control of *bureaucrats* and *bigots.* From all *this* it seems clear, although the individualism that good teaching requires may be hard to attain in our turbulent times, that unless some loopholes and exceptions are provided our system may crush the best that is in man.

JONATHAN SWIFT, "The Abolishing of Christianity"
(*Gulliver's Travels and Other Writings,* New York,
Modern Library, 1931)

Although I realize how weak and presumptuous it is to reason against the disposition of a world determined to abolish Christianity, I must confess that I do not yet see the absolute necessity of *extirpating* it from among us. *We* are much changed, in half an age, for I know some very old people who can remember when it would have been absurd to come to the defense of our antiquated and exploded gospel system. I do not presume to *defend, of course,* real Christianity—the restoration of which would be a wild and destructive project—but only nominal Christianity.

Permit me, *then,* to examine the wonderful advantages to the nation proposed by those who would *abolish* our present *system,* and to show, *finally,* the inconveniences which their innovation may possibly cause. To the *proposal* of the *first* great *advantage,* that it would enlarge and establish liberty of conscience, I answer that we need a *nominal* religion so that great wits, who love to be free with the highest objects, will be able to abuse and revile God: *otherwise* they will—of much more pernicious consequence—speak evil of dignities, abuse the government, and reflect upon the ministry. To the proposal of the *second great advantage,* that it would free the educated and unprejudiced man from the obligation of believing anything, I *answer* that he is already free to believe what he pleases, especially if the publication of his belief serves to strengthen the party in power.

It is *likewise* urged that the revenues now spent in the support of parsons and bishops would maintain at least two hundred *educated* and *unprejudiced* young men, to which I *answer* that in the country parish there ought to be at least one literate man, that *these revenues* probably would not support one hundred young profligates, and that the clergy, reduced by law to the necessity of a healthy low diet and moderate exercise, are the only great restorers of our English breed. *Still another advantage* proposed by the *abolition* of Christianity is the clear gain of one day in seven, which I call a perfect cavil, for business and recreation certainly go forward on Sunday as well as any other day in the taverns and coffee-houses and churches.

These innovators advertise an *even greater advantage* to the *abolishing* of Christianity, that it will utterly extinguish parties among us, to which I *again answer* that our love of faction is rooted much deeper in our hearts than phrases borrowed from religion, and founded upon firmer principles. *Once again,* it is objected as *absurd* that a set of men should be suffered—much less employed—to bawl *one day in seven* against the lawfulness of those methods most in use toward the pursuit of greatness, riches, and pleasure, which are the constant practice of all men alive on the other six. *But this objection* is a little unworthy of so refined an age as ours, when in the *pursuit* of gratifying a predominant passion men have always felt a wonderful incitement by reflecting it was a thing forbidden.

It is *further proposed* that with the discarding of religion will go those grievous *prejudices* of education, which under the names of "virtue," "conscience," "honor," "justice" and the like are so apt to disturb the peace of human minds, since they are so difficult to eradicate. *But* so effectual care has been taken to remove these *prejudices* by an entire change in the methods of education that the young gentlemen who are now on the scene seem not to have the least tincture of those infusions. Could the *abolishing* of Christianity do more? *And* not all are *gentlemen;* I look upon the mass of our people to be as staunch unbelievers as any of the highest rank, but I do conceive some notion of a superior power to be of singular use to the common people, as furnishing excellent materials to keep children quiet when they grow peevish, and providing topics of amusement in a tedious winter night.

Lastly, it is *proposed* that the *abolishing* of Christianity will unite Protestants by admitting to communion all those who are now shut out as dissenters on account of a few insignificant ceremonies. To *all this* I *answer* that there is one darling inclination of mankind which usually affects to be a retainer of religion; I mean the spirit of opposition that lived long before Christianity and can easily subsist without it. *This spirit,* were it not for Christianity, would be employed in contravention to the *laws* of the land and the *disturbance* of the public peace, which would be on a much sounder basis among us if there were convents and monasteries where the melancholy, the proud, the politic, and the morose could spend themselves and evaporate the noxious particles.

Now, having considered the *advantages* proposed by the *abolition* of Christianity, I should like to mention a few of the *inconveniences* which may attend the repeal of the *gospel system.* Our wise reformers, *for example,* have not considered what an *advantage* and felicity it is for great wits to be always provided with objects of scorn and contempt: where could the free-thinkers, the strong reasoners, the men of profound learning find a subject to take the place of Christianity, so calculated in all points to provide an opportunity for the display of their abilities? *Nor* do I think it wholly groundless that the *abolishing* of Christianity may perhaps bring the Church into danger, or at least put the senate [House of Lords] to the trouble of another securing vote. *In the last place,* I think nothing can be more plain than that by this expedient we shall establish what we chiefly pretend to avoid, popery. *And therefore,* if the *innovators* persist in their determination to *abolish* Christianity, I would humbly offer an amendment—the substitution of the phrase "religion in general" for the word "Christianity"—for we do not strike at the root of the evil however effectively we *annihilate* the *scheme* of the *gospel.* Of what use is freedom of thought if it does not father freedom of action, which is the sole end of all *objections* to Christianity? The quarrel is not against any particular points of hard digestion in the Christian *system* but against *religion in general,* which by laying restraints upon human nature is supposed the great enemy to freedom of thought and action.

Upon the whole, if Christianity must go, I think we should defer its departure to a time of *peace,* so that we may not discomfit our allies, who are Christians and because of the *prejudices* of their *education* proud of the appellation. *Certainly* we should not ally ourselves with the Turks, who still believe in God—more than is required of us at present. *To conclude,* I predict that whatever the *advantages* accruing to the *abolition* of Christianity, six months after the event the Bank and East India stock will fall at least one per cent. *And* since *that* is fifty times more than ever the wisdom of our age has thought fit to venture for the preservation of Christianity, there is no reason we should be at *so great a loss* merely for the sake of destroying it.

B. The *paraphrase* may be simply defined as a restatement of the original, its specific goal being clarification. It is most often, as the following sample indicates, applied to poetry. These are its characteristics:

1. *Suitable length.* Since the object is clarification or, in a sense, explanation, the paraphrase may be considerably longer than the original. Unlike the précis, the paraphrase is not content with essentials; *all* ideas and illustrations are used.

2. *Rearrangement of ideas in the original,* as necessary.

Again, the goal is to make meaning perfectly clear. Anything working toward this objective is legitimate.

3. *Maintenance of point of view,* as in the précis.

4. *Sacrifice of the language and style of the original in the interests of understanding.*

An original, followed by a paraphrase:

> GEOFFREY CHAUCER, "Chaucer's Wordes Unto Adam, His Owne Scriveyn"
>
> Adam scriveyn, if ever it thee bifalle
> Boece or Troylus for to wryten newe,
> Under thy long lokkes thou must have the scalle,
> But after my makyng thou wryte more trewe;
> So ofte a-daye I mot thy werk renewe,
> It to correcte and eek to rubbe and scrape;
> And al is thurgh thy negligence and rape.

[NOTE: A *scriveyn,* or *scrivener,* was in Chaucer's day a kind of secretary in that it was his profession to make precise copies of manuscripts. Before the invention of printing he was one of the two chief means of "book" production, the other being the reproducing of manuscripts in monasteries.]

> Scrivener Adam, if you ever get another chance to make copies of my translation of Boethius's *Consolation of Philosophy* or my poem *Troilus and Criseyde,* I hope you develop a case of the scabies if you don't do a better job of copying my originals. Because of your negligence and haste I have often been forced to do your work over again, by erasing and correcting it.

Assignments and Exercises

1. An examination of the essays by Stevenson, Russell, and Swift, to determine whether the sample précis depart in any way from the principles of good précis writing.

2. Précis of essays, to be selected by the instructor from the reading text.

3. Paraphrases of poems, selected by the instructor.

❦ Exposition in the Literary Essay

At some time during his freshman year the student will probably be faced with writing assignments on drama, fiction, and poetry. His total past experience in dealing with imaginative literature will very likely have consisted of "reports"— efforts at proving to the instructor, mainly by synopsis, that he has accomplished an assigned piece of "outside" reading.

Unless he finds himself seething with original ideas after studying a poem or play or story, he may because of his inexperience be at a loss as to how even to begin a critical essay, let alone provide a middle and an end. If it may be assumed that his reaction to a piece of imaginative literature is unformed, unsubstantial—he likes or dislikes it without quite knowing why—he requires, as a basis for substantial analysis, certain guidelines of procedure. If he has time, he can formulate these standards for himself after some quiet reading in a few of the works listed in Appendix I of this book. What follows (he should feel free to reject it as soon as he has a degree of literary sophistication) may nevertheless guide him until he has acquired some knowledge of critical literature.

CRITICISM AS EXPOSITION

1. The first of these standards carries with it the reassurance that he is not required to do anything different, in regard to rhetorical techniques, from what he has been doing. Unless he chooses to pick a fight with another critic, his critical essay is expository, at bottom *exposition of a thing*. The thing is a work of literature, the writer's purpose to enlighten the reader in regard to the work of literature. A slight complication of the problem will occur, it should be pointed out, when he must compare or contrast more than one work of poetry, drama, or fiction.

2. A second guide to critical procedure is the material on the organization of the literary essay appended to Chapter Five (pp. 138–139). Deserving special emphasis are the admonitions (a) to avoid beginning an essay with a biographical sketch of an author, (b) to avoid summarizing content, (c) to assume that the reader of the critical essay is familiar with the work under consideration, (d) when writing about more than one work, to deal with the same aspects of both works side by side, rather than separately.

3. The critical essay must have a plan, reflected in a thesis sentence and a sentence outline. These may be hazily expressed at first but will acquire substance as the writer visualizes the work of art under the strictures of the fourth standard, which is a fairly concrete means of evaluating the poem, the story, the play.

THE POEM

A poem tells a story, sings a song, or philosophizes. Whichever of these things it does, it probably should present a factual situation that the reader can easily visualize, be clear enough in meaning to be capable of some kind of interpretation, be unified (not diverse and fragmented), and be presented from a single point of view. If it does not accomplish all this, the writer has in hand sufficient ammunition for adverse criticism.

Similarly, he can reach a decision as to which of two or more poems is superior.

a. *The narrative poem.* Even though poetry is in a sense literary shorthand—it *suggests* infinitely more than it *says*—the narrative poem must in adhering to the requirements of any narrative present enough of a story to take the reader to a recognizable climax, a point of high excitement directly involving the success or failure of the enterprise (carried on by a hero, or central character) that is the focus of the narrative. Further, the narrative must be unified, and it must not (unless it is set in Arcadia or Faeryland) outrage the reader's imagination with too much of the fantastic and supernatural. Finally, the characters of the narrative poem must be recognizably human, and the development of their nature must be the ultimate purpose of the poem—not metaphor or plot or scenery.

b. *The song or lyric.* This kind of poem is admittedly more difficult to assess, but these are legitimate grounds for evaluation: (1) unity of impression (is the poet wrongly attempting to achieve more than one purpose?), (2) unity in point of view (if the poet looks up at a bird from the ground at one place in the poem and then looks down upon the bird from an aircraft in another part of the poem, unity of effect is destroyed), (3) unity of image (the bird should not be described as a dragon at one place in the poem and later described in more friendly terms).

c. *The philosophical poem.* All of the admonitions in regard to the lyric hold true here. But since the philosophical poem has as its reason for being the statement (explicit or implied) of an idea, the idea itself must be *clear, unified* (two equivalent or unresolvedly opposed ideas destroy unity), and *interesting.* If the idea fails to arouse a spark of interest in the reader, the poet may be dealing with the trivial. Poetry is not about trivialities.

Conclusion: An extended poem may be narrative, lyrical, and philosophical all at once. The neophyte is therefore well advised to practice assiduously on short poems before tackling long ones.

THE WORK OF FICTION

A short story or a novel has a framework of events called a plot. In the short story this framework is slight and covers a reasonably brief period of time. The purpose of plot in the short story (apart, again, from intrinsic interest) is (a) to present the central character or hero with a problem, (b) to tell the reader enough about the hero for the reader to make a prediction about how the hero will handle the problem, and (c) at the climax, to force the hero to try solving the problem. If plot essays more than this, unity in the story may be destroyed. If plot fails to do these three things, the story as a whole may fail. The critic, then, can successfully evaluate one or more short stories in regard to plot alone. For the novel—in a sense a closely knit *sequence* of short stories—considerations of plot are the same as for the short story, except for problems in extension of time: *complete* development of character obtains in the full-length work; the climax in the novel therefore exerts its tension upon all aspects of character at once. Again, plot or story line in the novel (although it must be interesting) cannot be the focus of reader fascination. Human character and human relationships are of paramount importance in fiction.

The critic must also examine plot to determine whether or not it is logically conceived. Plot in the work of fiction proceeds relentlessly by a succession of causes and effects. *Chance is ruled out*, although—witness the outrageous concatenations described in the newspapers—it may at times seem to rule human existence outside of fiction. But fiction has form; it is orderly; it is symmetrical.

Another convenient means of evaluating fiction is determining whether character is consistent. Just as chance is ruled out, so are involutions of character: a man does not, as Oscar Wilde long ago pointed out, pretend to be wicked through the course of a story and then turn out to be good. Similarly, once a novelist has established a character as weak, he does not at the climax become a tower of strength.

The strictures on point of view and unity of purpose and effect (the short story and the novel should aim at accomplishing *one* purpose, not several) applying to poetry are also especially useful in evaluating technique in a work of fiction. *The embryo critic is strongly advised, finally, to avoid decisions based on stylistic excellences or deficiencies.* Style can be analyzed, as the early chapters of this book make clear, but a critic of art needs experience before venturing into this arena. (What many professional critics do in this regard, by the way, is to reproduce a paragraph or two of the story or novel they attack or praise, and then to say categorically, "This is good style," or "This is bad style.")

THE PLAY

Plays, according to one critical tradition, are to be examined as to whether they observe the "three unities," (a) of time (a play should deal with a day in the lives of its characters), (b) of place (a play should have one geographical location), (c) of action (a play should not have two or more plots of relatively equal importance). These limitations have some validity, simply because the playwright should not confuse his audience, but probably only the unity of action is a sound basis for play analysis. To continue, the requirements of the drama are, by and large, the requirements of prose fiction. But they become especially vivid on the stage, for the playwright enjoys none of the narrative advantages inherent in prose fiction. He cannot set a scene, he cannot explore backgrounds, he cannot evoke a mood—except through conversation among his characters on the stage. For the dramatist conversation evokes the reason-for-being of fiction: human character, human relationships. Anything happening on the stage that interferes with or obscures conversation (slamming of doors, answering telephones) is therefore to be accounted a fault. Action should serve no purpose but to promote or implement conversation.

Chapter Seven

❀ ARGUMENTATION

It is not the contention of English teachers alone that there is nothing more important to be gained from exposure to college than the ability to write correctly, effectively, and reasonably. In whatever discipline, the effectiveness and reasonableness of a piece of writing often depend, as indicated in Chapter Five, upon whether it is necessary for the essayist to present an argument. He must know when and upon what grounds to say "I disagree"—a business of immense significance to him in evaluating the editorial content of what he reads as well as in rationally ordering the matter of his own work. In doing so he continues to use the rhetorical methods of exposition (since disagreement constitutes the only necessary distinction between exposition and argumentation), but in a special, probably more consciously artful and careful, way.

In general, several courses are open to him, according to the nature of his writing problem, as it involves (a) *active disagreement with a known argument,* (b) *refutation of an anticipated argument,* (c) *presentation of both sides of an issue, with a conclusion favoring one side,* or (d) *the apology, a confession of limitations and prejudices.*

EXAMPLES

(a) *Active disagreement with a known argument:*

(1) Some of our own people seem to get no satisfaction out of anything but chasing after dollars without let-up from year to year, save when they are asleep, or in church, or both. We recall a certain rich man who boasted that in the eighty-eight years of his career he had not once taken a vacation or wanted one. Naturally his way was the right way, and he proceeded to show it. "What right," asked he, "has a clerk to demand or expect pay for two weeks' time for which he renders no equivalent? Is it not absurd to suppose that a man who can work eleven and a half months cannot as well work the whole year? The doctors may recommend a change of air when he's sick; but why be sick? Sickness is an irreparable loss of time." I am not misquoting this very rich man: his signed pronouncement lies before me—the sorriest thing that ever I saw in print.

(2) Seriously, is it good for men and women and children to swarm together in cities and stay there, keep staying there, till their instincts are so far perverted that they lose all taste for their natural element, the wide world out-of-doors? In any case, although evolution be a very great and good law, yet is it not a trifle slow? How about you and me? Can we wait a few thousand years for fulfilment of the wise men's prophecy? We are neither coolies, nor mud-turtles, nor those other things with the awful name.

(3) Granting, then, that one deserves relief now and then from the hurry and worry that would age him before his prime, why not go in for a complete change while you are about it? Why not exorcise the devil of business and everything that suggests it? The best vacation an over-civilized man can have is to go where he can hunt, capture, and cook his own meat, erect his own shelter, do his own chores, and so, in some measure, pick up again those lost arts of wildcraft that were our heritage through ages past, but of which not one modern man in a hundred knows anything at all. In cities our tasks are so highly

specialized, and so many things are done for us by other specialists, that we tend to become a one-handed and one-idead race. The self-dependent life of the wilderness nomad brings bodily habits and mental processes back to normal, by exercise of muscles and lobes that otherwise might atrophy from want of use.

—Horace Kephart, *Camping* (New York:
The Macmillan Company), pp. 19–20.

(b) *Refutation of an anticipated argument:*

(1) It being the interest, then, of the very worst of them [the first human politicians], more than any, to preach up public spiritedness, that they might reap the fruits of the labor and self-denial of others and at the same time indulge their own appetites with less disturbance, they agreed with the rest to call everything which, without regard to the public, man should commit to gratify any of his appetites, VICE, if in that action there could be observed the least prospect that it might either be injurious to any of the society, or even render himself less serviceable to others; and to give the name of VIRTUE to every performance by which man, contrary to the impulse of nature, should endeavor the benefit of others, or the conquest of his own passions out of a rational ambition of being good.

(2) It shall be objected that no society was ever anyways civilized before the major part had agreed upon some worship or other of an overruling Power, and consequently that the notions of good and evil, and the distinction between *Virtue* and *Vice*, were never the contrivance of politicians, but the pure effect of religion. Before I answer this objection, I must repeat what I have said already, that in this *Inquiry into the Origin of Moral Virtue* I speak neither of Jews or Christians, but man in his State of Nature and ignorance of the true Deity; and then I affirm that the idolatrous superstitions of all other nations, and the pitiful notions they had of the Supreme Being, were incapable of exciting man to virtue, and good for nothing but to awe and amuse a rude and unthinking multitude. It is evident from history that in all considerable societies, how stupid or ridiculous soever people's received notions have been as to the deities they worshiped, human nature has ever exerted itself in all its branches, and that there is no earthly wisdom or moral

virtue but at one time or other men have excelled in it in all
monarchies and commonwealths that for riches and power have
been anyways remarkable.

—Bernard Mandeville, from *The Fable of
the Bees* (London, 1714).

(c) *Presentation of both sides of an issue, with a conclusion
favoring one side:*

(1) How often have we not been told that the study of
physical science is incompetent to confer culture; that it touches
none of the higher problems of life; and, what is worse, that
the continual devotion to scientific studies tends to generate a
narrow and bigoted belief in the applicability of scientific
methods to the search after truth of all kinds? How frequently
one has reason to observe that no reply to a troublesome argument tells so well as calling its author a "mere scientific specialist." And . . . I am afraid it is not permissible to speak of
this form of opposition to scientific education in the past
tense. . . .

(2) . . . I hold very strongly by two convictions. The first
is that neither the discipline nor the subject matter of classical
education is of such direct value to the student of physical
science as to justify the expenditure of valuable time upon
either; and the second is, that for the purpose of attaining real
culture, an exclusively scientific education is at least as effectual
as an exclusively literary education.

(3) I need hardly point out to you that these opinions, especially the latter, are diametrically opposed to those of the great
majority of educated Englishmen, influenced as they are by
school and university traditions. In their belief, culture is ob-
tainable only by a liberal education; and a liberal education is
synonymous, not merely with education and instruction in literature, but one particular form of literature, namely, that of
Greek and Roman antiquity. They hold that the man who has
learned Latin and Greek, however little, is educated; while he
who is versed in other branches of knowledge, however deeply,
is a more or less respectable specialist, not admissible into the
cultured caste. The stamp of the educated man, the university
degree, is not for him.

(4) I am too well acquainted with the generous catholicity

of spirit, the true sympathy with scientific thought, which pervades the writings of our chief apostle of culture to identify
him with these opinions; and yet one may cull from one and
another of those epistles to the Philistines, which so much delight all who do not answer to that name, sentences which lend
them some support.

(5) Mr. Arnold tells us that the meaning of culture is "to
know the best that has been thought and said in the world."
It is the criticism of life contained in literature. That criticism
regards "Europe as being, for intellectual and spiritual purposes,
one great confederation, bound to a joint action and working to
a common result; and whose members have, for their common
outfit, a knowledge of Greek, Roman, and Eastern antiquity, and
of one another. Special, local, and temporary advantages being
put out of account, that modern nation will in the intellectual
and spiritual sphere make most progress, which most thoroughly
carries out this program. And what is that but saying that we
too, all of us, as individuals, the more thoroughly we carry it
out, shall make the more progress?"

(6) We have here to deal with two distinct propositions. The
first, that a criticism of life is the essence of culture; the second,
that literature contains the materials which suffice for the construction of such criticism.

(7) I think that we must all assent to the first proposition. For culture certainly means something quite different from
learning or technical skill. It implies the possession of an ideal,
and the habit of critically estimating the value of things by comparison with a theoretic standard. Perfect culture should supply
a complete theory of life, based upon a clear knowledge alike
of its possibilities and its limitations.

(8) But we may agree to all this, and yet strongly dissent
from the assumption that literature alone is competent to supply
this knowledge. After having learned all that Greek, Roman, and
Eastern antiquity have thought and said, and all that modern
literatures have to tell us, it is not self-evident that we have
laid a sufficiently broad and deep foundation for that criticism
of life which constitutes culture.

(9) Indeed, to anyone acquainted with the scope of physical science, it is not at all evident. Considering progress only
in the "intellectual and spiritual sphere," I find myself wholly

unable to admit that either nations or individuals will really
advance, if their common outfit draws nothing from the stores
of physical science. I should say that an army, without weapons
of precision and with no particular base of operations, might
more hopefully enter upon a campaign on the Rhine, than a
man, devoid of a knowledge of what physical science has done
in the last century, upon a criticism of life.

—Thomas Henry Huxley, from
"Science and Culture," 1880.

(d) *The apology, a confession of limitations and prejudices:*

Call me, if you like, the fox who has lost his brush; I am
nobody's servant and have chosen to live on the outskirts of a
Majorcan mountain-village, Catholic but anti-ecclesiastical, where
life is still ruled by the old agricultural cycle. Without my brush,
namely my contact with urban civilization, all that I write must
read perversely and irrelevantly to such of you as are still geared
to the industrial machine, whether directly as workers, mana-
gers, traders or advertisers or indirectly as civil servants,
publishers, journalists, schoolmasters or employees of a radio
corporation. If you are poets, you will realize that acceptance
of my historical thesis commits you to a confession of disloyalty
which you will be loth to make; you chose your jobs because
they promised to provide you with a steady income and leisure
to render the Goddess whom you adore valuable part-time service. Who am I, you will ask, to warn you that she demands
either whole-time service or none at all? And do I suggest that
you should resign your jobs and for want of sufficient capital
to set up as small-holders, turn romantic shepherds—as Don
Quixote did after his failure to come to terms with the modern
world—in remote unmechanized farms? No, my brushlessness
debars me from offering any practical suggestion. I dare attempt
only a historical statement of the problem; how you come to
terms with the Goddess is no concern of mine. I do not even
know that you are serious in your poetic profession.

—Robert Graves, Foreword to *The White
Goddess,* amended and enlarged ed.
(New York, 1958), p. xi.

Laying the Groundwork for an Argument

Each of the foregoing examples of argumentation accomplishes, or attempts to accomplish, the same end, *proving a point or justifying a position.* Further, once his subject has been decided upon, each writer prepares to reach his end—lays the groundwork for proving his position—through roughly the same process: (a) *selection of a question, or matter to be inquired into,* (b) *statement of position (proposition),* (c) *selection or identification of issue(s), the point(s) to be argued,* (d) *definition of terms* (if required).

An examination of the passage from Horace Kephart's *Camping* will show how the process operates. Kephart's general subject is, of course, camping; every sentence of his famous book contributes somehow to a development of this subject. And as it turns out, the question under consideration in the passage is camping, too, that is to say, whether camping as a human activity is justifiable in the light of recent progress and "citification." Kephart's *proposition* is an affirmative statement of the *question,* delayed until the end of the passage so that he can concentrate upon the *issue, the point to be argued,* the crux of many an argument. Here the *issue* is the vacation, without which there would certainly be little or no camping. In choosing this *issue* Kephart immediately gains the reader's support, and quite likely the reader's endorsement of his argument: few would agree with the "certain rich man" on vacations—the lives of many, indeed, are bearable only because there is the vacation to look forward to. As for *definition of terms,* Kephart's proposition, a simple one, does not require it. But a sardonic *definition* from the rich man, "Sickness is an irreparable loss of time," further strengthens Kephart's position before he proceeds with his argument.

EXERCISES:

1. An examination of the selections by Mandeville, Huxley, and Graves with a view to locating the argument: (a) *formulation of*

the question, (b) *statement of position,* (c) *identification of issue,* (d) *definition of terms* (if any).

2. A similar examination of selections from the reading text, as assigned by the instructor.

3. The formulation of various questions of general concern (see any newspaper), and the identification of issues in regard to these questions.

Establishing a Position

Having put down the foundation for his argument by adopting a position and clarifying the issues at stake—*again, the proper selection of issue is a matter for continued emphasis*—the writer is free to build his argument along one of several lines, restricted by his original decision to present only his side of the question, to develop both sides of the question (as Kephart does), or, in an *apologia,* to deprecate the other side prejudicially (as Graves does). Obviously the primary consideration is to protect his own position by seeking the support of facts, authorities, the powers of reason.

A. SUPPORT THROUGH FACT

Of all methods of idea development the most reliable—because most vivid—is *illustration,* the citation of factual material or the reference to authority (see the section dealing with illustration in Chapter Four), for in using it the writer chooses at will the facts or authorities that fit his essay plan, ignoring or suppressing those which do not. Honesty, however, must be his habit of mind; he should take care not to invent illustrations, and he should adopt a position consistent with his beliefs. Of course he cannot adequately illustrate any idea unless he can distinguish between what is a fact and what is an idea, and use examples that are specific rather than general. If experience fails to supply concrete illustrations, he should have recourse to an encyclopedia, an almanac, or some other reference work.

The value of factual support to an argument is apparent in the following student-composed paragraphs.

The Question: Water skiing—sport or nuisance?
Position: Water skiing is a nuisance.
Issues: (1) Danger to skier, (2) detriment to fishing.
Definition of Terms: Sport (possibly).

THE LATEST THING IN COWBOYS

When does recreation cease to be a sport and become a menace? This is the year, as far as I'm concerned, and the sport turned menace is water skiing. The power cruisers are more numerous, the motors more powerful, the skiers more suicidal. Every lake or widened stream in the country is filled with these maniacs, racing at top speed without regard for their own safety or that of the helpless fisherman, whose anchored or slowly drifting craft is likely to be—and often is—swamped by tidal waves created in the wake of these daredevils. And what of the fish? Any angler will be glad to tell you the fishing is done for, unless you want to try for them late at night or very early in the morning, before the madness begins all over again. Skiing may be invigorating, and good exercise, and all that, but I insist that it's high time to restrict the skier's activities, by laws with teeth in them, even if the sporting goods houses go broke in the process.

Commentary: This is a well-organized paragraph owing to words used in a time sense at the beginning and at the end, and to repeated references to madness. Its style is fairly spirited, and it holds to the issues. But there is not one concrete illustration, although nearly every sentence can be strengthened with statistics, names, or anecdotal material. The final sentence, by the way, has a cliché.

Student's Revision: When does recreation cease being a sport, a way of having fun without bothering anybody, and become a menace? This is the year, as far as I'm concerned, and the sport turned menace is water skiing. Two years ago Lake Como, which my father says used to be a fisherman's paradise, had one docking facility, with accommodations for about twenty small boats. Once in a while, mostly on summer weekends, you would see a skier or two noisily parading across the water, but he was an irritation rather than a nuisance. Fishermen, who never bother anybody, had the lake pretty well to themselves. Last summer everything changed. A fellow named Jim Weber bought the docking facility, christened it *Weber's Marina,* built slips for at least a hundred power craft of all sizes, and in general turned a quiet fishing retreat into a Disneyland for water exhibitionists. In June there were three accidents involving water skiers, on the Fourth of July a water skier drowned and a fisherman's rowboat was rammed and sunk by an outboard cruiser. By Labor Day there were enough wounded to fill a good-sized hospital ward. This summer lived up to expectations, too; on each of the four Sundays in June there was a drowning in Lake Como directly attributable to water skiing mischief. As for fishing, you don't hear much about it nowadays—it's too dangerous. What has happened to Lake Como is happening, I suppose, to every decent body of water in the country, jammed with maniacs racing at top speed without regard for their own safety or that of the helpless fisherman, whose wisest course is to try for the fish that haven't scared off either late at night or very early in the morning, before the madness begins all over again. Skiing may be invigorating, and good exercise, and all that, but I insist that it's high time to restrict the skier's activities with punishing laws, even if the sporting goods houses go broke in the process. They won't, anyway, for fishermen are beginning to buy skin diving equipment in self defense.

Commentary: In conference with his instructor the student was advised to give some thought to the need for defining the term *sport;* hence the revised opening sentence. He was advised further to use specific illustrations from his own experience or recollection, and he did so with a satisfactory degree of effectiveness without sacrificing much of the original material, which he wanted to keep if possible. Upon submitting the revision he confessed to great difficulty in working illustrations into the paragraph. He was not sure that it had been improved.

EXERCISES:

1. An analysis of the paragraphs on water skiing, to determine the nature and extent of the improvement in the second paragraph, with suggested further improvements.

2. A search for and analysis of paragraphs and essays in the reading text which establish a position by support through fact.

3. As assigned by the instructor, the composition of one or more arguments establishing a position in this way.

B. SUPPORT THROUGH REFERENCE TO AUTHORITY

The second of the water skiing paragraphs cites an authority, "my father." Such an authority may or may not carry weight with the reader, depending upon his reverence or respect for the wisdom of ancestors. There are, then, several kinds of authority. Some are appropriate to or carry weight in certain situations; others would be of little consequence in the same situations. He who disagrees is obliged to make certain that his authorities are cited with pertinence to the issues.

1. Printed authorities. Because they have a kind of permanence lacking even to monuments of stone and steel, and because of civilized man's veneration for the printed word, published writings of almost any kind are particularly useful as authorities. For Western man the Bible pervades all aspects of his culture, and is consequently the pre-eminent authority, as the Koran and Bhagavad-Gita are for other cultures. It is not too much to say that all writers, professional and amateur, must be able to cite Biblical authority with ease. The conscientious writer's (and reader's) ready-reference bookshelf has therefore a well-bound copy of the "King James" (Authorized Version), with a concordance. Indispensable are the latest edition of a good desk dictionary (see Chapter Two), the works of Shakespeare, the foremost "literary" authority in the language, and Bartlett's *Familiar Quotations.* Among nonliterary printed works the American *Declaration of Independence* and *Constitution* are powerful authorities, as are the publications and commentaries of presidents, supreme court justices, evangelists, senators, corporation executives (the student is invited to compile a list, in order of descending authority), and experts upon certain aspects of contemporary or past life—historians, philosophers, college presidents, lawyers, teachers, chamber of commerce secretaries, doctors. The Eastern heart specialist Paul Dudley White, for example, became a sought after and widely quoted authority on physical culture following the coronary illness of President Eisenhower.

Here is a striking demonstration of how to argue from Biblical authority:

The Question: Can the Authorized Version be improved upon?

Position: Recent efforts to translate the Bible anew have failed to supplant the Authorized Version.

Issues: (1) The poetry of the Authorized Version *versus* the prose of recent translators, (2) the nature of religious feeling.

Definition of Terms: Religious feeling.

(1) Pursuing, of late, advanced researches into theological pathology, I have had the sad duty of reading certain "new," "modern," "American," and "idiomatic" translations of the New Testament, including those of the Rev. MM. Weymouth, Moffatt, Goodspeed, and Ballantine. All of these translators, I believe, are pious and righteous men, and every one of them undertook his task with the sole object of making Holy Writ more intelligible to the plain people, and hence more persuasive and precious. But I can only report professionally as a theologian that all of them, in my judgment, will go to hell for their pains.

(2) And richly deserve the singeings there in store for them. For all they accomplish, in putting the original Greek into familiar English, is to put it into English so flabby and preposterous that all the beauty is gone out of it. Consider, for example, the sonorous and magnificent line in the Lord's Prayer—thus in the authorized version: "Give us this day our daily bread." Well, this is what it becomes in the Weymouth version: "Give us

today our bread for the day." And this in the Goodspeed version: "Give us today bread for the day." And this in the Ballantine version: "Our bread for the coming day give us today."
And this in the Moffatt version: "Give us today our bread for
the morrow."

(3) Could vandalism go further? It is almost like arranging
Schubert's serenade as a waltz for the bagpipes. All the loveli-
ness is squeezed out of the line. Its ancient charm and elo-
quence vanish into thin air: it ceases to be a prayer and becomes
a mere demand. And is there any compensating gain in clarity?
Is an error in the authorized version rectified? Certainly not.
As a matter of fact, the four experts simply introduce confusion
and obfuscation into what was formerly crystal clear. Two of
them make it appear that the bread asked for is wanted at once;
the other two say that it will not be needed until tomorrow.

(4) I turn to the book of John, and to an episode that most
latter day preachers of the Word delicately avoid: the episode
of the woman taken in adultery. It is unpleasant reading for
vice crusaders, prohibitionists, and other such wowsers, for it
sets forth, in succinct and highly dramatic form, the basic principles of the Christianity actually preached by Christ. You recall,
no doubt, the great speech that confounds the scribes and
Pharisees, eager to put the woman to death: "He that is without
sin among you, let him first cast a stone at her." But perhaps
you have forgotten the superb dialogue that follows, between
Christ and the woman—the most stupendous scene in all drama,
sacred or profane. I quote it from the authorized version:

*When Jesus had lifted up Himself, and saw none but the
woman, He said unto her, Woman, where are those thine ac-
cusers? Hath no man condemned thee?*

*She said, No man, Lord. And Jesus said unto her, Neither do
I condemn thee; go, and sin no more.*

(5) Well, what do the modernizers make of this austere and
colossal beauty, this masterpiece of simple and lovely English,
as it was of Greek? Goodspeed, more discreet than the rest,
omits it altogether: I can't find it in his version of John. But
Weymouth tackles it boldly, and with this almost unbelievable
result:

Then standing up, Jesus spoke to her. "Woman," He said,

"Where are they? Has no one condemned you?" "No one, Sir," she replied. "And I do not condemn you either," said Jesus. "Go, and from this time do not sin any more."

(6) Imagine it! "No one, Sir"! And "do not sin any more"! But Ballantine, as impossible as it may seem, is still worse:

Jesus raised himself up and said to her, "Woman, where are they? Has no one sentenced you?" She said, "No one, Sir." Jesus said, "Neither do I sentence you. Go. From now on sin no more."

(7) And Moffatt, with a herculean effort, manages to be worse than Ballantine:

Raising Himself, Jesus said to her, "Woman, where are they? Has no one condemned you?" She said, "No one, Sir." Jesus said, "Neither do I; be off, and never sin again."

(8) Give your eyes to that "be off." And then ask yourself if a million centuries in hell will be enough for that translator!

(9) All of these dreadful perversions of incomparable beauty, as I have already said, are full of good intentions: they show enough, indeed, to pave hell from the Torquemada monument to the Avenue of Revivalists. What ails them is simply a gross misunderstanding, on the part of their rev. perpetrators, of the nature of religious feeling. These worthy gentlemen all seem to think that it is a product of ratiocination—that it arises out of logic and evidence, like the belief, say, that two and two make four. It does nothing of the sort. It begins, not as a series of ideas, but as a mystery, and it remains a mystery to the end. Religion is most potent to sway the mind, indeed, when the evidences of its objective truth are most vague and unconvincing —when it is apprehended, not as fact at all, but as sheer poetry, the very negation of fact.

—H. L. Mencken, from "Holy Writ,"
The Bathtub Hoax, ed. Robert Mc-
Hugh (New York: Alfred A. Knopf,
1958), pp. 165–168.

Commentary: Mencken is an expert at *slanted writing* (see section C, below), and so in order to soften the impact of his criticism he presents a sort of apology in the first and last paragraphs: "All of these translators . . . are pious and right-eous men"; "All of these dreadful perversions . . . are full of good intentions. . . ." And as a definer of terms Mencken will repay careful study. The first paragraph defines recent tendency to new Biblical translation as a disease; the final paragraph defines religious feeling as a mystery.

2. Unprinted authorities. Certain unprinted authorities, *old sayings*, for example, have a kind of permanence and, in fitting circumstances, substantial weight. The danger in using an apothegm lies, however, in the possibility of an offsetting maxim. "Look before you leap," but "He who hesitates is lost." *Tradition* is another kind of authority which is often effective. A person who calls himself a Jeffersonian, for instance, relies for authority upon political tradition accumulated about Jefferson's name for a century and a half. If he were alive, Jefferson might have difficulty recognizing some aspects of the tradition as Jeffersonian, but he remains the ultimate authority nevertheless. "The American way of life" is a similarly ambiguous use of tradition as authority. Its limitations are patent (see *argumentum ad hominem,* below). The best kind of unprinted authority, finally, is what has a good or at least an outside chance of being published. Oral statements of position by experts in whatever field—preachers, teachers, even parents—are to be regarded as authorities, provided the authority is identified. *In the last analysis, then, the substantial authority is an identified person.*
The following paragraphs sufficiently demonstrate the problems involved in citing unprinted authorities.

(1) When a white-robed scientist, momentarily looking away from his microscope or his cyclotron, makes some pronouncement for the general public, he may not be understood, but at least he is certain to be believed. No one ever doubts what is said by a scientist. Statesmen, industrialists, ministers of religion, civic leaders, philosophers, all are questioned and criticized, but scientists—never. Scientists are exalted beings who stand at the very topmost pinnacle of popular prestige, for they have the monopoly of the formula "It has been scientifically proved . . ." which appears to rule out all possibility of disagreement.

(2) Thus the world is divided into Scientists, who practice the art of infallibility, and non-scientists, sometimes contemptuously called "laymen," who are taken in by it. The laymen see the prodigious things that science has done, and they are impressed and overawed. Einstein said that matter could be converted into energy, and the atomic scientists went ahead and did it with the atomic bomb, and what other group of people have done anything so wonderful as that? Science has achieved so many things, and has been right so many times, that it is hard to believe that it can be wrong in anything, particularly for a layman, who does not have enough knowledge of the subject to be able to argue back. He might not even want to argue back, for the claims of science are extremely inviting. The benefits we have received from it are tremendous, all the way from television to penicillin, and there is no reason to suppose that they will stop. Cancer may be cured tomorrow, or the day after, and the nuclear physicists may easily find a way to end all the drudgery, and usher in the golden age. Mere laymen, their imaginations stupefied by these wonders, are duly humble, and regard the scientists as lofty and impeccable human beings.

—Anthony Standen, from *Science Is a Sacred Cow* (New York: E. P. Dutton and Company, Inc., 1950), pp. 13–14.

Commentary: "They Say It's Wonderful," the first chapter of *Science Is a Sacred Cow,* is an excellent example of the skillful use of expository techniques to develop a difficult argumentative position: the belief that science is infallible and beyond criticism is a dangerous delusion. At the outset he pays careful attention to the need for defining terms; the scientist is an exalted being, standing at the pinnacle of prestige, who practices the art of infallibility. The layman, on the other hand, is defined as a person who believes that the scientist practices the art of infallibility. Hence the layman regards the scientist as an authority, and through the expository technique of cause and effect Standen shows why the layman so regards the scientist, naming one authority, Einstein. While granting that science seems always to be right (the *apology*), Standen uses irony, or blame through praise, by calling the atomic bomb "wonderful" and by equating television with penicillin. In succeeding paragraphs he cites scientific authorities, often by name, to show that scientists have the prejudices of ordinary people.

EXERCISES:

1. The compilation of a list of printed and unprinted authorities, under various categories.

2. A search for and analysis of paragraphs and essays in the reading text which establish a position by support through authority.

3. The composition of an essay on "Holy Writ" which examines the latest translation of the Bible.

4. As assigned by the instructor, the composition of one or more arguments which establish a position by support through authority, or which do so by attacking the basis for authority in the manner of Standen.

C. SUPPORT THROUGH REASONING

Every college student—every college freshman, in fact—should be exposed to a basic course in logic, the "science" of thought. It is therefore not the purpose of this chapter to present a short course in logic but to help the inexperienced writer make certain that his line of reasoning is not fallacious at bottom, that his argument from point to point is logically connected—that the issues are pertinent to the question—and to indicate the possibilities for refuting an existing argument by recourse to reason alone.

Fortunately it is axiomatic that all men, however primitive or sophisticated their cultural backgrounds may be, reason ultimately in the same way, or ways. They do so, first of all, because apparently the human mind has inherent characteristics that cause it to deal with knowledge in a similar fashion regardless of race or environment. Also its operation is greatly affected by the very nature of the knowledge or experience that it collects, classifies, and analyzes. To put it another way, the brain has *a priori* qualities at birth, without regard to experience in this world; and it has *a posteriori* qualities, those developed through worldly experience. What a man knows and what he thinks he knows (prejudice) both have an *a priori* and an *a posteriori* basis.

Deduction. The mind deals, *a priori*, with knowledge through a logical process called the *syllogism*. The essence of this process lies in three statements: (a) *the major premise,* (b) *the minor premise,* (c) *the conclusion.*

(a) *The major premise.* This statement reaches a conclusion about *all* members of a class.

EXAMPLES

1. All mermaids have blue eyes.
2. Republicans hate Roosevelt.
3. Drunkards are poor risks.
4. All communists are liars and hypocrites.
5. Texans are happy people.

(NOTE: Each of these major premises can be invalidated, factually, by demonstrating that a member of the class does not fit the conclusion. For example, if a black-eyed mermaid were discovered in the Indian Ocean, the first premise would no longer be tenable.)

(b) *The minor premise.* This statement places a thing or an idea in the class of the major premise.

EXAMPLES

1. Henrietta Mood, who certainly ought to know, has been noising it about that her alleged sister Cecily is not a human being at all but a mermaid.
2. To avoid the winds of scandal, Claude Rhomboid and his bride Cecily left Puckering Valley for Pennsylvania, in America, and in due course were naturalized, voting the straight Republican ticket in 1936. (They are, for the moment at least, Republicans.)
3. Meanwhile Claude, more worried about the scandal than he cared to admit, became a steady, though secret, boozer.
4. Eight years after leaving England the Rhomboids discov-

ered, in the *Times Literary Supplement,* that Henrietta Mood had been imprisoned as a Communist spy.

5. Following World War II Claude and his all-too-human Cecily, radiant once more, took up residence in Ballinger, Texas, a small but friendly town that is growing pleasantly smaller.

(NOTE: Each of these minor premises has as its primary function the placing of a person in one of the all-inclusive classes of the foregoing major premises. To assign the conclusion of the major premise to a person would mean nothing. If Henrietta's sister Cecily were said to have blue eyes, for example, the minor premise would not fulfill its function in the syllogism. Many things other than mermaids have blue eyes.)

(c) *The conclusion.* This statement assigns the characteristic or conclusion of the major premise to the thing or idea of the minor premise.

EXAMPLES

1. Cecily has blue eyes (assuming Henrietta is right).
2. Claude and Cecily hate Roosevelt.
3. Claude is a poor risk.
4. Henrietta lied when she accused Cecily of mermaidness.
5. Claude and Cecily are happy.

(NOTE: Each of these conclusions follows inescapably from the major and minor premises upon which it is founded. The five syllogisms, then, are said to be valid, and the deductive operation of each syllogism—its reasoning process—cannot be criticized upon logical grounds. The only possible means of criticism lies in the factual content of the major premise: a member of the class must be found to whom the conclusion of the major premise does not actually apply. Finding this member of the class is an *a posteriori* operation, induction.)

Induction. *Induction* is the mental process through which the major premise of the deductive syllogism acquires substance, meaning, in the world of fact. Induction probably begins, curiously enough, with the "rhetorical" techniques of definition and classification, here assumed to be necessary modes of thinking. A young child may, for example, be faced with a need for distinguishing between fishes and birds and animals, all of which he has subconsciously defined as living things because they move of their own volition—dead things, he has decided, do not initiate self-movement. He concludes, classifying, that the distinction between animals and birds and fishes rests in habitat or environment. His conclusion is easy to state in a set of major premises:

(a) All living things in the water are fish.
(b) All living things in the air are birds.
(c) All living things on land are animals.

He has, in effect, by means of definition and classification provided a foundation for syllogistic, deductive reasoning. When eventually in the course of experience he finds a living creature that is equally at home in the water, in the air, and on land, he will re-examine his earlier conclusions and state them again (still subconsciously) so that they will accommodate the latest knowledge. That is to say, he learns a little and formulates an idea about what he has learned in a *hypothesis* or *theory*, which he may later reject as inadequate or continue to accept as it is strengthened through increased knowledge, until it attains the force of *law*, seeming always to be true. And if he refuses to reject inadequate ideas, closes his senses to experience, his education has ceased; his reasoning tends to involve attempts to find ways to reinforce his prejudices.

The major premise, then, in reaching a conclusion about *all* members of a class must result as far as possible from universal experience, from the examination of as many members of a class as can be found. Kephart's rich man is a case in point. His reasoning goes something like this:

> (a) *The first step*
>
> Major premise: A rich man is a good man.
> Minor premise: I am a rich man.
> Conclusion: I am a good man.

(b) *The second step*

Major premise: I never take vacations.
Minor premise: He takes vacations.
Conclusion: He is not a good man.

(c) *The third step*

Major premise: Anything causing a man to miss work is an irreparable loss of time.
Minor premise: Sickness causes a man to miss work.
Conclusion: Sickness is an irreparable loss of time.

COMMENT: No wonder Kephart termed the rich man's outburst "the sorriest thing that ever I saw in print." The syllogism of the first step is valid enough, but its major premise probably does not result from a detailed investigation of the careers of thousands of rich men. The major premise of the second step has a class with only one member. And the major premise of the third step attempts to put sickness in the same class with vacations, that is, to define the vacation as sickness.

Evidently if the writer intends to properly support an argument through reason, he must carefully examine its logic. To do so, to ensure the validity of his reasoning in an essay, the writer should acquire the habit of reducing it, *in writing*, to a syllogism or series of related syllogisms. Further, he should make it a practice to list his assumptions—especially those which he cares nothing about proving factually—so that he will make certain to dispose of them in some sort of apology.

EXERCISES:

1. Examination of the illustrative passages in this chapter, from Mandeville, Huxley, Graves, the writer on water skiing, Mencken, Standen, (a) to see what their assumptions are, (b) to arrange their ideas in syllogistic fashion.

2. As assigned by the instructor, similar work on essays in a book of readings.

3. The composition of essays developing an argument, at least in part, by support through reason, each essay to be accompanied

by (a) statements of assumption, (b) syllogistic analyses of the
reasoning process, as well as (c) the usual thesis sentence and outline (preferably a sentence outline).

Refuting the Opposition

A. PROOF OF INITIAL POSITION

Kephart could have chosen to refute the rich man by showing the logical deficiencies in his position. But instead Kephart
is content with the epithet "sorry"; it is more to his purpose
to support his own position, that camping is justifiable because
its activities return man to a normalcy that has been lost
through atrophy of his "moving parts" in the advance of civilization. Since camping as a kind of vacation is therefore useful,
the rich man is refuted by Kephart's argument that the best
kind of vacation in effect ultimately serves the purpose of an
employer like the rich man: the normal employee is a useful
employee.

B. SHOWING WEAKNESS IN THE OPPOSITION

Mandeville, on the other hand, decides to deal with the
position of those who object "that no society was ever anyways civilized before the major part had agreed upon some
worship or other of an overruling Power, and consequently
that the notions of good and evil, and the distinction between
Virtue and *Vice*, were never the contrivance of politicians, but
the pure effect of religion." Mandeville's answer is an effort to
demonstrate the weakness of the objection on the ground that
"man in his State of Nature" has such pitiful religious notions
that they are "incapable of exciting man to virtue, and good
for nothing but to awe and amuse a rude and unthinking
multitude."

Samuel Johnson's critical essay "Romances and Morality"
refutes the opposition in both of these ways. In the face of
an increasing volume of what today might be called realistic

fiction, Johnson takes the position that such fiction is an incitement to immorality in the young, who may well imitate fictional heroes in regard to both their good and bad actions. Fictional heroes, Johnson maintains, should be all good or all bad:

(1) There have been men indeed splendidly wicked, whose endowments threw a brightness on their crimes, and whom scarce any villainy made · perfectly detestable, because they never could be wholly divested of their excellencies; but such have been in all ages the great corrupters of the world, and their resemblance ought no more to be preserved than the art of murdering without pain.

(2) Some have advanced, without due attention to the consequence of this notion, that certain virtues have their correspondent faults, and therefore that to exhibit either apart is to deviate from probability. Thus men are observed by Swift to be "grateful in the same degree as they are resentful." This principle, with others of the same kind, supposes man to act from a brute impulse and pursue a certain degree of inclination, without any choice of the object; for, otherwise, though it should be allowed that gratitude and resentment arise from the same constitution of the passions, it follows not that they will be equally indulged when reason is consulted; yet, unless that consequence be admitted, this sagacious maxim becomes an empty sound, without any relation to practice or to life.

(3) Nor is it evident, that even the first motions to these effects are always in the same proportion. For pride, which produces quickness of resentment, will obstruct gratitude by unwillingness to admit that inferiority which obligation implies; and it is very unlikely that he who cannot think he receives a favor will acknowledge or repay it.

(4) It is of the utmost importance to mankind that positions of this tendency should be laid open and confuted; for while men consider good and evil as springing from the same root, they will spare the one for the sake of the other, and in judging, if not of others, at least of themselves, will be apt to estimate their virtues by their vices. To this fatal error all those will contribute, who confound the colors of right and wrong, and, instead of helping to settle their boundaries, mix them with so much art that no common mind is able to disunite them.

(5) In narratives where historical veracity has no place, I cannot discover why there should not be exhibited the most perfect idea of virtue; of virtue not angelical, nor above probability, for what we cannot credit, we shall never imitate, but the highest and purest that humanity can reach, which, exercised in such trials as the various revolutions of things shall bring upon it, may, by conquering some calamities and enduring others, teach us what we may hope and what we can perform. Vice, for vice is necessary to be shown, should always disgust; nor should the graces of gayety, or the dignity of courage, be so united with it, as to reconcile it to the mind. Wherever it appears, it should raise hatred by the malignity of its practices, and contempt by the meanness of its stratagems; for while it is supported by either parts or spirit, it will be seldom heartily abhorred. The Roman tyrant was content to be hated, if he was but feared; and there are thousands of the readers of romances willing to be thought wicked, if they may be allowed to be wits. It is therefore to be steadily inculcated that virtue is the highest proof of understanding and the only solid basis of greatness; and that vice is the natural consequence of narrow thoughts; that it begins in mistake and ends in ignominy.

–From *The Rambler,* No. 4:
Saturday, March 31, 1750.

Commentary: The second of the paragraphs from "Romances and Morality" states the position, reinforced by a quotation from Swift, of the supporters of realistic fiction: ". . . certain virtues have their correspondent faults, and therefore . . . to exhibit either apart is to deviate from probability." Johnson refutes by showing weakness; it (the position) does not allow for the operation of reason.

The fifth paragraph refutes by an attempt to prove initial position (Johnson's): according to Johnson the purpose of literature is to make vice abhorrent and virtue desirable.

The "argumentum ad hominem." If the writer knows what the prejudices of his reading audience are likely to be, it will certainly be to his advantage to address an appeal to these prejudices, so long as the appeal can be made under the guise of sweet reason. Both Mandeville and Johnson have done so. Mandeville, for example, in the phrase "rude and unthinking multitude" perhaps arouses a trace of prejudice in his readers, who do not care to think of themselves as ordinary men. And Johnson's classing Swift with the opposition is nicely calculated to warm the prejudices of the reading public for whom *The Rambler* was designed. In logical terms, such an appeal is called *argumentum ad hominem;* if it can be detected within an argument, then it is possible to refute the argument through exposing this weakness in a position.

Often it can be detected without much trouble. Here are a few obvious examples (as always, the student is invited to expand the list as he encounters specimens):

1. Anyone who believes in democracy will agree with me . . .
2. If you believe in our way of life . . .
3. Surely no right-thinking person . . .
4. All intelligent men will stand together when . . .
5. As a self-made man, I . . .

Logical fallacies.   Generally less obvious than the *argumentum ad hominem* are the logical fallacies resulting from improper or invalid *a priori* reasoning. Their detection, again, provides a valuable basis for refutation through weakness in position.

a. *The hasty generalization.* Kephart's rich man, in the section dealing with induction, has probably reached his first major premise (A rich man is a good man) through this syllogism:

Major premise: I am a rich man.
Minor premise: I am a good man.
Conclusion: All rich men are good men.

This is a hasty generalization. On the foundation of woefully inadequate evidence—which should be gathered by the proper use of inductive techniques—the rich man has erected a monument to the inseparability of wealth and goodness.

Recently a news magazine enjoying national circulation pub-

lished the results of a survey it had conducted in an attempt
to discover public opinion on a certain aspect of foreign policy.
Toward the end of the article its author revealed that the
"sampling" involved thirty-two persons in Atlanta, a business-
woman in North Hollywood, a Miami hotel executive, a New
Jersey businessman, a Chicago cost accountant, and a Florida
banker. The conclusion reached as to the American temper in
this particular poll was, on the face of the evidence presented,
a hasty generalization, especially since most of the persons
questioned were in business.

Hasty generalizations are commonplace enough. Advertising,
as witness these characteristic exaggerations, is an exception-
ally fertile producer.

1. Doctors recommend . . . (Two doctors? Three doctors?)
2. It's [name your brand] three to one. (For or against?
Were only four people polled?)
3. Join the switch to . . . (Did anyone switch besides the
pretty, though emaciated, girl in the advertisement?)
4. Do you use [name your brand]? Everyone else does.
(Indeed. Why, then, do stores bother to stock competing
brands?)
5. Nearly everybody in [name your geographic location]
reads the [name your publication]. (Beginning at what age?)

b. *The false analogy.* Lacking the *a priori* power to classify,
the mind would be unable to analyze what the senses perceive. This power, to put the matter simply, consists of recognizing likenesses and differences in things. To contrast, to
distinguish one thing from another, is to perceive that there
is a difference. To understand that two things are alike in
some way is to compare them, to draw an analogy. Discovering likenesses in unlike things is one of man's chief intellectual
and emotional delights. Without metaphor, without the striking verbal reflection of such discovery, poetry could not exist,
and good writing would lose much of its flavor. But just as
poetry can have false metaphors—John Donne's "A Valediction:
forbidding mourning" pretends that the souls of two parted
lovers are like the arms of a compass—so exposition or argu-

mentation in prose may develop an idea from a pretended, a false analogy, the discovery of a likeness where, in fact, none is demonstrable. The exposure of a false analogy, then, will often refute a position by striking at its assumptions. The following illustrations suggest how frequently the false analogy will be encountered.

> . . . in the very composure of man, there is manifestly discovered a summary abstract of absolute perfection, by the which as by an excellent Idea, or an exact rule, we may examine and exemplifie all other things.
> The Mathematicians have found out by their observance of the beautious and uniforme proportion of the body of man, and by the symetrie of the parts therof, their true scantlines and dimensions: yea by the laying of it in his full length, & then spreading the armes and legges to their widest compasse, they have contrived both the perfect square, and the exact circle: The square, by foure right lines at the foure uttermost points of the hands and feet; the circle, by rounding a line about those points, placing the center of their compasse upon the navell. The naturall Philosophers reduceth the vastnesse of the universal (comprehending all things that hath either being, or vegitation, or sense, or reason) unto this same well compacted Epitome of mans fabrifacture.

> . . . and as in every man there is both a quickning & ruling soule, and a living and ruled bodie; so in every civill state, there is a directing & commaunding power, & an obeying and subjected alleageance. For as neither the soule alone, nor body alone (if they should be severed) can be a man, so not the ruler alone, nor the subjects alone, can be a commonweale. Where all will rule, there is no rule, and where none doeth rule, there is all misrule. . . .

> —Edward Forset, from *A Comparative Discourse of the Bodies Natural and Politique* (London, 1606).

Commentary: Besides being a fascinating revelation of the vagaries of spelling and punctuation several hundred years ago, Edward Forset's treatise in defense of absolute monarchy

—already under attack from several quarters—is an extended argument from false analogy.

Assumption: Man is perfect.

The Question: Is monarchy preferable to a commonwealth form of government?

Position: Monarchy is the only proper form of government.

The Issue: A state is, or ought to be, like a human being.

Forset's lines of reasoning can be reduced, for the most part, to one syllogism.

Major Premise: The head rules the human body (which is perfect).

Minor Premise: The king is the head of the state (whose organization is like that of the human body).

Conclusion: Absolute monarchy is the perfect form of government (the king rightly rules the state).

Forset's argument can be refuted in at least three ways. His assumption, first of all, has little physiological basis in fact. Further, he attempts to demonstrate the truth of his assumption by appealing to still another assumption: Mathematics is a perfect science. A second means of refutation is to gather, inductively, evidence to disprove the contention of the mathematicians that a circle or square can be drawn about a person spread-eagled upon the ground—humans vary considerably as to their proportions. A third course is to point out the falsity of Forset's analogy; the human being is a physical entity, the state an abstraction.

There is no particular need, of course, to seek false analogies in seventeenth-century political pamphlets, for they abound in expressions of contemporary opinion.

"MARGARET AND MARIE"

A parallel in history between Britain 1961 and France 1788 can easily be drawn. Louis the Sixteenth and his Marie Antoinette, like Queen Elizabeth II and her playgirl sister Margaret, were reared in inconceivable luxury. Margaret married the wrong fellow, just as Louis married the wrong girl. The expense of Margaret's upkeep, borne by the public, is increasing by the minute.

The street-corner Frenchman in 1788 was as unhappy about high taxes as the pub-crawling Briton is today.

Louis and his bride had three palaces, all bulging with servants and toadies. Their town dwelling, the Louvre, is comparable to Buckingham Palace, and Fontainebleau has its counterpart in Margaret's Scottish castle.

Princess Margaret is lovely, spirited, and gay, as was Marie Antoinette, who is credited with saying "Let them eat cake" when told of a bread shortage.

The author of this student theme has not supplied Margaret with an equally vivid mot, and so Margaret's place in history is still dubious.

Here are a few possible false analogies plucked at random in a week's time from the editorial page of a metropolitan newspaper. An editorial essay concerned with a vital national problem is developed from each of them.

1. Society is like a machine.
2. The operation of a government is like the operation of a business corporation.
3. Armies are like watchdogs.
4. The public debt is like a private debt.
5. Elected officials are like servants.
6. Neighboring nations are like brothers.
7. Foreign aid is like private charity.
8. War is like a game.

EXERCISE:

Analyze these possibly false analogies to determine the extent to which the resemblances may reasonably be pushed.

c. *"Post hoc, ergo propter hoc"* (following this, therefore on account of this). The nature of the cause-and-effect relationship between events—natural phenomena of whatever description—involves a philosophical problem of considerable depth and complexity. Its resolution seems to be that there is never a *single* cause for any effect, that an effect has what amounts to a multiplicity of causes, all operating at the same moment. For the purpose of refutation by exposing a logical fallacy, however, it is enough to understand that two events closely following one after the other in time are not necessarily caused one by the other. That is to say, their time relationship may be the *only* way in which they are related.

Upon a humid and ominous summer day a casual stroller hears a clap of thunder and, immediately, the song of a bird. He concludes that the thunder has caused the bird to sing, but he certainly ought to qualify his deduction in the light of these questions:

1. Was the bird singing before the thunderclap and resting during the noise?
2. Was his song inaudible while it was thundering?
3. Did he suddenly decide to sing because a female of his species fluttered by?
4. Do birds react to thunder—can they hear it?

And if the stroller reduces his mental operation to a syllogism, he may feel inclined to abandon the business altogether.

Major Premise: Birds sing after thunder.
Minor Premise: It thunders.
Conclusion: A bird will sing.

Sometimes a person—even a professional writer—will assume, fallaciously, that certain effects have certain causes because "it ought to be that way." Good health ought to proceed from clean living, virtue and wealth should be boon causal companions, recognition should result from hard work. That these causes do not always produce the desired effects is notoriously the way of the world. Here is a classic example of argument based upon this fallacious conception of the cause-and-effect relationship:

> The principal object . . . proposed in these poems [*Lyrical Ballads*] was to choose incidents and situations from common life, and to relate or describe them, throughout, as far as was

possible in a selection of language really used by men, and at
the same time to throw over them a certain coloring of imagination, whereby ordinary things should be presented to the
mind in an unusual aspect; and, further, and above all, to make
these incidents and situations interesting by tracing in them,
truly though not ostentatiously, the primary laws of our nature:
chiefly, as far as regards the manner in which we associate ideas
in a state of excitement. Humble and rustic life was generally
chosen, because, in that condition, the essential passions of the
heart find a better soil in which they can attain their maturity,
are less under restraint, and speak a plainer and more emphatic
language; because in that condition of life our elementary feelings co-exist in a state of greater simplicity, and, consequently,
may be more accurately contemplated, and more forcibly communicated; because the manners of rural life germinate from
those elementary feelings, and, from the necessary character of
rural occupations, are more easily comprehended, and are more
durable; and, lastly, because in that condition the passions of
men are incorporated with the beautiful and permanent forms
of nature. The language, too, of these men has been adopted
(purified indeed from what appear to be its real defects, from
all rational causes of dislike or disgust) because such men
hourly communicate with the best objects from which the best
part of language is originally derived; and because, from their
rank in society and the sameness and narrow circle of their
intercourse, being less under the influence of social vanity, they
convey their feelings and notions in simple and unelaborated
expressions. Accordingly, such language, arising out of repeated
experience and regular feelings, is a more permanent and a far
more philosophical language than that which is frequently substituted for it by poets . . . in order to furnish food for fickle
tastes and fickle appetites of their own creation.

> —William Wordsworth, from *Preface*
> to *Lyrical Ballads*, 2nd ed. (London,
> 1800).

Wordsworth's *Preface* laudably argues for the simplification of
poetic diction. But the cause-and-effect relationships upon
which his argument is erected are open to some criticism.
According to the poet humble and rustic life, as opposed to
elevated and city life, presumably, causes (a) greater maturity

of the essential passions of the heart, (b) less restraint of these passions, (c) a plainer and more emphatic language of these same passions, (d) a greater simplicity of elementary feelings, (e) a more accurate contemplation of these feelings, (f) a more forcible communication of these feelings, (g) an incorporation of the passions of men with the beautiful and permanent forms of nature, (h) a purification of language, (i) a communication of feelings and notions in simple and unelaborated expressions. This is a large order. It means simply that Wordsworth wishes the conditions of eighteenth-century peasant life were ideal for the composition of great poetry. They were not, as Robert Burns well understood, and as Wordsworth himself must have suspected, for he names not one poet born and bred in humble country circumstances.

EXERCISE:

Examine the following causal statements for possible flaws in logic.
1. Smoking makes people happy.
2. Hair tonic attracts girls.
3. Close shaves make better baseball players.
4. Automation causes unemployment.
5. Speed causes accidents.
6. Haste makes waste.
7. Testing atomic weapons prevents aggression.
8. Socialized medicine means inadequate medical service.

d. *Begging the question.* All reasoning follows a circular and meaningless path unless it refers to experience. The paragraph taken from Wordsworth's *Preface* refers not to experience but to would-be, wished-for experience. For Wordsworth the best kind of man is the poet. In the sense that Wordsworth views the peasant as the best kind of man (because his is the best kind of environment), he is *assuming the truth of what he intends to prove.* He is *begging the question,* hence arguing illogically. The lawyer who in a courtroom parades character witnesses before the jury instead of marshaling evidence to overcome the evidence of the prosecution begs the question. The following syllogism lies behind the parade.

Major Premise: People without criminal records never commit crimes.

Minor Premise: He has no criminal record.

Conclusion: He did not commit the crime.

But criminals have to begin somewhere.

The advertiser recommending a particular brand of aspirin because doctors prescribe aspirin begs the question. The landlord arguing against slum clearance on the ground that poor people need a place to live begs the question. Calling Washington a political cesspool and then urging that it be cleaned up begs the question. H. L. Mencken in the selection toward the beginning of this chapter begs the question in assuming that the King James Version of the New Testament cannot be improved upon.

EXERCISE:

Analyze the logic of the following student-produced essay, especially in regard to whether it begs the question.

CHARITY?

(1) Yesterday I read in the *Times* two news stories which turned out to have a closer relationship than I first noticed. The first one had to do with American aid aimed at relieving distress in Brazilian areas whose population is in dire economic distress. The other story was about a secret warehouse full of illegal arms and Cuban military uniforms, somewhere near Sao Paulo.

(2) Our aid—thirty-four million dollars of it—has been allocated to a primitive northeastern area of Brazil inhabited by two and a half million *paisanos,* starving because of flood and drouths. If they occasionally live in better circumstances, they inhabit mud huts.

(3) But right next door to the mud huts, according to the story from Recife, are hidden military supplies and Che Guevara propaganda. Arms smuggling, further, is prevalent.

(4) Here we have a typical conflict between the forces of good and the forces of evil. All these people are starving. They are hungry without prospect of relief, sick without expectation

of cure or even attention. They want their children to grow up in a better society, and it doesn't take much to convince them that their society is bad. A Cuban agitator who says he can make it good will not be questioned very closely.

(5) Charity, or foreign aid if you want to call it that, is temporary and expensive, and if we were to try aiding all the needy people in the world, those in China for example, we would run out of money in about a week. The forces of freedom have faced the Communists in situations like this before, but they usually haven't coped successfully with the tactics of these international bandits. When there are emergencies, emergency relief should be sent, but charity never builds self respect or responsible local institutions. These go hand in hand with free enterprise and freely elected government.

(6) It is a source of some encouragement that the President says the charity will inspire "a policy of better use of the farm land." If revolution can be defeated by charity, it must spell hope as well as bread.

e. *Ignoring the question.* An argument begs the question if it assumes the truth of the arguer's position at the outset. If the arguer chooses to prove something other than what he has promised to prove, he is fallaciously *ignoring the question* to concentrate on an issue which is not pertinent to the question. Side issues, logically speaking, can always be developed to advantage in an argument, but it should never be pretended that a side issue is a main issue. Nor should the real issue be concealed, as in this student-composed "letter to the editor."

(1) The success of the Communists lately in getting college students to help them has been a great surprise to our democratic way of life. Mobs of students, armed with street weapons and aroused by Red agitators, have already overthrown the elected presidents of Turkey, South Korea, and Japan. And now riots like those abroad are happening on our own front porch, in San Francisco.

(2) Requiring hundreds of policemen to quell the disturbance, the San Francisco student riots have awakened thinking Americans to the fact that these students demonstrating for the Communist cause did not riot because they were hungry or be-

cause they were mistreated. No, they were sons and daughters
of the prosperous middle class, well fed and free as birds.
Communist propaganda would have us think that Socialism is
the religion of the lower classes. It wants us to believe that we
should turn away from God because of slums and disease. Communism is not, however, this kind of disease. It is a spiritual
and mental sickness, originating not with the poor, the unedu-
cated, the hard-working but with idle students. Almost every
Red leader originally became a Communist when he was a
university student, growing materialistic in philosophy and
atheistic in faith.

Ostensibly the writer is attacking Communism, but his real
target is the university. He ignores the apparent question—
how to prevent the spread of Communism—to focus upon one
kind of Communist. His ultimate purpose is clear, at any rate:
to destroy a system of university education in which free inquiry is permitted.

EXERCISE:

Analyze the following statements to determine possible questions and issues, pertinent and otherwise.

1. Raising teachers' pay will cure the teacher shortage.
2. Socializing medicine will prevent the patient from choosing
his doctor.
3. "Right to work" laws will reduce unemployment.
4. Federal aid means federal control.
5. Abolishing capital punishment would cost us more money
because of the greater number of prisoners to feed and house.

f. The *"non sequitur."* If what the arguer chooses to prove
has not even a side-issue connection with the question, it is
called a *non sequitur,* for it does not logically follow what
precedes it. The *non sequitur* is a favorite device of the poli-
tician, who realizes that shaking hands and kissing babies are
far more essential to his continuation in office than is a direct
statement of position on a public issue. The young hoodlum on
trial for his life, although he may be a perfect stranger to soap
and necktie and filial affection, appears in court attired more

properly and somberly than an undertaker, flanked by his weeping mother and other female relations. The sign in the finance company's window proclaims enthusiastic membership in the brotherhood of human charity. Instead of demonstrating the superior qualities of his "product," the advertiser displays testimonials from the young, the smiling, the beautiful, the athletic. And a responsible news magazine as part of a high-level critique of White House policy accuses the President's personal physician of inept prescription writing. All these are consciously intended *non sequiturs*, rooted in hypocrisy, and eventually exerting some influence upon human affairs and culture. In presenting an argument the student will wish to avoid formulating unintended *non sequiturs*, as in this class-room essay on "Certain Aspects of Freedom":

(1) Our way of life has variety as its essence. Variously we choose our form of worship. Variously we state our opinions on all matters within our mental abilities. Variously we meet and argue freely, on TV programs for example. Variously we educate our children, wherever we please, and we speak our minds on whether we think what they are getting in the schools is good. We enjoy free public library service (because of Andrew Carnegie, a capitalist), and we variously read what we like. Variously we choose our jobs, according to our talents and prejudices. We take all this variety for granted. Elsewhere in this world it is largely a dream.

(2) Why, then, are we regimenting ourselves increasingly, instituting a radical form of government which is already beginning to dictate what our children will study, what they will think, and what they will become in adult life? Is it not perfectly obvious that the burning of the books in the free libraries will be the next step? Since despite our various backgrounds we seem to stand in awe of a Harvard education, we have voted ourselves out of our variety. What we enjoy variously may not make us richer, but it is there for us to choose, variously. This is freedom.

EXERCISE:

A point-to-point analysis of the logical organization of this short essay, especially in regard to the *non sequitur*.

C. EXPOSURE OF SLANTED WRITING

Slanted writing, like the *argumentum ad hominem*, appeals to the prejudices of the reader, but it does so largely through diction, through deliberate choice of words and phrases loaded with connotative meaning. As already indicated, the selection from Mencken toward the beginning of this chapter is expertly "slanted" at the reader. It begins mildly enough, associating *pathology*, ordinarily a medical term, with theology. The beginning sentence of the third paragraph describes recent Biblical translation as *vandalism*. But the final paragraph is unrestrainedly slanted. The translations are *perversions*, their clergyman authors *rev. perpetrators* somehow compared to Torquemada, another clergyman with good intentions. It is possible to refute Mencken, then—to some extent—by pointing out that his language is not suited to a temperate and judicious discussion of the artistic merits of sacred literature translation. Intemperance is also a characteristic of these sentences, taken at random from the editorial page of a newspaper (slanted writing italicized).

1. Chief Justice Earl Warren's announcement that the United States must surrender its sovereignty will be hailed by *one-world traitors* as the "supreme law of the land."

2. There is a revival of political courage all over the country, and a determination in many other states to do what the *emboldened patriots* did in Texas this year, to the end that Congress shall be dominated by men who will override *those in high places* who have drawn up a *surrender* pattern.

3. Soviet Russia has been showing its muscles to the world again, this time while efforts are being made to rally Western powers to join in defense against *international gangsterism*.

4. The idea that unilateral action to frustrate Communist designs in this hemisphere would lose prestige for the United States in Latin America is *so much hogwash*.

5. Who says television isn't educational? We've seen enough *blackmailers* operate on the TV tube to know that Castro would keep increasing his demands. (There are at least two logical fallacies involved here, in addition to the slanted writing.)

6. The *dictatorial* planners in the federal establishment have as their total ambition the increasing of their influence and control over Americans.

EXERCISES:

1. Replace the italicized words and phrases in these sentences with objective, denotative terms.
2. A search for and analysis of material in current periodicals of opinion, news magazines, and newspapers which appears to contain logical fallacies or slanted writing.
3. The composition of several one-paragraph essays refuting the ideas in this material by exposure of fallacious reasoning and slanted writing.
4. A student review of the themes and paragraphs he has written thus far in the academic year, to see how often he has been guilty of fallacious reasoning or slanted writing.

Concluding the Argument

Several suggestions for writing a successful conclusion have been made in Chapter Five—return to and expand upon a so far undeveloped idea; examine the implications of the thesis; make a prediction. Additional suggestions applying to argumentation are needed, for whether or not the argument devotes much time to refuting the existing or anticipated opposition, it is probable that the arguer will wish to solidify his own position as a means of closing out the essay. He will do so with (a) *a brief summary of position,* (b) *a final emphasis upon its merits,* and, possibly, (c) *an apology.*

A. THE SUMMARY OF POSITION

By now the argument presumably has been developed in some detail; repeating it—even part of it—is likely to bore the reader. Hence the recommendation of Chapter Five, to save a specific and literal thesis statement for the end of the essay, is especially pertinent to argumentation. Failing this possibility, it is useful to state the position or thesis in a fresh and novel form, along with a new idea that the writer perhaps does not intend to develop. The final paragraph of *Areopagitica* (London, 1644), John Milton's classic advocacy of freedom of the press, addressed to members of Parliament, is an excellent case in point. Slanted writing is italicized.

And as for regulating the press, let no man think to have the honour of advising ye better than yourselves [the Parliament] have done in that order published next before this, "That no book be printed, unless the printer's and the author's name, or at least the printer's be registered." Those which otherwise come forth, if they be found mischievous and libellous, the fire and the executioner will be the timeliest and the most effectual remedy that man's prevention can use. For this *authentic Spanish policy* of licensing books, if I have said aught, will prove the most unlicensed book itself within a short while; and was the immediate image of a *star-chamber decree* [Parliament had recently abolished the Court of Star Chamber, an arbitrary instrument of royal tyranny] to that purpose made in those times when that court did the rest of those her pious works, for which she is now fallen from the stars with Lucifer. Whereby ye may guess what kind of state prudence, what love of the people, what care of religion or good manners there was at the contriving, although with singular hypocrisy it pretended to bind books to their good behaviour. And how it got the upper hand of your precedent order so well constituted before, if we may believe those men whose profession gives them cause to inquire most, it may be doubted there was in it *the fraud of some old patentees and monopolizers,* in the trade of bookselling; who, under pretence of the poor in their company not to be defrauded, and the just retaining of each man his several copy, (which God forbid should be gainsaid,) brought divers glossing colours to the house, which were indeed but colours, and serving to no end except it be to exercise a superiority over their neighbours; men who do not therefore labour in an honest profession, to which learning is indebted, that they should be made other men's vassals. Another end is thought was aimed at by some of them in procuring by petition this order, that having power in their hands, malignant books might the easier escape abroad, as the event shows. But of these sophisms and elenchs of merchandise I skill not: this I know, that errors in a good government and in a bad are equally almost incident; for what magistrate may not be misinformed, and much the sooner, if liberty of printing be reduced into the power of a few? But to redress willingly and speedily what hath been erred, and in highest authority to esteem a plain advertisement more than others have done a sumptuous bride, is a virtue (honoured lords and commons!) answerable to your highest actions, and *whereof none can participate but greatest and wisest men.*

Commentary:

1. Milton's position is that books should not be licensed by an agency of the government.

2. *The issues* (stated categorically): a. A book should not be destroyed because it partakes of immortality.

b. The Spanish Inquisition originated the practice of licensing books.

c. Virtue untested is not virtue.

d. A fool will be a fool with or without a book.

e. Qualified licensers do not exist.

f. Students will not bother to learn, nor teachers to teach, unless they are certain that knowledge is freely available.

g. Our good clergymen constitute the nation's armor against such things as bad books.

h. Knowledge is the basis of civilization.

3. In concluding his argument in the final paragraph, Milton returns to only one of these issues, that licensing is an "authentic Spanish policy."

4. He restates his position, or thesis, obliquely in the first sentence of the final paragraph.

5. He introduces new material:

a. Licensing is a star-chamber practice.

b. Licensing is reminiscent of the old practice—developed to a fine art under James I—of granting monopolies.

6. He apologizes: "if I have said aught"; "of these sophisms and elenchs of merchandise I skill not. . . ."

B. THE FINAL EMPHASIS ON THE MERITS OF A POSITION

Milton also makes two points by way of emphasizing the merits of his position: 1. He advocates no more than returning to Parliament's previous order in regard to printing, "That no book be printed, unless the printer's and the author's name, or at least the printer's be registered."

2. Members of Parliament themselves run the risk of being misinformed if they trust licensers to do a proper job.

The concluding paragraph of Joseph Addison's famous argument against feminine vanity (*The Spectator*, May 24, 1711) gracefully emphasizes the merits of his position, that beautiful women should learn to control their vanity because they will not always be young and pretty.

> Considering therefore that in these and many other Cases the *Woman* generally out-lives the *Idol*, I must return to the Moral of this Paper, and desire my fair Readers to give a proper Direction to their Passion for being admired: In order to which, they must endeavour to make themselves the Objects of a reasonable and lasting Admiration. This is not to be hoped for from Beauty, or Dress, or Fashion, but from those inward Ornaments which are not to be defaced by Time or Sickness, and which appear most amiable to those who are most acquainted with them.

C. THE APOLOGY

There is much to be said for leaving the reader in a good humor, however serious and pressing the nature of the argument. This is the ultimate purpose of the apology. Perhaps the most telling of all apologies is that of Jonathan Swift's *A Modest Proposal* (1729), which argues ironically that the woes of a subjugated and starving Ireland can be cured by slaughtering its young children for the table:

> I profess in the sincerity of my heart that I have not the least personal interest in endeavouring to promote this necessary work, having no other motive than the *public good of my country, by advancing our trade, providing for infants, relieving the poor, and giving some pleasure to the rich.* I have no children,

by which I can propose to get a single penny; the youngest being nine years old, and my wife past child-bearing. (Swift's italics)

EXERCISES:

1. As assigned by the instructor, an analysis of concluding paragraphs of arguments in the reading text, with the object of determining how the author has chosen to conclude his argument and evaluating his success in doing so.

2. The composition of several concluding paragraphs for projected argumentative essays, with complete sentence outlines for the essays. At least one paragraph should be devoted to each of the methods discussed in this section, and one should attempt to use all three.

A Final Word on Persuasion

The purpose of argumentation is persuasion. Men are dogmatic by nature, exceedingly difficult to change once they have reached a conviction. Hence the writer need not worry particularly about whether he has destroyed the opposition with hard and unassailable conclusions. In the first place, there is a good deal of reasonable argument that can be advanced on both sides of most questions. Also, in addition to demonstrating his own position, probably his real task is to sway the person who is not yet convinced, one way or the other. Here a suggestion is better than a demand, a whisper more audible than a shout, a bit of humor more effective than a statistic. To put it another way, an argument stands a better chance of succeeding if its author regards himself as an entertainer rather than a preacher.

Assignments

1. The composition of a list of questions on contemporary problems, suitable for essays developed mainly by argumentation.

2. The writing of several full-length (500–750 words) argumentative essays, at least two of them on both sides of one question.

3. As assigned by the instructor, extended analysis of argumentative essays in the reading text.

4. As assigned by the instructor, a detailed analysis of at least two of the essays in the list of suggested readings, which the instructor may well wish to expand.

Readings

Anthony Standen, Chapter One of *Science Is a Sacred Cow* (New York, 1950).

Samuel Johnson, "Romances and Morality," from *The Rambler* (Oxford, 1907).

John Milton, "Areopagitica," *Complete Poetry and Selected Prose* (Modern Library).

The Spectator for May 24, 1711 (New York and London, 1954).

Jonathan Swift, "A Modest Proposal," *Gulliver's Travels and Other Writings* (Modern Library).

Robert M. Hutchins, "Gate Receipts and Glory," *Saturday Evening Post*, Dec. 3, 1938.

Henry D. Thoreau, "On the Duty of Civil Disobedience," *Walden and Other Writings* (Modern Library).

Philip Wylie, "Common Women," *Generation of Vipers* (New York, 1954).

Sir Philip Sidney, *An Apologie for Poetrie* (London, 1928).

Oliver Goldsmith, "National Prejudices," *Essays* (London, 1765).

Washington Irving, "English Writers on America," *Selected Writings of Washington Irving* (Modern Library).

Bernard Shaw, "Better than Shakespeare," *Dramatic Opinions and Essays* (New York, 1907).

G. K. Chesterton, "A Defence of Nonsense," *The Defendant* (London, 1901).

H. L. Mencken, "The Sahara of the Bozart," *Prejudices: Second Series* (New York, 1920).

C. Northcote Parkinson, "Plans and Plants, or the Administration Block," *Parkinson's Law* (Boston, 1957).

E. B. White, "Freedom," *One Man's Meat* (New York, 1944).

E. A. Abbott, "A Square," *Flatland* (New York, 1952).

Philip Roth, "Positive Thinking on Pennsylvania Avenue," *The New Republic*, June 3, 1957 (and letters in the same periodical, June 24 and July 15, 1957).

Chapter Eight

❊ DESCRIPTION

In the preceding chapters we have been talking about *explaining* things to an audience, about *telling* an audience something, and about *persuading* an audience of the wisdom of some position we have taken. The time comes to most writers—and, in assignments, inevitably to the freshman writer—when he will want not to explain or tell or persuade, but simply to *show* his audience something. To do this requires what may often be a difficult transformation: the writer must take a piece of his experience, a place, an object, a person, and commit it so to paper that the reader will acquire the same view and the same feeling that the author has had in his own sensory reaction. In effect, the writer has to say, "Here is something you must see. This is what it was like, or what it seemed to be. This is the way it looked. This is the way I felt." And he must do this, remember, so well that the reader will experience not the thing itself, but the thing, the object colored and shaped and turned by the writer's sensory and sensitive reactions to it.

Very little writing is purely descriptive in this sense. Descriptive writing naturally is important to all other kinds of discourse. The argumentative little letter home trying rationally and emotionally to persuade papa to send more money will likely contain an ecstatic description of the darling frock on which it is to be spent. The laboratory report is essentially concerned with the exposition of procedure and result, but may also include description of the paraphernalia used in achieving that result. In short, being a record of what we see and sense, description is fundamental to our expression.

To write effective description, the writer must present his subject as he experienced it so that his reader will have essentially the same experience, although the author will *not* be interested in *reproducing* his subject on the page. In the first place, this is not possible; in the second place, even if it were possible, it would not be desirable. If reproduction of a tree were the same thing as description of a tree, or if it effected the same results, then the long history of painting would abruptly have ceased a day or so after the invention of the first camera. But reproduction is not the goal of the descriptive writer. He wants to present the subject as it has already impressed him. Thus his goal is not to reproduce, but to present his impression of the thing. He does not present the tree itself for his reader. He presents the tree as it was for him, in all its sad and gay seasonal strength and fall, its leafy associations for him.

Description necessarily relies for its effectiveness on sharp presentation of sensory images and impressions. However, description does not ordinarily arise from mere impressions collected at random. The author's next task is the selection of those impressions that will record the tree as it was. If the writer records all the impressions that came to him before that tree, he is apt to set down a great many totally irrelevant things. The act of transformation that makes for good description requires filtering impressions, weighing them, and discovering which ones capture the subject at hand. The exact height of a tree and the circumference of its trunk, for example, are not likely to help very much in the description of that tree. These are qualities which any tree may have. But careful description of the one limb bent low as with an appended weight, the grey, warped solitary board held high in a crotch of the tree by a bent nail, and the wavering initials JWC + PRA enclosed in a heart—these are features of that tree alone and, testifying as they do to the stages in some boy's growth, they are features that will help to present that one tree, that unique piece of experience, so that a reader can visualize it.

Sensory and sensitive impressions selected for their efficacy in allowing the reader to experience the thing described are, then, crucial to effective description. Their importance is illustrated in the following selection from a student paper, meant to be an essay in description:

(1) After the third game, we switched courts, which is a customary procedure in tennis. (2) Upon switching courts, I could see Milton Daniel dormitory directly in front of me. (3) Also, a distinct view of Tom Brown and Pete Wright dormitories was possible on my right. (4) As the match progressed, I noticed quite a few familiar faces going into and coming out of Pete Wright and Tom Brown. (5) At the finish of the second game in the second set, one of my friends came over to the tennis court from Tom Brown, which is located directly north of Pete Wright. (6) As we stopped to talk, a car load of girls we knew also stopped to talk to us. (7) After they left, my roommate and I resumed our tennis match.

At this point, perhaps it should be noted that the importance of visual and other sensual impressions is illustrated here by their absence. Nothing in this passage helps to *present* the scene as it was. Nothing tells us of its appearance. Consider the effect of this passage sentence by sentence, remembering that it was meant to be a piece of descriptive writing.

Sentence One:

The information that the two boys have switched courts is important for what it lets us know about the writer's point of view. Otherwise, this sentence contains nothing about sight, sound, smell, feeling, or other impressions that might convey the look of the scene.

Sentence Two:

This tells us only that a dormitory is directly in front of the writer. Save for its name, it could be any dormitory on any campus, for we are told absolutely nothing about it.

Sentence Three:

We know now that two more dormitories are visible, but that is all we know about them. We do not know their color, their size, their shape; we do not know if they are new, comfortable, or run-down; we do not know if they are hard, crowded, pushing places, or if they are tight little islands against professors and the public.

Sentence Four:

Now we have familiar faces, damned to remain forever anonymous because they are not made familiar *to us*.

Sentence Five:

Another anonymous friend. This sentence lets us know that time is passing, but that is all.

Sentence Six:

What a world of profit and delight the writer misses here. Girls are never just girls.

Sentence Seven:

Nothing.

This passage, of course, fulfills none of the functions of descriptive writing. To avoid such weakness and to learn more of the responsibilities of description, the author should consider two major features of descriptive writing: the tactics for arranging description and the related problems of observation and diction.

Strategies for Descriptive Writing

Description has much in common with other kinds of writing. Like exposition and argumentation, it should be *unified* and *coherent*. Also like other forms, it should be *well organized*. Some methods for achieving these qualities are discussed in the following sections of this chapter.

UNITY IN DESCRIPTION

Unity in writing, as we have seen before, is that quality characteristic of a piece of writing that is controlled by a central, dominating idea. All units of writing, regardless of their length, require unity. A long complex sentence, for example, is controlled and unified by the single independent clause it contains at some strategic place. The paragraph is controlled and unified ordinarily by a topic sentence, and the essay is similarly unified as it develops a single, dominating thesis. So, too, descriptive writing requires unity.

The method authors have traditionally found useful in unifying description is the exploitation of the *dominant impression*. The dominant impression in descriptive writing has something like the same function as the thesis in expository and argumentative writing, providing in much the same way both a beginning and a focal point for everything in the essay. The dominant impression is the striking, central feature of a person, place, or thing; it is that quality of the subject that one tends to notice first and remember longest. *Writers employ the method utilizing the dominant impression by subordinating every other impression to this central characteristic, or by describing all other features of the subject in such a way as to contribute directly to the establishment of a dominant impression.*

These are techniques not peculiar to descriptive writing. The caricaturist works by eliminating all secondary features, subordinating them out of existence, until the striking qualities, the characteristic qualities of a face remain alone and emphasized. A famous caricature of Al Jolson in blackface illustrates the method of dominant impression. Done on black paper, the caricature consists of nothing but two white-gloved hands and two white circles for eyes—all subordinate features have been omitted. Current editorial drawings of President Kennedy tend to concentrate on features suggesting youth, a shock of sometimes unruly hair, and a wide smile. Such a method can also be used in descriptive essays. In the passage that follows, observe how the author simply ignores anything that does not express the controlling impression he wants to present:

> From Amelia's children I learned not only gaiety and casualness and inventiveness, but the possibility that mere living may be delightful and that natural things which we ignore unless we call them scenery are pleasant to move among and gracious to recall. Without them it would probably never have occurred to me that to climb an aspen sapling in a gale is one of those ultimate experiences, like experiencing God or love, that you need never try to remember because you can never forget. Aspens grow together in little woods of their own, straight, slender, and white. Even in still weather they twinkle and murmur, but in a high wind you must run out and plunge among them, spattered with sunlight, to the very center. Then select your tree and climb it high enough for it to begin to wobble with your weight. Rest your foot-weight lightly on the frail branches and do most of your climbing with your arms. Now let it lunge, and gulp the wind. It will be all over you, slapping your hair in your eyes, stinging your face with bits of bark and stick, tugging to break your hold, roaring in your open mouth like a monster sea-shell. The trees around you will thrash and seethe, their white undersides lashed about like surf, and sea-music racing through them. You will be beaten and bent and buffeted about and the din will be so terrific your throat will invent a song to add to the welter, pretty barbaric, full of yells and long calls. You will feel what it is to be the Lord God and ride a hurricane.
>
>   —William A. Percy, *Lanterns on the Levee: Recollections of a Planter's Son* (New York: Alfred A. Knopf, 1941), pp. 54–55.

We are not told here of height, circumference, foliation, color, or location. The author has eliminated everything merely incidental to this dominant impression—pure innocent joy, compounded of movement, majesty, and mystery.

Instead of eliminating secondary impressions, the author may choose to subordinate them and handle them so that they will contribute to the strength of the dominant impression, getting something like the same effect an expert cameraman achieves when through the use of color filters he shades everything in his picture into one dominant mood or impression. This method is not uncommon to conversation. The young man who comes back to his room late in the night after his first evening in an espresso house, bursting into his room with "Man, that's the weirdest place I've ever seen," is using this method, particularly if he goes on to describe setting, furniture, lighting, and people encountered in such a way as to emphasize their weirdness.

Several strategies are useful in exploiting this method. Simple repetition can be effective—repetition of key words and phrases that set the mood or capture the impression, almost as in a refrain. Grammatical subordination is likewise effective, elements of the description not directly contributing to the emphasis of the dominant impression being relegated to subordinate grammatical elements in the sentence. A third method is less specific, resulting as it does not from manipulation on paper, but from the attitude of the writer. If the subject being described does create a striking mood or impression, often that mood or impression will control the writer's description, so that he sees everything in terms of that mood. All three of these techniques are illustrated in the passage that follows, which is taken from a longer account of two boys' visit to a circus ground as the circus is being set up:

> Talking in low excited voices we would walk rapidly back toward town under the rustle of September leaves, in cool streets just grayed now with that still, that unearthly and magical first light of day which seems suddenly to re-discover the great earth out of darkness. . . . At the sculptural still square

where at one corner, just emerging into light, my father's shabby little marble shop stood with a ghostly strangeness and familiarity, my brother and I would "catch" the first street-car of the day bound for the "depot" where the circus was—or sometimes we would meet some one we knew, who would give us a lift in his automobile. . . . The great iron-grey horses, four and six to a team, would be plodding along the road of thick white dust to a rattling of chains and traces and the harsh cries of their drivers. The men would drive the animals to the river which flowed by beyond the tracks, and water them; and as first light came one could see the elephants wallowing in the familiar river and the big horses going slowly and carefully down to drink.

Then, on the circus grounds, the tents were going up already with the magic speed of dreams. All over the place (which was near the tracks and the only space of flat land in the town that was big enough to hold a circus) there would be this fierce, savagely hurried, and yet orderly confusion. Great flares of gaseous circus light would blaze down on the seared and battered faces of the circus toughs as, with the rhythmic precision of a single animal—a human riveting machine—they swung their sledges at the stakes, driving a stake into the earth with the incredible instancy of accelerated figures in a motion picture. And everywhere, as light came, and the sun appeared, there would be a scene of magic, order, and of violence.

—Thomas Wolfe, From Death to Morning
(New York: Charles Scribner's Sons, 1932),
pp. 205–207.

Everything in this passage helps to establish a sense of magic, compounded of movement, of the striking order in chaos, and of the remarkable juxtaposition of strangeness and familiarity. The author uses repetition to achieve part of his effect. The word *still* appears twice, the words *magic* or *magical* three times, and words suggesting a sense of magic or wonder, such as *unearthly* or *ghostly*, three times. Subordination of incidental items is also used to good effect, as in the last sentence, where the approach of light and sun is subordinated to the sense of magic, order, and violence. Most noticeable, however, is the way the author controls his description with the reminiscent mood of magic and wonder, recalling the intense movement and the strangeness in a familiar setting. Beginning with the stillness of his familiar setting, the rustle of leaves, the cool street, the still light, and the "sculptural still square," he thrusts into that setting the world of movement and magic. Horses plod along the road, elephants wallow in the river, tents go up with "the magic speed of dreams"; there is a "fierce, savagely hurried" confusion, and men swing sledges with an "incredible instancy." Yet, he recalls, in this movement there was order, a "savagely hurried, and yet orderly confusion," a scene of "magic, order, and of violence." The sense of magic and wonder is further established by a sense of incongruity. The light is "unearthly and magical," the father's shop stands with a "ghostly strangeness and familiarity," and best of all, *elephants* wallow in a familiar river. In this way an adult writer recaptures the awe a boy felt.

In description, as in other kinds of writing, lack of unity is one of the common weaknesses. In exposition and argument, this lack of unity results usually from the writer's failure to develop a central thesis. In much the same way in description it results, usually from the writer's failure to develop a dominant impression. The writer ordinarily wants to treat his subject realistically, to present it as it is, but through his selection of details he can also decide what effect his subject is to create, and what mood or impression he wants to establish. The writer, in short, has to decide what he wants description to accomplish. The student essay that follows suffers from the common weakness; it is not unified because the author is uncertain as to desired effect, and as to dominant impression:

> Deep in the heart of Central Texas, far from the struggles of industry, lies a small stream known as Bushe Creek. The Bushe is no ordinary creek for it possesses a special kind of magic which belongs to it alone. This enchantment begins with the entrance of the long, narrow lane which leads to the stream. Bending lowly above, overhanging branches of huge elms interlock to form a tunnel of cool green leaves through which golden rays of sunlight filter softly to the dark, damp earth. The emer-

ald ceiling reveals a glimpse of blue sky as a gentle breeze ruffles the trees and whistles down the silent pathway. The stream pauses to form a quiet pool of crystal water surrounded by smooth, grey mud. The mirror-like surface of the pool is broken with tiny ripples as an invisible insect skims across the water and vanishes into the obscure edge. Beside the quiet liquid lies a decaying log. Its hollow grayness reflects softly against the blend of trees and sky pictured in the glassy stillness. A few feet beyond the pool rises a gentle hill of dense underbrush and forest. The breeze carries a fresh odor of spicy sweet cedar. The sun bakes a musty yet pleasant fragrance from the drying wildflowers.

From an opening in the pool, the Bushe continues on its busy way down a small fall. The crystal-clear water trickles over jagged, slime-green rocks and lands on a second but smaller pool. Near the shore is a heavy mass of flood waste that lies bleaching in the sun.

How many times I have stood with the clear, trickling waters cooling my feet and cleansing my mind! How many hours have I watched a water insect struggle for existence and compared his simple life with mine! This is the magic of the Bushe.

A number of things are wrong with this essay, especially some significant weaknesses in diction. The major problem is the lack of unity, which results from confused impressions. In the second sentence the author announces that the Bushe is "no ordinary creek," for it has its own unique special magic. He then reinforces this impression by telling us of the enchanting "tunnel of cool green leaves," the quiet pool, and the pleasant odors (the last sentence in the first paragraph, incidentally, is quite effective). Other items suggest a pleasant scene that might possess its own magic—the small fall, for example, and the "jagged, slime-green rocks." But an equal number of items and impressions *detract* from this sense of magic that has been asserted from the first of the essay. The "smooth, grey mud" is an interesting descriptive touch, realistic enough, but it does not in any way contribute to the sense of magic and peace elsewhere suggested, particularly since the word *mud* coming at the end of the sentence has a blunt, emphatic sound that calls attention to it. The decaying log, interesting in itself, similarly fails to add to the mood or impression that the author seems to have wanted to set. The greatest weakness occurs in the last paragraph. To be sure, introspection and meditation may be magical, or they may produce magical effects, but the author has not in any way shown here that the meditation of the final paragraph is related integrally with the descriptions of the first two paragraphs. The result is a broken-backed essay, two paragraphs working toward description, one paragraph lost in apparently unrelated thought.

Writing that is not unified destroys the effect of description, as it destroys any other kind of effort. The traditional and still useful method for assuring unity in description is the establishment of a dominant impression as a focus for the descriptive work.

COHERENCE IN DESCRIPTION

In earlier chapters the problem of coherence and continuity has been discussed at some length. This problem must also be a concern of the writer who would write good description. As in exposition and argumentation, the author is obligated to make his work hold together so that each element of the work will be the natural and easy consequence of the element it follows. The reader should be able to go through a work easily, aware always of its consistency, and able always to perceive the steps in its development without undue jolts to his sensibility. The method authors customarily have found most useful in achieving coherence for their work is the establishment and maintenance of a natural and consistent point of view.

Point of View. A writer's point of view indicates how and where he stands in regard to his subject. It makes clear to a reader what the writer's physical position or mental attitude is in relation to the subject. In this way, the point of view performs two services, one for the reader, one for the writer and indirectly for the reader.

First, a clearly defined point of view enables the reader to *know* the author of the work he is reading. Establishing his viewpoint, the author makes certain commitments to his reader: he acquaints him with his physical or mental attitude, which commits him to a way of seeing his subject. When this is done, the reader may read with greater ease, knowing there should be no inconsistencies in what he reads, expecting no shifts of position or attitude unless they are duly explained. Point of view is, of course, a descriptive device in itself, determining what portion of a subject is seen or from what angle it is seen. More, it is a means the writer has of committing himself to his reader, saying in effect, "This is what I am; this is the way things look to me."

Point of view also serves the writer directly by giving him a natural means of transition, or continuity. Once the point of view is established, the writer has a post to tie everything to. When he proclaims his point of view, the writer is himself the constant factor in the description, the standard to which everything relates. Since everything in the description will result from *his* perceptions, the writer has available to him a kind of natural continuity as the reader understands that what he reads comes from a single source looking at a single subject in a single way.

The point of view from which a writer chooses to describe his subject may be either primarily physical or primarily mental, depending on the nature of the subject and on the writer's relation to it. Any description is likely to be subjective; that is, it will be informed by the author's mental attitude, his mood, his feelings. Some descriptions, however, may be organized and controlled by predominantly physical factors.

The writer may choose, for example, to describe his subject from a *fixed* physical position, presenting his subject as he sees it from a given position that does not change throughout the description. In the following passage Nathaniel Hawthorne describes an old building from a fixed position outside the

building, beginning his description at the top of the building
and moving downward in the course of his description:

. . . here, with a view from its front windows adown this not
very enlivening prospect, and thence across the harbor, stands
a spacious edifice of brick. From the loftiest point of its roof,
during precisely three and a half hours of each forenoon, floats
or droops, in breeze or calm, the banner of the republic; but
with the thirteen stripes turned vertically, instead of horizon-
tally, and thus indicating that a civil, and not a military post
of Uncle Sam's government is here established. Its front is orna-
mented with a portico of half a dozen wooden pillars, supporting a balcony, beneath which a flight of wide granite steps
descends towards the street. Over the entrance hovers an enormous specimen of the American eagle, with outspread wings, a
shield before her breast, and, if I recollect aright, a bunch of
intermingled thunderbolts and barbed arrows in each claw.
With the customary infirmity of temper that characterizes this
unhappy fowl, she appears, by the fierceness of her beak and
eye, and the general truculency of her attitude, to threaten mischief to the inoffensive community; and especially to warn all
citizens, careful of their safety, against intruding on the premises which she overshadows with her wings. Nevertheless,
vixenly as she looks, many people are seeking, at this very
moment, to shelter themselves under the wind of the federal
eagle; imagining, I presume, that her bosom has all the softness
and snugness of an eider-down pillow. But she has no great
tenderness, even in her best of moods, and sooner or later,—
oftener soon than late,—is apt to fling off her nestlings, with a
scratch of her claw, a dab of her beak, or a rankling wound
from her barbed arrows.

The pavement round about the above-described edifice—
which we may as well name at once the Custom House of the
port—has grass enough growing in its chinks to show that it has
not, of late days, been worn by any multitudinous resort of
business. In some months of the year, however, there often
chances a forenoon when affairs move onward with a livelier
tread. Such occasions might remind the elderly citizen of that
period before the last war with England, when Salem was a
port by itself; not scorned, as she is now, by her own merchants

and ship-owners, who permit her wharves to crumble to ruin, while their adventures go to swell, needlessly and imperceptibly, the mighty flood of commerce at New York or Boston.

> —Nathaniel Hawthorne, Introduction to
> *The Scarlet Letter.*

Here there is no indication that the viewer has changed his physical position; everything described could be seen from the same station, presumably somewhere almost directly in front of the building. In the passage below a wider scene is described from a similarly fixed point of view:

> Two or three days and nights went by; I reckon I might say they swum by, they slid along so quiet and smooth and lovely. Here is the way we put in the time. It was a monstrous big river down there—sometimes a mile and a half wide; we run nights and laid up and hid daytimes; soon as night was most gone we stopped navigating and tied up—nearly always in the dead water under a towhead; and then cut young cottonwoods and willows and hid the raft with them. Then we set out the lines. Next we slid into the river and had a swim, so as to freshen up and cool off; then we set down on the sandy bottom where the water was about knee-deep and watched the daylight come. Not a sound anywheres—perfectly still—just like the whole world was asleep, only sometimes the bullfrogs a-cluttering, maybe. The first thing to see, looking away over the water, was a kind of dull line—that was the woods on t'other side; you couldn't make nothing else out; then a pale place in the sky; then more paleness spreading around; then the river softened up away off, and warn't black any more, but gray; you could see little dark spots drifting along ever so far away—trading-scows, and such things; and long black streaks—rafts; sometimes you could hear a sweep screaking; or jumbled-up voices, it was so still, and sounds come so far.
>
> —Mark Twain, *Huckleberry Finn.*

The nature of the fixed, predominantly physical point of view places certain restrictions on the writer, as the preceding passage illustrates. Once the writer takes a stance, once he adopts a fixed position from which to describe his subject, he must then also accept the conditions that the point of view sets. He can describe only what is apparent to his senses from that position. Hawthorne, for example, gives the reader the *front* of his building and the ground surrounding the front. From the position he has taken, he can do nothing else. Twain, describing the woods across the Mississippi River through the eyes of Huckleberry Finn, tells us that they are "a kind of dull line," because "you couldn't make nothing else out." For the same reason he speaks of scows and rafts as "little dark spots drifting along ever so far away."

This at first may seem to be a disadvantage, restricting the writer's freedom in his description. In some instances, it may indeed put the writer in a difficult position, for the fixed point of view means that he can give only a *partial* view of his subject. This kind of viewpoint may, however, have advantages that far outweigh any possible restrictions. In the first place, the fixed point of view is a readier device for effecting transition, there being always the constant, fixed viewer in the same place to act as a cohesive factor. In the second place, this viewpoint performs the important service of forcing the writer to focus clearly on a relatively small area. The necessity of seeing clearly the small view he sees may help the writer to present his account of that view better.

Some subjects call for description from a fixed position more than others. Larger scenes, landscapes, cities, ballrooms, and the like, can usually be handled better from a fixed position. By their nature, such scenes are too large and too complex for thorough description, even if the point of view is a shifting one. For this reason, the writer may work more effectively by devoting his whole attention to a smaller segment of his experience, being enabled in this way to get at the total impression of his subject for his reader.

Some subjects, on the other hand, call for more thorough coverage. A home, for example, or a small shop, a club room, a snack bar, a warm tavern—such scenes may be completely described if the author varies his approach. If the subject seems unsuited for description from a fixed point of view, or if for some other reason the author chooses not to use this kind of viewpoint, he may choose instead to describe from a *moving* point of view: in place of remaining fixed in one position relative to the subject, the author shifts his point of view, moving around and through his subject, looking here, then there, as his moving vantage point allows him to see his subject from different angles, according to some previously determined plan. This treatment is illustrated in the following passage. After the description of the Custom House from the outside, which was given a little earlier, the narrator goes inside the old building and describes what he sees as he moves about:

> . . . on ascending the steps, you would discern—in the entry, if it were summer time, or in their appropriate rooms, if wintry or inclement weather—a row of venerable figures, sitting in old-fashioned chairs, which were tipped on their hind legs back against the wall. Oftentimes they were asleep, but occasionally might be heard talking together, in voices between speech and a snore, and with that lack of energy that distinguishes the occupants of almhouses, and all other human beings who depend for subsistence on charity, on monopolized labor, or anything else, but their own independent exertions. These old gentlemen—seated, like Matthew, at the receipt of customs, but not very liable to be summoned thence, like him, for apostolic errands—were Custom House officers.

> Furthermore, on the left hand as you enter the front door, is a certain room or office, about fifteen feet square, and a lofty height; with two of its arched windows commanding a view of the aforesaid dilapidated wharf, and the third looking across a narrow lane, and along a portion of Derby Street. All three give glimpses of the shops of grocers, block-makers, slop-sellers, and ship-chandlers; around the doors of which are generally to be seen, laughing and gossiping, clusters of old salts, and such other wharf-rats as haunt Wapping of a seaport. The room itself is cobwebbed, and dingy with old paint; its floor is strewn with gray sand, in a fashion that has elsewhere fallen into long disuse; and it is easy to conclude, from the general slovenliness of the place, that this is a sanctuary into which womankind, with her tools of magic, the broom and mop, has very infrequent

access. In the way of furniture, there is a stove with a voluminous funnel; an old pine desk, with a three-legged stool beside it; two or three wooden-bottom chairs, exceedingly decrepit and infirm; and—not to forget the library—on some shelves, a score or two of volumes of the Acts of Congress, and a bulky Digest of the Revenue Laws. A tin pipe ascends through the ceiling, and forms a medium of vocal communications with other parts of the edifice.

In this passage the author moves into the building, describing the entrance as he does so, and thence into one of the rooms in the building, which is also described. The shifting of his point of view is indicated briefly and naturally by such phrases as "on ascending the steps," and "on the left hand as you enter the front door." Thomas Wolfe's description of the circus grounds, a passage from which was quoted in the discussion of dominant impression, is also presented from a shifting point of view:

. . . my brother and I would "catch" the first street-car of the day bound for the "depot" where the circus was—or sometimes we would meet some one we knew, who would give us a lift in his automobile.

Then, having reached the dingy, grimy, and rickety depot section, we would get out, and walk rapidly across the tracks of the station yard, where we could see great flares and steamings from the engines, and hear the crash and bump of shifting freight cars, the swift sporadic thunders of a shifting engine, the tolling of bells, the sounds of great trains on the rails.

And to all these familiar sounds, filled with their exultant prophecies of flight, the voyage, morning, and the shining cities —to all the sharp and thrilling odors of the trains—the smell of cinders, acrid smoke, of musty, rusty freight cars, the clean pine-board of crated produce, and the smells of fresh stored food— oranges, coffee, tangerines and bacon, ham and flour and beef— there would be added now, with an unforgettable magic and familiarity, all the strange sounds and smells of the coming circus.

The gay yellow sumptuous-looking cars in which the star performers lived and slept, still dark and silent, heavily and powerfully still, would be drawn up in long strings upon the tracks. . . .

Then, along the tracks, beside the circus trains, there would be the sharp cries and oaths of the circus men, the magical swinging dance of lanterns in the darkness, the sudden heavy rumble of the loaded vans and wagons as they were along the flats and gondolas, and down the runways to the ground. And everywhere, in the thrilling mystery of darkness and awakening light, there would be the tremendous conflict of a confused, hurried, and yet orderly movement. . . .

Then, on the circus grounds, the tents were going up already with the magic speed of dreams.

Without intruding into the flow of the description, Wolfe here indicates the movement of his point of view in several instances. He lets us know that the boys leave their part of town for the depot, informs us when they reach the depot, and shows them walking across the tracks to get to the circus grounds. Once there, they move about, their eyes falling on different parts of the scene, movements indicated by such phrases as "Then, along the tracks, beside the circus trains," and "Then, on the circus grounds, . . ."

The moving point of view gives the writer some advantages not available to him with the fixed point of view. Such a viewpoint allows the author to present his subject completely if he wishes, permitting him to view his subject in all its aspects. This treatment may also free the author to capture his subject in a series of shifting, kaleidoscopic impressions as he moves about. And such a rapid, impressionistic view is of course quite similar to our own view of things in many instances.

Whether the writer uses the fixed or the moving point of view, he has certain obligations to fulfill. If his writing is not to appear stilted and mechanical, the point of view he chooses must first of all be *natural*. A writer must not simply announce, "I am going to describe the Snack Bar in the Student Union." The description should be made to appear what it is, a part of the writer's experience. Readers will want to know how he got to the Student Union; they will also wonder why he is bothering to describe the place. Good description will usually satisfy these desires, letting the reader understand that the subject is a part of experience, not an arbitrary assignment, and letting the reader understand through the writer's attitude that the scene is after all worth describing. The writer is also obligated to make his point of view *consistent*. Once he has adopted a fixed position, he should stay with it. If the author is using a moving viewpoint, he will probably want to let his readers know that he is moving; otherwise they will hardly be able to accept the description. Such indication of movement needs to be unobtrusive, informing the reader without breaking the continuity of the writing.

All descriptions, even that from physical points of view, are informed by subjective attitudes. In some descriptions, however, the writer may almost entirely forsake the physical point of view in order to let his mood, his personality, his background filter his sensory impressions. A young woman concluding an objective description of a young man she has just met with "I wouldn't have him," would hardly find the same mode of description useful a year later when she is thoroughly devoted to the young man and consequently sees him in a slightly different light. This kind of description is likely to seem less orderly than that restricted to physical point of view. It depends, for example, not on an ordering of space or units, but upon the value or importance or lasting impact of impressions. This is also an immensely pleasurable and valuable kind of description: it is one way we have of confronting other people and discovering what they are like when they are not in our company, a way we have of communing with other men.

Descriptions employing a predominantly mental point of view may take any one of several forms, of which two are probably most common. In the first, the writer retains a physical point of view, but subordinates the physical position to his mood or feeling. The account of climbing aspens in a gale, quoted earlier, is an illustration. Description from a physical position is one of the necessities of the scene, but position is subordinated to the mood of awe and excitement created by the experience. A moving physical point of view is obvious in the description of the circus grounds given earlier, but again the physical position is less important than the sense of mystery and discovery that permeates the presentation.

A second common form that description from the mental point of view may take is movement by free association. Here, in the grip of some powerful mood, of some striking feeling, or of some special sense of value, the author appears to allow his mind and eye to wander about his subject, as in a revery. The following passage is a famous illustration of this technique:

I can call back the solemn twilight and mystery of the deep woods, the earthy smells, the faint odors of the wild flowers, the sheen of rain-washed foliage, the rattling clatter of drops when the wind shook the trees, the far-off hammering of wood-peckers and the muffled drumming of wood-pheasants in the remoteness of the forest, the snapshot glimpses of disturbed wild creatures scurrying through the grass—I can call it all back and make it as real as it ever was, and as blessed. I can call back the prairie, and its loneliness and peace, and a vast hawk hanging motionless in the sky with his wings spread wide and the blue of the vault showing through the fringe of their end-feathers. I can see the woods in their autumn dress, the oaks purple, the hickories washed with gold, the maples and the sumachs luminous with crimson fires, and I can hear the rustle made by the fallen leaves as we plowed through them. I can see the blue clusters of wild grapes hanging amongst the foliage of the saplings, and I remember the taste of them and the smell. I know how the wild blackberries looked and how they tasted; and the same with the pawpaws, the hazelnuts, and the persim-mons; and I can feel the thumping rain upon my head of hick-ory-nuts and walnuts when we were out in the frosty dawn to scramble for them with the pigs, and the gusts of wind loosed them and sent them down. I know the stain of blackberries and how pretty it is, and I know the stain of walnut hulls and how little it minds soap and water, also what grudged experience it had of either of them. I know the taste of maple sap and when to gather it, and how to arrange the troughs and the delivery

tubes, and how to boil down the juice, and how to hook the
sugar after it is made; also how much better hooked sugar tastes
than any that is honestly come by, let bigots say what they will.
— Mark Twain, *Autobiography*
(New York: Harper and Brothers, 1924),
I, 110–111.

Here the author is moving freely about in his description as
his mind moves by association through scenes of his childhood.
The typical sentence and clause beginnings indicate, moreover,
that it is a series of associations marked by a mood of reminiscence compounded of joy and of sadness, joy of pleasure recalled and sadness of pleasure gone.

Mental point of view enforces much the same obligations
upon the author as does physical point of view. The point of
view must allow the description to remain natural—nothing
can be more damaging to writing than the grafting upon it of
artificial and arbitrary mood. The point of view must also remain consistent. More disturbing to a reader than an unex-
plained shift of physical point of view is a sudden and
complete change of mood or feeling that cannot be accounted
for.

PROBLEMS IN COHERENCE AND POINT OF VIEW

Three kinds of weakness are frequent in descriptive writing:
stilted handling of the point of view, violation of the point of
view, and failure to exploit the point of view.

The first of these is illustrated in the following passage.
Remember that the descriptive point of view should be natural,
and that shifts in the point of view should be easy and comfortable.

An espresso coffeehouse provides an amazing picture to the
average individual, especially from the doorway.

The first attraction that meets the eye is the dark, hazy atmosphere hanging over the tables. The dull light seeping
through this cloud and trying its best to illuminate the room
seems only to die a few feet from its source and its only real

benefit is to cast weird shadows on the ceiling. Hundreds of burning brown and white, red-tipped, smoke-emitting "ready-rolls" cause the eyes to smart and play tricks on viewing this scene for the first time.

Across the narrow span of floor space from the door to the opposite wall, a shaggy, unshaven being of slight build is cracking the ivory keys on the board in front of him and sending forth a selection of notes that matches the strange voice ringing from the walls. Accompaniment is from two barrel-shaped, white-topped instruments being struck very hard by two sticks. This noise is ear-shattering and completely unnerving. Nevertheless this weird arrangement is sending crazy signals into the strangely dressed, pillow-lounging creatures, and they begin to stir restlessly. A sharp cat call causes the spine to tingle and the heart to thump faster. A dance has started between two glass-bearing hands and two smoke-yielding hands, causing considerable comment in the audience.

To the right and left of the door scantily clad tray bearers form a chain of endless walking, talking, and wiggling glass carriers. Two black eyes shine from behind a black curly beard and a deep voice says "There is a fifty cents' charge tonight." As I slowly turn away from the door, I wonder in amazement at all the excitement created here.

Although there are a few effective touches here, this little essay is marked by numerous weaknesses, not the least of which is a stiff, mechanical manipulation of the point of view. The one-sentence paragraph that introduces the essay sets the scene and the point of view—and incidentally dooms the essay to ineffectiveness. We can perhaps grant that the coffeehouse is an intriguing place, but we cannot read this sentence without recognizing an assigned chore. What is missing is the rest of the writer's experience that would give body to what he sees here. Particularly we may want to know the circumstances that brought him to the place. We may wonder further what he was doing standing in the doorway all that time. Had we seen the author in this situation, we should probably have concluded that he looked pretty silly. Reading his essay, we may conclude the same thing—his point of view is unnatural. The

introduction to each of the succeeding paragraphs emphasizes
the awkwardness. In the second paragraph he tells of the "first
attraction that meets the eye"—well enough. Then he directs us
first across the floor, then to the right and left of the door. To
be natural, his description needs to show that something directs
his attention to these two areas. He has, in effect, given us a *list*
when he should let his point of view determine his direction.
Little reason is given why the attention is directed first to the
atmosphere, then across the room, and then to the entrance.

A second common failing in descriptive writing occurs when
the author violates his point of view. Once he has chosen the
point of view from which he plans to work, the writer is committed to the consistent use of the same viewpoint. We do not
expect a gloomy man suddenly to leap into moments of inex-
plicable happiness any more than we expect a man standing
outside a house to describe what is inside. Consider the following passage, taken from a student essay written for a special
assignment in which the writer was to describe a familiar
scene from an unfamiliar point of view. For this assignment,
the writer adopted the viewpoint of an alien six inches tall.

> I shall never forget the day I first found out what a taxi was
> and decided to take one to the nearest zoo. I walked out of my
> house in the flowerpot near the Weston Arms Hotel's entrance
> and began trying to catch a taxi driver's eye. I climbed upon a
> dispenser for newspapers and began waving my arms rapidly. I
> watched in disgust as the first taxi drove by. Deciding then to
> take drastic measures, I began waving my arms and shouting
> at the top of my lungs, but to little avail. I'm afraid my voice
> was overshadowed by the monstrous noises of the cars going by.

This writer fails to accept the point of view that was earlier
established. A six-inch alien would, for example, have no term
for *our* zoo, and would probably not know what one is. Nor
would he have experience of hotels, flowerpots of a size he
could live in, or newspapers and their dispensers. His experience would not enable him either to know or to use these
terms. The writer has erroneously permitted his point of view
character, the alien, to talk about things he cannot talk about.

To such a creature a newspaper would be perhaps no more than a piece of some kind of white material, four or five times longer than himself, marked with ciphers of varying sizes. This, from *his* point of view, is what he would experience. The body of a description has to consist of experience available to the point of view from which it is presented.

A third weakness that frequently appears in descriptive writing is the failure to exploit the point of view. The writer's point of view is an enormously important factor in determining the effectiveness of both the content and the style of the description. Point of view provides the attitudes, the moods, the special physical angles of vision that are the writer's alone, and that can make his presentation a unique and valuable piece of work. Full development of these special angles of vision can make the written work vital and worthwhile; it means expression of views and visions not fully shared by anyone else and therefore all the more important to everyone else. Failure to exploit the point of view ultimately means failure to express one's person. The passage that follows, illustrating this weakness, is taken from a student essay describing a homecoming bonfire:

> As I sat in the shadows of a stadium that once played a memorable role in my high school career, I watched the bonfire now surrounded by the present gleeful youth of my old school. As if in a time machine my memories carried me back to the days when I was young and jubilant in my devotion to this school.
>
> The chants of the throng as led by the gay and jovial cheerleaders echoed in the stillness of the night, closing the span of time between my world of yesterday and today. Many were the lithesome figures swaying to and fro to the rhythm of the drum beat in the background. The enthusiastic cheers coming from the large group of loyal supporters of the most prominent football team in the history of the school made such a deafening roar that it seemed to shake the nearby buildings. . . .
>
> A hush fell over the excited crowd as the first strains of the highly-respected alma mater were rendered by the ever-faithful band. Reverence prevailed over the entire group until the last

note faded away. A short-lived silence reigned just before the thunderous fight song filled the air. At this signal the crowd dispersed, each to his own way.

Throughout the first paragraph and including the first sentence of the second paragraph, we are prepared for a continuing mood, the bittersweet mingling of present bliss and faded joy, a mood of reminiscence. This mood is established as the author tells us he sat "in the shadows of a stadium" that once played "a memorable role" in his life, and as he tells us of memories carrying him back to earlier days, closing the span of time. This mood of reminiscence, when it is fully developed, can be one of the most poignant and effective vehicles for description. Yet once we get into the second paragraph, we lose that mood as the author fails to develop his impressions while experiencing it. This is particularly noticeable in the last paragraph, where weak expressions such as "the highly-respected alma mater" and "the ever-faithful band" fail completely to suggest with any force the past joys that are recalled by present gaieties. Reverence before the alma mater and the excitement engendered by a "thunderous fight song" could be treated so as to evoke again the bittersweet mood, but the author fails to do so.

Methods for Organizing Descriptive Essays

Ideally, the writer's subject, his attitude toward it, his knowledge of it, and everything else involved in his point of view toward it should determine the way he goes about his description. Over the years, however, some methods have proved to be almost universally useful in the organization of description. If nothing else, they at least provide forms upon which a writer can depend if all else fails him.

1. *Spatial Organization.* When the writer is employing a predominantly physical point of view, and when he is describing a scene or object rather than a person, some kind of spatial organization may be suitable. Organization of this kind usually

consists of some systematic approach to the bulk of the subject or the space it occupies. The plan or movement of the essay may, for example, follow one of the following typical patterns:

> right to left
> left to right
> far to near
> near to far
> top to bottom
> bottom to top
> large to small
> small to large

2. *Chronological Organization.* In some few instances where time creates major changes in the subject, the writer may describe his subject at different times, arranging his essay either chronologically or according to some other principle of time arrangement. A writer could, for example, make good use of a chronological scheme in describing a landscape that changes sharply under varying light at varying hours of the day. A plan of reverse chronology which has often been used to good effect is movement from the present to the past in describing some scene long known and well remembered. This kind of organization may be employed with a point of view either predominantly physical or predominantly mental.

3. *Organization toward Climax.* A good plan can be worked out by presenting subordinate and contributing details of the subject first and then working with them toward final full establishment of the dominant impression. This, incidentally, has the good effect of reserving the major impression to that section of the essay which is normally most emphatic.

4. *Organization through Support.* A plan reversing the preceding organization can also be effective. The writer may choose to start off emphatically and attract his reader's attention with the best expression of the dominant impression. A description of incidental and contributing details would follow.

5. *Organization by Encounter.* This method has the double advantage of appearing casual and unstudied and of creating

an illusion of reality. With this method the writer has a good opportunity for duplicating his experience: he describes his subject as he encountered it, telling of what he saw first and going on then to describe the progress of his encounters.

6. *Organization by Association.* When the writer is using a viewpoint predominantly mental, he may wish to adopt the pattern of revery utilized by Mark Twain in the selection from his autobiography quoted earlier. A method rather difficult to use well and one that can easily be overused, it involves letting the description follow one's train of associations. Moving from one aspect of the subject to another by suggestion, the writer lets his organization be determined as one feature makes him think of another.

Observation and Diction in Description

Neither unification through dominant impression nor the achievement of coherence through proper handling of the point of view nor any kind of planning, however good, can make description effective unless the author's language records his experience truthfully and exactly. Probably the most common weaknesses in descriptive writing result from inexactness. Vague or generalized descriptions of images and impressions that could arise anywhere, from any scene or thing, always militate against good description. Another common failing occurs when writers, especially beginners, in an attempt to avoid this fuzziness fall into an exaggerated and equally inexact kind of expression usually called "flowery writing."

To be effective, description must make clear how the subject differs from all other subjects, illuminating its special qualities for the reader. Inexactness or vagueness of any kind of course prevents illumination, as the following sentences illustrate. They are taken from a student essay describing Gulf Hills, Mississippi.

> As we passed down the crowded streets of Biloxi, we could see many new motels, and there were people enjoying the cool, refreshing ocean which was so near to the streets.

The writer has told us nothing about this scene that might not also be true of a hundred others. He has told us nothing *exact*. For example, we learn that the streets are crowded, but no scene is presented to us. Are they crowded with cars? With people? With confetti? The author further tells us that he saw many new motels. Are these different? What is the author's actual experience? What style of architecture? What color? What are their names? A simple listing of the sometimes romantic names of motels would do more than the author has done to suggest the character of Biloxi motels. And consider that "cool, refreshing ocean." What we need to know is exactly what the ocean looked and smelled like. Was it cool, but muddy? Was it blue, green, brown, or mottled?

> As we started down the long, winding road, we could see the beautiful homes with the even more beautiful golf course winding between and in back of them.

Of these homes, we know only that they are beautiful, and it is entirely likely that our vision of beauty is not the author's. Of the golf course we know only that it is more beautiful than the homes. Since the word *beautiful* conveys no meaning the first time it is used, we might say at the risk of sounding flippant that the golf course is more nothing than the homes.

The essay quoted earlier describing the homecoming bonfire is also guilty of similar inexactness, as the following sentences indicate:

> As I sat in the shadows of a stadium that once played a memorable role in my high school career, I watched the bonfire now surrounded by the present gleeful youth of my old high school.

The crucial phrase is "the present gleeful youth," indicating their *mood* but telling us nothing of their *appearance*.

> The chants of the throng as led by the gay and jovial cheerleaders echoed in the stillness of the night, closing the span of time between my world of yesterday and today.

The mood of the cheerleaders is suggested, but again nothing of their appearance is even hinted at. And yet young cheer-

leaders are a fine sight, their sometimes colorful or even spec-
tacular dress, the glad limberness of their bodies, the strength
of their voices, even the very lines of face and body embodying a symbolic moment of youth. But the author does not tell
us about these things.

He does tell us a little later that

> Many were the lithesome figures swaying to and fro to the
> rhythm of the drum beat in the background.

Doing so, he makes himself guilty of a second kind of weakness, "flowery writing." The phrase "lithesome figures" sounds
good, but it does not tell a reader much. *Lithesome* is a good
word, of course, but a useless word unless it is given a local
habitation, unless we can *see* the lithesomeness embodied in
these particular forms. A little further on in his essay, this
author mentions the appearance of the football team:

> The cheer from the crowd burst forth with renewed vigor as
> the idolized football team appeared in the surrounding brilliance
> from the growing light of the bonfire.

"Burst forth," "with renewed vigor," and "idolized football
team," aside from being clichés, are specimens of flowery
writing, the author here operating under the misapprehension
that sounds and syllables equal good description. If only the
author had described simply what he heard and saw—telling,
for example, how the crowd recognized the team as the light
from the growing bonfire touched their faces when they
stepped forward.

Faithful description of what one sees and senses—this is the
key to good description. And, assuming the writer has the
methods for organizing and continuing his essay, the steps to
good description are two: *close observation,* and *precise expression of the circumstances of this observation.* One of the
principal features of good description is the accuracy and full-
ness of the author's observation. Remember Huck Finn's description of the sunrise:

> The first thing to see, looking away over the water, was a kind
> of dull line—that was the woods on t'other side; you couldn't

make nothing else out; then a pale place in the sky; then more paleness spreading around; then the river softened up away off, and warn't black any more, but gray. . . .

The precision of the record is one reason for the effectiveness of this short description of what a boy would see, no more, no less.

Often, the minute detail, the incidental item usually overlooked furnishes the exactness that the writer needs and helps him to capture the experience itself—and precision, of course, requires painstaking observation, as in the passage that follows, taken from Mark Twain's autobiography after the passage previously quoted:

I know how a prize watermelon looks when it is sunning its fat rotundity among pumpkin vines and "simblins"; I know how to tell when it is ripe without "plugging" it. I know how inviting it looks when it is cooling itself in a tub of water under the bed, waiting; I know how it looks when it lies on the table in the sheltered great floor-space between house and kitchen, and the children gathered for the sacrifice and their mouths watering. I know the crackling sound it makes when the carving knife enters its end and I can see the split fly along in front of the blade as the knife cleaves its way to the other end. . . .

We have all seen a watermelon cut open, and we have all probably noticed that the melon does indeed split open ahead of the knife—but we might not have thought to say so in a description. Yet it is this kind of regard for the details of experience that makes description good. To say that the knife splits the melon open is accurate enough, and we would not fuss about it. But to tell us that in fact the melon splits ahead of the knife is to get the experience itself before us.

Observation alone does not make description. The observation must be ordered precisely. The passage above, in addition to illustrating the preciseness of observation necessary, also illustrates the preciseness of diction that makes good description. Unusual words and long words are rare. Nouns, the names of things, are predominant. Attributive adjectives (which beginners often mistakenly assume to be the bulwark of description) are few, and of those that do occur, one, *fat,* is plain, straightforward, and unmistakable in intent, and another, *crackling*, has the additional descriptive effect of onomatopoeia.

The language must be precise, every word exactly coinciding with its referent. For this reason nouns and verbs are likely to be more telling than adjectives and adverbs, though these forms do have their effect. But men share many long-run experiences; they hold much of experience in common. Hence if the writer can *name* his experience precisely, and if he can precisely name the actions involved in that experience, the names themselves will evoke in the minds of his readers many of the sensory impressions he wants to create:

> In the morning they rose in a house pungent with breakfast cookery, and they sat at a smoking table loaded with brains and eggs, ham, hot biscuits, fried apples seething in their gummed syrups, honey, golden butter, fried steak, scalding coffee. Or there were stacked batter-cakes, rum-colored molasses, fragrant brown sausages, a bowl of wet cherries, plums, fat juicy bacon, jam. At the mid-day meal, they ate heavily: a huge hot roast of beef, fat buttered lima-beans, tender corn smoking on the cob, thick red slabs of sliced tomatoes, rough savory spinach, hot yellow cornbread, flaky biscuits, a deep-dish peach and apple cobbler spiced with cinnamon, tender cabbage, deep glass dishes piled with preserved fruits—cherries, pears, peaches. At night they might eat fried steak, hot squares of grits fried in egg and butter, pork-chops, fish, young fried chicken.
>
> —Thomas Wolfe, *Look Homeward, Angel*
> (New York: Charles Scribner's Sons,
> 1929), p. 68.

Assignments

1. Read and discuss the descriptive techniques of assigned essays in a reading text. Note the point of view the author uses in each instance, and if he is using the method of dominant impression, show how each detail in the essay contributes to that impression.

Examine the diction to determine whether the author is using concrete words, words essentially denotative or connotative, noting especially any words that evoke a sensory response.

2. Write a descriptive paragraph using each of the methods mentioned in the section "Methods for Organizing Descriptive Essays."

3. Write a descriptive essay on a subject agreed upon by you and your instructor.

Readings

Reference

Chapter Two of this book.

Mark Twain, "Fenimore Cooper's Literary Offenses," *The Portable Mark Twain* (New York, 1946).

Illustrations

Thomas Hardy, *The Return of the Native* (Modern Library).

Charles Dickens, *A Tale of Two Cities* (Modern Library).

Ernest Hemingway, *A Farewell to Arms* (New York, 1929).

Thomas Wolfe, *Look Homeward, Angel* (New York, 1929).

Mark Twain, *Huckleberry Finn* (Modern Library).

————, *Autobiography* (New York, 1924).

Charles Lamb, "Poor Relations," "Old China," in *Complete Works and Letters* (Modern Library).

William L. Laurence, *Dawn over Zero* (New York, 1946).

Daniel Defoe, *Robinson Crusoe* and *A Journal of the Plague Year* (Modern Library).

Chapter Nine

❋ NARRATION

Men have, we suppose, always argued and explained and described. These are natural modes of expression. An equally natural mode, probably an older, and certainly a more direct, is the fourth of the classical kinds of discourse, narration. Tales passed on from father to son beside a fire, myths orally repeated, fables, legends, Scriptural parables, the works of Homer himself—these are all specimens of narrative writing. Later men, with greater sophistication but less art, have endeavored to interpret, to explain, to describe phenomena of nature and of human activity that narrators had presented directly, making ideas and principles and feelings live in the actions of people or of personifications. Narration, although selective in much the same way as other modes of writing, is a direct presentation of experience, dramatizing for an audience the words and the deeds of men. It is, therefore, another and possibly more forceful means men have for confronting other men, knowing them best through action, reaction, and word.

As such, narration is therefore commonly used to preserve

human experience, to preserve actions and series of actions. It takes its form in this preservation; its purposes may vary widely. The writer of narrative may seek formally or informally to preserve human actions; but he may also seek through narration to serve other purposes, such as explanation or persuasion. Narration is thus closely related to other forms of discourse, often using techniques typical of other kinds of writing, often fulfilling the functions of other kinds of writing. But, well done, it is invariably the most dramatic of the classical modes of discourse since by definition its concern is with things being done, with creatures performing.

Narrative writing is, then, a natural form of discourse and one that often employs the methods of other forms. The five-year-old who, having no knowledge of abstractions and no vocabulary to express them, reports in woeful indignation that "I was playing with the rope and David pushed me and he said it was his and he took it away from me and then he stuck out his tongue and he's ugly," *narrates* her troubles and in so doing *explains* her vision of the injustice of it all. Autobiographical and biographical writing and all kinds of historical writing reveal the author's use of exposition, description, and argumentation, as well as his narrative of life in motion.

The narrative writer, as readings in biography and fiction clearly demonstrate, must necessarily make use of description. We are not likely to believe in people or in their actions unless we are also provided ways of *knowing* them directly, by seeing their persons and by seeing the situation in which they go about their several actions.

The narrative also quite obviously must use on occasion some methods of exposition, since we may not always understand actions without explanation. Narration has indeed close affinities with some kinds of exposition: narrative writing and exposition of sequences (discussed in Chapter Six) are clearly related. Both are determined by a time scheme of some kind since both involve a progression through time.

Despite this similarity, there is a sharp distinction between exposition of sequences and narrative writing. Exposition of sequences is organized by some chronological plan, as is narration, but they differ in at least one major respect. The writer of this special kind of exposition is engaged in explaining a process, a series of related events. Almost invariably both he and his audience know from the start what the *end* of that series will be, it being his purpose to explain not isolated events but a sequence the nature of which the audience ordinarily knows from his title or his introduction. In narrative writing, on the other hand, while the author always knows, the audience seldom knows what the outcome of the progressive actions will be. On those occasions when the audience does know the outcome of a series of actions, it becomes the writer's obligation, as we shall see later, to maintain some suspense nevertheless by withholding information and by other methods. Since the author's purpose is to narrate the events, the audience is obliged to wait and to discover the conclusion.

A writer might, for example, set out to explain the sequence of actions that makes an automobile run. To do so, he will have to use a chronological plan: gasoline is put into the tank, it flows then through tubes to the motor, where mysterious explosions and things take place in the pistons and thereabouts and then the car moves (actually, of course, it is probably indulgent elves who propel the car along). The audience knows from the start what will happen in the end—unless either the writer or the automobile has crossed wires. But the writer of narration is usually writing about unique things, about individual people doing things so that, knowing people, the audience has no way of anticipating the conclusion of the narration. This kind of writing, narration, is the province of this chapter.

Problems and Techniques in Narration

Although narrative discourse is in many ways natural to us, and although its commonly chronological plan may be easily grasped—especially by time-obsessed minds of the twentieth century—writers nevertheless experience frequent difficulty with this form. Probably the most common problems the narrative writer encounters are revealed in the following student essay:

WEEKEND AT A TYLER LODGE

A few months ago Don Crabtree, a schoolmate of mine, and I went to spend the weekend at a private hunting and fishing lodge located a few miles out of Tyler, Texas.

Tyler and the surrounding countryside was not like the sun-baked, dry, flat and sometimes sandy terrain usually associated with Texas. It flourished with large stands of pine and other native trees common to that part of the country. The rolling hills were covered with soft green grass and wild flowers.

When we were approaching the outskirts of Tyler, we turned off on a small side road covered with gravel. Bordering the roadway was waist high grass and an occasional cornfield. Now and then we saw weatherbeaten cardboard signs advertising the local politicians who were up for election.

Soon we came to a large wrought iron fence braced by two brown brick pillars which formed the gateway to the lodge. The driveway to the lodge followed the curve of a small lake. The lake was about a quarter of a mile long and almost the same distance in width. Tall, slender cattails and various other water plants fringed the water's edge. A large grove of pine trees extended the entire length of the drive.

The lodge was surrounded by a low burnished wire fence upon which was mounted the white, sun bleached antlers of deer that had been killed during past hunting seasons. It was a large two-story log cabin with a large screened-in back porch. The interior was comfortably furnished with lounges and easy chairs to sit and pass away the time in.

It was about five thirty in the afternoon when we finally got unpacked and settled. Don and I, eager to try fishing in the lake, hurried down to the shore where there was a small weather-worn dock much in need of repair which groaned and squeaked as we walked upon it. We discovered two ten-foot aluminum flat boats tied to the dock. They were mounted with small trolling motors covered with a thin film of grease and smelling strongly of gasoline. We carefully boarded one of the boats and slowly glided out into the lake. A small frog, frightened by our appearance on the water, hopped his way from lily pad to lily pad. Shadows from the tall pine trees were creeping their way across the smooth surface of the water, creating various shades of green. Beautiful lilies, green moss and thick patches of lotus lined our way for a short distance until we reached deep water.

When we were about in the center of the lake, we dropped our small lead anchor and began to fish. After fishing for several hours without any success, it began to grow dark. There was no moon which made it difficult to see, so we prepared to return to the dock. Don couldn't get the motor started, and as I stepped to the back of the boat to help him, the front end rose up in mid air causing it to sink immediately in about twenty feet of water, leaving us stranded in the middle of the lake. We quickly decided to swim for the dock rather than the bank because of snakes. As we swam for the dock, our progress was hampered many times as we became entangled in the moss and lily pads. I thought to myself how beautiful these water plants seemed only a few hours ago and now as an obstacle to our safety they appeared ugly and sinister. Our clothes were a burden too, which slowed our progress and tired us. It seemed hours since our boat had overturned and I thought we would never reach the dock; however we finally reached it and lay there for a while until we were rested and could breathe normally again, before returning to the lodge.

We were depressed for a while after our return to the lodge, but a shower, a change of clothes and a good night's rest made us feel better.

Returning to our homes the next day, we reflected gravely that we were grateful to be alive; and we were firmly convinced that we would never trust a flat boat again.

Demonstrated here are major weaknesses which occur through failure to manage successfully four stylistic problems crucial to good narration. Other problems may undoubtedly occur in narration, but these are so important and so pervasive that successful narrative writing depends directly on the writer's ability to master them. For the sake of discussion, we may term these (1) the problem of particularity, (2) the problem of chronology, (3) the problem of suspense, and (4) the problem of viewpoint.

THE PROBLEM OF PARTICULARITY

One of the recurring themes in this book has been the necessity of establishing fully and precisely what one means, or what one wishes to present. Chapters Two, Three, Six, and Eight especially deal with the critical issue of making words express experience and of making words evoke experience. This is likewise a problem of narration: the writer cannot deal in ideas and ghosts, he must present *men* doing things. He cannot summarize their actions, coldly rehearsing each event in its inevitable place in a deadly sequence; he must *dramatize* events, making the reader focus on individual character and specific action in a specific place. Unlike description, which typically presents impressions indirectly as they are filtered through the consciousness of the writer, narration at its best gives the reader impressions of the events *directly*. To achieve this effect successfully, the writer is obliged to re-create reality faithfully, selecting those details of appearance, action, and conversation that give the events their peculiar quality.

The student essay quoted above fails to achieve any of these effects, fails to satisfy any of these requirements. Consider some of the weaknesses. Since we never know anything about the writer's companion except his name, it is difficult to visualize him floundering in a lake in the dark of night, struggling for a shore that seems hours away. Such a predicament should reveal a great deal of a man's character, but this does not happen here. In paragraph six we are told that the two boys are eager for fishing, that they hurry to the shore, that they discover some boats, and that they board one of them carefully. We do not, however, *see* their eagerness or their hurry. We do not experience the discovery, and we cannot watch as they board the boat. We are not given enough details of movement, appearance, and speech to be able to witness these things *as they happen*, yet, given such details, one can see eagerness and hurry and other things. In the following paragraph we learn of the boat's capsizing, at which time we learn that the two "quickly decided to swim for the dock," their progress being hampered by moss and lily pads. This is not narration. In the dark of the night, entangled in moss and lily pads, still clothed, and minus a boat, even the most rational and calm among us do a bit of threshing, perhaps even yelling a bit, and possibly feeling a moment's panic. This is what we want in the narrated action—the things that happened as they happened in all their immediacy.

One of the things lacking here, in other words, is the sense of particularity. We cannot be too concerned about this sequence of events because the author has not made it urgent and real for us. How did that moss feel wrapped about the leg? What were the thoughts of water snakes that ran through the mind? How did they swim? What was that sudden shock like when the boat went under? It is as if the author had given a summary of a play when what we wanted was to see the living drama.

THE PROBLEM OF CHRONOLOGY

Narration is usually identifiable by chronological organization of some kind. It is, however, easy to be misled by what seems to be the easiest of all schemes of organization. Simple chronology will rarely lead to effective narration. In this, as in other forms of writing, the writer has the opportunity to create order out of the chaos we usually live. A good part of all our lives is spent doing things that do not matter very much in the long run—items in the daily routine, things we do without thinking. Another good part of our lives we spend doing nothing at all. While at times it may be the author's purpose to dramatize such activities in his narrative, the narrative writer is most often concerned with those moments that reveal character, with those crucial actions that show men and women as they are. Thus in narrative writing, as in other kinds, the writer has among the first of his duties the selection of those revelatory moments that do have meaning. He cannot, of course, simply ignore all other moments, not even those humdrum moments when we wait around to be real. What he can do is to pace his writing so that he dwells emphatically on moments of interest and crisis and so that he minimizes the others, subordinating them, or using them for transitional purposes. Consider once again the student essay quoted above.

The sequence of events in this essay is as follows:

Paragraph 1—two friends go to hunting and fishing lodge
Paragraph 2—no action; description
Paragraph 3—approaching a town, they turn on a side road;
      they see billboards
Paragraph 4—they reach a fence and apparently go up a driveway to the lodge
Paragraph 5—no action; description
Paragraph 6—they hurry to the shore
      they discover two boats
      they board one of them
      they glide out into the lake
Paragraph 7—they drop anchor and fish
      they prepare to return
      one can't start motor
      the other offers to help and boat sinks
      they decide to swim for the dock
      their progress is hampered
      one thinks of the change in the scenery
      clothes become burdensome
      time passes and one despairs of reaching dock
      they reach dock and rest
Paragraph 8—they are depressed
      they feel better with a shower
Paragraph 9—they feel grateful, but distrust flat boats

All of the events in this sequence appear in independent constructions. Not appearing here are important items which the author relegated to subordinate elements: being stranded in the middle of the lake, being concerned about snakes, and being slowed and tired by wet clothes. Forgetting these important omissions, consider the sequence in its main elements.

Six paragraphs and eight steps in the action pass before we get even close to the crucial events surrounding the dark swim. As a result, the reader has no sense at all of the urgency or of the mental and spiritual turmoil the author apparently wanted to present in his account of how what had been a pleasant scene suddenly became sinister and ugly. The problem is that we are taken calmly through so many stages in the action that when the crucial events occur, they appear to be merely further steps in a tiresome sequence of events about which it is unnecessary for us to bother since the author himself hasn't presented any real dismay or alarm. The author of this essay obviously should have gotten us to the dark swim more quickly by minimizing many of the early steps in the sequence of actions.

THE PROBLEM OF SUSPENSE

Closely related to the problem of chronology is the corollary matter of maintaining suspense. The establishment and maintenance of suspense is of critical importance in narration for at least two good reasons. First, since the narrative writer is engaged in dramatically re-creating reality to show people in action, he is obliged to accept *all* of reality as his province. And we all know that we do not know certainly what will happen at six o'clock tonight—this is one of the essential truths about life, that it is unpredictable. Thus, though the writer knows perfectly well what is to become of his characters, he usually finds it best to withhold this information from his readers in order to help create the illusion of reality. The writer of the student essay quoted above has served this purpose reasonably well. We do not know and cannot know at any point early in the narration what will happen later.

But we do not really care what happens later in the essay. And the principal reason why we do not care is that the author has not considered another reason for maintaining suspense, a stylistic or artistic reason. Because most of us enjoy suspense, our interest in an essay will usually continue if the author deliberately withholds information or whets our fancy in some other way. In the student essay under discussion we do not know what is to happen, but we do not care especially because the author has not in any way prepared us for what is to come. The dunking and the difficult swim are so far removed from the first events he tells of that by the time we get to these important incidents at the end of the essay we have lost interest. Our interest is further diminished because the tone of the essay is too even, there being no appreciable difference between the account of fishing and the account of sinking in the dark water.

One method authors have traditionally found useful for maintaining reader interest through suspense is called *foreshadowing*. The narrator is always in one of two basic situations in regard to his reader, both of which require suspense for best effects. In much narrative writing the readers do not know what is to happen; here some natural suspense is apparent. In some narrative writing—that, for example, which records well-known events—the readers already know what is to happen later. In both cases the technique of foreshadowing is useful. In the first situation, illustrated in the student essay, the author may relieve some of the tedium of simple chronology and attract the interest of his readers by foreshadowing, or presaging, later events—not revealing them fully, but forecasting just enough of them to let the reader know that there *is* an end to this narration, that there is purpose in this sequence of events. In the second situation, where the readers already know the outcome of the action the author is narrating, this technique may be used to divert the readers' attention from the known ending, to keep his attention on the immediate action with hints of the consequences to enliven and give meaning to the early stages in the action.

THE PROBLEM OF POINT OF VIEW

One last major problem the narrative writer faces is the question of how he stands in relation to the actions he is recording. The writer's point of view is important to all kinds of writing, helping to determine both the manner and the effect of his presentation (see the discussion of point of view in Chapter Eight, "Description"). Point of view is especially important in narrative writing because it largely controls the immediacy, the liveliness of the actions that are being presented. Since the writer wants to narrate actions dramatically as if they were happening, he must choose the point of view that is appropriate to his subject, that will allow him to present his subject most fully and in most vivid detail, and that will allow him to create a sense of immediacy and urgency.

Three points of view have, used in the right situations, proved uniformly successful. The first is often called the *omniscient-author* point of view. Utilizing this method, the author removes himself from the actions he is narrating; from his detached position he can see and know all that has happened in the sequence of events he is interested in. Most historical narrative and most biographical narrative are presented from this point of view, the actions being already over and the author necessarily removed from them in space and often in time. The writer of historical narrative, though he may not know certainly everything that has happened in his province, undertakes to discover as nearly as possible the complete truth through research, reading, and other means of inquiry. Narrative presented from this point of view is traditionally in third person, past tense.

In an effort to achieve greater immediacy and intenser dramatic effect, many authors prefer to avoid the omniscient-author technique. This method almost inevitably reminds the reader that the events being related are past, and also, usually, that the author is no longer involved in them. To avoid the more common and traditional point of view, then, some authors prefer where possible to present their narrative as if seen and told by a participant and eyewitness. This technique obviously cannot be used very satisfactorily with much historical narrative, where, by the very nature of the subject, we are interested in the pastness of the events, not their immediacy. Nor can this method be used often in biographical narrative, the biographer not always being an intimate acquaintance of his subject. However, the method is patently appropriate to auto-biographical narrative, where the author is free if he wishes to present significant moments of his life in the first person, utilizing present tense where feasible to create the illusion of actions currently occurring.

On some occasions, neither of these methods seems fitting. At times the author may feel that he cannot in justice presume to omniscience in historical matters or in biographical affairs. At times, the author may feel that first-person management of autobiographical narrative is inadequate since we seldom appear to others as we do to ourselves. In both instances, a third alternative is possible, although its use is closely restricted. Authors at such times as these sometimes use a multiple, shifting point of view, viewing the action first from one vantage point, then from another. In historical and biographical narrative, for example, letters, diaries, journals, interviews, and other sources of information occasionally will permit an author to assume the viewpoint of different persons involved in the action he is narrating. Similar resources, as well as conversations and other personal communications, may occasionally permit the author to assume points of view other than his own even in autobiographical narrative.

Whatever the point of view he chooses to employ, the author is bound to observe some precautions (see "Some Problems in Coherence and Point of View," Chapter Eight). First, he is obligated, once he has adopted a point of view, not to violate that viewpoint by revealing in his narrative facts, feelings, or nuances that would not be available to him from that point of view. Second, he is obligated not to shift his viewpoint, *unless* he carefully prepares his reader for the shift and justifies the shift by the needs of the narrative.

Difficulty with the point of view is another problem revealed in the student essay given above. In one sense at least the point of view here is right. Neither the omniscient-author method nor the multiple viewpoint would be useful here, primarily because we are concerned with the actions and reactions of the central figure. The use of the first-person participant point of view is appropriate, then, but there remain some qualifications. The action here is too clearly past. From the first sentence onward the author tells us much too obviously that this action is over and done with. As a consequence, we once again are prevented from experiencing the suspense that should be a cardinal attraction of narrative writing. There is patently no reason for us to be alarmed.

SUMMARY

We have seen that the student essay fails because the scenes and actions are not presented in their solidity, because the pacing is wrong, because the element of suspense is totally lacking, and because the point of view does not permit any sense of urgency or immediacy. Re-written with these problems in mind, the essay comes off somewhat better:

> Don and I had hurried down to the shore as soon as we got unpacked and partially settled. The small dock of buckling grey boards, some flopping loose as we stepped on them, groaned and squeaked as we passed. We found two ten-foot aluminum flat boats tied up. They were mounted with small trolling motors covered with a thin film of grease and smelling of gasoline. They looked useful and safe enough. We eased carefully into one of them and glided out into the lake. A small frog, frightened by our appearance, hopped his way from lily pad to lily pad. Shadows from the tall pine trees were creeping their way across the surface of the water, falling in black-green stripes across the green water mottled with reflections. Lilies, green moss hanging eerily downward, and thick patches of lotus lined our way for a short distance through the life-crowded water until we reached the deeper middle.
>
> When we were about in the center of the lake, we dropped our small lead anchor and began to fish. Drowsing in the late afternoon quiet, I held my line out and idled. The countryside around the lake was alien to me, unlike the sun-baked flat and sandy terrain I knew better. It flourished with large stands of pine and other native trees. The rolling hills were covered with

grass and wild flowers. We had arrived at the lodge by a country road through waist-high grass and thick cornfields and along a driveway curving by the lake past the cattail and pine-clump fringe of the lake.

We had fished for several hours without luck. Darkness came fast, the last light that sometimes lingers cut off here by the thick growth around the lake. And there was no moon. When we were both ready, Don turned to the motor. It wouldn't start.

I moved to the back of the boat to help him. Almost with my movement the front end of the boat reared bluntly into mid air and the boat sank immediately, falling away before me even as I tried to move toward Don. We were left, alone in the darkness at the middle of the lake.

I tore to the surface, ripping at the water with my arms in unreasoning urgency. Don was nowhere to be seen. Then as my breathing quietened and my own flailing diminished I heard him somewhere near, blowing and threshing. In the darkness I could think of nothing but the darkness of the plant-strewn, teeming water along the shore, and so I set out for the dock, hoping to miss as much as I could. Don swam alongside me. The alien scene oppressed me as I swam, the crawling, moving sensation I had of the water destroyed the impression of beauty I had had only hours before. Plants and lilies and moss were no longer colors and images in the darkness. They were things, curling and brushing and sometimes clinging to my legs, ugly and sinister movements in the water, holding me back, even as my clothes drug at my legs and arms.

In the dark strange water we lost sense of time, tiring and tiring more. At last a shape of darkness loomed over us. We had reached the dock. For a long time we lay there, resting, trying to find normal breath. Constant in my mind were dire thoughts on flat boats.

The essay is still no work of art, but some improvements have been made. In the first place, the author has now moved his starting point nearer to the crucial moment of the capsizing. Description of the scene is somewhat better realized, as in the description of the dock and the water in the first paragraph. The sentence "They looked useful and safe enough" serves to establish at least a moment's unrest and suspense, as we realize that safety *was* a consideration and that the safety *may* be a matter of appearance only. The "moss hanging eerily downward" and the "life-crowded water" near the end of the first paragraph intimate uneasiness and prepare for the concern that appears manifested later. The flashback description in the second paragraph gets the background and setting out of the way more quickly than in the first version and without letting the description interrupt the movement. The new emphasis in this description on the strangeness of the countryside helps to establish the narrator's sense of danger later, as does the darkness stressed in the third paragraph. The two short simple sentences at the end of the third paragraph help to set a tone of urgency by their brevity. Rearranging his work in this way, the author has all of the fourth, fifth, and sixth paragraphs for the critical moments in the water. These moments are given more nearly their proper emphasis by the new attention to description of the things in the water and of the narrator's actions in the water.

Forms for Narration

We have seen briefly how particularity, pacing, suspense, and point of view largely control the effect of narration. These are problems the successful management of which is vital to all kinds of narrative writing. Whether he is writing about John Pelham's death on the Rapidan in the Civil War, about a moment when he himself reached a kind of maturity, or about the events constituting the Dred Scott case, the narrative writer will want to present people in all their solidity doing interesting and believable things; he will want to pace his telling so that we may get to the dramatic moments quickly; he will want to maintain our interest by continuing suspense; and he will want to unify and dramatize the telling by an appropriate point of view.

Some other characteristics of narrative form may be briefly suggested. Because timing, suspense, point of view, and some of the other features of narrative to be mentioned below are pervasive, informing the entire narrative work, point by point illustration is neither feasible nor desirable. The student should for this reason take special notice of the readings listed at the end of the chapter, all illustrative of the principles of narrative form.

STANDARDS COMMON TO ALL NARRATION

The problems discussed above are not peculiar to any special forms of narration, but are common to all forms. Closely related are some further necessities of narration:

1. The narrative writer is free of time. He may alter its progressions, however, in order to achieve his desired effect, making events apparently isolated reveal their actual connections by moving them closer together, separating events superficially related so that their incoherence will be demonstrated, piling all of time into a moment so that the influence of the past may be graphically demonstrated. Narrative writers have often found useful two ways of manipulating time for effect: they sometimes simply rearrange chronology to get at urgent events faster and more connectedly. This method, however, is of only very limited use in factual narration. The second method commonly used is the *flashback*, a deliberate movement backward in time. If at a crucial moment in the narration events out of the past have direct bearing on present actions, if they influence or clarify these actions, then the writer is free to summon them up. But whether his chronology is continuous or broken by flashbacks, whether he writes biography, autobiography, or history, *the narrative writer needs always to devote his attention to moments of revelation, when persons and actions show up clearly for what they are.* A man's character and the significance of his actions emerge in the process of his day's work, to be sure, but they present a sharper image at a moment of crisis when *all* the character and significance that have been established over the years are suddenly called directly into play.

2. To get to these moments of revelation, the writer must

choose his beginning place well so as not to lose his reader through unnecessary exposition and description. *He will want usually to start near the moment of revelation he seeks to narrate, using either highly connotative description or the flashback to reveal necessary background for the action or actions.* If, for example, one wishes to narrate how they brought good news of battle from Aix to Ghent, it is not necessary to relate the events of the battle itself. The bearing of the news is the pertinent sequence of events, though of course the author may through description suggest the urgency of the battle or through flashback reveal important moments in the battle that make the bearing of the news significant.

POSSIBLE PLANS FOR NARRATION

Particularity and point of view are not so much parts of the *plan* for narrative writing as they are aspects of the author's vision and understanding. Since timing and suspense are, however, subject to planning, some traditionally useful methods of organization may be suggested.

1. Two arrangements have often been found effective for getting the author quickly to his narrative moments. The first is a pure chronological method in which the author first establishes background and antecedent actions, then proceeds to the subject actions. This plan is most often used in historical narrative, the very nature of which stresses continuity. The second plan calls for the author to start directly into his narration, pausing at appropriate moments of temporary calm or other respite from action to gather in flashback the necessary background for the actions at hand. These plans may be varied in many ways:

antecedent actions-description-narration
antecedent actions-narration-description-narration
description-antecedent actions-narration
description-narration-antecedent actions-narration

2. Typical plans for establishing and maintaining suspense may also be suggested. One method is illustrated in the re-

vised student essay presented above. This plan involves the use of foreshadowing, which by descriptive effects and by nuances of mood and tone prepares the reader for reversals and developments in the fortunes of the people in the narrative. The narrative writer may also make use of all our delusions in order to maintain suspense. He may allow us to feel that all is well with his characters, only to reveal that events have an unfortunate outcome; this method is also used to some extent in the revised student essay. Or he may lead us to believe that all goes poorly in his narrative with dire consequences threatening, only to discover a fortunate ending. For example, a narrative about a student who because of shyness withdraws from the society of his fellows might well adumbrate the most wretched kind of solitary life for the student, attracting our sympathy in this way so that we are all the more pleased when, contrary to our expectations, he finds in his isolation a great love and a great knowledge.

Assignments

1. Examine and criticize the following theme in the light of suggestions in this chapter.

BEARLY MISSED

It was a cool, cloudy Friday morning in April. The calm of the early morning was gratifying to my friend, Frank, and me, as we started on our long awaited fishing trip.

We woke up early that morning and could hardly wait to start plugging away at the large mouth blacks we knew were hiding in the cove at Nigger's Bluff.

We loaded up Frank's poor excuse for an automobile and were just about to drive off when I heard the ever-familiar echo of my dog's barking. Telling Frank that I could not leave my dog, Tippy, behind, I opened the door and with one happy bound he jumped in and we were on our way at last.

Our happy trio arrived at Nigger's Bluff at six o'clock, and we were soon nestled in the broad shoals of the cove. The water was still, shimmering bright, like a fresh glass of champagne, and not a sound could be heard for miles around. Frank was the first to throw his line into the water. He arched it high and gracefully. It slid into the clear water with a dull "thunk." He started reeling in his line ever so carefully and cautiously, as if he were about to put the finishing touches on a great hand-painted masterpiece. Every part of our bodies was tensed, ready for the action of the first strike. But to our surprise, nothing happened. That run of bad luck continued throughout the morning and into the early afternoon.

I suggested we return to the car, pack some food, and take a hike through the peaceful countryside. Frank was against that idea, as he knew that this was bear country. I assured him that no harm would come to either of us. Frank consented, after much deliberation, and we started on our way through the calm countryside.

After hiking several miles Frank and I came upon some tracks we thought to be those of a large wildcat. We set Tippy on the trail of this animal and he raced ahead with great delight. When he got about two hundred yards from us, he stopped and let out a number of high-pitched yelps. Frank and I ran to see what he had caught and were surprised to see what it was. We saw that the tracks were really those of a bear cub. We caught the cub after a few minutes of quick maneuvering.

Just then we heard a sound of rustling leaves and snapping twigs. I saw the hair on Tippy's back rise as if someone had just placed him on a hot electrical wire. Frank and I wheeled around and our glance was quickly met by that of an enraged female grizzly. I was sure I saw a small flame of hate flickering in her bloodshot eyes as she rushed for us. Cold pangs of fear, like thousands of sharp pins, ran through my body, as I watched the bear bowl Frank over with one hasty slap of her big paw. A dull, sickening sensation crept over me as I had no idea what to do.

Tippy was suddenly a ball of fury as he jumped between the frenzied bear and Frank. Shaking off the nauseating fear that had gripped me, I utilized all of my power and put Frank on my shoulder. I carried him to the safety of a close rock forma-tion, and watched the battle still raging between the dog and the bear. Tippy was darting back and forth, nipping at the bear's nose, but still managing to keep out of her reach. The bear gave one desperate lunge, but Tippy dodged and raced quickly away. The bear, sensing no more trouble, gathered the cub to her side and disappeared into the woods.

Frank was coming to and was obviously in pain as thick, red blood was spurting from a gaping wound in his arm. I helped him back to the car, where my heroic dog was waiting for us. Putting them both in the car, I headed directly for the nearest hospital. The doctor told me that Frank was a very lucky boy not to have lost his arm.

Frank was discharged from the hospital in two weeks and I went to visit him at his home. He told me that he would go fishing with me again, but if I ever got the idea to go hiking again, it would be by myself.

2. Prepare a detailed chronology of your own life. From this list select moments, actions, or series of actions which might be appropriate for narration, explain how the account of these things might be made suspenseful, and indicate the appropriate point of view for each narrative.

3. Subject to further instructions from your professor, write an autobiographical essay, a biographical essay, and a historical essay.

Readings

Daniel Defoe, *Robinson Crusoe* and *A Journal of the Plague Year* (Modern Library).

James Boswell, *Life of Samuel Johnson* (Modern Library).

Benjamin Franklin, *Autobiography and Selections from His Writings* (Modern Library).

John Aubrey, *Brief Lives* (Ann Arbor, 1957).

Thomas Carlyle, *The French Revolution* (New York, 1859).

Bruce Catton, *A Stillness at Appomattox* (New York, 1953).

James Anthony Froude, "The Execution of Mary Queen of Scots," from *The History of England from the Fall of Wolsey to the Defeat of the Spanish Armada* (New York, 1906).

Francis Parkman, *The Oregon Trail* (Modern Library).

John Dos Passos, the "Camera Eye" sections of *U. S. A.* (Modern Library).

James Thurber, "University Days," *My Life and Hard Times* (New York, 1933).

Chapter Ten

❋ THE RESEARCH PAPER

In essence, the research paper describes an investigation and publishes the findings of that investigation. Ideally, the investigation, in whatever area of human activity—theology, philosophy, mathematics, science, art, law, social relationships, various kinds of history, linguistics, economics, military tactics —aims at discovery, at increasing knowledge. But the investigation may as well, and as profitably, have as its purpose the ordering, the consolidation, of present knowledge in a particular field. In any case, and in any field of interest to man, the methods of research are the same: After acquiring a general knowledge, the researcher narrows his scope, concentrates upon perhaps only a single aspect of his field. He does so through conscious or unconscious choice, under direction possibly from a superior or by "feel." If he has a fortunate sensitivity to a certain kind of problem—most intelligent men are endowed with this sixth sense, whether they realize it or not—he may "vibrate" to its presence, and make an extraordinary discovery where others have passed a thousand times without experiencing the slightest spark of intellectual electricity.

These striking discoveries are of course rarities, but nothing can be achieved by way of discovery or consolidation unless the researcher knows his field. Hence it must be deliberately restricted; man's exploration of the universe of facts and ideas has been in recent years pushed so rapidly on all frontiers that any effective piece of research is necessarily highly specialized.

Once the researcher's findings are "in," he publishes the results in a paper of suitable length (and it is a good idea for even the college freshman writing his first term paper to imagine that he is doing so for publication). This paper employs, as required, all the techniques that the student has mastered after diligent and repeated practice in exposition, argumentation, description, and narration. The nature of the research paper dictates, however, mastery of one additional technique—*documentation*. It is easily acquired, for it is purely mechanical as to form and almost completely conventional in content. To document a paper is simply to supply the reader with information as to sources, (a) *unless a source is perfectly obvious,* for example, a dictionary, and (b) *unless it is likely to be a matter of common cultural experience,* like the source for a familiar Biblical quotation or a Shakespearean apothegm, or the author of $E = MC^2$.

The first term paper with which the freshman hopes to demonstrate his competence in all these techniques may be in one of four or five disciplines, among them history, a foreign language, English, a physical science (the formalized laboratory report is a special kind of research paper). In a great many colleges and universities—perhaps a majority—a standard part of the freshman English course is a research paper. Usually it is designed in such a way that the student can carry over to other courses what he has learned about the research paper in English, even though the subject matter of the paper is restricted to topics connected with literature and literary history. This is a valid approach to the term paper problem, for if the English instructor were required to supervise research papers in areas outside his specialty, he would find it difficult to exercise control over content. He would probably find himself teaching footnotes instead of writing.

Hence this chapter deals exclusively with the problems of research and composition in English and American literature and literary history. The usual freshman course in English will have sufficient readings in the literatures of both England and the United States: a smattering of poetry, a group of short stories, one or two plays, a novel. The instructor may permit the student to choose his research paper subject from among these types, concentrating perhaps upon one or more works by a particular author, or comparing works of a kind by two authors. The possibilities here are infinite, since there are a great many literary figures well worth studying and writing about.

Another approach, and one that finds increasing favor among students and faculty alike, is the "controlled" research paper that uses as its source materials a famous work of literature— *Walden, The Scarlet Letter, Huckleberry Finn*, for example— and an accompanying volume of critical articles of various kinds, and by a number of authors, designed by the editor of the volume to provoke a flow of ideas in the student and to provide ample material for classroom discussion of the work, upon which every member of the class writes a paper. The instructor who adopts this approach finds that it has advantages: (a) it fosters coherent and concentrated classroom work; (b) if he restricts his students to the use of these sources alone, he can with little difficulty check the accuracy of quotation and documentation in their papers; (c) students will not be competing for books and periodicals in the library, which if comparatively small can be quickly drained of its resources; (d) students will become acquainted with kinds of sources whose existence they may not have suspected; (e) plagiarism will be markedly reduced.

It has serious disadvantages, however: (a) the student may be forced to write a paper on a subject in which he has little interest; (b) the class risks being committed, unwittingly, to a biased or limited viewpoint (of the editor of the "control" volume); (c) a search for pertinent books and essays will be discouraged; (d) the student will not properly learn what the resources of the library are. Not much can be done about the first two of these difficulties, but the instructor can remedy the others by requiring the use of secondary source materials supplementing those in the control volume.

Finding Source Materials

A PRELIMINARY NOTE ON LIBRARY RESOURCES

Among the resources of a college library are books (including theses and dissertations, if the college or university has a graduate school), periodicals, newspapers, pamphlets, government documents, and manuscripts. If the library has an "open stack" system, the student in most cases can, once he has learned the location of what he wishes to read, find and remove from the shelf the desired material. A "closed stack" system requires the student to submit a written request for the material at one of probably several loan desks. Under either system he needs to determine whether the library has a particular item on its shelves.

1. *Books.* Rare books, theses, and dissertations in the library may be catalogued and shelved in special ways, which can be explained by the reference librarian. All other books are indexed in the library's card catalog. That is, for most books the card catalog has a card filed under the author's name (the main entry), a card filed under the title, and a card (perhaps several) filed under the subject or subjects treated by the book. The illustration on p. 290 shows three cards for the same book.

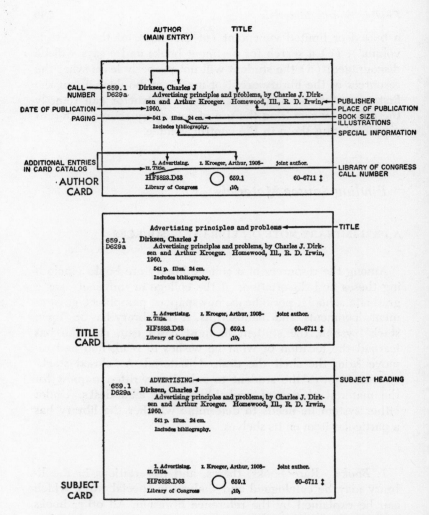

There is also a card in the catalog filed under "Kroeger, Arthur," so that the student who has heard about a book by Kroeger can find it without difficulty. It is worth noting that the number in the lower left-hand corner of the card is the Library of Congress call number; whenever possible, college libraries purchase catalog cards (already printed and ready for the card catalog, except for library call numbers and typed headings) directly from the Library of Congress.

The student need not expect the classification system upon which the call number is based to be in universal usage. Certain private libraries, like the Folger Shakespeare Memorial Library in Washington, D.C., have special classification systems suited to their special needs. The system originated by the Library of Congress—the greatest of all libraries—has been adopted by a number of other libraries, but the chances are good that the student will find his own college library employing the Dewey Decimal Classification system, under which the call number consists usually of two lines. The first line states the classification number (dealing with books on the same subject); the second line states the book number (arranging a book within a subject group). These are the subjects covered by the Dewey system:

000-099	General Works
100-199	Philosophy, Aesthetics
200-299	Religion
300-399	Social Sciences, Sociology
400-499	Philology (Languages)
500-599	Pure Science
600-699	Applied Science
700-799	Fine Arts, Recreation
800-899	Literature
900-999	History, Geography

In order to find items in the card catalog intelligently, the student will keep these further "peculiarities" in mind:

a. Catalog cards are *never* alphabetized by a beginning article (*a, an, the,* or a foreign equivalent). Hence, if the first word of a title is an article, the card will be filed under the second word.

b. In most libraries catalog cards are filed *word by word,* not letter by letter. Note the difference between the two systems.

Word by Word	*Letter by Letter*
New Jersey	Newark
New Series	New Jersey
Newark	New Series
Newton	Newton

c. Abbreviations (*St.—Saint; Mrs.—Mistress; Dr.—Doctor*) are filed as if they were spelled out.

d. Surnames beginning with *Mc, Mac,* and *M'* are filed together as if they all began *Mac.*

e. Catalog cards for books *by* an author are filed before cards for books *about* him.

f. A subject heading is as specific as a catalog librarian can make it (hence, the searcher should, if he is investigating pugilism, look for material under *pugilism* or *boxing* rather than *athletics*).

EXERCISES:

1. An essay describing other peculiarities of catalog cards.

2. An essay comparing and contrasting the Dewey and the Library of Congress classification systems, with some attempt to reach a conclusion as to which is preferable.

If a book is *not* indexed in the library's card catalog, then it is not in the library (this statement holds true for reference books—dictionaries, encyclopedias, indexes, bibliographies, yearbooks, directories, atlases, handbooks—as well as for books designed for reading from cover to cover). There is no library that has a copy of every book ever printed, but a book that has been printed can usually be found somewhere. To help find books that are not locally available, certain large libraries —the Library of Congress and the University of Texas library, for example—maintain *union card catalogs*. Such a catalog has file cards from other libraries, and it is understood that a local library can under certain circumstances borrow books from libraries elsewhere.

Still another kind of library book catalog is often available to the student—the printed and bound catalog of a particular library. Such catalogs are the *Library of Congress Catalog of Printed Cards*, the *Library of Congress National Union Catalog*, and the British Museum's *General Catalogue of Printed Books*. Since the printed volumes cannot themselves be enlarged, these catalogs are periodically expanded with printed supplements. The Library of Congress, for example, publishes quarterly accession lists represented by its printed cards.

A final source of book information that the student needs to know about is the cumulative book index. Here the standard work is the *United States Catalog*, the first edition of which listed books in print to 1912. Successive editions carried on this work to 1933. The first supplement, *The Cumulative Book Index*, published in 1938, indexed books for the period 1933-1937, and *The Cumulative Book Index* is now published twice a year.

EXERCISE:

If the library has available to students either the *Library of Congress Catalog of Printed Cards* or *The Cumulative Book Index*, a listing of at least ten books from either or both of these sources that are *not* indexed in the library card catalog.

2. *Periodicals.* Very few libraries index periodicals in the card catalog for books. A library may choose not to index its periodical holdings, but it is customary for a file of some sort to be maintained—a separate card catalog or perhaps a vertical display file located at the periodicals loan desk. In either case, this information is furnished: (a) the name of the periodical, and (b) a list of the published volumes (with dates), *a check mark by the number of each volume in the library.*

Ordinarily this file is not where the student will begin his search for periodical materials. Armed with a subject, he will consult one of several available periodicals indexes for information on recent or not-so-recent magazine articles dealing with the subject:

Poole's Index to Periodical Literature, 6 volumes covering the period 1800–1906. A valuable tool is Marion V. Bell and

Jean C. Bacon, *Poole's Index, Date and Volume Key* (Chicago, 1957).

19th Century Readers' Guide to Periodical Literature, 1890–1899, 2 volumes in 4 parts.

Readers' Guide to Periodical Literature (begins with 1900, is now published quarterly).

The International Index to Periodicals (2 volumes of this for 1907–1919 are entitled *Supplement to Readers' Guide*), now published quarterly and dealing with the humanities and social sciences.

Usually these works index a magazine article under both author and subject headings. The student will wish to consult the preliminary pages of the index volume, which explain the indexing system and furnish a list of the periodicals indexed (a librarian, by the way, has probably checked the titles locally available).

The student may discover that his library does not subscribe to a periodical that he needs to consult. In this case he will have recourse to the *Union List of Serials* (or one of its various supplements, among them *New Serial Titles,* published monthly), which will tell him from what library the required title can be obtained. A librarian will then arrange either to borrow the volume of the periodical from a nearby library, or to have the material photostated—the student bearing the cost in either case.

3. *Newspapers.* Most college libraries subscribe to several daily newspapers. It is customary to keep current issues on racks in a reading room. Back issues may be available only on microfilm, or not at all. If back issues are kept, the student will wish to become acquainted with *The New York Times Index* (begun in 1913 and now published twice a month), a useful source for historical information in *The New York Times* and other good newspapers as well.

4. *Pamphlets, government documents,* and *manuscripts.* If they are cataloged, these library materials are handled in special ways. The student will consult the reference librarian—

often an encyclopedia of important information—as to their availability and use.

Once the instructor has decided whether he wishes to use a control volume, the student is ready to settle, at least tentatively, upon a subject. This subject is ultimately determined by the student's own ideas about the writer (or writers) he has been studying. The works of this writer—his poems, plays, stories, novels, diaries, letters, autobiography, canceled checks, and other various personal documents—are called *primary sources*. These are all-important to the researcher; it is not too much to say that the best kind of research paper depends *only* upon primary sources.

Books and articles written *about* this writer by other authors are called *secondary sources*. Here the term *secondary* is especially significant: the researcher must produce a paper which places *secondary* reliance upon such sources. A research paper whose materials are taken mostly from secondary sources is more often than not worthless. The ideas in the paper need not be particularly original, but they certainly should be developed from a beginning analysis of primary sources.

Generally speaking, the researcher can locate primary sources in his library by consulting the card catalog. Secondary sources, however, are so numerous and of such variety, because of the proliferation of periodicals since the eighteenth century, that the card catalog (which lists books and perhaps a few articles) is only a starting place. That is, the researcher's responsibility is to make reasonably sure that he knows what has been written on his subject and whether he should refer to it in his own paper. He will be tempted, because of their apparent convenience and completeness, to look up secondary sources in the library's inviting stock of general periodicals indexes. These guides must be used with caution in view of their lack of selectivity and tendency to emphasize ephemeral publications. The researcher may be forced to resort to these indexes, in the absence of satisfactory subject bibliographies. But fortunately bibliography as a scientific tool of research has progressed tremendously in recent years. In no discipline has the advance been greater than in literary bibliography. The researcher will possibly discover that his writer, if important enough, is the subject of one or more book-length bibliographies covering both primary and secondary sources. He will learn, too, that there are valuable bibliographies of periods and of literary types—drama, poetry, and fiction, for example. He must also consult cumulative and annual literary bibliographies, which are issued both in books and as parts of well-known scholarly periodicals. These are basic (and once again the student is invited to expand the list):

A. *The Guide to Literary Study.*

> Richard D. Altick and Andrew Wright, *Selective Bibliography for the Study of English and American Literature.* New York, 1960. This invaluable work should be in every student's personal library, whether or not he plans to pursue literary studies.

B. *The General Bibliography of Literature: English*

> *The Cambridge Bibliography of English Literature,* 4 vols. Cambridge, 1941. *Supplement* (vol. 5), Cambridge, 1957.
> *The Concise Cambridge Bibliography of English Literature.* Cambridge, 1958. Every student of literature should own this inexpensive book.

C. *The General Bibliography of Literature: American*

> Robert E. Spiller, et al., *Literary History of the United States,* vol. 3. New York, 1948. *Supplement,* New York, 1959.
> Jacob Blanck, *Bibliography of American Literature.* New Haven, 1955–. Vols. 1–3 (Henry Adams—Bret Harte) have appeared at this writing. Indispensable.
> Floyd Stovall, *Eight American Authors.* New York, 1956.
> Lewis Leary, *Articles on American Literature, 1900–1950.* Durham, 1954.
> Clarence Gohdes, *Bibliographical Guide to the Study of the Literature of the U. S. A.* Durham, 1959.

D. *The Serial Bibliography of Literature: General*

Modern Humanities Research Association, *Bibliography of English Language and Literature*. Annual since 1920.

"Annual Bibliography," *PMLA: Publications of the Modern Language Association of America*. Annual (April issue) since 1922. International in scope since 1957. Indispensable.

English Association, *The Year's Work in English Studies*. Annual since 1921.

E. *The Serial Bibliography of Literature: English*

"Literature of the Renaissance," *Studies in Philology*. Annual (April issue) since 1917. [In April and May, 1961.]

"Shakespeare: An Annotated Bibliography," *Shakespeare Quarterly*. Annual (Spring issue) since 1950.

"English Literature, 1660–1800," *Philological Quarterly*. Annual (April issue through 1948; July thereafter) since 1926.

"The Romantic Movement: A Selective and Critical Bibliography," *English Literary History*. Annual, 1937–49. Thereafter in *Philological Quarterly*. Annual (April issue) since 1950.

"Current Bibliography," *Keats-Shelley Journal*. Annual since 1952.

"Victorian Bibliography," *Modern Philology*. Annual (May issue), 1933–57. Thereafter in *Victorian Studies*.

"Current Bibliography," *Twentieth-Century Literature*. Quarterly since 1955.

F. *The Serial Bibliography of Literature: American*

"Articles on American Literature Appearing in Current Periodicals," *American Literature*. Quarterly since 1929, except for the first two volumes (annual).

"Articles in American Studies," *American Quarterly*. Annual (Summer issue) since 1955.

EXERCISES:

1. A short essay on the location of basic reference works in the library.

2. The compilation of a list of the most useful reference works in the library (general and specialized), with a short statement for each work as to its contents and their arrangement.

3. A search for each of the bibliographies listed above. A brief statement as to how the contents of each of these bibliographies are arranged.

4. A search for bibliographical materials in literary periodicals not listed above.

5. A search for and listing of nonliterary subject bibliographies. Brief statements as to the nature and arrangement of their contents.

Using Source Materials: Compiling the Bibliography

Having decided upon a subject and become familiar enough with his primary sources to have worked out a bibliography of these sources and a preliminary plan for the research paper, the student begins to examine secondary sources, listing those that are pertinent to his inquiry and making notes as to how he intends to use these sources. This list of secondary sources is called a working bibliography. Its compilation, calling for meticulous care on the researcher's part, requires the use of 3″ x 5″ or—better—5″ x 8″ file cards, one card for each book and each article whose use is contemplated. The file card (written on one side only) will have this information:

1. The heading SECONDARY SOURCE (cards for primary sources are so labeled)
2. Library call number (if the source is a book)
3. A bibliographical entry in *final form*
4. A note on contents and how they can be used

The bibliographical entry on the card, since it is in final form, will be reflected in the bibliography which comes at the end of the research paper. These are its essentials:

(a) *For the book*

1. Author's name (last name first, since the bibliography, generally speaking, is alphabetized by author), followed by a period

2. Title of book, followed by a period
3. City of publication, followed by a comma
4. Year of publication, followed by a period

NOTES: These four essentials *must* be accounted for in the bibliography. Others to be included, as necessary, are (a) *name of editor,* (b) *edition,* (c) *title of series,* (d) *number of volumes.* There is one additional problem, the citation of a work which the researcher has not himself seen, but which he wishes to quote or paraphrase from another work which in turn quotes or paraphrases it.

The *long form* bibliographical entry, now obsolescent, also includes the name of the publisher. If this is used, it comes after the city of publication (*now followed by a colon*) and is followed by a comma.

For the typed paper (and this convention should be observed as well on the file card) the second and all succeeding lines of the entry begin beneath the *third character* of the first line, *which itself begins on the margin.*

SAMPLES

1. *All-inclusive form*

```
Smirk, Julian P.  My Life, ed. Walter Norm.  5 vols.
   3rd ed.  (Vols. III-VII, "The Smirks of ·Texas.")
   New York, 1949.
```

2. *General form*

```
Smirk, Julian P.  My Life.  New York, 1949.

Further, Wells J., and Fenwick Reed Basking.  Our
   Wives.  New York, 1949.  [If a periodical article
   has more than one author, the same procedure is
   to be followed.]
```

3. *Edited book*

```
Livid, Horace M.  Nebraska Boyhood, ed. Walter Norm.
   New York, 1952.

Patent, Willis R., ed.  A Congress of Poems.  New
   York, 1950.
```

4. *An edition*

> Apsey, Willard Robert. Cowpunching in Idaho. 2nd
>   ed. New York, 1951.
>
> Fitz-Bascom, Charles. A Look Back at New England,
>   ed. Fenwick Basking. 3rd ed. New York, 1953.

5. *One of a series with a general title*

> Plodder, Earnest. Mark Twain Country Byways.
>   "Western Cattle States," Vol. III. New York, 1949.

6. *A book in several volumes*

> Chortle, Warren L. The Indiana Outlook. 4 vols.
>   New York, 1962.
>
> Jaeger, Talbot Jones. The Ohio Answer. Vol. III of
>   The Snyder Papers. New York, 1963.

7. *The citation of a book from another book* (the same procedure to be followed for articles)

> Kenning, Beowulf. The Sordid Muddlebys. New York,
>   1940. Quoted from Julian P. Smirk, My Life. New
>   York, 1949. [Here, since there is no need to in-
>   vert the author's name for the purpose of alpha-
>   betizing, it is followed by a comma.]

NOTES:

1. For the typed bibliography, titles of books and names of periodicals or newspapers *may or may not be underlined* (indicating printed italics), as the author wishes; his practice must be consistent, however. Capitalized are the first letter of the first word, and of nouns, pronouns, adjectives (but *not* articles), adverbs, and verbs.

2. The foregoing samples deal with most of the bibliographical problems that are likely to arise. They by no means exhaust the subject. Numerous additional samples (for both bibliography and footnote form) may be consulted in William Riley Parker, comp., *The MLA Style Sheet,* rev. ed. (New York, 1951); and Kate L. Turabian, *A Manual for Writers of Term Papers, Theses, and Dissertations,* rev. ed. (Chicago, 1955). Both of these inexpensive paperbacks should be in the student's personal library.

(b) *For the periodical or newspaper*

1. Author's name (last name first), followed by a period

2. Title of article or story, in quotation marks, followed by a comma (*the comma precedes the second quotation mark*)

3. Name of periodical or newspaper, followed by a comma

4. Volume (or number) of the periodical or newspaper (*no punctuation follows*)

5. Date of volume or number, enclosed in parentheses (*a comma immediately follows the second parenthesis*)

6. *Inclusive* page numbers of the article or story, followed by a period (*notice, in the samples that follow, that if the volume number is furnished, there is no abbreviation for the word "page(s)" before the page number or numbers*)

SAMPLES

1. *General form*

Wilt, Arthur L. "A Sketch of My Existence," Atlantic Digest Annual, XXI (1957), 333–347. [It is assumed that this periodical is published but once a year.]

Wordsworth, Deanna. "Reluctantly West," Oregon Biographical Quarterly, XXIII (1958), 401–408. [This publication comes out four times a year, but the pages are numbered consecutively through- out the four issues.]

2. *Special forms*

Snyder, K. Elmore. "Round about the Mississippi," South Dakota Recollections, LXIII (Spring, 1959), 23–45. [This publication comes out several times a year, its pages being renum- bered in each issue.]

Widdle, G. P. "A Sketch from the Nineties," Vir- ginia Confederate Memories, No. 1 (Autumn, 1960), pp. 48–106.

Widdle, G. P. "A Sketch from the Nineties," Vir- ginia Confederate Memories, LX (1960), no. 3, pp. 105–107.

Muddleby, Frank R. "The Kenning Descendants," Colorado Intelligencer, Jan. 3, 1963, p. 17. [A newspaper article.]

"The Furbish Papers," <u>Old</u> <u>Times</u> <u>in</u> <u>Arizona</u>, Jan.
5. 1963, pp. 21–23. [A magazine article, anony-
mous.]

(c) *For the reference work*

"The Catamount," <u>The</u> <u>World</u> <u>Book</u> <u>Encyclopedia</u>, III,
1275.

"Cattle," <u>Encyclopaedia</u> <u>Britannica</u> (1955 ed.), V,
46–51. [If the reference work is a single
volume, the abbreviation for <u>page(s)</u> must be
used.]

(d) *For the unpublished work*

Odlum, Keithly. "Artistic Self-Deceit in the
Small Towns of America." Unpublished MS, undated, in the archives of the Kingsville, Missouri, Historical Association.

Wibb, Benjamin. "The Influence of the Plodder
Family upon Kingsville, Missouri, after 1900."
Unpublished typescript, 1955, owned by Keithly
Odlum.

David, Melinda Catherine. "The Plodders and
Fence-cutting." Unpublished Master's thesis,
Department of History, University of Texas, 1959.

(e) *For the interview*

Wagg, Ormond. Personal conversation, Feb. 3, 1960.

Muddleby, Frank R. Tape recorded analysis of some
Wagg family records, Mar. 21, 1961.

—————. Interview, Mar. 22, 1961, based on the
taped analysis of Mar. 21. [The use of the solid
line, eight spaces long, to indicate that the
source is that of the previous entry is optional.
Either way, consistency is mandatory.]

Using Source Materials: Note Taking

The working bibliography, alphabetized, becomes a final
bibliography when the researcher has discarded (or set aside
for future reference) the file cards for sources that he does
not care to use in the actual process of composing the research
paper. *Hence the final bibliography is a classified and alphabetized record only of the specific sources referred to in the*

course of the paper. Sources of additional interest in regard to the topic under consideration need not be mentioned, unless the writer feels impelled to list them in a special section appended to the bibliography. Since he is not likely to have assembled an exhaustive list of such references, he should resist the temptation to show that he has consulted more than he has referred to.

As soon as he has decided to use a source, whether he plans to quote, paraphrase, or merely refer to it, he should copy the quotation or make careful notes and write down the final footnote, just as he has done for the bibliography. For this purpose he may use another set of file cards—large ones, it is hoped—or sheets of note paper. The footnote supplies much the same information that the bibliography entry has, and it similarly begins with a capital letter and ends with a period. There are five differences between them, however: (a) *the footnote does not invert the author's name;* (b) *by and large the footnote does not employ periods as internal punctuation;* (c) *the footnote encloses publication data in parentheses;* (d) *the footnote cites specific page numbers in giving credit;* (e) *the first line of the footnote is indented as a paragraph is, the second line returning to the margin.* There follow, in the same order, sample footnotes for the bibliographical entries cited above.

Book, all-inclusive form

> Julian P. Smirk, My Life, ed. Walter Norm (5 vols.; 3rd ed.; "The Smirks of Texas"; New York, 1949), III, 23. [The third item inclosed in parentheses designates the title of the series of which the volume is a part.]

Book, general form

> Julian P. Smirk, My Life (New York, 1949), pp. 21-22.

Book, more than one author

> Wells J. Further and Fenwick Reed Basking, Our Wives (New York, 1949), p. 27. [The same procedure is to be followed for periodical articles having more than one author.]

Book, edited

Horace M. Livid, Nebraska Boyhood, ed. Walter Norm (New York, 1952), pp. 27–28.

Willis R. Patent, ed., A Congress of Poems (New York, 1950), pp. 101, 103. [The cited material is not on consecutive pages.]

Book, edition

Willard Robert Apsey, Cowpunching in Idaho, 2nd ed. (New York, 1951), p. 301.

Charles Fitz-Bascom, A Look Back at New England, ed. Fenwick Basking (3rd ed.; New York, 1953), pp. 301–302.

Book, one of a series with a general title

Earnest Plodder, Mark Twain Country Byways (Vol. III, "Western Cattle States"; New York, 1949), p. 1.

Book, one of several volumes

Warren L. Chortle, The Indiana Outlook (New York, 1962), IV, 333–334. [As with the article form, the abbreviation for page(s) is not used with a volume number.]

Talbot Jones Jaeger, The Ohio Answer (Vol. III, The Snyder Papers; New York, 1963), pp. 23–25.

Book, cited from another book

Beowulf Kenning, The Sordid Muddlebys (New York, 1940), p. 67, quoted from Julian P. Smirk, My Life (New York, 1949), p. 21. [The same procedure is to be followed for articles.]

Article, general form

Arthur L. Wilt, "A Sketch of My Existence," Atlantic Digest Annual, XXI (1957), 333–334. [The title of this periodical indicates that it is published but once a year. It may be published more often, but at any rate the form of the footnote indicates that the pagination throughout the year is consecutive, as it is with most periodicals of a non-popular nature.]

Deanna Wordsworth, "Reluctantly West," Oregon Biographical Quarterly, XXIII (1958), 401. [This pub-

lication comes out four times a year, the pages being
numbered consecutively throughout the four issues.]

Article, special forms

    K. Elmore Snyder, "Round about the Mississippi,"
<u>South</u> <u>Dakota</u> <u>Recollections</u>, LXIII (Spring, 1959), 45.
[This periodical comes out several times a year, its
pages being renumbered in each issue. As appropriate,
a month may be used instead of a season.]

    G. P. Widdle, "A Sketch from the Nineties,"
<u>Virginia</u> <u>Confederate</u> <u>Memories</u>, No. 1 (Autumn, 1960),
pp. 105–106. [Volume numbers are not assigned to
yearly accumulations of this periodical. Note that the
abbreviation for <u>page(s)</u> must be used.]

    G. P. Widdle, "A Sketch from the Nineties,"
<u>Virginia</u> <u>Confederate</u> <u>Memories</u>, LX (1960), no. 3, p.
105.

    Frank R. Muddleby, "The Kenning Descendants,"
<u>Colorado</u> <u>Intelligencer</u>, Jan. 3, 1963, p. 17. [A news-
paper article, for which the day of the week (preceding
the day of the month, and followed by a comma) may also
be supplied if desired. This is also the form for an
article or story in a magazine published more than once
a month, whether or not a volume number is available.]

    "The Furbish Papers," <u>Old</u> <u>Times</u> <u>in</u> <u>Arizona</u>, Jan.
5, 1963, p. 21. [An anonymous article in a magazine or
newspaper.]

Reference work

    "The Catamount," <u>The</u> <u>World</u> <u>Book</u> <u>Encyclopedia</u>,
III, 1275.

    "Cattle," <u>Encyclopaedia</u> <u>Britannica</u> (1955 ed.), V,
46. [If the reference work is a single volume, the
abbreviation for <u>page(s)</u> must be used.]

Unpublished work

    Keithly Odlum, "Artistic Self-Deceit in the Small
Towns of America," unpublished MS, undated, in the
archives of the Kingsville, Missouri, Historical Association, pp. 3–4. [Assigning page numbers to manuscripts, which often do not employ such numbers, is
something of a problem; it is complicated a bit in
regard to manuscript leaves with writing on both sides.
These "rules" may be applied with confidence: (1) Although they are not numbered, the recto (facing) and

verso (reverse) sides of a manuscript leaf may be
designated as pages by the researcher for his own convenience. In the footnote these numbers are enclosed
in brackets to indicate that the numbers are not on the
manuscript. (2) A manuscript leaf with writing on the
recto side only should be designated "folio," and in
the footnote its number (bracketed if not on the leaf
itself) should be preceded by the abbreviation for
folio(s). (3) If the manuscript has leaves some of
which have writing on both sides and others of which
do not, the researcher should use the designation
"leaf" before the number (again bracketed if not on the
leaf itself), which is followed by the abbreviation
for recto or verso.]

Benjamin Wibb, "The Influence of the Plodder
Family upon Kingsville, Missouri, after 1900," unpublished typescript, 1955, owned by Keithly Odlum, pp.
23-27. [As a rule typescripts use the recto of a sheet
only; brackets may be required if the pages have no
numbers, however.]

Melinda Catherine David, "The Plodders and Fence-
cutting," unpublished Master's thesis, Department of
History, University of Texas, 1959, p. 36.

Interview

Ormond Wagg, personal conversation, Feb. 3, 1960.

Frank R. Muddleby, tape recorded analysis of some
Wagg family records, Mar. 21, 1961.

Frank R. Muddleby, interview, Mar. 22, 1961,
based upon a tape recorded analysis, Mar. 21, 1961, of
some Wagg family records.

Standard abbreviations for bibliography and footnotes. The
foregoing sample forms for footnotes and bibliography have
standard abbreviations wherever possible, to save space. These
strictures govern the use of abbreviations:

1. Once an abbreviation is employed, it must be employed, in
similar situations, throughout the research paper.

2. The bibliography entry for a work cited in a footnote uses
all abbreviations found in the footnote, except for abbreviated titles
of periodicals.

3. Abbreviations are not proper in the *text* of the research paper.

4. If the researcher invents an abbreviation, as for a work to which he often refers, he must justify the invention in the first footnote which has the shortened form.

5. The names of most literary periodicals have standard abbreviations (see, for example, the lists in the *MLA Style Sheet* and in *PMLA's* April bibliography), which certainly should be utilized in footnotes. They are not proper in the bibliography, however.

6. A number of standard abbreviations are of foreign origin. Since they *are* standard, they have been sufficiently Anglicized—and Americanized—and need not be underscored to indicate italics. Examples: passim, viz., e.g., and all those listed below.

7. One hitherto, or until recently, accepted abbreviation is obsolescent and will be avoided: *op. cit.*, "in the work cited." A second or succeeding footnote citation of a work already cited fully will use the author's last name (or full name if other writers cited have the same last name) and a page reference: Smirk, p. 321.

A list of abbreviations, with meanings, follows. Spacing should be observed with care.

1st, 2nd, 3rd, 4th, 5th, 6th, 7th, 8th, 9th (etc.)

A.D. (Precedes numerals.)

B.C. (Follows numerals.)

anon. anonymous

art., arts. article(s)

b. born

bibliog. bibliography, -er, -ical

biog. biography, -er, -ical

ca. about (Used before approximate dates.)

cf. compare (Never use when *see* is meant.)

ch., chs. chapter(s)

col., cols. column(s)

comp. compiled, -er

d. died

diss. dissertation

ed., edd. editor(s), edition(s), edited by

ed. cit. edition cited

e.g. for example (Preceded and followed by commas.)

enl. enlarged

esp. especially

et al. and others

etc. and so forth

ex., exx. example(s)

fac. facsimile

fasc. fascicle (Division of a book published in parts.)

fig., figs. figure(s)

fl. flourished, reached greatest development or influence

fol., foll. folio(s)

front. frontispiece

hist. history, -ical, -ian

ibid.   in the single title cited in the note immediately preceding

i.e.   that is (Preceded and followed by commas.)

illus.   illustrated, -or, -ion(s)

introd.   introduction, introduction by

lang., langs.   language(s)

MS, MSS   manuscript(s) (Spell MS. with a period when referring to a specific manuscript.)

n., nn.   note(s), footnote(s)

N.B.   take notice, mark well

n.d.   no date

n.n.   no name

no., nos.   number(s)

n.p.   no place of publication

N.S.   new series, new style

O.S.   old series, original series, old style

p., pp.   page(s) (Do not begin a footnote with this abbreviation. Omit if volume number precedes.)

par., pars.   paragraph(s)

pl., pls.   plate(s)

pref.   preface

pseud.   pseudonym

pub., pubs.   published (by), publication(s)

q.v.   which see

reg.   registered

resp.   respectively

rev.   review, -ed (by), revised (by), revision

sc.   scene

scil.   namely, to wit

viz.   namely, to wit

sec., secs.   section(s)

ser.   series

sic   thus, so (Between square brackets as an editorial interpolation. Not an exclamation.)

sig., sigg.   signature(s)

st.   stanza

St., SS.   Saint(s) (feminine Ste.)

s.v.   under the word or heading

tr.   translator, -ion, -ed (by)

v.   see

v., vv.   verse(s)

vol., vols.   volume(s) (Omit "Vol." and "p." when these items are supplied.)

v.s.   against

Composing the Research Paper

THE FIRST DRAFT

When the researcher settles down to write, he does so with the knowledge that his investigation is finished. He has consulted all sources, primary and secondary; he has a thesis and a fairly firm working outline that, it is hoped, accounts for every paragraph in the projected paper. And he has something to say, it is again hoped, within the framework of the advice offered in the section on The Organization of the Literary Essay at the end of Chapter Five.

How he works his ideas into sentences and paragraphs and a coherent whole now depends partly on the "system" advocated by this book and partly—as of course it has from the start—on the writer's personality and eccentricities. They may dictate that he write an initial draft in pencil on large sheets of lined paper, or that he produce a typed first version. In either case, the observance of a few well-tested rules of procedure will simplify the process considerably.

1. He should leave plenty of room between the lines, and wide margins, for revision and correction.

2. He should write on one side of a sheet.

3. Remembering that his own ideas are of primary importance, he should severely limit the length of quotations and paraphrases.

4. As he uses these materials, he should compose *complete* footnotes, *numbered consecutively,* on pages separate from those for his text.

    a. Footnotes are numbered consecutively, in Arabic numerals, throughout the paper.

    b. At the instructor's discretion, they will (in the final typed version) appear beneath the textual matter to which they refer or all together on separate sheets at the end of the paper. The latter system is preferable.

    c. The first footnote reference must be complete, like the samples above.

    d. Second and succeeding references to the same work will be as brief as possible, but not ambiguously so. (1) If only one work by a writer is cited, succeeding references to that work will give the last name of the writer and the page number(s). (2) If more than one work by the same writer is cited, *all second and succeeding references must use a title (or short title) with the writer's last name and the page number(s).* (3) An immediately succeeding second reference *may, at the footnoter's discretion,* employ the abbreviation *Ibid.* (which need not be underscored), with the page number(s), as appropriate: Ibid., if not accompanied by page number(s), means "in the same work on the same page(s)."

    e. Footnote and bibliography information for the same work must be consistent in content and physical appearance—especially in regard to abbreviations.

In the following footnotes—presumably for a short paper, *only one work by any one writer is cited* (it is obvious why first names are necessary). The samples appearing earlier in this chapter are mostly used.

  [1] Julian P. Smirk, *My Life* (New York, 1949), pp. 3–4.
  [2] Ibid.
  [3] Ibid., pp. 99–101.
  [4] Beowulf Kenning, *The Sordid Muddlebys* (New York, 1940), p. 101.
  [5] George Smirk, *Gray Days and Gold in California* (San Francisco, 1957), p. 395.
  [6] Kenning, pp. 333–334.
  [7] Frank R. Muddleby, "The Kenning Descendants," *Colorado Intelligencer,* Jan. 3, 1963, p. 17.
  [8] George Smirk, pp. 405–409.
  [9] "The Furbish Papers," *Old Times in Arizona,* Jan. 5, 1963, p. 21.
  [10] Muddleby, p. 17.
  [11] "The Catamount," *The World Book Encyclopedia,* III, 1275.

The following footnotes, apparently taken from a somewhat shorter paper, explain how to handle more than one work by the same author.

  [1] Julian P. Smirk, *My Life* (New York, 1949), p. 46.
  [2] Julian P. Smirk, *My Life,* ed. Juliana Smirk (New York, 1952), pp. 3–5.
  [3] Ibid., p. 9.
  [4] Julian P. Smirk, ed., *A Congress of Poems* (New York, 1950), pp. 101, 103.
  [5] Smirk, *My Life,* p. 203.
  [6] Smirk, *My Life,* ed. Juliana Smirk, p. 293.
  [7] Juliana Smirk, ed., Introduction to Smirk, *My Life,* pp. xx-xxi.

The following footnotes embody more than one work by the same writer and works by writers bearing the same surname.

[1] Julian P. Smirk, *My Life* (New York, 1949), pp. 3–4.

[2] Ibid.

[3] Julian P. Smirk, *My Life*, ed. Juliana Smirk (New York, 1952), p. 349.

[4] Julian P. Smirk, *The Smirk Outlook* (New York, 1962), III, 247.

[5] Julian P. Smirk, *My Life*, ed. Juliana Smirk, p. 1.

[6] George Smirk, "The Influence of the Smirk Family upon Kingsville, Texas, after 1900," unpublished typescript, 1955, owned by George Smirk, Jr., p. 25.

[7] George Smirk, Jr., "The Smirks and Fence-cutting," unpublished Master's thesis, Department of History, University of Texas, 1959, p. 36.

[8] George Smirk, "The Influence of the Smirk Family," p. 27.

[9] Julian P. Smirk, *My Life*, pp. 33–49.

[10] George Smirk, Jr., "The Smirks and Fence-cutting," p. 48.

THE SECOND DRAFT

After a period of soul-searching, correcting, and changing, the researcher is ready to produce a typed copy of his paper that will differ from the final copy, in regard to form, in only one respect: spacing between the lines. *He will triple-space the second draft throughout,* so that there will be plenty of room for further changes. Otherwise the second draft will closely resemble the final draft as to margins, the system of indentation, and other aspects of form. The footnotes, however, will continue to be on separate pages, and they will be compared carefully with the bibliography, which is the last section of the second draft.

Now it is a good idea for the researcher to put his paper aside for a day or two, so that when he returns to it he will see his work in a fresh light; style is a basic consideration, and he should be concerned at this stage of composition with rhetorical matters above all else. There is no good reason why he should resist the impulse to make extensive revisions and to delete parenthetical material ruthlessly. A second draft may therefore look like a pile of scrap paper by the time conscientious editing is accomplished. And it may be necessary to type another "second" draft.

FORM IN THE FINAL DRAFT

The chief problem of the final draft is form, not rhetoric. Since form is a purely mechanical matter—granting both student and instructor have reached an understanding as to what proper form consists of (the student should never hesitate to ask the instructor what he prefers)—perfection of form is an obligation, a kind of absolute consideration. Perfect form, that is, does not enhance the merit of a research paper; but imperfect form damages the paper considerably. These are the basic aspects of form:

1. The arrangement of contents
   a. The cover sheet
   b. The outline
   c. The text
   d. The notes (unless they accompany the text)
   e. The bibliography
2. Title and subtitles
3. Page numbering
4. Margins
5. Indentation
   a. For the cover sheet
   b. For the outline page
   c. For the text
   d. For notes
   e. For bibliography
6. Spacing—vertical and horizontal
   a. For the cover sheet
   b. For the outline

   c. For the text (including set-off prose or poetry quoted)

   d. For the notes

   e. For the bibliography

Before typing the final draft—and he should do the work himself—on good white paper 8½ x 11 inches in size (Turabian recommends twenty pound weight paper with at least 50 per cent rag content), the writer should prepare a checklist of form, the important details of which are summarized below, in accord with the Turabian and MLA manuals. If these manuals disagree on some point, as all such manuals do, the *MLA Style Sheet,* and particularly its Supplement, is adhered to.

1 (a). THE COVER SHEET.

This page has the following information, centered on the page, double-spaced between items:

Title of paper (all capital letters)

Name of author, in normal order

Title of course

Date of submission

1 (b). THE OUTLINE PAGE(S).

At the top of this page is the title of the paper, just as it appears on the cover sheet. Next is the thesis sentence. Then comes the word "Outline" centered on the page (*not* in quotation marks; first letter capitalized). The outline itself follows, the Roman numeral headings beginning at the left-hand margin. (The student is referred to Chapter Five for the form of a complete outline.)

1 (c). THE TEXT.

The title of the paper, as on the cover sheet, is at the top of the first page of text, which itself is double-spaced throughout, except for set-off quotations and subtitles.

1 (d). THE NOTES.

If the notes are not at the bottom of the page to which they refer, they will be on a separate sheet following the text, headed NOTES (all capital letters).

1 (e). THE BIBLIOGRAPHY.

This is the next page(s). Unless the instructor wishes categories (i.e., primary sources, secondary sources, books, articles), all items in the bibliography will be put into a single list, with a precise heading, for example, LIST OF WORKS CONSULTED, LIST OF WORKS CITED, or SELECTED BIBLIOGRAPHY, capitalized throughout.

2. TITLE AND SUBTITLES.

The title of the paper, in capital letters, appears on the cover sheet, on the first page of the outline, and on the first page of text.

Subtitles are seldom used, unless the paper is quite long. When used, subtitle is centered on the page and underscored. Capitalized are the first letter of the first word, and of nouns, pronouns, adjectives (but not articles), adverbs, and verbs.

3. PAGE NUMBERING.

All pages (except for the cover sheet) are numbered in the upper right-hand corner, three-fourths of an inch below the top edge:

    a. the outline page(s) in lower case Roman numerals (i, ii);

    b. the remaining pages (text, notes, bibliography) in Arabic numerals, consecutive to the end.

4. MARGINS.

Leave at least one and one-half inches of margin at the left, so that the binder can be accommodated. Other margins are at least an inch. EXCEPTION: Titles are two inches from the top edge of pages, including notes and bibliography titles.

5. INDENTATION.

a. Cover sheet: all items centered on page.

b. Outline page: title centered; "Outline" centered; "Thesis" and Roman numeral headings begin on margin. (See Chapter Five for outline form in detail.)

c. Text:

(1) Paragraphs are indented eight spaces.

(2) Prose quotations are indented four spaces (and observe the right-hand margin).

(3) Poetry quotations are centered on page.

d. Notes: The first line of a note is indented eight spaces, beginning with the raised Arabic numeral (which is *not* followed by punctuation). The second and succeeding lines of a note return to the original margin. These rules apply whether the notes appear at the bottom of pages to which they refer, or are listed separately.

e. Bibliography: To indicate alphabetizing, the first line of the bibliography item begins at the margin. The second and succeeding lines begin beneath the third character of the first line.

6. SPACING.

a. Cover sheet: double-space between items.

b. Outline page(s):

(1) After title, triple-space.

(2) Double-space thesis sentence.

(3) Triple-space after thesis.

(4) Triple-space after "Outline."

(5) Double-space the outline throughout.

c. Text:

(1) Triple-space after title (before and after subtitles).

(2) Double-space all text (including quotations which are "run-on" in the text, in quotation marks).

(3) For prose quotations which are set off (more than two lines *and* at least two sentences), single-space within the quotation; triple-space before and after the quotation.

(4) For poetry quotations which are set off (two lines or more), single-space within the quotation; triple-space before and after the quotation. (See also page 371, paragraph 3.)

d. Notes:

(1) If footnotes are to be at bottom of pages, triple-space between the last line of text and the first line of footnotes.

(2) Do *not* type a separating line between text and footnotes.

(3) Single-space within footnotes.

(4) Double-space between footnotes.

(5) The last line of footnotes on a page must be above the normal bottom margin.

(6) If the notes are on a separate page(s), triple-space after the title; thereafter follow rules 3, 4, and 5.

e. Bibliography:

(1) Triple-space after title.

(2) Single-space within items.

(3) Double-space between items.

The Sample Research Paper

A student-composed research paper is reproduced here, in final form after the student's corrections and revisions had been accomplished following conferences with his instructor. The essay was written in the second semester of the freshman year, in a class using a "control" volume of critical essays along with Mark Twain's *Huckleberry Finn*.

The writer was a student in his middle twenties, a Korean War veteran whose high school education had not been completed and whose ability in composition upon entering college was quite poor. As the paper demonstrates, he rapidly developed. His essay uses footnotes at the bottom of pages to which they refer. He chose *not* to underscore book titles in the bibliography.

The essay is especially noteworthy for its solid reliance upon transition devices, and for (a) *emphasis upon primary use of primary sources,* (b) *emphasis upon primary use of primary sources,* (c) *emphasis upon primary use of primary sources.*

SOME ASPECTS OF JIM'S SPEECH

IN <u>HUCKLEBERRY</u> <u>FINN</u>

Carl D. Lane

English 311b. 75

April 20, 1959

i

SOME ASPECTS OF JIM'S SPEECH
IN <u>HUCKLEBERRY FINN</u>

Thesis: Although Mark Twain was not as thorough in representing Jim's dialect as he said he was, his reproduction of the way Jim probably talked is basically accurate and consistent. (11)

Outline

Introduction: I decided to see for myself whether Twain's use of dialect forms in <u>Huckleberry Finn</u>, as he explains it, is satisfactorily accurate and consistent. (1)

I. An examination of successive passages in which Jim appears shows that Twain was, fairly often, guilty of oversights in representing Jim's speech. (2-4)

II. But an examination of other passages shows that Twain was remarkably consistent in representing Jim's speech, even after a hiatus of several years in writing the novel. (5-8)

III. And he was particularly good at stressing certain syllables when, logically, they ought to be stressed. (9-10)

Thesis (11)

1

SOME ASPECTS OF JIM'S SPEECH

IN <u>HUCKLEBERRY</u> <u>FINN</u>

Explaining his representation of the six or
seven country dialects in <u>The</u> <u>Adventures</u> <u>of</u>
<u>Huckleberry</u> <u>Finn</u>, Mark Twain says: "The shadings
have not been done in hap-hazard fashion, or by
guess-work; but pains-takingly. . . ."[1] Upon first
reading the novel, I did not particularly notice
these shadings. But after studying Jim's speech
as exemplifying what Twain calls "Missouri negro
dialect," I concluded that about one-third of the
words are variously spelled, as many as three different ways in a single conversation. How "painstaking" Twain really was seemed to me still an
open question despite some evidence as to his
attention to detail in notes which he made while
writing the book,[2] and despite an apparently gen-

---

[1] Mark Twain, <u>Adventures</u> <u>of</u> <u>Huckleberry</u> <u>Finn</u>,
ed. Henry Nash Smith (Boston, 1958), leaf 32v.
Hereafter citations from <u>Huckleberry</u> <u>Finn</u> will be
indicated by page numbers, in parentheses, in my
text.

[2] This evidence is on page two of the "Group
B" notes ("Let Jim say putty for 'pretty' and
nuvver for 'never'") and on pages two, six, eight,
and thirteen of the "Group C" notes ("Huck says
Nuther," for example). See Bernard De Voto, <u>Mark</u>
<u>Twain</u> <u>at</u> <u>Work</u> (Cambridge, 1942), chapter 2.

eral agreement as to Twain's close attention to
dialectal matters, unstressed syllables being
dropped with some consistency in words like 'bove,
'way, b'long, b'lieve, and k'leck (but not in
business and powerful, probably a Twain oversight).[3] What I should like to do here, then, is
to examine different spellings and different
stresses of certain words to see whether Twain
intended them so, that the words would have more
meaning and sound as nearly as Jim would have
sounded if he himself could have put them in
writing.

There seems to be an evident oversight on
Twain's part in the first important conversation
in which Jim figures, when he is telling Huck's
fortune. Jim says: "What he's a-gwyne to do,"
and "but every time you's gwyne to git well agin."
(underscore mine) I can find no inflection to
warrant the difference in spelling, since both
forms are preceded by an 's and followed by to.
Again, Jim uses de most of the time as in the
same conversation: "De bes' way is to res' easy en

[3] James Tidwell, Mark Twain's Representation
of Negro Speech, Vol. XVII of American Speech, ed.
William Cabell Greet (New York, 1942), p. 174.
This paper will not undertake to develop the possibility that a number of apparent oversights on
Twain's part can be accounted for by his knowledge of variations within dialect forms.

let de old man take his own way." However, in
another sentence in the same paragraph Jim employs another corruption of the: "en 'tother one
is black." (p. 17) The seems to be more effective
this way, or it has rhythm—if you could call it
that. Similarly, I find is attached to another
word as 's in unstressed positions: "Dey's two
gals flyin' 'bout you in yo' life," "Dat's good,"
(p. 17) and "What you want to know when good
luck's a-comin' for?" (p. 37)

    The next important conversation of Jim's
comes when he first sees Huck on Jackson's Island.
Jim thinks Huck is a ghost and says: "doan' hurt
me—don't." (p. 36) Here Twain begins to use
don't only in stressed positions, and henceforth
unstressed doan'. There are other cases involving
pronunciation of final t in stressed syllables:
"but mind you said you wouldn't tell," (p. 38)
instead of wouldn' tell, and in the same sentence
mind instead of mine. Didn't is used instead of
didn' on a few occasions, for example, "en I said
if I didn't git it I'd start a bank myself." (p.
40) In the same conversation Jim tells Huck: "I
'uz powerful sorry you's killed." Powerful instead of pow'ful seems to be another oversight,
unless stress continues to be a deciding factor.

    In the next episode is an example of his

4

using <u>and</u> in four different ways. <u>En</u>, the customary form, is ordinarily unstressed: "Ef you's
got hairy arms en a hairy bres'." (p. 40) "De cow
up'n died on my hans'." (p. 40) <u>An'</u> is used in
stressed positions in sentences: "Mighty few—an'
dey ain' no use to a body." (p. 40) Hence, <u>and</u>
used by Jim is evidently a lapse on Twain's part.
In the same conversation Jim uses the word <u>busi-
ness</u>, which drops the unstressed syllable in
American speech generally. Also in the same sentence there is a difference in the spelling of
<u>because</u>, which has been spelled several times as
<u>kase</u>, for example, "kase it's down in de bills dat
you's gwyne to get hung." (p. 17) When Twain
spells <u>because</u> as <u>bekase</u>, it is stressed in that
particular instance. In this conversation Jim
uses <u>don't</u> in the stressed form again.

During the course of Jim and Huck's argument
over King Solomon and Frenchmen, when Jim uses
words like <u>more</u>, <u>door</u>, <u>poor</u>, and <u>boarding-house</u>,
he consistently drops the <u>r's</u>: "A harem's a bo'd'n-
house," "Dey's plenty mo'," and "Po' little chap."
(p. 67) And Twain has consistently changed words
that have <u>oi</u> in them to <u>i's</u>, for instance, <u>biler-
factry</u> in "en den he could shet down de biler-
factry," and in the same conversation, <u>pints</u> in
"Doan' talk to me 'bout yo' pints." (p. 67)

5

The next time we meet Jim, he is very much excited about finding Huck still alive. Jim says: "Hain't you been gone away?" (p. 72) instead of ain' or ain't that he would normally use. Two examples of these two spellings from the same passage are: "en you ain' dead," the unstressed form, and "ain't it so," the stressed pronunciation. In the same place Twain is again guilty of an oversight in failing to drop the unstressed syllable in away. Furthermore, in the same episode Jim correctly says island more than once. (p. 72) On the other hand, Jim is using many new words that he has not used thus far in the book: whah, in "whah is I"; drownded, in "you ain' drownded"; reck'n, in "I reck'n I did dream it"; fren's, in "puts dirt on de head er dey fren's en makes em ashamed." (p. 73) Here Twain is evidently making the words read as they would sound had Jim been speaking them, and spelling words correctly in order not to obscure meaning.

In the next "Jim" episode Twain has returned to composing Adventures of Huckleberry Finn after a hiatus of several years.[4] We could expect a corresponding lapse in Jim's dialect, but the unstressed syllables of words like fas' for fast, las' for last, lan' for land, and 'fraid for afraid

[4] De Voto, p. 38.

are consistently dropped. (p. 95) But at this
point a new problem arises; Twain spells _of_ in
four different ways. _Er_, the most frequent spelling, is unstressed as in "one er dem." (p. 95)
_O_ is an extremely short form which appears in two
types of expressions: "stacks o money" and "O'
course." (p. 95) _Ur_ is an unstressed _of_ before a
vowel: "She don't b'long to none ur em." (p. 95)
_Of_ is a stressed form, occurring in "to see what
wuz gwyne to come of it." Twain has spelled _of_ in
one other way, which will be discussed in a
moment.

    When we next see Jim, he and Huck are dis-
cussing the way kings "carry on." Jim uses the
stressed _don't_ twice: "Don't it s'prise you de way
dem kings carries on, Huck," and "Why don't it,
Huck?" (p. 129) This is certainly in keeping with
the consistency of Jim's dialect in stressed pronunciation. In the same passage Jim says: "I doan'
hanker for no mo' un um, Huck"—this is at least
the second time that Twain uses _un_ for _of_ when it
is not stressed (the first is on p. 72).

    Shortly thereafter Jim is telling Huck how
he has mistreated his daughter. Jim uses _uz_ and
wuz for _was_: "din I went into de yuther room en uz
gone 'bout ten minutes," (p. 131) obviously unstressed. Again, "What makes me feel so bad dis

time, uz bekase I hear sumpn over yonder on de
bank." (p. 132)　And here are several good examples
of the stressed form <u>wuz</u> being used, right alongside the unstressed form: "but looky here Huck,
who wuz it dat uz killed in dat shanty, ef it
warn't you?" (p. 37)　"But dey wuz people
a-stirrin' yet," (p. 38) and "My, but I wuz mad."
(p. 131)

　　　　In the last important dialogue in which Jim
figures, he is protesting to Tom that he does not
want any spiders or rattlesnakes in the hut with
him.　There are very few dialectal words I have not
already discussed.　<u>Rattlesnakes</u>, <u>goodness</u>, and
<u>gracious</u> (p. 218) are all spelled correctly, I
think to help the reader recognize them.　Earlier,
I said that Twain had probably overlooked the word
<u>powerful</u> spelled correctly (p. 40).　In this con-
versation he properly leaves the unstressed syllable out: "I lay he'd wait a pow'ful long time
'fo' I ast him." (p. 218)

　　　　We can readily see that Mark Twain was not
as thorough in representing Jim's dialect as he
said he was.　A number of inconsistencies which he
could easily have remedied have been pointed out.
Furthermore, many words that are spelled in the
"dictionary" way are not words that would be hard
to write in dialect form; instead, they seem to be

owing more to poor proof reading than to not knowing how to write them. However, I do not think
Twain was basically inconsistent in reproducing
Jim's dialect, just negligent and, at times, possibly ignorant of the history of certain word
forms, for example, pint for point, which is now
considered illiterate but was good English in the
eighteenth century: the Negroes got it from their
masters, who had adopted it from their forefathers
in England, and did not alter their own usage when
pint fell into disrepute among the white gentry.

9

LIST OF WORKS CITED

De Voto, Bernard. Mark Twain at Work. Cambridge, 1942.

Tidwell, James. Mark Twain's Representation of Negro Speech. Vol. XVII of American Speech, ed. William Cabell Greet. New York, 1942.

Twain, Mark. Adventures of Huckleberry Finn, ed. Henry Nash Smith. Boston, [1958].

Assignments

1. An examination of several issues of a learned periodical, and a written analysis of the contents of these issues.

2. The formulation of several possible subjects for research papers (the latitude of choice depending upon whether the instructor decides to use a "control" volume).

3. The compilation of working bibliographies for two of these subjects—the form of each item to be final.

4. The composition of a short (500 words) research paper, accenting proper form.

5. The composition of a full-length (1500–2500 words) research paper, possibly an extended version of the shorter paper.

6. An expository essay on library facilities in a particular subject area, with specific recommendations for improvement of these facilities (based on a study of one or more bibliographies in the subject area and, possibly, on library shortcomings revealed in the process of research for the long paper).

Reference Readings

(If the instructor does not wish to assign many or all of these to the class as a whole, he may ask for individual oral reports.)

Chapter Five of this book

William Riley Parker, comp., *The MLA Style Sheet*, rev. ed. (New York, 1951).

Kate L. Turabian, *A Manual for Writers of Term Papers, Theses, and Dissertations*, rev. ed. (Chicago, 1955).

Blanche McCrum and Helen Jones, *Bibliographical Procedures & Style*, a Manual for Bibliographers in the Library of Congress (Washington, D.C., 1954).

Richard D. Altick and Andrew Wright, *Selective Bibliography for the Study of English and American Literature* (New York, 1960) (see, especially, "Some Books Every Student of Literature Should Read," pp. 109–110, and "A Glossary of Useful Terms," pp. 111–124).

Richard Altick, *The Scholar Adventurers* (New York, 1950) (Introduction).

Jacques Barzun, *The House of Intellect* (New York, 1959) (Chapter 9).

Douglas Bush, "Scholars, Critics, and Readers," *Virginia Quarterly Review*, XXII (1946), 242–250.

Howard M. Jones, *One Great Society* . . . (New York, 1959) (Chapters 6, 7, 11).

Howard M. Jones, "The Social Responsibility of Scholarship," *PMLA*, LXIV (1949), Supplement, pt. 2, pp. 37–44.

Austin Warren, "The Scholar and the Critics," *University of Toronto Quarterly*, VI (1937), 267–277.

Austin Warren, *Literary Scholarship, Its Aims and Methods* (Chapel Hill, 1941) (Chapter 3).

"The Aims, Methods, and Materials of Research in the Modern Languages and Literatures," *PMLA*, LXVII (1952), no. 6, pp. 3–37.

Merle Curti, ed., *American Scholarship in the Twentieth Century* (Cambridge, Mass., 1953) (Chapters 1, 4).

Jacques Barzun and Henry Graff, *The Modern Researcher* (New York, 1957) (Parts 2, 3).

R. B. McKerrow, "Form and Matter in the Publication of Research," *PMLA*, LXV (1950), no. 3, pp. 3–8.

Henry M. Silver, "Putting It on Paper," *PMLA*, LXV (1950), no. 3, pp. 9–20.

Chauncey Sanders, *An Introduction to Research in English Literary History* (New York, 1952) (Part 3, Chapters 4, 5, 6, 7; Part 4).

THE HANDBOOK-GLOSSARY

INTRODUCTION

This is a concise, two-part manual of word and sentence usage designed to supplement the desk dictionary. Part One is a descriptive analysis of sentence elements and their relationships. In Part Two both handbook and glossary materials are combined and alphabetized, with the correction key, to facilitate their use. Wherever possible, the student will be referred to appropriate parts of chapters in *A College Rhetoric,* and cross-referencing is often resorted to. But except where undue repetition would otherwise result, each item in Part Two is intended to be self-contained, so that corrections and revisions in student essays can be accomplished without much searching for the principle that applies. The writer will do well, however, to look carefully through the Handbook-Glossary before attempting to revise his first paper.

Remedial exercises have been dispensed with (although there are numerous illustrations), on the theory that the student will usually be able to correct his mistake when it is pointed out to him.

The instructor in making his comments will probably wish to use the symbol *Gl* for matters of usage listed alphabetically in the glossary but not covered by the correction key. And he may wish to add his own list of verbal nightmares to what is here.

Part One

�֍ SENTENCE ELEMENTS AND THEIR RELATIONSHIPS

The structure of the English—or the American English —sentence is simple: its meaning and its stylistic effects are achieved mainly through word order, although to establish meaning some words (irregular verbs, certain pronouns) change in form, and others (regular verbs, nouns, adjectives, adverbs) often have special endings. By the time the student reaches college, he is presumed to have mastered the problems connected with sentence structure and meaning. Hence the following descriptive analysis of sentence elements and their relationships is a concise review of necessary knowledge rather than a thoroughgoing grammar. The books listed below are recommended to the writer who wishes to acquaint himself further with the history and complexities of English—the greatest of all means of communication, of contemplative and artistic expression.

Baugh, Albert C. *A History of the English Language.* Rev. ed. New York, 1957.
Curme, George O. *Parts of Speech and Accidence.* Boston, 1935.
Curme, George O. *Syntax.* Boston, 1931.
Fowler, H. W. *A Dictionary of Modern English Usage.* New York, 1944.

Fries, C. C. *American English Grammar*. New York, 1940.

Fries, C. C. *The Structure of English*. New York, 1952.

Jespersen, Otto. *Essentials of English Grammar*. New York, 1933.

Long, Ralph B. *The Sentence and Its Parts*. Chicago, 1961.

Mencken, H. L. *The American Language*. 4th ed. New York, 1936. *Supplement I*, 1945; *Supplement II*, 1948.

I. Primary Sentence Elements: the Parts of Speech

As a glance at any page of a dictionary demonstrates, a great many words serve as more than one part of speech. The following discussion of the parts of speech has as its basis, therefore, the understanding that its function in the particular sentence determines what part of speech a word (or a phrase) is. Further, the eight parts of speech—nouns, pronouns, verbs, adverbs, adjectives, prepositions, conjunctions, interjections—can be grouped according to function: nouns and pronouns are *naming* words, verbs *describe action* or situation, adverbs and adjectives *modify*, prepositions and conjunctions *connect*, and interjections *intensify*, in an independent way.

A. *Nouns*

CLASSES OF NOUNS

A noun denotatively names a person, a place, a thing, an idea, a quality. Nouns are classified in several ways:

    1   2   3   4   5   6
proper or common, concrete or abstract, mass, collective.

1. *Proper nouns* are names of people or particular geographical locations. Certain things, like institutions, are also designated by proper nouns. Proper nouns are distinguished by capital letters.

EXAMPLES: Cy Long, Jr., the President, the Pope, General Maxwell Taylor (persons); the Gulf of Mexico, New York City, Idaho, Mount Everest (geographical locations); the *Queen Mary* (ship); the Maxwell (automobile); Houghton Library, Harvard College, Mercantile National Bank, the Empire State Building (institutions).

2. *Common nouns* are all other kinds of nouns.

3. *Concrete nouns* (embracing the class of proper nouns) name particular things, or kinds of things.

EXAMPLES: boy, ship, leaf, tomato, head of cabbage, desk.

4. *Abstract nouns* name ideas or qualities.

EXAMPLES: boyhood, philosophy, religion, love, justice, crime.

5. *Mass nouns* assign general rather than particular names.

EXAMPLES: ice, water, wheat, tomatoes, furniture, iron.

6. *Collective nouns* name groups of things which may be regarded as single things (but at times they seem to be plural in nature).

EXAMPLES:

trio	group	army
company	audience	crowd
womankind	herd	class
dozen	orchestra	team
mob	jury	faculty

FORMS OF NOUNS

A noun may be a single word (*stick*), a compound word (*yardstick*), or a hyphenated word (*bull's-eye*). The dictionary should be consulted if there is any doubt as to whether a combination is hyphenated.

1. *Plurals* of nouns are formed by adding *s* or *es* to the singular form (*opiates*, the *Joneses*), but there are enough exceptions (*cries*, *thieves*, *staves*, *children*, *feet*, *women*,

alumnae) that, again, the dictionary should be consulted if there is any question in the writer's mind.

2. Nouns have special *case* forms for the *possessive case* only. The possessive case of nouns is indicated in three ways:

a. By adding *'s* to all singular—and a few plural—nouns for which the addition produces an *s* or *z* sound (*girl's, animal's; mother-in-law's; women's, children's*). Only the apostrophe is added to plurals ending in *s* (*girls', animals'*).

b. By an *of* phrase (the poems *of Colquitt,* the words *of Milton*).

c. By the double possessive, combining the *of* phrase and the *'s* ending (that rascally cat *of Susan's*).

3. Certain nouns have masculine and feminine forms:

EXAMPLES: actor, actress   masseur, masseuse
            alumnus, alumna   master, mistress
            executor, executrix   comedian, comedienne

FUNCTIONS OF NOUNS

In the sentence a noun may function as the subject of a verb, the object of a verb, the object of a preposition, a predicate noun after a linking verb, an appositive, and a modifier of verbs or sentences.

1. *Subject of a verb:* Feckless *Furbish* fumbled four times in the first frame.

2. *Object of a verb:* Coach Widdle banished *Furbish* from the locker room.

3. *Object of a preposition:* His teammates never gave the game ball to *Furbish.* (indirect object of the verb)

To *Furbish* the love of his classmates was a matter of complete indifference.

Football with *Furbish* was a pastime, not a profession.

4. *Predicate noun after a linking verb:* The goat of the town, of course, is *Furbish.*

5. *Appositive:* The man *Furbish* does not much resemble the boy.

Our quarterback, *Furbish*, has apparently forgotten the art of the forward pass.

6. *Modifier of verbs or sentences: Afternoons,* Furbish punts a bit, blocks less.

Furbish lost his midseason form *years* ago.

B. *Pronouns*

CLASSES AND FUNCTIONS

A pronoun can serve *nearly* all the functions of a noun in a sentence (it being difficult to conceive of a sentence in which a pronoun could serve as a modifier of a verb or the sentence). See the table on page 339.

1. *Personal pronouns,* substituting for the names of people, function in subjective, objective, or possessive capacities.

Subjective: He fumbled four times in a row.

Objective: Coach Widdle banished *him* from the locker room.
His teammates never gave *him* the game ball.
To *him* the respect of his fellows meant little.
We didn't mean to hit *him* so hard.

Possessive: The game ball is *his.*

2. *Relative* or *reference pronouns* refer to preceding nouns (or pronouns). The relative pronoun agrees with its referent in gender and number.

WRONG: A person *that* is in trouble needs help.
RIGHT: A person *who* is in trouble needs help.
WRONG: A horse *who* is blind is no good.
RIGHT: A horse *that* is blind is no good.
WRONG: Jones's house, *that* is just down the street, seems to be on fire.

RIGHT: Jones's house, *which* is just down the street, seems to be on fire. (*Which* is proper for nonrestrictive usage.)

WRONG: The man *who* we owe all our troubles to is Jones.

RIGHT: The man *whom* we owe all our troubles to is Jones. (object of the preposition, case being determined by function within the phrase or clause)

3. *Interrogative pronouns* begin questions.

Who stole my heart away?
Which is the lucky girl who has the next dance with Claude?
Whatever happened to Charlie Furbish?

4. *Reflexive pronouns* are used as objects of verbs when the subjects of the same verbs are identified with the objects (I hit *myself* on the head) and as intensifiers of personal pronouns or nouns (He *himself* has said it; Jane *herself* has no recollection of borrowing the book).

5. *Reciprocal pronouns* (*each other, one another*) may be most easily defined as plural reflexives.

Two persons: Jane and John have known *each other* too long.

More than two persons: Furbish and Claude and Henrietta have known *one another* for exactly one hour.

6. *Demonstrative pronouns* distinguish between alternative antecedents.

Singular: Here are two new automobiles. *This* has greater horsepower; *that* has more solid coachwork.

Plural: Here are numerous examples of abstract painters in one room. *These* on this wall are cubist-abstract; *those* on that wall are spherical-abstract.

7. *Numeral pronouns* refer, usually successively, to one or more of a group or series.

Cardinal numbers: Here we have a likely bevy of blushing bathing beauties. *One* is short, *two* are tall, and *three* seem ill at ease.

Ordinal numbers: There, on the other hand, is a crowd of gross and gawky boys. The *first* is grinning, the *second* shuffles nervously, and the *third* frankly stares.

8. *Indefinite pronouns,* of which there is a large number, more or less indefinitely single out items in a group or series, or refer to a whole group (or a part of it), rather unspecifically.

EXAMPLE: Here, once again, is a crowd of gross and gawky boys. *Some* are short; *others* are tall. *All* are vaguely repulsive.

NOTE: When possible, the possessive case of the indefinite pronoun is formed with *'s.* (What is tax money? *Everybody's* seems to be *nobody's.*)

TABLE OF PRONOUNS

Personal Pronouns

		Subjective	Objective	Possessive
1st person	Singular:	I	me	mine
	Plural:	we	us	ours
2nd person	Singular:	you	you	yours
	Plural:	you	you	yours
3rd person	Singular:	he, she, it	him, her, it	his, hers, of it
	Plural:	they	them	theirs

Relative Pronouns

who, whoever	whom, whomever	whose
that	that	of that
which, whichever	which	of which

Interrogative Pronouns

who, whoever
what, whatever
which

TABLE OF PRONOUNS—*Continued*

Reflexive Pronouns

1st person	*Singular:*	myself	myself	of myself
	Plural:	ourselves	ourselves	of ourselves
2nd person	*Singular:*	yourself	yourself	of yourself
	Plural:	yourselves	yourselves	of yourselves
3rd person	*Singular:*	himself, herself, itself	himself, herself, itself	of himself, herself, itself
	Plural:	themselves	themselves	of themselves

Reciprocal Pronouns

each other   one another
(two)   (more than two)

Demonstrative Pronouns

Singular: this, that, such, same, the former, the latter, the first, etc.

Plural: these, those

Numeral Pronouns

Cardinal numbers: one, two, three, etc.

Ordinal numbers: first, second, third, etc.

Indefinite Pronouns

EXAMPLES:

all	someone
another	everyone
some	few
any	many
none	much
anybody	several
nobody	something
somebody	other
each	neither
both	either

C. *Verbs*

CLASSES AND FUNCTIONS

A verb describes an action or situation in which its subject is involved. Like nouns and pronouns, verbs are classified in various ways: finite or complete,¹ infinite or incomplete,² regular or weak,⁴ irregular or strong,⁵ transitive,⁶ intransitive,⁷ linking, auxiliary or helping.⁸ Verbs are additionally distinguished in form by the *principal parts,* which are the basis of showing time relationships: (a) the *present* or "bare infinitive" form, (b) the *past* form, and (c) the *perfect* form. The principal parts of the verb *do,* for example, are *do, did, done.* The student who is in doubt as to the principal parts of a verb he wishes to use should consult the dictionary.

1. *Finite* or complete verbs. Every complete sentence has a finite verb as well as a subject (the subject being "understood" in commands). The finite verb agrees with its subject in *person* and *number,* and *it conveys a definite time sense,* expressed in its *tense* (see the conjugation of *know,* pp. 347–349). Further, if there are other verbs in the same sentence, the *time relations expressed must be mutually consistent* (see the chart of time relationships and the accompanying examples, pp. 350–351). Finally, *there must be a consistency of time relations from sentence to sentence, and from paragraph to paragraph* (see the discussion of *shifts,* p. 365).

2. *Infinite* or incomplete verbs. These are also known as *verbals.* They in themselves convey no sense of person or number; their time sense, when appropriate, depends upon that of a finite verb with which they are associated.

a. *Infinitives* are of two kinds: *pure infinitives* and *"to" infinitives.*

The *pure* (or "bare") *infinitive* is the first principal part of a verb (*do, have, walk, run, go*). It is used with auxiliary verbs to form verb phrases (*can fight, may run, shall jump*), and as a kind of adverbial modifier after certain verbs (I helped him *hold* the freshman for paddling). NOTE: The infinitive form of *be* is *be*, although its principal parts are *am, was, been*.

The *"to" infinitive* has the first principal part of the verb preceded by the preposition *to*. This valuable sentence element serves several purposes:

> *Subject:* **To fumble** is sinful.
>
> *Object:* I like *to smoke*.
>
> *Predicate after linking verb:* To smoke is *to live* a little.
>
> *Adjectival modifier:* I wish I had money *to burn*.
>
> *Adverbial modifier:* They moved *to halt* the merger.

NOTE: In cases similar to the following example, the subject of the infinitive is in the objective case: I knew *it* to be him. (Hence *him*, although after a linking verb, is in the objective case to agree with *it*.)

The *present infinitive* has the time sense of being at the same time or later than the time of a governing finite verb: Here he comes *to ask* you for the money.

The *perfect infinitive* has the time sense of being before the time of the governing finite verb: Today, though tired, I am glad *to have finished* with last night's assignment.

b. The *gerund*, or *verbal noun*, is the *-ing* infinitive form (*rowing, throwing, growing*). It serves any noun function in the sentence.

> *Subject:* For Furbish *throwing* the football is an unattainable art.
>
> *Object:* He prefers *kicking* it.
>
> *Predicate noun:* Understanding Furbish is *comprehending* stupidity.

Appositive: Claude's basic occupation, *loafing,* seems to suit him.

Sentence modifier: Playing well, Furbish stays in the game.

The *present gerund* has the same time sense that the present infinitive has: *Seeing* Furbish on the field was a unique experience, in a way.

Similarly, the *perfect gerund* indicates time before that of the governing finite verb: *Having seen* Furbish once at cricket was enough.

NOTE: In most cases the subject of the gerund takes the possessive case: *Her* coming roused Furbish to new heights of vainglory.

c. The *participle,* or *verbal adjective,* assumes the *-ing* infinitive or the third principal part (*done, known, walked, thrown*) forms. It functions as an attributive or predicate adjective.

Attributive: Claude gave Henrietta a *knowing* look.

Predicate after linking verb: The turkey at last is *done.*

Participles convey a certain time sense, in context:

Present: Furbish on the field has a *sidling* gait.

Past: Furbish was a *known* fool back home.

Perfect: The service *having been sung,* the choir left the stalls.

Like finite verbs, participles can take objects:

Following the pretty girl, Furbish stubbed his toe.

Like adjectives, participles can be modified adverbially:

Furbish began *weaving crazily* down the field.

Participles may be used in *absolute phrases,* modifying sentences:

Judging from his weight, Furbish will never make the team.

NOTE: Sometimes such phrases are *dangling modifiers;* see *absolute phrase,* p. 382.

3. *Regular* or *weak* verbs. Most verbs are "regular" in that the second and third principal parts (the *past* and *perfect* forms) are formed simply by adding -*d* or -*ed* to the pure or "bare" infinitive form (*walk, walked, walked; carve, carved, carved*). If the student is in any doubt as to whether a verb is regular, he should consult the dictionary.

4. *Irregular* or *strong* verbs. Some verbs form the second and third principal parts by a change in vowel (and sometimes by other changes): *rise, rose, risen; come, came, come; begin, began, begun; speak, spoke, spoken*. Again, the student who has forgotten his conjugations should consult the dictionary.

NOTE: The verb *be* (*am, was, been*) is so irregular that it has eight forms that must be committed to memory: *be, am, is, are, was, were, being, been.*

5. *Transitive* verbs. The transitive verb takes an object (or *receiver of the action*): Furbish *flung* the football far down the field.

                   S   V   O

Many verbs are used both transitively and intransitively (without an object); the dictionary always notes whether a verb can be used in both ways.

6. *Intransitive* verbs. The true intransitive verb, which *cannot take the passive form,* does not require an object to complete sentence meaning: Claude *lies* (i.e., falsifies).

7. *Linking* verbs. Linking verbs, which may be regarded as intransitive, require predicate nouns or predicate adjectives (sometimes these are "understood") to complete their meaning: Furbish *was* never captain of the team.

         S   LV   PN

Be is the most commonly used linking verb. Many such verbs have to do with the senses (*taste, feel, smell*). If a form of *be* can be satisfactorily substituted for a verb in a sentence, that verb is a linking verb.

8. *Auxiliary* or *helping* verbs. An auxiliary verb is used with another verb to form a verb phrase to establish *time* or *voice.* The most commonly used auxiliaries are *be, do, have,* which are fully conjugated, as are the less commonly used *get, let, need, used.* Also important as auxiliaries are *can, could; may, might; shall, should; will, would; must; ought.* These are exceedingly limited as to conjugation, having only the forms listed here.

NOTE: The *passive voice* poses a special writing problem (see the Handbook-Glossary entry, p. 407). The student should never use a verb in the passive voice unless he has no other stylistic alternative.

Definition: In the passive construction the normal object of a verb becomes its subject, although it is still the receiver of the action: *The ball was thrown to third base.* (Here the normal subject of the verb has vanished from the sentence, to its disadvantage. The following sentence is even worse: *The ball was thrown* WILDLY *to third base.* Here the reader will certainly wish to know who threw the ball.) Some grammarians consider the passive verb to be intransitive.

The retained object. Note the difference between the following sentences:

         S   VT   IO   O
    The team gave Furbish the game ball.

         S   PV   O
    Furbish was given the game ball. (Here *ball* is called a *retained object.* The indirect object has become the subject of the now passive verb, which nevertheless still has an object.)

A NOTE ON MOOD

Nearly all verb expression is in the *indicative mood,* which in general deals with the world of fact, and ideas about the world. Occasionally, however, the speaker or writer is called upon to deal with fact in a *conditional* or *contrary-to-fact* manner. Upon such occasions his verbs assume the *subjunctive mood* or the *conditional mood* (used mostly in conjunction with the subjunctive mood). The subjunctive mood is used for commands and for contrary-to-fact expressions, such as hopes or wishes.

> *Command:* *Be* a villain.
> *Wish:* Heaven *help* the working girl.
> *Hope:* *May* I *live* a hundred years.
> *Recommendation:* I ask that you *watch* Furbish closely.
> *Conditional:* I *shouldn't care* to be Furbish.
> *Subjunctive with conditional:* If I *were* you, Furbish, I *should change.*

CONJUGATION OF THE VERB **KNOW**

*Principal parts: **know, knew, known***

INDICATIVE MOOD

Active Voice   *Passive Voice*

PRESENT TENSE

Singular	*Plural*	*Singular*	*Plural*
I know	we know	I am known	we are known
you know	you know	you are known	you are known
he (she, it) knows	they know	he (she, it) is known	they are known

PAST TENSE

I knew	we knew	I was known	we were known
you knew	you knew	you were known	you were known
he knew	they knew	he was known	they were known

FUTURE TENSE

I shall know	we shall know	I shall be known	we shall be known
you will know	you will know	you will be known	you will be known
he will know	they will know	he will be known	they will be known

PRESENT PERFECT TENSE

I have known	we have known	I have been known	we have been known
you have known	you have known	you have been known	you have been known
he has known	they have known	he has been known	they have been known

PAST PERFECT TENSE

I had known	we had known	I had been known	we had been known
you had known	you had known	you had been known	you had been known
he had known	they had known	he had been known	they had been known

FUTURE PERFECT TENSE

I shall have known	we shall have known	I shall have been known	we shall have been known
you will have known	you will have known	you will have been known	you will have been known

CONJUGATION OF THE VERB **KNOW**—*Continued*

FUTURE PERFECT TENSE—*Continued*

he will have known	they will have known	he will have been known	they will have been known

THE PROGRESSIVE TENSES (*active voice*)

Present: I am knowing, you are knowing, he is knowing, we are knowing, etc.

Past: I was knowing, you were knowing, he was knowing, we were knowing, etc.

Future: I shall be knowing, you will be knowing, etc.

Present Perfect: I have been knowing, you have been knowing, he has been knowing, etc.

Past Perfect: I had been knowing, etc.

Future Perfect: I shall have been knowing, you will have been knowing, etc.

THE EMPHATIC TENSES (*active voice*)

Present: I do know, you do know, he does know, we do know, etc.

Past: I did know, you did know, he did know, we did know, etc.

CONDITIONAL MOOD
(*used alone or with the subjunctive*)

Active Voice	*Passive Voice*
PRESENT TENSE	
Singular: I should know, you would know, etc.	I should be known, you would be known, etc.
Plural: we should know, you would know, etc.	we should be known, you would be known, etc.
PERFECT TENSE	
Singular: I should have known, you would have known, etc.	I should have been known, you would have been known, etc.
Plural: we should have known, you would have known, etc.	we should have been known, you would have been known, etc.

SUBJUNCTIVE MOOD

Active Voice	*Passive Voice*
PRESENT TENSE	
Singular: if I, you, he know	if I, you, he be known
Plural: if we, you, they know	if we, you, they be known
PAST TENSE	
Singular: if I, you, he knew	if I, you, he were known
Plural: if we, you, they knew	if we, you, they were known

CONJUGATION OF THE VERB **KNOW**—*Continued*

FUTURE TENSE

Singular: if I shall know, if you will know, etc.

if I shall be known, etc.

Plural: if we shall know, if you will know, etc.

if we shall be known, etc.

PRESENT PERFECT TENSE

Singular: if I, you, he have known

if I, you, he have been known

Plural: if we, you, they have known

if we, you, they have been known

PAST PERFECT TENSE

Singular: if I, you, he had known

if I, you, he had been known

Plural: if we, you, they had known

if we, you, they had been known

FUTURE PERFECT TENSE

Singular: if I shall have known, if you will have known, etc.

if I shall have been known, if you will have been known, etc.

Plural: if we shall have known, if you will have known, etc.

if we shall have been known, if you will have been known, etc.

IMPERATIVE MOOD

PRESENT TENSE *(only)*

know

be known

INFINITIVES

PRESENT TENSE

to know

to be known

PRESENT PERFECT TENSE

to have known

to have been known

PARTICIPLES

PRESENT TENSE

knowing

being known

PAST TENSE

known

been known

PRESENT PERFECT TENSE

having known

having been known

GERUNDS

PRESENT TENSE

knowing

being known

PRESENT PERFECT TENSE

having known

having been known

THE TIME RELATIONSHIPS OF TENSES

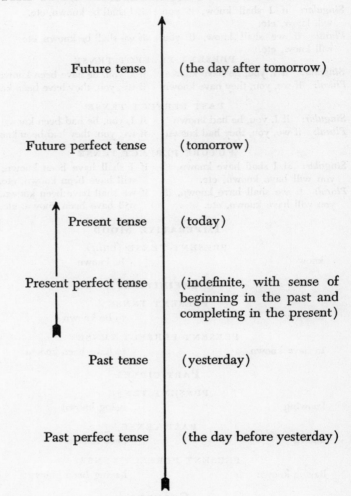

Future tense   (the day after tomorrow)

Future perfect tense   (tomorrow)

Present tense   (today)

Present perfect tense   (indefinite, with sense of beginning in the past and completing in the present)

Past tense   (yesterday)

Past perfect tense   (the day before yesterday)

NOTE: The future perfect and past perfect tenses must be used with the future and past tenses, *not by themselves.*

EXAMPLES:

(verbs italicized)

1. John Warren *likes* a back yard full of collies. (present tense, indicative mood, active voice)
2. John Warren *has* always *liked* the company of dogs. (present perfect tense, indicative mood, active voice)
3. Karl *served* as a squinting modifier in our book. (past tense, indicative mood, active voice)
4. By the time the meal *will end* (or *ends*) Pete *will have set* a new record for stowing away the celery. (future tense, indicative mood, active voice; future perfect tense, indicative mood, active voice)
5. Pete *had finished* the celery at lunch, and at supper *bestowed* a loving glance upon the carrot dish. (past perfect tense, indicative mood, active voice; past tense, indicative mood, active voice)
6. Our whole family *is known* for its hereditary irascibility. (present tense, indicative mood, passive voice)
7. Pete *was caught* invading the refrigerator at midnight. (past tense, indicative mood, passive voice)
8. Probably he *will have been seen* entering the kitchen tomorrow night, just before the clock *will strike* (or *strikes*) twelve. (future perfect tense, indicative mood, passive voice; future tense, indicative mood, active voice)
9. If I *were* you, I *should padlock* the refrigerator. (present tense, subjunctive mood, active voice; present tense, conditional mood, active voice)
10. If I *had been* you, I *should have padlocked* the refrigerator. (past perfect tense, subjunctive mood, active voice; past perfect tense, conditional mood, active voice)

D. Adverbs

Adverbs describe or modify verbs, other adverbs, adjectives, clauses, and sentences.

> *Verb modifier:* After the game Coach Widdle will speak *quietly.*
>
> *Adverb modifier:* Coach Widdle speaks quietly *enough.*
>
> *Adjective modifier: Quietly* friendly Coach Widdle despairs of Furbish.
>
> *Clause modifier: Consequently* Furbish feels frustrated. (also sentence modifier)
>
> *Clause modifier: When* Furbish feels frustrated, he beds down.

FORMS OF ADVERBS

In general adverbs formed from adjectives add *-ly* to the adjective form: *loud, loudly; loose, loosely.* But they may retain the adjective form: Hers was the *first* pretty face he had seen. There are many adverbs that are not formed from adjectives (see the list of transition devices, pp. 134–137).

MEANINGS OF ADVERBS

In an extended sense adverbs answer the questions how? when? where? why? how far? how positively? Examples follow.

> *Adverbs of manner:* carefully, quietly, secretly, differently
>
> *Adverbs of time:* early, initially, finally, always, soon
>
> *Adverbs of place:* here, there, everywhere, above, below, downstairs
>
> *Adverbs of degree:* quite, partially, completely, fairly, nearly
>
> *Adverbs of cause and effect:* hence, consequently, therefore
>
> *Adverbs of condition:* yes, no, undoubtedly, certainly, maybe

COMPARISON OF ADVERBS

The *comparative* and *superlative* forms of adverbs add *-er* and *-est* to the *positive* form (*soon, sooner, soonest*), or prefix the positive form with *more* and *most* (*often, more often, most often*). When in doubt as to which method to use, the student should consult the dictionary.

E. *Adjectives*

Adjectives modify or describe nouns (and sometimes pronouns). Usually they are placed before the nouns they modify (sometimes after, for special effect), or after linking verbs, as in: His forehead is *warm*.

TYPES OF ADJECTIVES

Adjectives are *descriptive* (describing a quality of the noun), *limiting* (pointing at the noun), *proper* (proper nouns serving as limiting or describing adjectives). Descriptive adjectives, *except for participles,* are regularly compared; they may be modified by adverbs. Usually limiting adjectives are neither compared nor modified. Proper adjectives are not compared. Examples follow.

> *Descriptive:* muddy [muddier, muddiest] football; very muddy football
>
> *Limiting:* this gridiron, his mistake, a hoecake, four girls
>
> *Proper:* the Dutch line, Alexandrian culture [many common nouns are also used as adjectival modifiers]

Certain adjectives, with limiting articles, serve as subjects or objects.

> *Subject: The unwashed* are people, too.
>
> *Object:* I cannot bear to contemplate *the miserables* of this world.

COMPARISON OF ADJECTIVES

Adjectives are compared in the same two ways that adverbs are (see above). Again, the dictionary should be consulted in doubtful cases.

F. *Prepositions*

Prepositions are *introducing* words (sometimes phrases) for words, phrases, or clauses. Prepositions have certain shades of adverbial or conjunctive meaning, usually meaning in connection with what they introduce. Since meaning is connected with all prepositions (and since their use, in all modern languages, is highly idiomatic), some care should be exercised in their selection. Dictionaries indicate the right preposition to be used with many words. The most commonly used prepositions are *at, in, on, to* (indicating position or movement); *of, by, for, from, with* (indicating various shades of situation).

TYPES OF PREPOSITIONS

Possibly the sensible way to classify prepositions, which are great in number, is according to whether the sense conveyed is of *motion, position, time,* or *situation* (this last an admittedly nebulous classification).

> *Motion:* into, across, against, around, down, over, between, out of, under, through, up, past
>
> *Position:* in, on, under, between, against, above, below, near, over, upon, aboard, amid, at, before, behind, beneath, beside, inside
>
> *Time:* after, before, during, ahead of, past, since, until, till, within
>
> *Situation:* about, as far as, because of, ahead of, as to, at, concerning, contrary to, despite, due to, owing to, in spite of, in view of, like, on account of, since, through, with

FUNCTIONS OF PREPOSITIONS

Prepositions are used to indicate grammatical function in a sentence (*to* with the infinitive, *to* before an indirect object, *of* to show possession) and to introduce words, phrases, and clauses (see the description of phrases and clauses, pp. 356–358).

G. *Conjunctions*

Conjunctions introduce or connect sentence elements (words, phrases, clauses). They may have, and often do have, additional meaning (but usually not within a construction following a conjunction). A conjunction should be selected with care therefore. See the meanings attached to transition devices, pp. 134–137.

TYPES OF CONJUNCTIONS

Conjunctions are classified as to whether they connect parallel constructions (*pure* or *coordinating conjunctions*), connect adverbial clauses with independent clauses (*subordinating conjunctions*), or are used instead of pure conjunctions between independent clauses in the same sentence (*conjunctive adverbs*).

The *pure conjunctions* are *and, or, but, nor.* The elements they connect must be equivalent grammatically. Examples follow.

> *Between words:* Neither Henrietta *nor* Claude is happy.
>
> *Between phrases:* Furbish is always under a cloud *or* over a barrel.
>
> *Between clauses:* I shall retreat not when I should *but* when I am afraid.

A list of the usual *subordinating conjunctions* follows:

why	till	in order that	as long as
while	though	if	as if
where	that	how	as
when	so that	before	although
unless	since	because	after

(See the Handbook-Glossary entries for *as, because, if—whether, where, while.*)

Conjunctive adverbs (*so, however, nevertheless, consequently,* etc.) are often used as connectives between independent clauses. Such a connective must be preceded by a period or a semicolon (see RULE 3, pp. 49–50). Conjunctive adverbs are handy as transition devices, but since the compound sentence in itself is mediocre stylistically, it is a good idea to reserve the conjunctive adverb for emergency use (see *Clarity through Subordination*, pp. 52–59).

H. *Interjections or exclamations*

Interjections (*oh! ah! alas!* etc.) are "violent" intensives used adverbially, for the most part. The writer of expository or argumentative essays need not resort to their use unless he is directly quoting a source that uses them.

II. Larger Sentence Elements:
Phrases and Clauses

Phrases and clauses serve the same purposes that words serve in the sentence.

A. *Phrases*

A phrase is a sentence unit of at least two words. Considered as a unit, it has neither a subject nor a verb (although it may *be* a verb). Adroit manipulation of phrases (and to a somewhat lesser extent clauses) is the key to a sentence style characterized by vigor and variety. Phrases may be classified in several ways: noun, verb, adverb, adjective, prepositional, conjunctive.

1. The *noun phrase* is a noun with modifiers that cannot be deleted from the sentence without materially altering the meaning of the noun.

Subject: The first three chukkers were Furbish's.

Object: Furbish threw *one strike* while on the mound.

Predicate noun: Hers were *all hearts.*

Appositive: The Big Game, *Harvard against Yale,* does not stir Furbish.

Gerund: His learning Widdle's plays takes little of Furbish's time.

Infinitive: To learn Widdle's plays is to comprehend the infinite.

2. The **verb phrase** may be defined as all the words in a sentence that compose a finite verb (*was going, had been done, will be happening*).

3. The **adverbial phrase** is usually two adverbs together constituting a modifier (*fairly fully* understood, *rather fairly* stated).

4. The **adjective phrase** consists of two or more adjectives describing or modifying the same noun (*angry old* Furbish, *little red* Russian, *wrinkled, aging, palsied* football coach).

5. The **prepositional phrase** consists of a preposition and its *object* (a "bare" infinitive, a pronoun, a noun or noun phrase). The prepositional phrase is used syntactically to compose an infinitive (*to live*) or to indicate the possessive case (the neigh *of a horse*). Examples of other uses of the prepositional phrase follow.

As a noun: *Out of sight* is *out of mind.*

As an adverb: *With all my heart* I welcome Coach Widdle's retirement.

As an adjective: The girl *with the three blue eyes* is a Burrows creation.

6. The **conjunctive phrase** is a conjunction with an adverb (*and also, and not, but not*).

B. *Clauses*

A clause consists of a *subject* and a *finite verb* (except for the command, in which the subject is "understood").

1. The **independent clause** states a complete idea. It can stand alone as a sentence. Its ultimate meaning, of course,

depends on context, that is, upon what has preceded it and what will follow it as expressions of facts or ideas. The independent clause, then, is the basis of sentence style: an incomplete sentence, since it does not express an idea completely, is improper in the expository or argumentative essay.

2. The *dependent clause,* since it does not state a complete idea, depends for the completion of its meaning upon the independent clause. Further, the dependent clause reinforces the meaning of the independent clause, either *restrictively* (dropping the dependent clause from the sentence would alter its meaning) or *nonrestrictively* (the dependent clause furnishes additional, but not necessary, information).

a. The *noun clause.* The noun clause is used in place of a noun. It may serve as a *subject* (*What Furbish does* no longer matters to Joan), as an *appositive* (The rule *that you mustn't rough the kicker* was odious to Furbish), as an *object* (Claude gives Henrietta *what she needs in the way of affection*), as a *predicate noun* (Furbish is *what a ball player ought never to be*).

b. The *adjective clause.* The adjective clause describes or modifies a noun or pronoun.

Restrictive: The girl *whom Furbish loves* is nobody else's.

Nonrestrictive: Joan, *who is pretty in a negative sort of way,* is Furbish's girl.

c. The *adverb clause.* The adverbial clause is used like an adverb in modifying verbs or whole sentences. An adverbial clause beginning a sentence is followed by a comma.

Restrictive: Furbish weeps *when he sees movies of his games.*

Nonrestrictive: Furbish always closes the door of his room, *whether there is a draft or not.*

The following section, "The Relationships of Sentence Elements," has examples of basic sentence patterns.

III. The Relationships of Sentence Elements

THE SIMPLE SENTENCE

1. Subject–verb:

Betsy capitulated.
  S   VI

Begone!   [command; subject
VI   "understood"]

To be punished irritates.
   Phrase   VI

Fred's being a champion speller
        verbal
figures.
VI

2. Modifier–subject–verb; subject–modifier–verb; subject–verb–modifier:

In the classroom Mrs. Rall whispers.
   Mod   S   VI

Mrs. Rall consistently teaches.
  S   Mod   VI

Mrs. Rall shouts under certain cir-
  S   VI   Mod
cumstances.

3. Subject–verb–object:

Mrs. McAlister throws erasers.
      S   VT   O

Take back your flowers.   [command]
VT   O

Dr. Snyder wants to know.
   S   VT   Phrase

MacLaine deplores paper grading.
          VT   verbal

Abbreviations

S	subject
O	object
IO	indirect object
NCl	noun clause
AjCl	adjective clause
AvCl	adverb clause
VI	intransitive verb
VT	transitive verb
E	expletive
PN	predicate noun
PA	predicate adjective
Mod	modifier
LV	linking verb

4. Subject–verb–indirect object–object:

Rita throws me kisses.
S   VT   IO   O

Give me your wilted violets.   [command]
VT IO   O

5. Subject–verb–object–indirect object:

Rita throws kisses at me.
S   VT   O   IO

Take pity on me.   [command]
VT O IO

6. Subject–linking verb–complement:

Allan was devastated.
S   LV   PA

Dr. Williams became chairman.
S   LV   PN

7. Expletive–verb–subject:

It is a long day.
E LV   S

It is saucers and cups breaking.
E LV S   S

There are fifty million Frenchmen,
E   LV   S
more or less.

There is lipstick on Claude's collar.
E LV S

[As an expletive *it* always takes a singular verb.]

[As appropriate, *there* as an expletive takes either the singular or the plural verb.]

8. Compound subject–compound verb–compound object:

Jim and Patsy danced and sang
S   S   VT   VT
roundelays and virelays.
O   O

9. Subject with modifiers–verb with modifiers–object or complement with modifiers:

Jim, bald and aging, and flushed and
  S   Mod   Mod

pretty Patsy madly danced the
        S   Mod   VT

twist, southern version.
  O   Mod

[Modifiers may precede or follow what is modified.]

10. Subject–passive verb–modifier:

The eraser was thrown with deadly
  S   VI   Mod

aim by Eilene.
  Mod

11. The question:

Why is there no rainbow in the sky?
 LV E   S

What is the matter with Hortense?
  S LV   PN

Does he love you in December as
 V   S   V   O
in May?

12. The exclamation:

I fall upon the thorns of life! I bleed!
S VI   Mod   S VI

[The structure is that of the declarative sentence.]

13. Special subjunctive expressions:

Heaven lend a hand to college pro-
  S   VT   O   IO
fessors.

[hope or wish]

The accolade of the board of regents
           S

descend upon us.
  VI

[prayer]

14. Special word order for emphasis or variety of effect:

Forth fled the faculty from the meeting.
Mod VI   S   Mod

Between Professors Williams and Snyder sat their victim,
                        Mod   VI   S
a freshman.

THE COMPLEX SENTENCE
(*See the key to structure, p. 76*)

1. Adverbial clause-independent clause:
   After he had spent two weeks on the campus, Philip
                       A-1
   decided against buying books.

2. Independent clause-adverbial clause:
   Philip decided against buying books *because the library*
                                       A-2
   had all he wanted.

3. Independent clause interrupted by adverbial clause:
   Philip decided, *although his conscience hurt him a bit,*
                              A-3
   against book buying.

4. Noun clause as subject of a sentence:
   What Philip has done will not alter book store policies.
      N-1

5. Noun clause as object of a verb:
   As usual, his mother deplores *what Philip has done.*
                                   N-2

6. Noun clause as object of a verbal:
   It is certainly deplorable to do *what Philip has done.*
                                 N-2

   It gives me a guilty feeling, knowing *what Philip has*
                                   N-2
   done.

7. Noun clause as object of a preposition:
   My objection to *what Philip has done* is based on a
                              N-3
   personal code of morals.

8. Adjective clause modifying a noun:

The ignorant college graduate *who stands before you*
  Adj
is our friend Philip.

Old ignorant Philip, *who stands before you even now,*
  Adj
owns a uranium mine.

9. Adjective clause modifying a pronoun:

He *who is our benefactor* is ignorant, bookless Philip,
  Adj
the millionaire.

10. Forms of relative pronouns in adjective clauses:

The man in uniform *who* stands behind Philip is his chauffeur.

He *whom* we are all indebted to is ignorant, bookless Philip, the millionaire.

The horses *that* run last are destined for the glue factory.

Of Human Bondage, which I read sleeplessly last night, is surely a classic.

(*Who* and *whom* refer to people; the restrictive *that* and the nonrestrictive *which* refer to things.)

THE COMPOUND SENTENCE

Two or more simple sentences brought together in one sentence:

Aubyn whistled, and Lyle dropped obediently to one knee.

Cedric snorted, Hortense snuffled, and Claude scratched his head. [series]

Patsy guffawed; Jim turned away from his self-portrait in disgust.

Jim may be disgusted; nevertheless I think it a good likeness.

THE COMPOUND-COMPLEX SENTENCE

The complex and the simple sentence brought together in one sentence:

Jim shows his disgust when he thinks of the self-portrait, but it is his face.

Two or more complex sentences brought together in one sentence:

When he sees the portrait, Jim smiles, but he does not know what I think of it.

(There are numerous other possibilities for clause combination. The student is nevertheless well advised to avoid writing compound sentences.)

PARTICULAR PROBLEMS OF SENTENCE ELEMENT RELATIONSHIP: PRONOUN REFERENCE AND SUBJECT-VERB SHIFTS

A. Pronoun reference

Many writers, professionals among them, employ the *demonstrative pronouns* THIS and THAT as references to foregoing sentences or ideas. To do so is inexact. For the precise writer a pronoun should refer to a *noun,* a *noun clause,* a *construction used as a noun,* or a *pronoun* (but ultimately to a noun). Intelligent subordination usually clears up the difficulty.

Inexact reference: Shakespeare's Globe Theatre was erected next to a tavern, across the river south of London. *This* was because the people of London proper did not want theatres and taverns near their homes.

Better: Shakespeare's Globe Theatre was erected next to a tavern, across the river south of London, because the people of London proper did not want theatres and taverns near their homes.

Relative or *reference pronouns* must agree with their antecedents in *gender* (masculine, feminine, neuter) and *number* (singular, plural). Similarly, pronominal adjectives referring to nouns or pronouns must reflect the gender and number of their referents (antecedents).

Poor: The *Ryndam* is my favorite ship. *Her* groceries are always superb, and *it* is always on time.

Worse: A fellow has to watch *his* step. *They* can make mistakes in *their* sleep. *It* is *his* responsibility, not *theirs*.

B. Subject-verb shifts

Once the writer has adopted a point of view, *objective* or *subjective,* he should maintain it scrupulously throughout the essay. Failure to do so leads to considerable awkwardness and inevitable error. Consider the following example, which needs to be rewritten from one point of view.

I don't know what's the matter with me these autumn days. One gets up in the morning feeling pretty good, and then he is suddenly swept up in a wave of pure ennui. You can't conduct a day's business if you don't feel like it. I may retire.

Failure to understand the sequence of tenses (see p. 350) and to preserve a uniform attitude toward time also causes error and sorely damages style. Consider these sentences:

I got up yesterday feeling pretty good—the sun shining, the birds singing—good old eleven o'clock. But when I cut myself shaving, cataclysm begins to be the general design. My hair won't part, the cat has been meowing, and the coffee tasted bad. I had had an irresistible desire to return to bed. Oh, I do not resist it.

IV. Punctuation as Reinforcing Sentence Element Relationships

(See also pp. 48–52)

A. *External punctuation*

As appropriate to the meaning, the sentence ends with a *period* (*declarative sentence*), a *question mark,* or an *exclamation mark.*

Declaration: Furbish has at last turned away from athletics.

NOTE: The period ending a quotation *precedes* the final quotation mark: Someone at some time must have said, "Good neighbors make good fences."

Question: But will Furbish's new resolve last the day out?

Exclamation: We must call the police!

B. *Internal punctuation*

Internal punctuation marks are *commas, semicolons, colons, dashes, parentheses,* and *brackets.* In an extended sense all of these sentence conventions indicate pauses, some more significant than others.

1. *The comma.* The comma is used *to separate clauses, to set off nonrestrictive or parenthetical sentence elements,* and *to indicate a variety of special situations.*

a. *Separating clauses*

Between two independent clauses, and preceding one of the conjunctions *and, or, but, nor:*

Susan and Sally sing sad songs over the telephone, *and* the operator always listens in.

Separating a series of three or more independent clauses, if *and* precedes the final clause:

Susan and Sally sing sad songs, the operator listens in, *and* Susan's and Sally's mothers become increasingly morose.

Following an introductory adverbial clause:

When Susan and Sally sing sad songs over the telephone, the cats go outside.

b. *Setting off nonrestrictive or parenthetical sentence elements*

Certain introductory constructions:

Dr. Jones, your patient's pulse is pounding. (*noun of address*)

Yes, Philip Furbish is under observation. (*sentence modifier*)

To be sure, his malady is not catching. (*loose modifier*)

To live a little, you have to be brave a little. (*introductory verbal phrase*)

On the afternoon of the very next beautiful day, he retired. (*long introductory phrase*)

The first team quarterback having been chosen at last, Furbish retired to the dressing room. (*absolute phrase*)

When Joan first met Furbish, she blushed prettily. (*adverbial clause*)

Loose modifiers ending the sentence:

Wells is a fine foundation man, *however.* (*adverb*)

Furbish is a beaten man, *in a sense.* (*phrase*)

Crenshaw is certainly a dedicated interlinguist, *as we all know.* (*adverbial clause*)

Sentence interrupters:

Crenshaw, *then,* must know Esperanto pretty well. (*adverb*)

Crenshaw knows, *on the whole,* more languages than any of the rest of us does. (*phrase*)

Crenshaw knows, *I think,* at least seven languages. (*clause*)

Crenshaw seems to believe, *when you come right down to it,* in being diplomatic about estimating the literary value of Esperanto. (*adverbial clause*)

Nonrestrictive appositives:

My youngest brother, *Jack,* is a wily poker player. (*nonrestrictive*)

BUT: Our friends *the Heflins* live on Melvin Avenue. (*restrictive*)

Nonrestrictive adjective clauses:

Lazy musicians, *who are probably in the majority,* make sour sounds. (*nonrestrictive*)

BUT: The musician *who practices assiduously* will succeed. (*restrictive*)

c. *Separating items in a list or series* (see *independent clauses in a series,* under [a] above)

When you go to a game with Furbish, take a hand warmer, a pocket radio, a jug of coffee, sun glasses, and ear plugs. (*series of words or phrases*—NOTE the comma before *and*)

Four courses were offered in the spring term: English 311, 324, 331, and 340. (*list*)

d. *Separating adjectives modifying a noun in the same way*

Jane is a pretty, radiant girl.

John is an oafish, loutish, lovable husband.

BUT: John is an oafish *and* loutish *and* lovable husband.

e. *Enclosing the second and succeeding items in dates and addresses*

Friday, *February 3, 1963,* will be a significant day. (*date*)

Susan and Pete's ambition is to live at The Cloisters, *43 Whim Drive, Reading, Valley Mills, Hampshire,* when in England. (*address*)

f. *Enclosing degrees and titles*

Ephraim Wugg, M.D., is our family physician. (*degree*)

The students have great faith in Philip Furbish, Chairman of the Board of Visitors. (*title*)

g. *In numbers, separating groups of three digits* (working from the *final* digit)

4,010   34,010   134,010   1,134,010

h. *With quotations* (see the section *quotation marks,* pp. 371–372)

i. *For clarity.* It is extremely doubtful that a comma should be given the task (in some other way than already discussed) of clarifying the sentence, which should be rewritten so that it will not have to depend upon a punctuation mark to make its meaning clear and precise.

2. *The semicolon.* As already indicated, the semicolon separates independent clauses in the same sentence that are *not* connected by one of the conjunctions *and, or, but, nor.* Some writers use the semicolon between independent clauses, even though they are connected by one of the pure conjunctions, especially if one or both of the clauses is heavily punctuated. The student would do well to use a period instead of a semicolon, in most cases, *unless both clauses are closely related in content and virtually equivalent as to importance of idea.* The following examples demonstrate the proper use of the semicolon.

Joan clung to a bush; Philip went sliding on down the hill.

Claude on most occasions acts like a cynical realist; nevertheless Henrietta clings to her ideals.

Even in the face of adversity, an adversity which he could not but contemplate with horror—increased by nameless terror—Coach Widdle struggled to win football games; and he knew he could not.

3. *The colon.*

a. The colon follows a *formal introduction* (i.e., an independent clause), as in the following examples.

Coach Widdle sent four men to the showers: Furbish, Crull, Mudge, Wormsey.

Wormsey had ruined several costly pieces of equipment: a face guard, a pair of cleated shoes, somebody's shoulder pads.

b. The colon may replace the semicolon between two independent clauses in the same sentence, if the first clause may be said to *cause* the second:

Furbish's miserable performance on the field seemed to distress Joan: she stopped loving him when the final gun went off.

c. The colon may be used instead of a comma before direct quotations introduced by *He said* and the like. The writer's usage should be consistent in this regard. See the sample research paper in Chapter Ten.

Joan commented wryly: "There goes my man."

OR

Joan commented wryly, "There goes my man."

d. The colon is customarily employed between the hour and minute numbers of a time expression:

Promptly at 4:30 P.M. Joan left the stadium for home.

e. Bibliography or footnote items citing a publisher use the colon as follows:

[1]George Widdle, *Losing Football* (New York: Ace Co., 1947), p. 27. (footnote)

Widdle, George. *Losing Football*. New York: Ace Co., 1947. (bibliography)

4. *Dashes and parentheses.* These punctuation marks are used to set off sentence interrupters (or "asides") if the nature of the interruption appears to be such that a comma is insufficient to the case. The student will avoid depending upon such punctuation crutches. The following examples demonstrate correct usage.

I realize—oh, how my head hurts!—that I need treatment.

Coach Widdle (our hero once) has gone into insurance.

His employer—believe it or not—is none other than Philip Furbish.

Widdle has begun to noise it about that Furbish (his employer) tyrannizes poor Joan (Widdle's secretary).

5. *Brackets.* Most student typewriters do not have square bracket keys, but it is well worth a small charge to have them added to the keyboard. Any symbol not on the keyboard, however, can be reproduced in the typed paper (a blank space must be provided) with black ink, neatly applied. Brackets are used for two purposes: (a) *to set off parenthetical material that in turn is within other parenthetical material;* (b) *to set off editorial comment within direct quotations.*

Jack has a good book on the subject (*Ice Houses* [New York, 1957]) that I should like to borrow from him.

After reading *Ice Houses* Jack commented, "Now I know where Edwina [a girl he fancies] gets her standoffishness."

C. *Quotation marks*

(*See also italics, p. 374*)

Quotations are either direct ("I see her, all right," Jack said) or indirect (Jack said that he could see her all right). Direct quotations, mostly cited from printed sources or as conversation, are enclosed in quotation marks. If the need arises to cite a direct quotation within a direct quotation, the conventional *double quotation marks* (" ") are used for the exterior quotation, *single quotation marks* (' ') for the interior quotation. An analysis of the usual quotation conventions follows.

1. In making a reference to *titles,* the writer indicates *book, periodical,* and *newspaper* names with *italics* (on the typewriter, by underlining). The titles of *parts* (articles, poems, chapters, columns, editorials, stories) of these publications are enclosed in quotation marks.

The latest issue of *Northern Lights* has a poem entitled "Eskimos." (See Chapter Ten for further examples.)

2. In calling attention to a word or phrase of perhaps peculiar usage or significance, a colloquialism for example, the writer will enclose it in quotation marks. *Words used as words and foreign terms are italicized.*

Tommy Wood used to call coffee the "toddy for the body."
Among the *demimonde* not much is said of Tommy nowadays.

3. For the research paper, quotations that are set off are not enclosed in quotation marks. But direct quotations *within set-off quotations* are enclosed in double quotation marks.

I often think of what Browning says:

"Not wounded, sir, but dead," he said, or thought
He said, or ought to've said, to make a rime.

But perhaps that is not what Browning says.

4. When conversation is reproduced, it is proper either to indent for a new paragraph when the speaker changes, or to continue with the same paragraph, provided that the material is closely related.

An example of conversation follows. The student should notice (a) that short phrases introducing direct quotations need not be followed by commas or colons, (b) that periods or commas at the end of quotations are put before the close-quotation mark, (c) that semicolons and colons, unless parts of quoted material, follow close-quotation marks, (d) that the same convention applies to question marks and exclamation points, (e) that the continuation of an interrupted quotation does not begin with a capital letter after the open-quotation mark unless a new sentence begins.

The meeting of the Shirley Street and Bellaire Drive North Small Item and Middle Adolescence, Not to Say Early Maturity, Society began on the floor of the television room, with two cats looking on.

"When I am five," Melinda began, "*really* I'll be alive." She smiled secretly.

Pete whispered, mostly to himself, "Isn't it time for the Baylor game?"

Other whispers were heard: "My whistle works"; "I can read books." David and Cathy looked at the dead eye of the big box. "'Captain Kangaroo' comes on in a minute," they said simultaneously.

Susan, her mind on college, stroked Little Cat absently, said "Ouch!" when the cat objected. "I think I'll like 'Captain Kangaroo.'"

V. Sentence Mechanics as Reinforcing Sentence Element Relationships

A. *Capitals*

Capitalize the following:

1. The first word of a sentence.

2. Proper nouns and adjectives derived from proper nouns:

Geoffrey Chaucer	Spanish
Indian	Saturday

Negro	Rhine River
Byronic	Trinity Mountain
The War Between the States	July
Baptist	Halloween

3. Important words (the first word, nouns, pronouns, verbs, adverbs, adjectives—but not *a, an, the,*) in titles of books, articles, magazines, and other published materials:

The Rape of the Lock
Saturday Review
Gulliver's Travels
The Complaint, or Night Thoughts

4. References to deity:

God
Saviour
Men of the church seek to abide by His will.

5. Titles when they precede names or when they are used in place of names:

I wrote a letter of protest to Senator Silvercreek.
They saw the Senator in his office.
The President came in early this morning.

6. The first word of a line of verse unless the poet uses a lower case letter.

7. The first word of a direct quotation:

Lyle said, "We have a deadline; let us write."
Jim pleaded, "Do I have to?"
Lyle said, "Yes, right now."

8. The points of the compass when they are used to indicate geographical regions:

Hold on to your Confederate money; the South will rise again.

B. *Numbers*

1. For numbers above one hundred, use digits except when the number occurs at the beginning of a sentence.

2. For numbers up to one hundred, use words except for numbers used in dates, addresses, page references, sums of money, and hours when either a.m. or p.m. is used.

C. *Abbreviations*

In college writing abbreviations are usually inappropriate. There are, however, some standard and commonly used abbreviations that are acceptable in ordinary writing:

1. Titles before proper names: Dr., Mr., Mrs., Mme.
2. Titles and other designations following proper names: M.D., Jr., Sr.
3. Government agencies and other organizations: TVA, FBI, A.F.L., UNESCO.

D. *Italics*

Show italics in both longhand and typewritten manuscripts by underlining. Italics should be used in the following situations:

1. To indicate titles of books and periodicals:

Gulliver's Travels is the greatest satire of all.
Last summer Pete sold subscriptions to the *Saturday Evening Post*.

2. To designate words being used not for their meaning but as words:

The word *of* is a preposition.
Lyle dislikes the word *structure* when it is used as a verb.

3. To indicate foreign terms:

The *pas de deux* was especially scintillating as performed by Cathy and Pete.

4. Sparingly, to indicate emphasis:

Whatever else he may be, Dryden is *not* dry.

E. *Apostrophes*

Use the apostrophe in the following instances:

1. To indicate possession: John's car, Keats' (or Keats's) poetry, Pete's paper route.
2. Where the context permits, to indicate contractions (not usually appropriate in college writing except when the writer is reproducing conversation):

> Jim said, "David doesn't usually practice playing the violin voluntarily."

3. To indicate plurals of numbers, letters of the alphabet, and words considered as words: six *x*'s, the 1950's, four *have*'s.

F. *Hyphens*

Use the hyphen in the following circumstances:

1. To divide a word between syllables when it is necessary to carry part of the word over to the next line.
2. To separate a prefix from the root word when

a. The prefix ends and the root word begins with the same vowel: re-elect, pre-eminent. (Some well-known words are customarily written without the hyphen, however: cooperate, coordinate).

b. The prefix and root word together could be confused with another word: re-collect "to collect again"; recollect, "to remember."

c. The prefix comes before a proper noun: anti-Communist, pre-Roosevelt.

3. To divide compound adjectives: a rough-talking man, an eighteenth-century writer.
4. To divide the words of the written forms of numbers from twenty-one to ninety-nine: forty-six, thirty-one, sixty-eight, one hundred and sixty-eight.

5. To divide words in many commonly used word groups: son-in-law, great-grandfather, mother-in-law.

6. To separate the prefix and root word of most compounds with *self* and *ex:* self-sufficient, ex-husband, self-governing, ex-Communist.

G. *Quotations*

1. For spacing of quotations and other information on the use of quotations, see Chapter Ten, pages 315–316; and pages 371, 410.

2. A special problem that occurs in quotations is the use of ellipsis marks to designate that material has been omitted from the quotation.

a. If words within a sentence that is quoted are omitted, three spaced periods are used to indicate the omission:

"The business of a poet," said Imlac, "is to . . . remark large properties and large appearances."

b. If words at the end of a sentence are omitted, the three spaced periods are added to the period marking the end of the sentence:

"The business of a poet," said Imlac, "is to examine not the individual but the species. . . ."

H. *Spelling*

Spelling English words can be a perilous undertaking. No doubt there dwells deep in the mind of many a student smarting from multitudes of red-circled words the private conviction that there was in the early writers who helped determine English spelling a streak of wild irresponsibility. No one can deny that English spelling has its confusing features; still, it can be mastered; many have done so.

Good spelling depends upon intimate familiarity with thousands of words and with even more thousands of sounds that combine to make words. Constant reading is therefore one good method of improving spelling. Familiarity does not necessarily breed contempt; in this case it may even breed assurance in spelling. Some further suggestions for improving spelling are given below.

1. Regard the dictionary as a natural appendage to your body, to accompany you continuously like a left arm or a right ear. No writer, good or bad, assured or panic-stricken, should set about writing without a good dictionary close at hand. See Chapter Two, page 26, for a list of standard dictionaries.

2. Consult the following basic rules for help in spelling several large groups of common words:

a. In one-syllable words ending in a single vowel followed by a single consonant, double the final consonant before adding a suffix beginning with a vowel:

drum	drumming
sit	sitting
run	running
bat	batting
swim	swimming

In words of more than one syllable with stress on a final syllable ending in a single vowel followed by a single consonant, double the final consonant before adding a suffix beginning with a vowel:

defer	deferred
confer	conferred
control	controlled

b. Put *i* before *e* to give the long *e* sound except after *c*:

relieve	belief
relief	achieve
believe	niece

Put *e* before *i* to give the long *e* sound after *c*, or to give
the long *a* sound:

receive	freight
deceive	neighbor
	weigh

Exceptions: either, neither, seize, weird

c. In words ending with -*ce* (pronounced *s*) or -*ge* (pronounced *j*), retain the *e* before suffixes beginning with *a, o,*
or *u*:

notice	noticeable
courage	courageous
peace	peaceable
change	changeable

Drop the *e* before suffixes beginning with *i* or *e*:

notice	noticing
encourage	encouraging

d. In words ending with a silent *e*, drop the *e* before suffixes beginning with a vowel, retain it before suffixes beginning with a consonant:

love	lovable	lovely
use	usable	useful
arrange	arranging	arrangement

e. Form the plural of nouns ending in *y* preceded by a
consonant by dropping the *y* and adding -*ies*. Form the
present tense, third person singular of verbs ending in *y*
preceded by a consonant by dropping the *y* and adding -*ies*:

baby	babies
sky	skies
try	tries
marry	marries

3. Proofread carefully. Carelessness or haste is responsible
for a large proportion of misspelled words. Most writers can
discover the majority of words they have misspelled—probably

as many as seven out of ten—by exacting care in proofreading. In order to proofread well, observe the following conditions:

a. Some time should pass between the writing and the proofreading. Even the most expert proofreader is likely to miss his own mistakes if he goes over his work immediately after finishing it. When he is close to his work, a writer tends to read what he had in mind, not what he has on paper.

b. Proofread slowly, where possible reading the work aloud at a rate slower than normal speech.

CORRECTION KEY

Ab	Abbreviations	Jar	Jargon
Abs	Absolute phrase	LC	Lower case required
Adj	Use adjective instead of adverb	Log	Faulty logic
		Loos	Loose sentence
Adv	Use adverb instead of adjective	M	Mood
		ME	Misplaced emphasis
Agr-1	Agreement of subject and verb	MM	Misplaced modifier
		Ms	Careless mistake
Agr-2	Agreement of pronoun and antecedent	N	Wrong footnote form
		Narr	Poor narration
Am	Ambiguous modifier	Neo	Neologism
Amb	Ambiguity	Non	Nonce word
Ap	Omitted apostrophe; misused apostrophe	No ¶	No paragraph
		NP	No punctuation needed
Awk	Awkward construction	Num	Numbers
Bib	Wrong bibliography form	Om	Omission
C	Clauses	Out	Relationship of outline and text
Ca	Case		
Cap	Capitals required	P	Punctuation
Cl	Cliché	Para	Parallelism
Clar	Clarify	Paren	Parentheses and brackets
Co	Collective nouns	Pas	Weak use of passive verb
Coll	Colloquialism	Per	Periodic sentence
Comp	Comparison	Pr	Pronouns
Con	Illogical connective	Pts	Parts of speech
Cont	Contractions	PV	Point of view
CS	Comma splice	¶	New paragraph
Dan	Dangling modifier	Q	Quotations
Dash	Dash	Red	Redundancy; wordiness
Desc	Poor description	Ref	Pronoun reference
Dev	Inadequate idea development	Rep	Needless repetition
		Res	Restrictive modifiers
Di	Diction	Rhet	Rhetorical questions
Ex	Exclamations	S	Sentence elements
Exc	Excessive coordination	Sh	Shifts
Exp	Expletive	Sp	Spelling
F	Fragment	Spl	Split infinitive
FS	Fused sentence	SS	Confused sentence structure
Gen	Generalization; a specific statement is needed	Stl	Poor style; confusion of stylistic levels
Gl	Glossary	Sub	Subordination needed
Hy	Hyphenation	Syl	Syllabication
ID	Failure to follow indicated idea development	T	Tense sequence
Id	Unidiomatic phraseology	Thes	Relationship of thesis, outline, and text
Ill-C	Illogical coordination		
Ill-S	Illogical subordination	Ti	Relationship of title and text
Illus	Illustration needed	Tr	Transition device needed
Inc	Incomplete construction	V	Verb forms
Int	Introductions	WO	Unconventional word order
It	Italics	WV	Weak verb

Part Two

❊ THE ALPHABETIZED HANDBOOK-GLOSSARY

A, *an*   *A* precedes words beginning with a consonant sound. The long *u* sound, as in *use*, will be treated like a consonant sound.

An precedes a vowel sound.

EXAMPLES:

a hotel	an oyster
a humorist	an upper plate
a university	an honest man
a European	an honor

Ab   ***Abbreviations***   Except for a.m., p.m., A.D., B.C., D.C., Dr., Mr., Mrs., St., and the like, abbreviations are not permissible in the text of an essay.

Crutches like etc. and & (the ampersand) are particularly reprehensible. Nearly as bad are clipped words: ad, auto, gym, exam, math, O.K., prof, prom.

(the) above   Although it may at times be the only solution to a reference problem, *above* as a noun reference to material in the same composition is vague and awkward. Probably *above* should be limited to preposition use.

AWKWARD: As I said above, Frenchmen walk with their arms folded behind their backs.
BETTER: As I have already said . . .

Abs   *Absolute phrase*   The style of a sentence can often be improved by reducing an adverbial clause —at the beginning or at the end of a sentence—to what is called an absolute phrase, which appears to be an independent construction. But expanding it into an adverbial clause will demonstrate its close grammatical relationship to the rest of the sentence. Examples of improving by this kind of subordination follow.

ORIGINAL: After Claude had finished milking the cows, he called Cecily to taste the foaming liquid.
REVISION: The cows milked, Claude called Cecily . . .
ORIGINAL: Claude walked along slowly, while the calves bawled and clattered at his heels.
REVISION: Claude walked along slowly, the calves bawling and clattering at his heels.

Caution: An apparent absolute phrase which cannot be expanded into an adverbial clause bearing a proper grammatical relationship to the rest of the sentence is a *dangling modifier* (see **Dan**) and must be revised out of the sentence.

A.D.   A.D. precedes the numerals.
B.C. follows the numerals.

EXAMPLES:
Cecily's real birth date is A.D. 1919.
Vergil was at the peak of his career in 20 B.C.

absolutely   As an intensive, this word contributes absolutely nothing to a sentence.

accept vs. except (verbs)   To *accept* is to receive, permissively.
To *except* is to exclude.

EXAMPLE:
> With sincere regret we accept your decision to except old Claude from the ordinary requirements of Kingsville Country Club membership.

Adj   *Use adjective instead of adverb*   An adjective must describe or modify a noun or pronoun.

An adverb must describe or modify a verb, adjective, or adverb.

Some confusion has arisen in regard to certain adverbs wrongly used as adjectives (and adjectives wrongly used as adverbs) because *-ly* is often added to an adjective to form an adverb.

RIGHT: I feel bad (i.e., *sick*).
WRONG: I feel bad about how I have been treating the Rhomboids.
WRONG: I sure wish I could go riding today.
WRONG: I feel real good today.
RIGHT: I feel very well today.
WRONG: He was sick as a child.
RIGHT: He was sickly as a child.

Adv   *Use adverb instead of adjective*

affect vs. effect (verbs)   To *affect* is to change.
To *effect* is to cause.

EXAMPLES:
> The humidity affects my sinuses.
> The committee effected a change in the club constitution.

aggravate   This verb does not mean "irritate" or "annoy."

WRONG: If you aggravate Cecily, she will overcook the roast.
RIGHT: Illness has aggravated Cecily's congenitally bad disposition.

Agr-1   *Agreement of subject and verb*   1. A verb and its subject agree in person and number.

2. Distributive pronouns (*anybody, anyone, everybody, everyone, nobody, none*) require the singular verb.

3. Certain collective nouns (*couple, jury, dozen, offspring, politics, team,* and the like) may take either the singular or the plural verb, depending upon the writer's point of view, which must be consistent.

4. The expletive *it* requires a singular verb.

EXAMPLES:
It is I who blackballed Claude.
It was they who threw me out of the club instead.

5. The expletive *there* does not govern the verb.

EXAMPLES:
There are those who feel that Cecily has murder in her heart.
There is a fellow who worships her nevertheless.

Agr-2   *Agreement of pronoun and antecedent*   A pronoun (or pronominal adjective) agrees with its antecedent in gender and number.

WRONG: A person should watch their step when climbing his neighbor's trellis.
RIGHT: Anyone who climbs his neighbor's trellis risks gunfire.

all right   This expression (signifying "O.K.") verges on the colloquial.
Alright is illiterate.

all together vs. altogether   *Altogether* is an adverb.

EXAMPLES:
We all went together to the picnic.
Cecily is not altogether wrong in daily examining the contents of Claude's wallet.

Am *Ambiguous modifier* A modifier must not be capable of reference to either of two words or constructions.

WRONG: Smirk said when he was through writing he was going in to Kingsville.

RIGHT: Smirk said he was going in to Kingsville as soon as he finished his writing stint for the day.

Amb *Ambiguity* Sentence meaning must be clear. No sentence element should be capable of more than one interpretation.

EXAMPLES:

Cecily says she is going to keep bucking horses.
Claude says he is going to keep riding horses.

and, or, but, nor These are the pure conjunctions. It is proper to begin a sentence with any of them.
See RULE 3, p. 49.

any *Either* designates one of two things.
Any designates more than two things.

EXAMPLES:

Claude owns a palomino and a Shetland pony, both manhaters. It would be a mistake to saddle either of them.

Cecily's string of polo ponies is characterized mainly by longevity. Any pony of hers can be outrun by either of Claude's.

Ap *Omitted apostrophe; misused apostrophe* 1. An apostrophe is proper in the following circumstances:

a. To indicate possessive case of nouns and indefinite pronouns.

EXAMPLES:

a day's misadventures
a newspaper's circulation
Cecily's wild horse

the *Chronicle's* reliability
Juliana's master's thesis
Jones's newspaper
the Joneses' (the family's) financial empire
anybody's old shoe
someone's poison

b. To form plurals of numbers, letters, and words referred to as words.

EXAMPLES:
the tense 1960's
the ABC's of counter-gamesmanship
the *do's* and *do not's* of pipsqueakery

c. To form contractions (*but* contractions should be avoided in the text of an essay).
2. An apostrophe is *not* proper in the formation of the possessive case of personal pronouns.

WRONG: It's, their's, her's
RIGHT: Its, theirs, hers

Arabic and Roman numerals   See ***Numbers,*** pp. 405–406.

around   *Around* and *about* should not be used in similar situations.

WRONG: Old Claude has formed the habit of dropping in around four o'clock for a martini.
RIGHT: Singing softly, we gathered around the supine Claude.
WRONG: Numerous couples stood around the dance floor.
RIGHT: The fleeing Cecily ever before him, Claude ran around and around the elm tree.

as   *As* should not be substituted for *because.*

WRONG: As I had had enough fun for one evening, I left off kicking Muddleby.
RIGHT: Because (or *since*) Muddleby harbors grudges, he has cut me dead ever since.

as vs. like   In comparisons or implied comparisons use *as* before phrases and clauses, *like* before nouns and pronouns.

WRONG: As Jones his associate, Wells has an inordinate love of sloth.
RIGHT: Like Jones his associate . . .
WRONG: Like Maine goes, so goes Vermont.
RIGHT: As Maine goes . . .
WRONG: I love like she loves.
RIGHT: Old grudge-harboring Muddleby behaves like me.

as good or better than   Exclude this monstrosity from the sentence.

as of, as of now   *Now* or *at* is more exact, and therefore preferable.

WRONG: As of four o'clock, Cecily and Claude celebrated the arrival of an heir.
RIGHT: Reginald Rhomboid was born at four o'clock.
WRONG: As of now, I am through eating candy.
RIGHT: I am through eating candy.

awful, awfully   As intensives these words contribute little to the meaning of a sentence. *Awful* means "awe-inspiring"; to be *awfully* bored is probably not to be *awe-inspiringly* so.

Awk   *Awkward construction*   This is admittedly a catchall; at times an instructor marking an essay is forced to employ this symbol because he honestly does not know what to say about a sentence. It is grammatically correct, perhaps, and it is not exactly unidiomatic; but it needs revision—or exclusion from the paragraph.

B.C.   B.C. follows the numerals.

EXAMPLE:
Homer was writing epics before 800 B.C.

because   A clause commencing with *because* is an adverbial construction and cannot serve as the subject of a verb. Substituting *that* for *because* will usually correct the error.

WRONG: Because Claude is an Englishman is no reason to serve him scones for tea.

RIGHT: That Claude is an Englishman . . .

below   Like *above*, *below* as a noun reference to material in the same composition is vague and awkward. Probably *below* should be limited to preposition use.

See *above*.

beside vs. besides   *Beside* is a preposition of place. *Besides*, meaning "in addition," "else," may well be limited to adverb usage.

EXAMPLES:

Eating buttered scones, Claude sat cozily beside his enemy Muddleby.

There were others besides the Smirks who were armed for the ensuing fray.

better   Since *better* is both adjective and adverb, it is a poor verb. *Improve, enhance,* or *surpass* are all better words.

WRONG: Claude bettered his situation by emigrating to Texas.

RIGHT: Claude improved . . .

Bib   *Wrong bibliography form*   See Chapter 10, pp. 299–302.

Bible, Biblical (the Scriptures)   Capitalize but do not italicize.

big   Avoid using *big* if its approximate meaning is "important."

POOR: The Smirks are big people in Kingsville.

bunch   This noun is appropriate only when designating an arrangement of flowers or vegetables.

C   *Clauses*   A clause must have a *subject* (noun or pronoun) and a *complete* or *finite verb*. A finite verb can be distinguished from a verbal (infinitive, gerund, participle) because its meaning is *complete* in regard to tense, person, number, and mood. It is a matter of basic importance for the student to have a sound knowledge of the clause structure of sentences, for his mastery of style depends greatly upon it.

There are four kinds of clauses:

a. *The independent clause.* This kind of clause states a complete idea. The simple sentence is an independent clause.

b. *The noun clause.* This kind of dependent, or subordinate, clause functions like a noun in the sentence, (1) as a subject of a verb, (2) as a complement after a linking verb, (3) as the object of a verb, (4) as the object of an infinitive, (5) as the object of a preposition.

c. *The adverbial clause.* This kind of dependent clause functions like an adverb in the sentence, modifying or describing verbs, adverbs, or adjectives.

d. *The adjective clause.* This kind of dependent clause functions like an adjective in the sentence, modifying or describing nouns or pronouns.

Ca   *Case*   1. The English language has long since been streamlined in regard to case forms (subjective, possessive, objective), so that there is not much excuse for the student's using a wrong form.

2. The case form of a pronoun, then, depends upon its function as a subjective, objective, or possessive word.

3. Nouns show case only in regard to their possessive form (see **Ap**).

4. The subject of a gerund takes the possessive form.

Study the following examples:

Cecily is *she*. (subjective case, after a linking verb)

Claude is chasing *her* again. (objective case, after a transitive verb)

It comes to be *he* who does the cooking. (subjective case, after the infinitive of the linking verb)

I knew it to be *him*. (objective case, to agree with *it*)

Claude's going fishing left Cecily decidedly gay. (subject of a gerund)

His going fishing left her free to spend the day with her secret friend Mrs. Muddleby. (subject of a gerund)

I don't care *who* you are. (subjective case, complement of linking verb)

It matters not to me *who* comes to the lodge. (subject of *comes*)

Can you tell me *whom* she is going to the promenade with? (object of *with*)

I don't care *whom* you take to the promenade. (object of *take*)

Hers is not so hard a life as she makes it out to be. (referring to *her life*)

can vs. may (verbs)　　*Can* involves the ability to do something.

May involves permission or possibility.

EXAMPLES:

I can do anything better than you.

I may exert my influence in Claude's behalf, but I doubt it.

May I intercede on Claude's behalf?

cannot　　One word.

Cap　　**Capitals required**　　A proper noun—defined as a noun which cannot take a limiting modifier—is capitalized.

Titles: The first word and nouns, pronouns, verbs, adjectives (but *not* articles), and adverbs in titles require capitals.

certainly   This is a good transition word, but it should not be used as an intensive.

claim   This verb is not to be used meaning "declare," "maintain," "charge."

WRONG: Cecily claims that Claude has no right to spy on her.

RIGHT: The Rhomboids claim dominion over a ranching empire of several acres.

Cl   *Cliché*   The writer should strive continually to express himself without resorting to trite, exhausted metaphors. The chances are that if he has heard an expression once, it is a cliché.

See Chapter 2, p. 42.

Clar   *Clarify*   The meaning of a sentence must be expressly clear, especially in regard to the sentences which precede and follow it.

See Chapter 3, pp. 48–67; Chapter 4, pp. 82–84.

Co   *Collective nouns*   Certain collective nouns (*couple, jury, dozen, offspring, politics, team,* and the like) may take either the singular or the plural verb, depending upon the writer's point of view, which must be consistent. Care must be exercised to ensure agreement of reference pronouns once the point of view has been established.

Coll   *Colloquialism*   There are various levels of informal expression. Some such expressions are appropriate to essay writing, but the colloquialism—especially because of its triteness—is not. Terms like *cute, date* (for an appointment or escort), *enthuse, guy,* and *irregardless,* common in beginning college essays, impoverish rather than enrich one's style. A colloquialism, further, is not legitimized by enclosing it in quotation marks.

See Chapter 2, pp. 19–23.

Comp   *Comparison*   1. There are two ways of comparing adverbs and adjectives: (a) adding *-er, -est,* (b) using *more, most.* If the writer is uncertain as to which course is right, he should consult the dictionary.

2. Comparisons must be complete and logical. Study the following examples.

WRONG: Muddleby's face is more angular than a horse.
RIGHT: Muddleby's face is more angular than a horse's.
WRONG: Cecily's garden has more radishes.
RIGHT: Cecily's garden has more radishes than Angela's; Cecily's garden has more radishes than it had last year.
WRONG: Angela is the prettiest of our two wives.
RIGHT: Angela is the prettier . . .
WRONG: Angela is the loveliest girl.
RIGHT: Angela is lovely.
WRONG: Cecily's approach to marriage is more unique than Angela's.
RIGHT: Neither Cecily nor Angela is unique in her approach to marriage. (Absolutes cannot be compared.)

compare vs. contrast   To *compare* is to deal with similarities.

To *contrast* is to demonstrate differences.

EXAMPLES:
Cecily has the figure of a Venus, the brain of a chipmunk. (comparison)
Shall I compare thee to a summer's day?
Thou art more lovely and more temperate . . . (contrast)

Con   *Illogical connective*   Connectives do not merely link; they also have meaning. This meaning must be consistent with the context of the sentence.

See the section on transition devices in Chapter 5.

Cont   *Contractions*   Contractions should not be used in the text of an essay unless it is necessary to reproduce an original, as conversation.

contrast (verb)   See *compare vs. contrast.*

convince vs. persuade   A person may be *persuaded* to do a thing, but he may not be *convinced* (i.e., be possessed by conviction) that he is doing the right thing.

WRONG: Claude convinced me to sign a deed to share water rights with him.
RIGHT: Claude persuaded me . . .

couple   This collective noun should not be used meaning "two."

WRONG: A couple of boys were whooping it up . . .
RIGHT: Two boys were whooping it up . . .

CS   *Comma splice*   Two independent clauses in the same sentence must be separated by (a) a comma followed by a pure conjunction, or (b) a semicolon.

See RULE 3, pp. 49–50.

Dan   *Dangling modifier*   Unless it is used adverbially, a loose modifier at the beginning or end of a sentence must have a specific grammatical relationship to a noun or pronoun. Phrases beginning with *thus, thereby,* or *with* are particularly suspect. Study the following examples.

WRONG: Driving along the highway to Kingsville, the rattlesnakes were numerous.
RIGHT: Approaching Kingsville, we saw numerous rattlesnakes along the highway.
WRONG: Born in 1919, Cecily's youth was spent in Sussex, Surrey, and Hants.
RIGHT: Cecily, born in 1919, spent . . .

WRONG: The barbed-wire fence was cut, thus causing the bawling and clattering calves to spill all over the highway.

RIGHT: When the barbed wire fence was cut, the bawling and clattering calves spilled all over the highway.

WRONG: With all of the means at my command, Cecily is quite unmanageable.

RIGHT: Even though I use all of the means at my command, Cecily is quite unmanageable.

Dash   *dash*   As a stylistic device—witness its recurrence throughout this book—the dash is a convenient contrivance to indicate sharp turns in thought and to enclose parenthetical material. The beginning writer will for the most part try to get along without it, however, for he may otherwise find it peppering his pages and interfering with the composition of coherent and well-considered sentences.

See RULE 6, p. 51.

dates   Two ways of giving dates are in common use now.

The standard form: September 25, 1929.

The military form now commonly accepted: 25 September 1929.

definitely   Meaning is not intensified by the use of this adverb.

Desc   *Poor description*   Study the appropriate section in Chapter 8, and revise according to its principles.

Dev   *Inadequate idea development*   A paragraph must develop its topic fully. Study the appropriate section in Chapter 4, and rewrite the paragraph in accord with its principles.

Di   *Diction*   The choice of a word is dictated by considerations of propriety (in regard to its level of usage) and exactness in denotation and connotation. Consult the dictionary.

different   A contrast employing *different* should be complete. *Different from* is infinitely preferable to *different than.*

WRONG: Juliana is so . . . so different.
RIGHT: Juliana is not like other girls.
WRONG: Juliana's smile is different than that of other girls.
RIGHT: I want a girl who is different from other girls.

disinterested vs. uninterested   *Disinterested* means "impartial."
Uninterested means "lacking interest."

WRONG: It is hard to be uninterested about taxes.
RIGHT: It is hard to find a disinterested newspaper during a political campaign.

due to   Despite a general tendency (abetted by radio and television) to blur meanings, the precise writer may wish to reserve *due to* for situations in which something is expected to happen. Otherwise *owing to* or *because of* will be appropriate.

RIGHT: The train is due to arrive at ten.
WRONG: Due to certain circumstances beyond our comprehension, Cecily walked home from the party.
RIGHT: Because of certain circumstances . . .

each other   Use *each other* in contexts involving only two people: The two authors, facing a deadline, were shouting down the hall at each other.

effect (verb)   See *affect.*

either   See *any.*

et cetera, and so forth   Never use either of these expressions. To do so is an admission that the writer does not know what to say next.

Ex   ***Exclamations***   Unless quoting another speaker or writer who has done so, never use an exclamation mark in exposition or argumentation.

Exc   ***Excessive coordination***   See Chapter 3, pp. 52–56.

             except (verb)   See ***accept.***

Exp   ***Expletive***   The expletive is a device making for sentence variety. It is not the subject of a verb but indicates, in effect, that the subject comes later.

             The expletive *it,* however, requires a singular verb.

             The expletive *there* does not govern the verb. See ***Agr-1.***

             extra   This adjective should not be used as an adverb meaning "unusually."

             WRONG: Cecily is behaving extra nice today.
             RIGHT: Cecily is behaving especially well . . .

F   ***Fragment***   In student essays the use of a fragmentary or partial sentence is indefensible.

             (the) fact that   This phrase should be edited out of the sentence if it is possible to do so. If what follows it *is* a fact, and not merely an opinion, the situation will be readily apparent to the reader.

             POOR: The fact that Cecily has bought a polo pony is known to one and all.
             BETTER: That Cecily has bought . . .

             farther, further   *Farther* indicates distance.
             Further indicates time or quantity.

             EXAMPLES:
             Claude's miserable acreage is farther down the road.
             The audience asked Smirk to speak further on his subject.
             The further we go into the matter, the later it gets.

feature   This is a good noun. Avoid using it as a verb.

WRONG: Cecily is featuring round steak for supper.
RIGHT: Cecily's entree for supper is *boeuf bourguignon*.

fellow man   Replace this awkward phrase with *people*.

few, fewer, vs. little, less   *Few* has to do with number.
Little indicates quantity.

EXAMPLES:
Fewer than five people stayed for the finish of Smirk's attack on Muddleby.
There was a little round steak on the platter. In fact, what she called *boeuf bourguignon* amounted to less than two pounds of tough calf.

(the) field of   This phrase is redundant when used with a noun designating the field.

fine   Unless this adjective is used in a more or less technical sense, it does not mean much.

POOR: I feel fine, and it's a fine day; so let's go for a fine walk.
RIGHT: A fine gold wire is used to wrap these filaments.
RIGHT: Some mills grind exceedingly fine.
RIGHT: We read fine print at the expense of our vision.

fix (verb, noun)   Legitimately this word has to do with making an object firm or finding where an object is.

POOR: Bill fixes bicycle tires for a living.
POOR: Bill has gotten himself in an awful fix.
BETTER: Claude fixed the picnic table in the ground to keep Cecily from spilling the punch.
BETTER: With our telescope we attempted to establish a fix on the astronaut's capsule.

flammable   There is no logical or etymological reason to substitute this term for *inflammable*. It (*flammable*) is a **neologism** (which see) coined by an illiterate fire extinguisher salesman.

FS   *Fused sentence*   Two independent clauses have been married without any connecting device. See **CS** (*comma splice*) and RULE 3, pp. 49–50.

-ful   Do not tamper with a standard word by adding *-ful* to it. This stricture applies as well to *-ize* and *-some*.

fun   Never use this noun as an adjective.

BAD EXAMPLES:
"This is going to be a fun house," Cecily chortled as Claude pushed her across the threshold.
"We'll have a fun time, for sure," Claude replied somewhat grimly.

funny   This adjective has been used in various contexts and has probably come to mean virtually nothing at all.

Gen   *Generalization*   A specific statement is needed. Beginning writers are afflicted with a penchant for generalization, for dealing with the abstract rather than the specific.

POOR: Everybody at school has a new frock for the promenade.
BETTER: That awful Henrietta Mood has a new frock for the promenade.

get   This verb has a myriad of meanings, or half-meanings. It should be used only when no other verb will serve.

Gl   *Glossary*   Glossary discussions are alphabetized in combination with the handbook material.

he or she   *He* is usually sufficient.

WRONG: Someone will volunteer, but I don't know who he or she will be.

RIGHT: Someone will volunteer, but I don't know who he will be.

Hy   *Hyphenation*   1. Although there is a general tendency to discard the hyphen in combined words (quasi-political, communist-inspired), the writer should consult the dictionary when in doubt about whether to hyphenate.

2. The rules for dividing words into syllables can be learned, but the writer confronted with the necessity to split a word at the end of a line will be wise to rely on his dictionary. He will be even wiser to make it a practice *never* to split a word.

ID   *Failure to follow indicated idea development*   See Chapter 4, pp. 85–94.

Id   *Unidiomatic phraseology*   See Chapter 3, pp. 68–71.

(the) idea that   This phrase should be edited out of the sentence if it is possible to do so. If what follows *is* an idea, the situation will be readily apparent to the reader.

POOR: The idea that Cecily knows more about polo ponies than Cynthia does is absurd.

BETTER: That Cecily knows . . .

if vs. whether   *If* is properly used in conditional situations.

Whether, often accompanied by *or not,* is proper when alternatives are proposed.

POOR: I do not know if I will take Cynthia to the promenade.

BETTER: I do not know whether . . .

RIGHT: If it rains, I shall not go to Cynthia's.

RIGHT: Whether it rains or not, Cynthia will go without me tonight.

Ill-C   *Illogical coordination*   See Chapter 3, pp. 59–62.

Ill-S   *Illogical subordination*   See Chapter 3, pp. 56–59.

Illus   *Illustration needed*   See Chapter 4, pp. 102–103.

image   This noun has been badly mauled by the practitioners of *madisonese* (see p. 42). It is well for the writer to reserve it for reference to a poetic device.

Inc   *Incomplete construction*   In the interest of clarity incomplete or "understood" sentence elements may need revision.

individual   In reference to a *person,* this noun is imprecise. Perhaps *individual* should be restricted to adjective use.

POOR: Claude is a crusty individual.

BETTER: Claude is crusty.

Int   *Introductions*   A formal introduction is a complete statement (independent clause). It is followed by a colon.

An informal introduction (usually a subject and a verb) is followed either by a comma or by no punctuation.

See RULE 8, p. 51.

is when   A definition employing this phrase is illogical. The verb is sufficient.

WRONG: A tiger is when a big cat has stripes.

RIGHT: A tiger is a big cat with stripes.

It   *Italics*   1. To italicize, underline (do not use quotation marks).

2. Italics apply to words referred to as words, foreign words, book titles, names of ships, periodicals, and newspapers.

3. The titles of parts of books, periodicals, and newspapers are enclosed in quotation marks.

4. See the sections on bibliography and footnotes in Chapter 10.

it seems, it would seem, I would say   All writing should be clear and forceful, never apologetic. Such expressions as these should therefore be edited out of the sentence, even though some commentators on our suffering language allow the use of the "polite subjunctive." If for no other reason, its use by politicians, who seldom make direct statements, disqualifies the polite subjunctive.

-ize   Resist the temptation to manufacture verbs by adding -ize to adjectives or nouns.

Jar   **Jargon**   Specialized language, as of a technical profession, sport, or sect, has no place in the serious writer's vocabulary, especially if such language tends to be colloquial. Witness words like *aforesaid* (legal jargon), *angle* (noun meaning *aspect* or *position*), *and/or*, *case* (when it means *instance* or *example*), *contact* (commercial verb), *finalize*, *line* (denoting *occupation*), *party* (denoting *person*), *plus* (mathematical symbol), *said* (legal adjective), *struck out* (baseball term, describing various types of failure).

See Chapter 2, p. 42.

just   As an intensifier, *just* adds nothing to a sentence.

key   Avoid using this noun as an adjective.

POOR: Our tackle threw a key block downfield.

BETTER: Our tackle threw a downfield block. (All blocks are "key" blocks.)

LC   *Lower case required*   Avoid capitalizing words for emphasis.

lend vs. loan   *Lend* is the verb.
           Loan is the noun.

like   See *as vs. like.*

little, less   See *few, fewer.*

locate   If properly used, this verb requires an object.

POOR: We decided to locate in Kingsville, or rather Cecily did.
BETTER: We decided to live in Kingsville . . .
RIGHT: If I can locate the property, I will buy it.

Log   *Faulty logic*   All elements of a sentence must have logical as well as precise grammatical relationships with other elements of the sentence.
           See Chapter 3, pp. 56–62.
           See the section on logic in Chapter 7.

Loos   *Loose sentence*   A loose sentence has parenthetical elements added to it after its central meaning has been established. Too many such sentences in an essay sorely damage its style.
           See the discussion of the periodic sentence, Chapter 3, pp. 66–67.

M   *Mood*   Although its occurrence is not frequent in English, the subjunctive mood continues in use for (a) commands, (b) conditions contrary to fact, (c) conditions impossible to fulfill.

EXAMPLES:
           Cecily, *hand* me the ice tongs and the flyswatter. (command)

If I *were* you, I should not cross the Rubicon tonight. (condition contrary to fact)

I wish I *were* a butterfly, so I could flit away. (condition impossible to fulfill)

may   See *can vs. may.*

ME   *Misplaced emphasis*   See Chapter 3, pp. 53–56.

MM   *Misplaced modifier*   A modifier or describer must stand as close as possible in the sentence to the word or construction modified.

AWKWARD: Cecily has wavy hair like an Arabian horse.
BETTER: Like an Arabian horse, Cecily . . .
MISLEADING: Claude first saw Cecily at the age of thirty.
WRONG: A great man, Cecily loves her Claude.
WRONG: A rainy, miserable day, Agatha stayed home on Thursday.

A special kind of misplaced modifier is called the squinting modifier, a modifier that may ambiguously refer to either of two terms it falls between: The car in which Karl was driving calmly slid off the road.

Calmly here may refer to either *driving* or *slid.* It should be moved to make the reference clear.

Ms   *Careless mistake*   The writer should proofread his work carefully before submitting it, (a) to make sure that he has written exactly what he wanted to write and (b) to remedy illegible handwriting.

must   This verb should not be used as a noun or adjective for emphasis.

WRONG: Seeing Elizabeth Taylor's latest motion picture is a must.
RIGHT: Try not to miss Elizabeth Taylor's latest motion picture.

myself   It is pretentious humility to use *myself* for *I* or *me*.

WRONG: Claude and myself rode the range looking for strays.
RIGHT: Claude and I . . .
WRONG: Cecily accompanied Claude and myself as we made the fence circuit.
RIGHT: Cecily accompanied Claude and me . . .

N   *Wrong footnote form*   See Chapter 10, pp. 303–306.

Narr   *Poor narration*   Review the principles of narration in Chapter 9, and revise the weak material according to these principles.

neither   *Neither* designates one of two alternatives. *None* designates one of more than two alternatives.

EXAMPLES:
Claude owns a palomino and a Shetland pony. Neither is worth a nickel.
Cecily's string of polo ponies is characterized mainly by longevity. None of them is worth as much as Claude's palomino.

Neo   *Neologism*   Before consenting to add a new term or expression to his stock of idioms, a person should consider whether the neologism is consistent with the flavor of the language he has been using and, more important, whether it adds to the range of his expression. At this writing *A-O. K.* is a case in point.

nice   This adjective should be reserved for the senses "demanding close discrimination," "demanding delicate handling," or "displaying close discrimination."

> WRONG: The ever glorious Cecily is not always nice to me.
>
> BETTER: The ever glorious Cecily sometimes treats me badly.
>
> RIGHT: Keeping Agatha home evenings is always a nice problem in domestic strategy.

Non   *Nonce word*   The nonce word is a term formed and used for a particular occasion. But it is habit-forming.

BAD EXAMPLE:
Compared to Cynthia, Cecily is stupid about polo-poniology.

no one   Two words.

none   See *neither.*

No ¶   *No paragraph*   The material that follows this symbol should be part of the paragraph preceding it.

NP   *No punctuation needed*   Excessive punctuation damages style.

Num   *Numbers*   1. Spell out numbers below 100; use numerals thereafter.

2. Hyphenate combinations (e.g., thirty-nine).

3. Do *not* spell out dates or serial numbers (except of course in a direct quotation).

4. The numbers which indicate not just number only but sequence (first, second, fourth, fifth) are ordinal numbers. Ordinal numbers do not require the suffix *-ly*.

5. Use Roman numerals to designate main headings in an outline, volume numbers of periodicals, acts of plays, and, in lower case, scenes of plays. Arabic numerals are used in most other situations.

I	1	20	XX
II	2	21	XXI
III	3	40	XL
IV	4	50	L
V	5	100	C
VI	6	200	CC
VII	7	400	CD
VIII	8	500	D
IX	9	1000	M
X	10	1500	MD
XI	11	1962	MCMLXII
XII	12		
XIII	13		
XIV	14		
XV	15		

off of   Recast sentences in which there are two consecutive prepositions.

POOR: Claude leaped off of his galloping horse.
BETTER: Claude leaped from his galloping horse.

Om   *Omission*   Proofread carefully to make sure that all idioms are complete, that no word has been carelessly omitted.

one another   Use *one another* in contexts involving more than two people: The authors and their editors were all shouting at one another.

Out   *Relationship of outline and text*   Outline and text must be consistent in organization and content.
See Chapter 5, "Developing the Outline and Staying with It."

P   *Punctuation*   See Chapter 3, pp. 48–52.
See *Int.*
See *Q.*

Para   *Parallelism*   Sentence elements that are equivalent or coordinate in meaning should be similarly parallel in grammatical structure.
See Chapter 3, pp. 62–65.

Paren   *Parentheses and brackets*   1. Parentheses may be used in the text to enclose parenthetical material that interrupts the flow of the sentence. But it is preferable to rewrite the sentence, integrating the parenthetical material in its context.
See RULE 6, p. 51.
2. Brackets usually inclose editorial comments within a direct quotation. They may be drawn in by hand on a typescript.

EXAMPLES:
Claude said, "Cec [Cecily] has forsaken me for that rascal Muddleby."
On the sign were the words "Abadon [*sic*] liquor and be saved."

Pas   *Weak use of passive verb*   Verbs in the passive voice severely limit the possibility of emphasis in a sentence.

POOR: The calf was roped, thrown, tied, and branded by the lanky old cowboy, whose cigarette never left his mouth in the process.
BETTER: A cigarette stuck in the corner of his mouth, the lanky old cowboy roped, threw, tied, and branded the bawling calf.

Per   *Periodic sentence*   See Chapter 3, pp. 66–67.

per cent   Two words.

persuade   See *convince vs. persuade.*

phase   This noun should not be used unless change is implicit in the context of the sentence.

WRONG: There are many phases to higher education.
RIGHT: There are many aspects . . .
RIGHT: The moon is in its final phase this month.
RIGHT: There are several important phases in the training of a gaited horse.

point(s) Often this noun has little meaning, for it deals with the general rather than the specific.

POOR: Despite her temper, Cecily has her points.
BETTER: Despite her temper, Cecily has the positive virtues of forthrightness and, occasionally, a sense of humor.

Pr *Pronouns* 1. Nouns do not have separate forms for the nominative and accusative cases, but personal and relative pronouns do have separate forms for these cases. Function in the sentence of course determines the proper form for the pronoun.
See *Ca.*
2. A pronoun agrees with its antecedent in gender and number.

WRONG: A person that is in trouble needs help.
RIGHT: A person who is in trouble . . .
See *Agr-2.*

3. *Which* and *that* should not be used as hazy references to materials in previous sentences or paragraphs. A pronoun should always refer to a noun or another pronoun, or a noun clause.

POOR: After mulling over the decision for half the day we decided to go riding. Which we did.
WEAK: One rainy day Henrietta left Cecily and Claude alone at tea. That is why they are married today.

4. *This* is much used as a reference to sentences or ideas or paragraphs which precede it. Any sentence beginning with *this* should therefore be examined closely to see (a) whether it refers to a

noun, pronoun, or noun clause; (b) whether effective subordination can eliminate the need for using this hazy reference word.

POOR: Henrietta and Cecily had a violent quarrel after Claude left the house. This is why they do not speak to each other.

BETTER: Henrietta and Cecily have not spoken to each other since their quarrel following Claude's departure from the house.

Pts   *Parts of speech*   It is function in the sentence that determines the part of speech to be used. Listed herewith are the parts of speech, with their functions.

1. The *noun* names a person, place, or thing. It may serve as (a) the subject of a verb, (b) the subject of a gerund, (c) an appositive, (d) the object of a verb, verbal, or preposition, (e) the complement of a linking verb.

2. The *pronoun* serves in place of the noun.

3. The *verb* states or describes action, condition, existence, state of being.

4. The *adjective* describes or modifies nouns or pronouns.

5. The *adverb* describes or modifies verbs, adjectives, adverbs.

6. The *preposition* relates a noun or phrase or clause to some other element of the sentence.

7. The *conjunction* links clauses, phrases, words.

8. The *interjection* is an independent word indicating emotion. It is often used as an introductory or transition device.

PV   *Point of view*   Once a point of view has been adopted, it should be scrupulously maintained throughout the composition.

See the discussion of *point of view* in Chapter 9.

BAD STYLE: I don't see how I can put up with Claude's lying and cheating much longer. *You* leave the house for ten minutes, and he is writing lies in his diary. *One* doesn't like to say it, but *I* don't think he can be trusted. (changes in point of view italicized)

¶   *New paragraph*   When the writer begins to consider an important new idea, he should begin a new paragraph.

Q   *Quotations*   Study position of punctuation in the examples which follow. (See also pp. 315–316, 371.)

EXAMPLES:
Claude said, "Cecily was sick yesterday."
Did Claude say, "Cecily was sick yesterday"?
The supine Claude groaned, "Am I still alive?"
"I'm afraid so," Cecily replied.
"I hurt all over," Claude answered, "but I am bound to improve."

quite   As an intensive *quite* seldom contributes to the emphatic quality of a sentence.

real   This adjective cannot be used as an adverb.

WRONG: Despite his thrashing at the hands of the Muddleby brothers, Claude feels real pert.
RIGHT: Claude feels very fit despite . . .

really   Like *quite, really* seldom intensifies the meaning of what it modifies.

(the) reason is because   Usually the logical error involved in this construction can be corrected by substituting *that* for *because.*

WRONG: Lately Agatha has been playing tennis with her left hand. The reason is because she recently learned that she is left-handed.
RIGHT: Angela likes to swim on her left side. Her reason is that she likes to wave at people with her right hand.

Red   *Redundancy; wordiness*   Delete any word or phrase or expression in the sentence that needlessly repeats what has already been said, or which says what does not need to be said.

> WRONG: The Rhomboids are having adjustment trouble as Texans in this modern world of today.
> BETTER: The Rhomboids are having trouble adjusting to life in Texas.
> WRONG: As I have already said, politics in Texas is largely a matter of the social group one belongs to, which is what I have been saying all along.
> BETTER: As I have said abundantly, politics in Texas is largely a matter of the social group one belongs to.

Ref   *Pronoun reference*   A pronoun refers ultimately to a noun (which is sometimes "understood" if it is a name). The reference must be clear and explicit.
>   See *Agr-2.*
>   See *Pr.*

Rep   *Needless repetition*

Res   *Restrictive modifiers*   See RULE 4, p. 50.

Rhet   *Rhetorical questions*   Some writers favor the rhetorical question as a stylistic device. It consists of asking oneself a question and then answering it, an awkward procedure at best, and one to be avoided if possible.

> POOR: What am I going to do about Cecily's gossiping? I am going to do this: I am going to stuff my ears with cotton.
> BETTER: The only remedy for Cecily's gossiping is stuffing the ears with cotton.

> *run* (verb)   Like *get,* this verb has a myriad of meanings, or half-meanings. It should be used only when no other verb will serve.

S   ***Sentence elements***   Basic elements in the sentence are the subject (the thing the sentence is *about*) and the predicate (saying something *about* the subject). Hence a sentence can consist of as few as one (an unadorned command) or two words (a noun or pronoun and a finite verb). But the subject and predicate can be described and expanded almost infinitely, in regard to variety.

Some obvious patterns involving variety are indicated on page 76. If the instructor has marked the sentence with the symbol "S," it is understood that its elements need rearranging for the sake of variety.

Sh   ***Shifts***   A discourse begun in the present tense should preserve the time relationships implicit in this tense throughout. Similarly, if the system of time relationships is based on a verb in the past tense at the beginning of a composition, all verbs throughout the composition must be temporally consistent with this verb.

BAD EXAMPLE:
Yesterday morning being sunny, I went to Forest Park to practice some iron shots. But scarcely *have* I *arrived* when it *begins* to clabber up, and soon I *was looking* for practice balls in a driving rainstorm. (shifts italicized)

See *PV.*

Note: It is proper, in describing the events of a work of fiction, to use the present tense (the *historical present tense*); for fiction, because it is permanent, is always with the reader in a present sense.

Shall vs. will; should vs. would   1. Precise writers use *shall* for the first person future tense in preference to *will.*

2. Precise writers use *should* in preference to *would* for first person conditional statements.

EXAMPLE:
I should go to church Sundays if I were you.

side   Like *point*, this noun should not be used meaning "aspect."

POOR: There are many sides to Cecily that I simply do not understand.
BETTER: There are aspects of Cecily's nature . . .

simply   As an intensive, this adverb contributes little to sentence emphasis.

smart   Avoid using this adjective meaning "intelligent."

so   As an intensive, *so* must be used in a completed comparison.

POOR: I felt so bad this morning.
BETTER: I felt so bad this morning that I went back to bed.

-some   Do not tamper with a standard word by adding *-some* to it.

Sp   ***Spelling***   Bad spelling is a reliable illiteracy index. Pride in one's inability to spell is a reliable idiocy index.

Spl   ***Split infinitive***   In itself the split infinitive is not incorrect, but the writer will avoid interposing an adverb between *to* and its infinitive unless satisfied that the style of the sentence is improved thereby.

SS   ***Confused sentence structure***   The instructor marking papers will use this symbol as a last resort.

Stl   ***Poor style; confusion of stylistic levels***   All of Chapter 3 applies to this problem.

structure   This is a noun, not a verb.
See the discussion of *madisonese,* p. 42.

Sub   ***Subordination needed***   Study Chapter 3, pp. 52–58.

such   Like *so, such* as an intensive must be used in a completed comparison.

POOR: I feel such a fool.
BETTER: I feel foolish.
RIGHT: I felt such a pain that I stopped working.

Syl   ***Syllabication***   1. When typing a paper, do not divide a word if no more than two letters are to be taken to the next line.
2. Similarly, do not divide a word if fewer than three letters precede the hyphen.
See *Hy.*

T   ***Tense sequence***   Study the following examples of time relationships between verbs.

Cecily *looks* better to me today than she *did* yesterday.
Cecily *has* always *looked* like a doll, but today she *looks* like Raggedy Ann.
Cecily *looked* better yesterday than she *had looked* for a long time.
By the time you *arrive* (or *will arrive*) tomorrow, Cecily *will have plastered* on her makeup.

that vs. which   The precise writer will begin restrictive modifiers with *that,* nonrestrictive modifiers with *which.* (But see the quotation from Johnson on p. 63.)

EXAMPLES:

The horse that you hear neighing behind the barn is Cecily's favorite.
The third house from the end, which seems to be on fire at the moment, is the site of all-out war between Claude and Cecily.

Thes *Relationship of thesis, outline, and text* Thesis, outline, and text must be consistent in content and organization.
See Chapter 5, sections III–V.
See *Out.*

Ti *Relationship of title and text* The title of an essay should be short and interesting. It should also, if at all possible, imply the thesis and indicate what the essay as a whole is about.

Titles 1. For the typed paper, all of the letters in the title of the paper are capitalized.

2. For the handwritten paper and in references to titles (especially when they are enclosed in quotation marks), the first letter of these items is capitalized: (a) the first word, (b) nouns, (c) pronouns, (d) verbs, (e) adverbs, (f) adjectives (but not *a, an, the*).

EXAMPLE:
"It Is a Sad Day in October with the Coming of the Snow and Ice"

too This adverb should not be used meaning "very."

POOR: Agatha does not sit her horse too well.
BETTER: Agatha does not sit her horse very well. (One can hardly do something *too* well.)

top This adjective does not denote excellence. "Top authority," for example, is clearly redundant.

Tr *Transition device needed* See the list of transition devices in Chapter 5, pp. 134–137.

truly This intensive is virtually meaningless.

type A person should not be referred to as a *type*.

POOR: Gwendolyn is the type of girl I could fall for.
BETTER: Gwendolyn interests me strangely.

uninterested   See *disinterested vs. uninterested.*

up   As an adverb used to intensify the meaning of a verb, *up* has little to recommend it. Deleting *up* from the following examples improves them.

Unfortunately, Reginald has learned from Claude to gobble up his food.

Observe the sylphlike Cecily as she stacks up the saucers.

Note: Occasionally the idiom, as in "chained up," seems to demand retention of *up.*

V   **Verb forms**   If in doubt as to the principal parts of verbs, consult the dictionary.

very   It is doubtful that *very* as an intensive contributes very much to the sentence.

where   *Where* should not be substituted for *that* to introduce a dependent clause.

WRONG: I see in the papers where Gwendolyn has at last sued Muddleby for breach of promise.
RIGHT: I see in the papers that . . .
BUT: Gwendolyn's garden is the place where affidavits grow.

whether   See *if vs. whether.*

which   See *that vs. which.*

while   *While* does not mean *although.* Therefore it should not be used to introduce a clause unless it specifically means "at the same time" or "during the time that."

POOR: While it is natural that Cecily should spoil Reginald a bit, Claude is certainly right in asserting that a bit of the rod will advance his son's education.
BETTER: Although it is natural . . .
RIGHT: Cecily fondled Reginald while Claude was, undetected, pinching the child.

will vs. would   See *shall vs. will.*

-wise   Do not tamper with standard words by adding *-wise* to them.

WO   *Unconventional word order*

WV   *Weak verbs*   Avoid using verbs whose denotative meaning is weak or ambiguous.

EXAMPLES:
have, get, run, be, do, go.

Appendix I:

SUGGESTIONS
FOR THE STUDY OF
IMAGINATIVE LITERATURE

Since this book deals throughout with the problems of effective style, every section presumably has at least indirect bearing upon the study of imaginative literature and specifically upon writing that results from that study. Special sections of the book, however, may have more direct bearing on this study than others. The section titled "Organization of the Literary Essay" (Chapter Five, p. 138), the one titled "Exposition in the Literary Essay" (Chapter Six, p. 186), and all of Chapter Ten, which uses the literary research paper as illustration for its discussion of research techniques, should be useful to the student both in his freshman composition course and in any subsequent study of literature alone. The bibliography that follows may also be of specific use in the study of literature since the works included, in addition to their intrinsic value, provide both literary and historical background and clear demonstration of the methods men have used in studying lit-

419

erature. The works listed here are important to any university student who would know his heritage, who would comprehend his present, and who would confront his future. And they are necessary to the student whose major concern is the study of literature.

This list is neither comprehensive nor systematically selective. The student may find further supplementary materials through diligent use of the bibliographical guides given in Chapter Ten.

DRAMA

Aristotle, *Poetics*
Giraldi Cinthio, *On the Composition of Comedies and Tragedies*
Lodovico Castelvetro, *A Commentary on Aristotle's Poetics*
Lope de Vega, *The New Art of Making Comedies*
Ben Jonson, *Timber: or, Discoveries*
Thomas Heywood, *An Apology for Actors*
John Milton, Preface to *Samson Agonistes*
John Dryden, *An Essay of Dramatic Poesy*
William Congreve, *Letter Concerning Humour in Comedy*
John Dennis, *The Usefulness of the Stage*
John Dennis, *On the Vis Comica*
Charles Lamb, "On the Artificial Comedies of the Last Age"
William Hazlitt, *Lectures on the English Comic Writers*
George Meredith, "An Essay on Comedy"
Friedrich Nietzsche, *The Birth of Tragedy*
Henri Bergson, *Laughter*
George Bernard Shaw, *Prefaces*
Francis Fergusson, *The Idea of a Theater*
Alan Thompson, *The Anatomy of Drama*

POETRY

Horace, *The Art of Poetry*
Longinus, *On the Sublime*
Sir Thomas Elyot, *The Governor*, Book 1, Chapter X
Sir Philip Sidney, *A Defense of Poesie*
Samuel Daniel, *A Defense of Ryme*
Nicholas Boileau-Despreaux, *The Art of Poetry*
Joseph Addison, Spectator no. 409

Alexander Pope, *An Essay on Criticism*
John Dennis, *The Advancement and Reformation of Poetry*
Edward Young, "Conjectures on Original Composition"
Samuel Johnson, *The Lives of the Poets*
Joshua Reynolds, Discourse XIII
William Wordsworth, Preface to *Lyrical Ballads*
Samuel Coleridge, *Biographia Literaria*
Percy Bysshe Shelley, *Defence of Poetry*
Ralph Waldo Emerson, "The Poet"
Edgar Allan Poe, "The Poetic Principle"
Edgar Allan Poe, "The Philosophy of Composition"
Matthew Arnold, "The Function of Criticism"
Matthew Arnold, "The Study of Poetry"
John Ruskin, "Of the Pathetic Fallacy"
Thomas Stearns Eliot, "Tradition and the Individual Talent"
T. E. Hulme, *Speculations*
Robert Frost, "The Constant Symbol," in his *Collected Poems*
José Ortega y Gasset, *The Dehumanization of Art*

FICTION

Henry James, "The Art of Fiction"
R. P. Blackmuir, ed., *The Art of the Novel*
Henry Fielding, Preface to *Joseph Andrews*
Henry Fielding, Part One of each book in *Tom Jones*
Emile Zola, *The Experimental Novel*
William Dean Howells, "Criticism and Fiction"
E. M. Forster, *Aspects of the Novel*
Percy Lubbock, *The Craft of Fiction*
Joseph Conrad, Preface to *The Nigger of the Narcissus*

Appendix II:

SUGGESTED SYLLABI

Given below are a basic syllabus and three alternate plans, any one of which may be useful with this book. One precautionary note is appropriate here. Instructors may find it beneficial to limit the number of text essays they use *in class* (outside of class, of course, the students should be reading constantly). Careful examination of an essay on *all* levels— diction, sentence and paragraph style, organization, exploitation of the traditional techniques of discourse, subject matter —takes a great deal of time. This kind of examination of a few essays is, however, probably more useful than briefer examination of many.

Syllabus for a One-Year Course in English Composition

Weeks	Class Discussion	Exercises and Assignments
1–2	Introduction Diction Close examination of diction in two essays	Chapter One and Exercises Chapter Two and Exercises Analysis of diction in essays other than those discussed in class

Weeks	Class Discussion	Exercises and Assignments
3–4	Sentence Style Examination of sentence style in the two essays discussed above	Chapter Three and Exercises Analysis of sentence style in essays other than those discussed in class
5–6	Paragraph Style Examination of paragraph style in the two essays discussed above	Chapter Four and Exercises Analysis of paragraph style in essays other than those discussed in class
7–8	Preparation Organization Examination of organization of the two essays discussed above	Chapter Five and Exercises Analysis of organization, extensive outlining of essays other than those discussed in class
9–16	Exposition Remainder of first semester should be devoted to careful study of expository technique, thorough study of essays at the instructor's discretion. Special attention should be given where possible to class examination of student essays	Chapter Six and Exercises Six to eight 500-word essays

(Second Semester)

Weeks	Class Discussion	Exercises and Assignments
1–3	Argumentation Examination of essays, current newspapers, and magazines. Here and throughout semester class discussion of student essays	Chapter Seven and Exercises At least one argumentative essay Analysis of argumentative techniques in outside reading
4–6	Research Methods	Chapter Ten and Exercises A research paper
7–8	Description Examination of essays	Chapter Eight and Exercises At least one descriptive essay
9–10	Narration Examination of essays	Chapter Nine and Exercises At least one narrative essay

Weeks	Class Discussion	Exercises and Assignments
11–16	The remainder of the semester may be devoted to (a) further study of the techniques of argumentation, description, and narration, with extensive writing; (b) an introduction to literature, with extensive writing; or (c) both of the above.	

Some Alternate Plans

1. The syllabus given above calls for rather extensive study *before* the student writes any full-length essays. If the individual instructor prefers to have his students begin writing essays immediately, he might find the following plan useful. Appropriately rearranged, the exercises and assignments given above could be used.

Weeks 1–6	Introduction, Ch. 1
	Preparation, Ch. 5
	Exposition, Ch. 6
Weeks 7–8	Diction, Ch. 2
Weeks 9–10	Sentence Style, Ch. 3
Weeks 11–12	Paragraph Style, Ch. 4
Weeks 13–16	Further study of exposition
Second Semester	As in syllabus above

2. Both the plans given above are for freshman courses in which the complete year is devoted to the study of composition. In many universities a one-year English requirement includes a semester's study of composition and a semester's study of literature. In such instances, the following one-semester plans for this book might be useful. With some deletions necessitated by time limitation, the exercises given above could be used.

a. Essay writing delayed as in first syllabus

Week 1	Introduction
Week 2	Diction
Week 3	Sentence Style
Week 4	Paragraph Style
Week 5	Preparation

Weeks 6–9	Exposition
Weeks 10–11	Argumentation
Weeks 12–13	Description
Weeks 14–15	Narration
Week 16	Summary

(Study of research withheld until second semester for use in conjunction with study of literature)

b. Essay writing undertaken from the beginning

Weeks 1–3	Introduction
	Preparation
	Exposition
Week 4	Diction
Week 5	Sentence Style
Week 6	Paragraph Style
Week 7	Further study of organization
Weeks 8–9	Further study of exposition
Weeks 10–16	As in Plan above

❀ INDEX

*[The following materials are not indexed:
(1) Readings, (2) Bibliographies in Chapter Ten.]*

A

426

Correction Key*

Ab	Abbreviations	
Abs	Absol	
Adj	Use a	
Adv	Use a	
Agr-1	Agree	
Agr-2	Agree ante	
Am	Ambig	
Amb	Ambig	
Ap	Omitte apos	
Awk	Awkwa	
Bib	Wrong	
C	Clause	
Ca	Case	
Cap	Capital	
Cl	Cliché	
Clar	Clarify	
Co	Collect	
Coll	Colloqu	
Comp	Compa	
Con	Illogica	
Cont	Contra	
CS	Comma	
Dan	Dangling modifier	**Log** Faulty logic